# TITANIC

## & HER SISTERS

## OLYMPIC &
## BRITANNIC

# TITANIC
## & HER SISTERS
## OLYMPIC &
## BRITANNIC

PRC

This edition published in 2004 by
PRC Publishing Limited
The Chrysalis Building
Bramley Road, London W10 6SP
An imprint of **Chrysalis** Books Group plc

ISBN 1 85648 689 3

Printed and bound in China

PAGES 6-7: Titanic *leaving Southampton, 10 April, 1912. From a painting by Stuart Williamson.*

# CONTENTS

# INTRODUCTION

On a bitterly cold April night in 1912, the liner *Titanic* struck an iceberg in mid-Atlantic and slowly sank, leaving only 705 survivors huddled in twenty lifeboats. Around them, 1,523 men, women, and children drowned or froze to death before rescue could arrive. Despite the subsequent losses of many thousands of lives in various 20th century transport accidents on land, in the air, or at sea, no disaster in history is so readily conjured up by the mention of a single word as the dramatic loss of the 'unsinkable' *Titanic* on the night of 14-15 April, 1912.

The 'Olympic' class ships (as they were known), were the largest and most luxurious liners ever built, their sheer size giving an overwhelming feeling of safety and security. This was backed by the knowledge that they incorporated the best traditions of British shipbuilding and the latest techniques of design and construction. This story starts long before that fateful night however, in the hearts and minds of men who wanted to build the very biggest and the very best ships in the world. This book is a comprehensive guide to how and why these three fine sisters — *Olympic*, *Titanic* and *Britannic* — came to be built and the effect they were to have upon the world in the early stages of the 20th century.

Their beginnings are completely intertwined with that of their owners, the White Star Line, founded in Liverpool by Henry Threlfall Wilson and John Pilkington in 1845. In 1863, the line acquired its first steamship, the 2,033 ton *Royal Standard*. In an ominous premonition of things to come, she suffered a collision with a large iceberg on 4 April, 1864, whilst on the return from her maiden voyage to Melbourne. Following this accident the line experienced financial difficulties and the company was liquidated, bankrupted by a debt of £527,000 to the Royal Bank of Liverpool. Its sole remaining assets — consisting of the name, house flag, and the residue of any business good-

*BELOW: White Star publicity material: a cutaway of* Olympic, *the first in the new class.*

WHITE STAR STEAMER "OLYMPIC", 46,439 TONS.

*LEFT: A postcard of* Titanic.

ABOVE: Titanic leaving Southampton, 10 April,
1912. From a painting by Stuart Williamson.

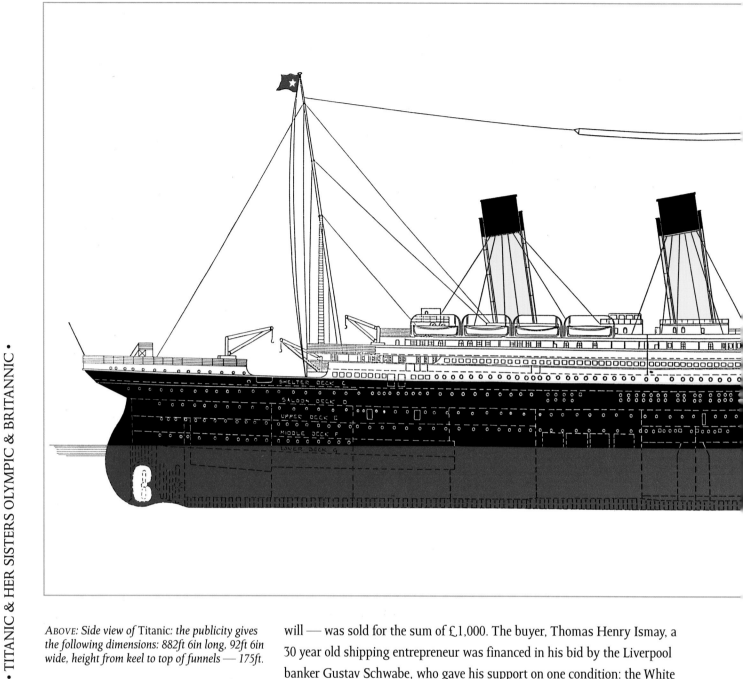

*ABOVE: Side view of* Titanic: *the publicity gives the following dimensions: 882ft 6in long, 92ft 6in wide, height from keel to top of funnels — 175ft.*

will — was sold for the sum of £1,000. The buyer, Thomas Henry Ismay, a 30 year old shipping entrepreneur was financed in his bid by the Liverpool banker Gustav Schwabe, who gave his support on one condition: the White Star Line must order its new ships from the Belfast shipbuilders Harland & Wolff, of which his nephew, Gustav Wolff, was the junior partner. The chain of events which would lead to the commissioning and building of the *Olympic*, *Titanic* and *Britannic* over 40 years later were, from that moment, set irrevocably in motion.

The White Star Line prospered but underwent a significant change of ownership when it was purchased in 1902 by the American I.M.M. Group, run by shipping magnate J. Pierpont Morgan. Although the White Star Line was now totally American owned, its ships still flew the British red ensign and continued to be manned exclusively by British officers and crews, maintaining the appearance of a British shipping line.

By the turn of the century the major seafaring nations were striving to gain the major share of the lucrative market formed by the massive flow of emigrants to the United States — the main contenders in this race were the mercantile fleets of Britain and Germany. At the end of the 19th century and in the early years of the 20th, German companies launched the world's largest liners and the *Kaiser Wilhelm der Grosse* soon proved that she was also the world's fastest by capturing the prestigious Blue Riband (also inflicting a major blow to British pride). There then followed a string of progressively larger and faster, world beating German ships which finally forced the British to take action. The British Parliament approved a bill which enabled the Cunard Line to take advantage of government subsidies to build two liners which could restore British prestige. These were to be the *Lusitania* and *Mauretania*. Built for speed, they succeeded in winning back the Blue Riband and, without stinting on luxury, could carry 560 first class, 475 second class and 1,300 third class passengers. Fares ranged from over £200 for the most luxurious cabins to around £20 for 'steerage' passengers. With the *Lusitania* and *Mauretania* set to dominate the British based transatlantic market in the years up to World War I, J. Pierpont Morgan was determined that his White Star Line would not be outdone and when in 1907 ambitious plans were submitted for two (later three) new 45,000 ton luxury liners he eagerly accepted. By July 1908 the preliminary design work had progressed enough for Harland & Wolff to make a formal proposal to the

16

*ABOVE: The last minutes of* Titanic, *from a painting by Stuart Williamson.*

*RIGHT: Stylised sectional view of the 'Olympic' class — the 'largest steamers in the world'.*

directors of White Star and its owners. This was accepted and on 31 July, 1908, Harland & Wolff was authorised to begin construction of two new ships, the first to be named *Olympic* and the second *Titanic*. Subsequently, in 1911, a third ship was also ordered, and the name *Gigantic* was chosen, this was later changed to *Britannic* as a direct consequence of *Titanic*'s sinking. Despite the superstitious change of name, the *Britannic* was to have a very short life. Employed as a hospital ship following her completion in November 1915, she sank after hitting a mine some twelve months later. The *Olympic* was more fortunate and survived until being gracefully retired in 1935. Work on *Titanic* began on 31 March, 1909, six months after the keel was laid for *Olympic*, and on May 31, 1911 she was launched. With celebrations completed, work continued on the immense task of fitting out the ship. Despite some last-minute modifications, *Titanic* was ready for her sea trials on 1 April, 1912, although these were delayed until the following day due to

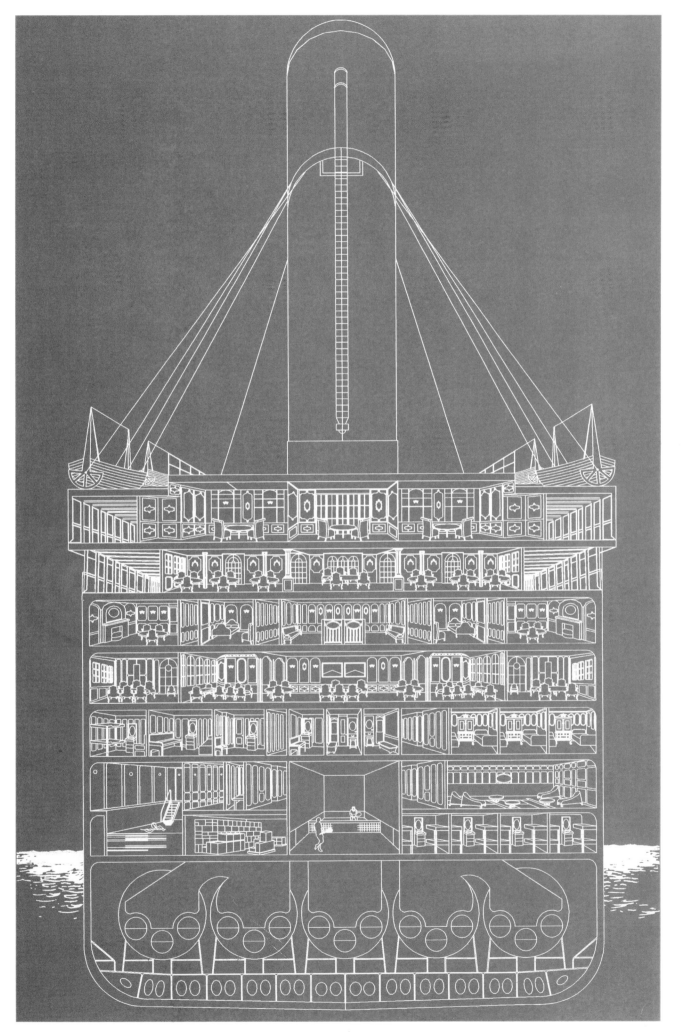

adverse weather conditions. Having successfully completed her trials, the *Titanic* sailed out into the Irish Sea, leaving Belfast forever and setting course for Southampton (her port of operation). She arrived there just before midnight on the night of 3 April, in time to prepare for her maiden voyage. She sailed, on schedule, on 10 April, 1912, and eventually met her destiny at position 41° 46' North, 50° 14' West. The loss of the *Titanic* on her maiden voyage showed, not for the first time, that man's greatest efforts in the fields of engineering and technology could be brought to nothing by the implacable forces of nature. Today, almost a century after the event, the demise of the *Titanic* still fascinates and interests new generations and is a constant source of news, disclosures, speculation and conjecture. Why should this be? There is of course an interest in the purely technical aspect of the vessel — the search to understand the factual details of the ship itself examine the circumstances of the sinking, as well as the subsequent rescue effort and the courtroom dramas. While these matters in themselves are obviously of great fascination, there is, perhaps, another part of the drama which grips the imagination even more strongly. The *Titanic*, with its accommodation strictly apportioned in three separate classes (first, second, and third), and its possible 2,436 passengers served in varying degrees of luxury by a crew of 892, was a microcosm of socio-economic life ashore at the time, where the upper classes were, for the most part, insulated from the sufferings and privations of the poor. When the ship went down, this class division was maintained: casualties among the third class or 'steerage' passengers were proportionately twice as great as those of first class.

The aftermath of the sinking was felt on both sides of the Atlantic, as families, rich and poor, mourned for their drowned relatives. As more news

*BELOW: A rat fish circles the wreck site.*

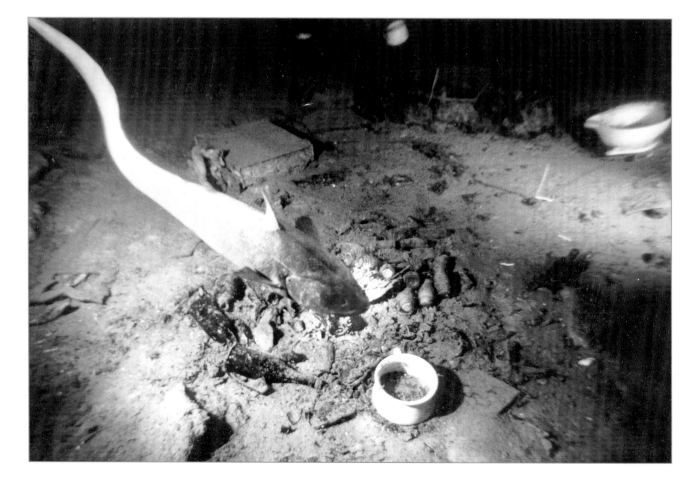

leaked out, the world was swept by tales of incidents associated with the sinking, ranging from scenes of panic and selfishness to tales of heroism and self-sacrifice, including the often quoted story of the ship's band playing popular airs as the giant liner slipped slowly beneath the waves. Memorial services were held, and the inevitable inquires began, both in London and New York. Each of these fell short of blaming the captain and his crew exclusively and cited numerous other factors which had contributed. However, Captain Lord of the *Californian* was found guilty (by the British Board of Trade inquiry into the *Titanic* disaster) of negligence and failing to maintain a proper watch. He was subsequently dismissed as a master. A number of appeals, the most recent by his grandson in 1987, have upheld the original findings of the court of inquiry. There was much discussion, too, over the conduct of Bruce Ismay, the chairman of the White Star Line who was on board for the ill-fated maiden voyage. But by far the most telling finding was that although the ship complied fully with the regulations of the day, there was only enough lifeboat accommodation to carry a little over a quarter of the 3,500 souls which the ship could accommodate when fully loaded.

So strong is the fascination with the name, that the ship has not been allowed to rest undisturbed. The hull of the *Titanic*, carrying all the cargo and passengers' baggage loaded at Southampton, acted as a magnet to the minds of adventurers and entrepreneurs. Almost as soon as the ship sank there were plans to salvage the wreck, spurred on by rumours of gold and other treasure reportedly stowed aboard. However, was not until the mid 1980s that the exact position of the wreck was established, some miles from the position originally calculated at the time of the sinking. Eventually though, the first underwater photographs were taken. This event threw the *Titanic* back into the headlines, and further expeditions were planned, although there was again controversy over whether the ship should be regarded as a protected grave or whether it would be permissible to salvage items from the wreck for public display. In the event, much was recovered in a French-led expedition in 1987, with other items being salvaged in later expeditions. Exhibitions in the United States, France, and Britain attracted thousands of visitors, proof that the story of the *Titanic* holds as much allure today as it has ever done in the past. More recently, the Hollywood blockbuster movie, James Cameron's *Titanic*, has beaten all box office records and has become the most successful film of all time. For this film, an almost full scale, landlocked replica was lovingly created and every modern computer based special effect technique conceivable was used to give the modern world an accurate impression of how the ship appeared at the time of its fateful maiden voyage. In addition to Cameron's latest rendition of the disaster, there several other histories of the *Titanic* in the cinema, with an example as early as 1912, the year she sank. There was a resurgence of films about the ship in the fifties with the essence of the disaster even resonating into other films seemingly unconnected. Most recently, and following on from the success of Cameron's film, the Discovery Channel hosted a global live TV extravaganza from the wreck site in August 1998, broadcasting from a flotilla of international research vessels. This event beamed live pictures of *Titanic*'s decaying hull into the homes of millions, and broadcast footage of

ABOVE: *Builder's model of the* Titanic.

the largest section of *Titanic* that has ever been brought to the surface. The section of her hull named 'The Big Piece', is a barely recognisable orange chunk, rusting and as brittle as glass, that will soon be all that we have left of her tremendous main shape. Discovery Channel's operation also highlighted the immense damage that 'rusticles' are causing to her remains — these strange micro-organisms are eating away at the iron in the wreck at a rate of one and a half tons a day. Decay is now accelerating at such an alarming rate that a conservative estimate maintains that within less than 80 years the wreck will have collapsed in on itself becoming nothing more than an iron deposit on the bottom of the north Atlantic Ocean. However, the most enduring image of *Titanic* is not from the present but of a graceful ship, slipping slowly beneath the waves on a starry April night, all her lights blazing as the band played valiantly on. This is the picture that is painted, indelibly, into the history of this century.

# GLOSSARY

| | |
|---|---|
| Aft | in, near or to the stern of the ship. Phrase applies all over the ship: i.e. moving aft. |
| Abaft | in the stern half of the ship. |
| Amidships or midships | in, or towards the middle of the ship. |
| Bilge | huge curve at the bottom of the hull. |
| Beam | width of vessel. |
| Breast hook | connecting piece at bow. |
| Bridge (deck) | control centre of the vessel. |
| Bow | very fore end of the ship. |
| Bulkhead | watertight divisions inside the hull. |
| Bunker | compartment for coal. |
| Caulk | make watertight. |
| Companionway | internal stairway. |
| Cutter | small rowing tender. Similar to the lifeboat. |
| Cranked (girder) | angled. |
| Davit | small crane for loading supplies and cargo. |
| Deadlight | cover for porthole. |
| Displacement | figure in tons equivalent to the weight of water displaced by the vessel. |
| Dog steps | Angle bars used as climbing rungs. |

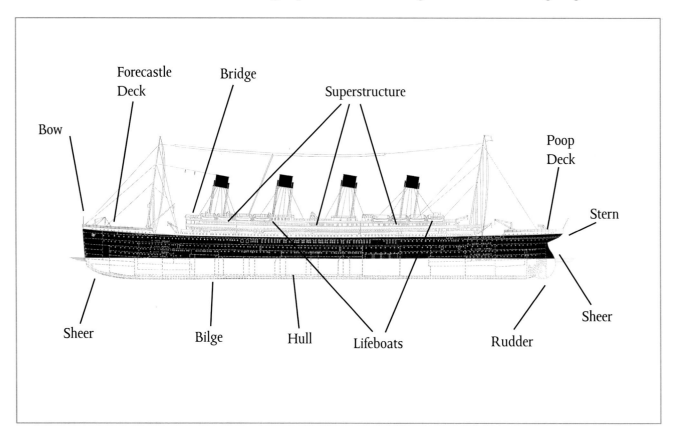

| | |
|---|---|
| Fathom | Measurement of depth (6 ft). |
| Fore | the front, bow part. Phrase applies all over the ship: i.e. moving fore. |
| Forecastle | forward part of the ship where crew are traditionally accommodated. |
| Forefoot | the first four feet of the bow |
| Gin | hoisting equipment: type of crane. |
| Gripe wire | lashing holding lifeboat in place. |
| Gross tonnage | carrying capacity of the vessel. |
| Hawse pipe | pipe for anchor chain main deck to side of vessel. |
| Hull | the body of the ship. |
| Halyards | rope for raising or lowering signals on the masts. |
| Helm | steering wheel. |
| Jacob's ladder | rope ladder with wooden rungs. |
| Joggles | overlapping of exterior plates on hull. Each plate has an in and out joggle. |
| Knot | measurement of speed, one nautical mile per hour or roughly 1.3 m.p.h. (nautical mile = 6,080 ft). |
| Lanyard | short rope used for securing or fastening. |
| Orlop deck | the lowest deck. |
| Port | 1. left hand side when facing forward. 2. to turn the ship to the left. 3. loading hole in the side of the ship. |
| Poop (deck) | the aftermost and highest deck. |
| Rivets | bolts for holding plates together. |
| Rudder | flat iron piece hinged vertically at the stern for steering. |
| Sheer | upward slope of hull at bow and stern. |
| Stern | the rear part of the vessel. |
| Starboard | 1. right hand side when facing forward. 2. to turn the ship to the right. |
| Superstructure | the raised structure separate from and above the hull. |
| Shelter (deck) | enclosed upper deck. |
| Toggle screw | fastening for watertight hatch cover. |
| Keel | composed of centre keel girder. Keel plate and then keel bar itself. |
| Tanktop | steel floor plate that rests on keel and supports engines and boilers etc. |
| Ton | 20 hundredweight (cwt), 1,016 tonnes. |
| Watertight doors | mechanically operated doors allowing access through watertight bulkheads |
| Well (deck) | space on main deck surrounded by superstructure and Poop and Forecastle decks Allows access to storage areas in ship by means of hatches |

Number of people on the *Titanic*

Maximum Possible Load

| | |
|---|---|
| Crew | 892 |
| Passengers | |
| First | 708 |
| Second | 510 |
| Third | 1,216 |
| Total | 3,326 |

There is some argument about the number of people on the *Titanic* on its maiden voyage after leaving Queenstown and the number of survivors. The immigration officer, E. J. Sharpe, noted as follows:

Actual Load

| | |
|---|---|
| Crew | 892 |
| Passengers | |
| First | 427 |
| Second | 179 |
| Third | 1,710 |
| Total | 2,208 |

Survivors/Fatalities
The widely accepted figure for total survivors is 705.

The widely accepted figure for total fatalities is 1,523, although 1,522 was the figure given in the inquiries.

It can be seen that the official record of 2,208 on board does not tally with the accepted figures for survivors and fatalities.

Lifeboats
Number of places in lifeboats:
14 standard @ 65 per boat = 910
2 cutters @ 40 per boat = 80
4 collapsibles @ 47 per boat = 188
Total = 1,178

# HARLAND & WOLFF

24

*ABOVE: View over Olympic's Poop Deck back toward Titanic, still on the slipway. The two graving docks visible in the picture are the Thompson and Alexandra docks.*

*BELOW: Edward J. Harland.*

The roots of the Harland and Wolff shipyard in Belfast can be traced through a rich vein of seafaring tradition that runs through the heart of Northern Ireland. Documents dating back over 300 years give an indication of the increasing importance attached to the trade, and a steady series of improvements were enacted during the 18th century to improve Belfast Lough, and thus ease navigation. In 1775, the American Revolution robbed British ship-owners of a major source of new tonnage — the shipyards of the East Coast — and this encouraged enterprising Scottish shipbuilder William Ritchie to invest in new works on reclaimed land where Garmoyle Street, part of the Laganside redevelopment, now stands. Ritchie's venture met with great success, and encouraged further investment through to the turn of the 19th century. In March 1820, the hull of one of the first steam ships built by a British yard, the 115 ft *Belfast*, was launched by Ritchie and McLaine. It was the first in a long line of famous vessels whose ghosts now haunt Belfast Lough.

In 1820, William MorisonPirrie, the grandfather of the future Harland & Wolff chairman, came to Belfast as the representative of his father's company. Pirrie energetically promoted the need to improve the approach channels to the Lough, which were full of silt and consequently too shallow, and was one of the driving forces behind the decision to straighten the channel by making two cuts across the meandering approaches. The first cut was opened in January 1841, and ensured that Belfast would continue to maintain its position as Ireland's major port. However, the expansion of Belfast shipbuilding had been insignificant when compared to the meteoric rise in the industry on the Thames, Tyne, Wear and Clyde. The need to improve the channel and quayside facilities hampered development on the Co. Antrim shore of the River Lagan during the late 1840's, prior to the opening of the cut, and the Harbour Commissioners had been largely unsuccessful in their attempts to encourage more shipbuilders to invest in the area. Most of those who were persuaded or who were already operating in the area, opted for the more tangible and immediate profits of the ship-repair industry and by the mid-19th century the Belfast ship-building industry seemed to be in danger of foundering.

Pirrie was undaunted. He was appointed in 1852 by the Harbour Commissioners to chair a committee which would investigate the proposal from one of the owners of the Belfast Iron Works that they should establish a shipyard on Queen's Islands. An enthusiastic Pirrie eventually persuaded the Commissioners of the commercial viability of the plan, and it was unanimously agreed that bids should be invited through English and Scottish newspapers for the purchase of land on the island, on which to construct

*ABOVE: G. W. Wolff.*

*BELOW: The principal families behind Harland & Wolff.*

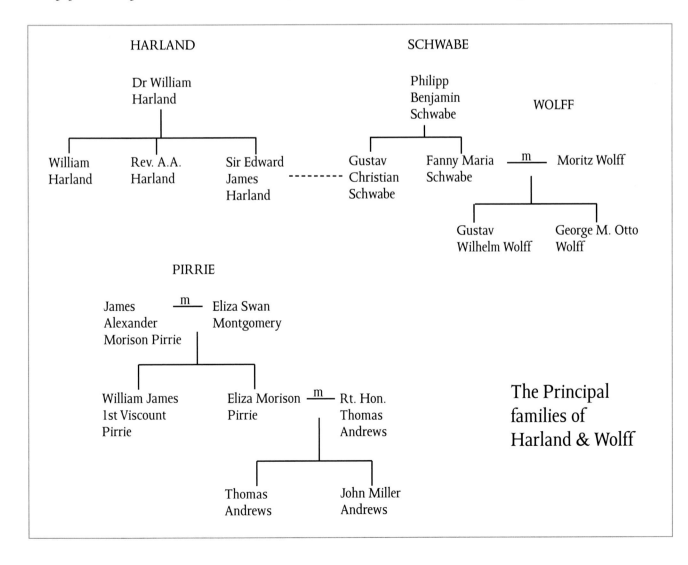

HARLAND

Dr William Harland

William Harland

Rev. A.A. Harland

Sir Edward James Harland

SCHWABE

Philipp Benjamin Schwabe

Gustav Christian Schwabe

Fanny Maria Schwabe —m— Moritz Wolff

WOLFF

Gustav Wilhelm Wolff

George M. Otto Wolff

PIRRIE

James Alexander Morison Pirrie —m— Eliza Swan Montgomery

William James 1st Viscount Pirrie

Eliza Morison Pirrie —m— Rt. Hon. Thomas Andrews

Thomas Andrews

John Miller Andrews

The Principal families of Harland & Wolff

shipbuilding yards.

The owners of the iron works sold up in early 1853 to Liverpudlian engineer Robert Hickson. Hickson consequently established the yard that was to give schooling to the founder of the mightiest of the Belfast yards, Edward Harland of Harland & Wolff, which grew from modest beginnings to be a shipyard that rivalled any in the world, and has a central role in the seafaring history of the British Isles. Harland's early career is documented in more detail elsewhere in this book, but suffice to say that he was an enthusiastic and talented engineer who had set himself on a career in engineering from an early age (much to the chagrin of his father, Dr. William Harland, who wished him to study as barrister). Among Harland's peers were men such as George Stephenson, who more than any other forged the path for Britain to become the greatest industrial nation of the 19th century. Harland worked his apprenticeship at Stephenson's works in Newcastle, and through family connections was later employed as a journeyman by J. & G. Thomson's works in Clydebank. After a short contract with Thomas Toward at Newcastle, Harland took up an appointment as the manager of Robert Hickson's shipyard in Belfast, and on those shores he was to establish a mighty shipbuilding dynasty that exists to this day.

Financial difficulties, in the form of outstanding loans to the Ulster Bank, afflicted Hickson's yard in 1855 and unhappy relations between Harland and the workforce were early stumbling blocks but proved insufficiently serious to prevent the yard completing a contract for a 1,237 ton ship, the

*RIGHT: Olympic in the graving dock. The propeller in view — 16 ft in diameter and made from manganese bronze — was driven by the turbine.*

*BELOW: A funnel heads towards the outfitting dock.*

*Khersonese*, which was launched in October 1855. Harland presided over the building of three more iron-sailing ships during the following two years at Hickson's yard. In 1857 he laid the groundwork for the partnership that would bring him considerable fame and fortune when he employed the nephew of a family friend , Gustav Wolff, to assist him at the yard. Harland was by now an experienced shipbuilder, eager to start his own yard, yet he was unsuccessful with applications made to Liverpool and other municipal bodies. Fortune appears to have been on his side, for the very next spring a financially disadvantaged Hickson offered Harland his yard, lock, stock, and barrel, for the sum of five thousand pounds. Financial support for the new venture was forthcoming from Gustav Schwabe, the wealthy benefactor who had steered Wolff in to Harland's employ. And so it was that on 1 November 1858, the firm's name changed to Edward James Harland & Company. Wolff was recalled from service at sea and placed in charge of the drawing office.

Contracts were immediately and fortuitously forthcoming. The most substantial was an order from John Bibby & Sons for three 1,500 ton iron steamers, and the limited size of Hickson's yard prompted Harland to purchase the small semi-derelict yard vacated by Thompson & Kirwan's Belfast Shipbuilding Company to complete the contract. With additions to the machine shops and the construction of a sail makers loft, Harland was able to combine the two yards and in 1859, the first year of operations, the company completed the *Bebington* (the last ship to be constructed by Edward James Harland & Company) and the *Venetian* (the first product of the partnership between Harland and Wolff). These two were the first of Bibby's trio of vessels. During the early 1860s the company expanded rapidly, establishing shipbuilding techniques that became standard practice across all the Belfast yards. With nearly 1,000 employees the yard was at full capacity. Most of these men were Protestant, not because of any official sectarian policy but because the skilled tradesman needed for the company were either

*RIGHT: Harland & Wolff workforce.*

*BELOW: Queen's Road, Belfast, c. 1912, showing the Harland & Wolff engine works.*

from Britain or the Protestant majority in Belfast. Their skills met with acclaim, for Bibbys ordered a further six vessels from the yard. These vessels were constructed with upper decks made entirely from iron, an innovation that increased the strength of the hull immeasurably and permitted a significant lengthening of its length (and thus cargo capacity) without a need to increase the beam.

The unofficial partnership between Edward Harland and Gustav Wilhelm Wolff was formally ratified on 11 April, 1861, 'in the trade or business of building and repairing iron ships and engines and doing all work connected with said trade'. Harland and Wolff entered their partnership with little working capital, yet found no difficulty in winning contracts for their new venture, launching 16 further vessels in the years 1862 to 1864.

During construction of a new graving dock and service basin at the south end of Queen's Island friction, between Catholic navvies employed for the job and Protestant shipwrights in Harland & Wolff's yard exploded into violence, but the unrest was rapidly quashed by the stern warnings of Harland. More serious was the sharp recession in the shipbuilding industry that followed the end of the American Civil War in 1865. Much of the work in the British and Irish yards had been for American merchants who needed fast steamships to run the Union blockades to southern mills. Profits fell drastically in 1866, but the future of the partnership was brightened when Harland & Wolff was approved for naval construction by the Admiralty in 1867. Facilities on Queen's Island were greatly improved by the opening of

*RIGHT: Harland & Wolff built over 75 ships for the Oceanic Steam Navigation Company, which ran the White Star Line. This list shows those up to Britannic.*

*BELOW: Entrance to the Harland & Wolff works.*

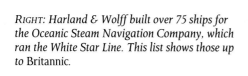

| No | Name | Vessel type | Launch date | Delivery date |
|----|------|-------------|-------------|---------------|
| 73 | *Oceanic* | Passenger ship | 27/8/1870 | 24/2/1871 |
| 74 | *Atlantic* | Passenger ship | 26/11/1870 | 3/6/1871 |
| 75 | *Baltic* | Passenger ship | 8/3/1871 | 2/9/1871 |
| 76 | *Republic* | Passenger ship | 4/7/1871 | 21/1/1872 |
| 77 | *Adriatic* | Passenger ship | 17/10/1871 | 31/3/1872 |
| 79 | *Celtic* | Passenger ship | 8/6/1872 | 17/10/1872 |
| 80 | *Gaelic* | Cargo ship | 21/9/1872 | 7/1/1873 |
| 81 | *Belgic* | Cargo ship | 17/1/1873 | 29/3/1873 |
| 83 | *Britannic* | Passenger ship | 3/2/1874 | 6/6/1874 |
| 85 | *Germanic* | Passenger ship | 15/7/1874 | 24/4/1875 |
| 140 | *Woodhopper* | Hopper barge | 18/6/1880 | during 1880 |
| 141 | *Arabic* | Cargo ship | 30/4/1881 | 12/8/1881 |
| 142 | *Coptic* | Cargo ship | 10/8/1881 | 9/11/1881 |
| 152 | *Ionic* | Cargo/Passenger ship | 11/1/1883 | 28/3/1883 |
| 153 | *Doric* | Cargo/Passenger ship | 10/3/1883 | 4/7/1883 |
| 171 | *Belgic* | Cargo ship | 3/1/1885 | 7/7/1885 |
| 172 | *Gaelic* | Cargo ship | 28/2/1885 | 18/7/1885 |
| 175 | *Callao* | Sailing ship | 1/1/1885 | 26/1/1885 |
| 176 | *Santiago* | Sailing ship | 17/1/1885 | 4/3/1885 |
| 208 | *Teutonic* | Passenger ship | 19/1/1889 | 25/7/1889 |
| 209 | *Majestic* | Passenger ship | 29/6/1889 | 22/3/1890 |
| 210 | *Cufic* | Livestock carrier | 10/10/1888 | 1/12/1888 |
| 211 | *Runic* | Livestock carrier | 1/1/1889 | 16/2/1889 |
| 236 | *Nomadic* | Livestock carrier | 11/2/1891 | 14/4/1891 |
| 237 | *Tauric* | Livestock carrier | 12/3/1891 | 16/5/1891 |
| 251 | *Naronic* | Livestock carrier | 26/5/1892 | 11/7/1892 |
| 252 | *Bovic* | Livestock carrier | 28/6/1892 | 22/8/1892 |
| 267 | *Gothic* | Passenger ship | 28/6/1893 | 28/11/1893 |
| 269 | *Megantic* | Passenger tender | 28/3/1891 | 6/6/1891 |
| 270 | *Cevic* | Livestock carrier | 23/9/1893 | 6/1/1894 |
| 283 | *Pontic* | Baggage tender | 3/2/1894 | 13/4/1894 |
| 293 | *Georgic* | Livestock carrier | 22/6/1895 | 8/8/1895 |
| 309 | *Delphic* | Passenger/Cargo ship | 5/1/1897 | 15/5/1897 |
| 316 | *Cymric* | Passenger ship | 12/10/1897 | 5/2/1898 |
| 317 | *Oceanic* | Passenger/Cargo ship | 14/1/1899 | 26/8/1899 |
| 322 | *Afric* | Passenger ship | 16/11/1898 | 2/2/1899 |
| 323 | *Medic* | Passenger/Cargo ship | 15/12/1898 | 6/7/1899 |
| 325 | *Persic* | Passenger/Cargo ship | 7/9/1899 | 16/11/1899 |
| 332 | *Runic* | Passenger ship | 25/10/1900 | 22/12/1900 |
| 333 | *Suevic* | Passenger ship | 8/12/1900 | 9/3/1901 |
| 335 | *Celtic* | Passenger ship | 4/4/1901 | 11/7/1901 |
| 337 | *Cedric* | Passenger ship | 21/8/1902 | 31/1/1903 |
| 340 | *Arabic* | Passenger ship | 18/12/1902 | 21/6/1903 |
| 341 | *Athenic* | Passenger ship | 17/8/1901 | 23/1/1902 |
| 343 | *Corinthic* | Passenger ship | 10/4/1902 | 14/7/1902 |
| 346 | *Ionic* | Passenger ship | 22/5/1902 | 15/12/1902 |
| 352 | *Baltic* | Passenger ship | 21/11/1903 | 23/6/1904 |
| 358 | *Adriatic* | Passenger ship | 20/9/1906 | 25/4/1907 |
| 394 | *Laurentic* | Passenger ship | 10/9/1908 | 15/4/1909 |
| 399 | *Megantic* | Passenger ship | 10/12/1908 | 3/6/1909 |
| 400 | *Olympic* | Passenger ship | 20/10/1910 | 31/5/1911 |
| 401 | *Titanic* | Passenger ship | 31/5/1911 | 2/3/1912 |
| 421 | *Zealandic* | Passenger/Cargo ship | 29/6/1911 | 12/10/1911 |
| 422 | *Nomadic* | Passenger tender | 25/4/1911 | 27/5/1911 |
| 423 | *Traffic* | Passenger tender | 27/4/1911 | 27/5/1911 |
| 432 | *Ceramic* | Passenger ship | 11/12/1912 | 5/7/1913 |
| 433 | *Britannic* | Passenger ship | 26/2/1914 | 8/12/1915 |

the Harbour Commissioners' Abercorn basin and Hamilton graving dock that same year. As it turned out, the first Admiralty order was completed at a loss, and for the next decade a roller coaster pattern of profit and loss was to dog the yard.

One of the most important contracts in the history of the Harland & Wolff yard was received in 1869 from the newly formed Oceanic Steam Navigation Company, which was established to capitalise on the expanding Atlantic trade routes by Thomas Ismay in competition with the Cunard and Inman lines. The order for five 420 ft steamers required a total re-equipping and modernisation, with four new berths constructed in the south-west part of the yard. At this time relations with the Harbour Commissioners were occasionally strained, partly because of their delay in extending the partners' lease to 31 years. However, work continued apace and healthy profits were registered in 1870.

Over the following two years industrial action to reduce the length of the working week was to force a concession from the British confederation of shipyard owners and political unrest over the Home Rule question again boiled over into social disturbance in the summer of 1872. Despite these problems, the partners had cause to be satisfied with a total return for the years 1871 and 1872 of over £42,000.

Shipbuilding experienced a boom during the early 1870s, with navigation companies locked in head-to-head competition over the fiercely contested north Atlantic route. The trickle of immigrants to North America and Canada had become a flood, many of them carried stateside on vessels built at Harland & Wolff. By 1875 the business had grown from a tiny works with

*BELOW: While the technology on board was state of the art for its time, that on the dockside could be more traditional — as well as rail and steam-traction engine power, horses were also used.*

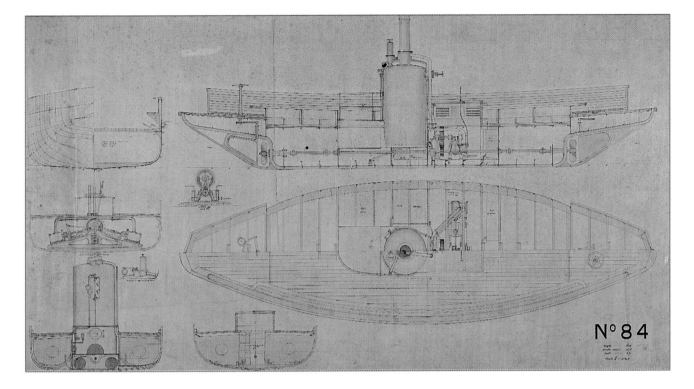

N° 8 4

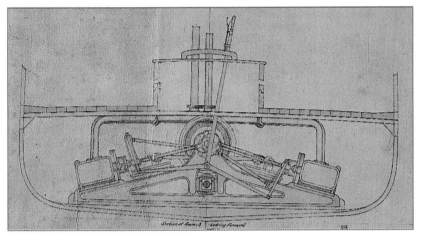

*ABOVE AND LEFT: This little ferry boat, owned and operated by the Belfast Harbour Commissioners, brought workers to Harland & Wolff across the River Lagan.*

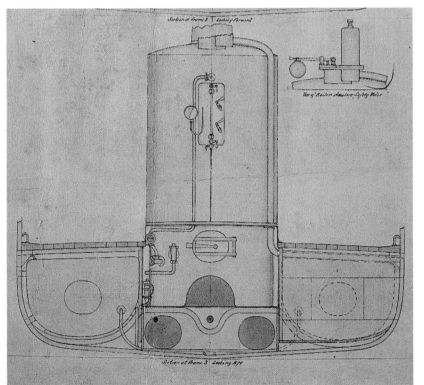

34

*ABOVE AND RIGHT: Edward Harland championed steam as a motive power, following in his father's footsteps — Dr William Harland had designed and patented a steam-powered carriage in 1827. Edward was to find his enthusiasm for steam was unappreciated in the shipping world at that time, but he did achieve a notable success with his revolutionary hull design of* Jane Porter. *This incorporated a new type of iron deck, with the internal spaces between the frames filled with cement rather than the traditional wooden wedges or chocks. The deck itself was also covered with cement and tiles providing an immensely strong and watertight construction.* Jane Porter *was yard No 5 and was delivered on 15 September, 1860.*

*FAR RIGHT:* Grecian *(Harland & Wolff Yard No 7) was delivered on 30 January, 1861. She was not the first for the Bibby Line (that had been* Venetian *in 1859) but she saw the start of a relationship that prospered over the years. She is notable for her improved hull form that was based on an increased length without any corresponding increase in beam or width, giving greater cargo capacity and passenger accommodation — the 'Belfast bottom' that was characterised by flat bottom allied to a square bilge.*

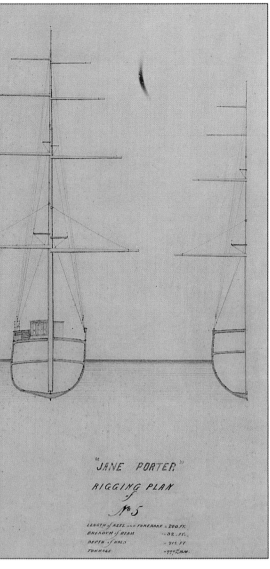

"JANE PORTER"

RIGGING PLAN

№ 5

LENGTH OF KEEL AND FORERAKE 200 FT.
BREADTH OF BEAM 32 FT.
DEPTH OF HOLD 21.5 FT.
TONNAGE 777.78M.

one berth, employing 48 men, to a large yard with six slips and a workforce of over 1,000, who built ships that sailed to the four corners of the globe. Undoubtedly much of this success was due to the confidence of investors such as Gustav Schwabe, John S. Bibby and Thomas Ismay, but the successful working relationship of the two partners and the skill of their workforce must be credited too. It was at this time that Harland & Wolff decided to reconstruct their partnership to embrace the yard manger, Walter H. Wilson, his brother, Alexander B. Wilson, who was in charge of engine design and installation, and the chief draughtsman William J. Pirrie.

The new partnership coincided with another serious decline in the shipbuilding industry, which was to last until 1880. Orders were few and far between, but with commitment and energy from the new partners and the experience and capital of the old, the company survived. Harland & Wolff both reduced their commitments gradually, but an upturn in profits in 1878 allowed the partners to invest in their own engine works by acquiring the business of Alexander McLaine & Sons for £7,000. At the same time they leased property from the Harbour Commissioners on the Queen's Road in Belfast. This expansion was partly spurred by increasing competition from the Co. Antrim side of the River Lagan from the Ulster Iron Works company and Workman Clark & Company. Both posed a threat to Harland & Wolff, and only by staying ahead of the competition could the partners expect to win future contracts. The massive investment in the engine works damaged the company profits, as did the small return on contracts completed in 1879, but confident investment by the partners was rewarded when between 1882 and 1884 another boom in the shipbuilding industry was experienced. By this time the engine works were in full operation and, with Pirrie's legendary

THE
GRECIAN AND ITALIAN.

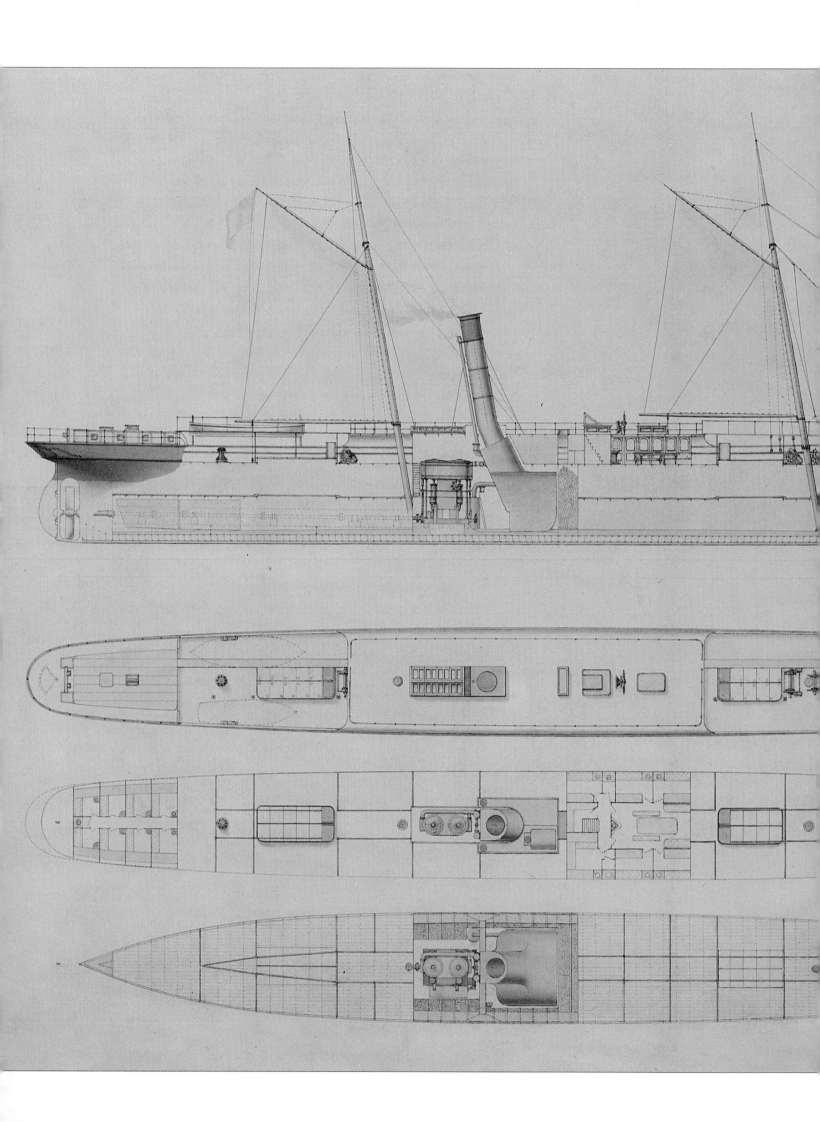

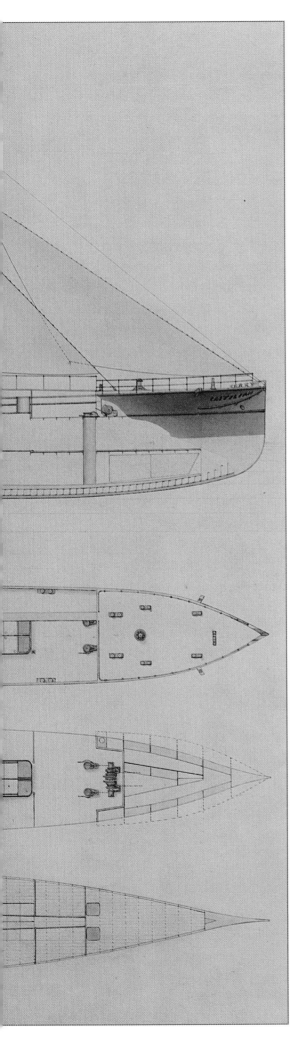

skills as a salesman, the order books were again full. Another asset to the company was Walter Wilson, the partner charged with much of the engineering and design management. He was a prudent and imaginative inventor with an engineer's eye for improvement and efficiency much in the mould of Edward Harland. These were boom years for the yard, and the success encouraged both of the original partners to cease their involvement in the management, and hence its profits and losses, by 1884.

A depression once again descended on the industry at the end of 1883. As freight rates continued to plummet, thousands of tons of shipping was withdrawn and few new vessels were commissioned. The partners had fortuitously invested in their own ships and had survived recession before by building ships at cost to encourage future contracts; but now they were forced to impose an unpopular wage cut on the riveters and platers in March. Nevertheless, relations with the Oceanic Steam Navigation Company, in which the partners held shares, were intensified and once again the company weathered the storm.

Increasing political unrest over Home Rule, and the likelihood that it might succeed, convinced the partners of the need to hedge their bets and prepare for a withdrawal to the British mainland. To this end a limited liability company was established by the partners, both old and new, to protect themselves should it prove necessary to sell the Queen's Island works. The new limited company was known as the Queen's Island Shipbuilding & Engineering Company which, as the new owner of the Harland & Wolff

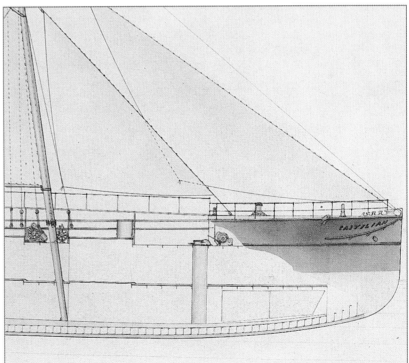

ABOVE AND LEFT: Another vessel for the Bibby Line, Castilian was delivered on 15 July, 1862. She marked a progression in Harland & Wolff ship design and, in particular, engine technology. While the basic condenser engine design was still employed, it had been much improved since the launch of the Grecian, with the result that power output and reliability had been increased by about half again.

works, presided over one of the most turbulent times in the yard's history. The weak order book, combined with the threat of Home Rule, had sapped the commitment of the Protestant workforce to Queen's Island and scores sought refuge in mainland yards. Even when a Conservative government won a huge majority at the July 1886 election, affirming public support for the Unionist cause, tension in the city and yard remained high for some time.

Developments in shipbuilding technology forced the partners to invest heavily in machine tools during the late 1880s, although this fortunately coincided with an upturn in business with contracts from the White Star Line, P & O and the Admiralty. By June 1888 it became clear that there was no longer a need for the partnership to continue. Another factor in its dissolution was Harland's increased involvement with politics (in 1887 he became Member of Parliament for North Belfast); it was considered unethical to benefit directly from government contracts and the name was officially changed to Harland & Wolff Limited, with all assets and liabilities transferred to the limited company under the management of Pirrie and Walter Wilson. Wolff increasingly concentrated on his expanding Belfast rope works.

The 1890s offered the same fluctuation of fortunes. Slump again followed boom but, through astute management and change in the company's financial structure, Harland & Wolff were able to build ships much more cheaply than their main competitors. The scheme was highly complex, involving deferral of profits until ships were finished and represented a very great risk, causing some concern to both Pirrie and Wilson. However, it was a great success at a time when shipbuilders were facing difficulty, and in the early 1890s the Company constructed more vessels than any other yard in the United Kingdom. Over fifty vessels were delivered, totalling almost 250,000

BELOW: *Delivered on 24 December, 1862,* Worrall *marked Edward Harland's entry into the world of shipowning on his own account. He had agreed to the construction of this classic sailing vessel in partnership with the principal owner, local merchant James Worall, who would oversee the operation and manning of the vessel. In return, Harland would reduce the building cost in direct proportion to the number of shares he would hold. The partnership proved successful: his share — just under a third — on average paid him a financial dividend of £1,900 per annum.*

"THE WOODLAWN"

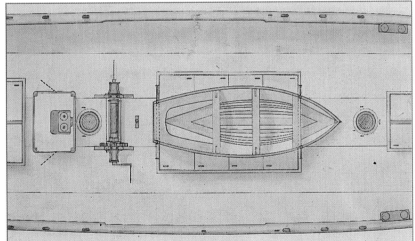

*ABOVE AND LEFT: This tiny vessel — Woodlawn — was completed in just over four months, the keel being laid on 22 February, 1868, and shows that simple sailing vessels were still in use despite the introduction of steam power.*

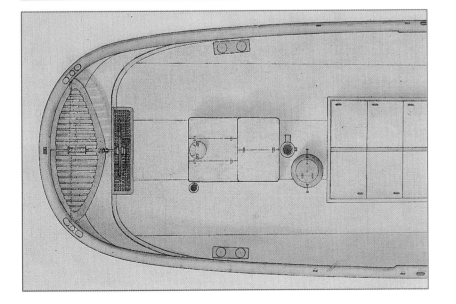

tons. Almost 7,000 men were employed, and further investment was made in a new sawmill, extensions to the engine works, and the internal tramline system. In February 1893, however, it again proved necessary to consider a move from Belfast as the second Home Rule Bill was introduced. After it was narrowly beaten in the House of Lords serious consideration was given to relocating to Liverpool, but in the eventuality no such decision was taken and political outlook for the company improved greatly when the Liberal government promoting Irish Home Rule was defeated at the ballot box. Instead, fresh difficulties were encountered during the mid-1890s — profits dwindled sharply and serious fires at both the timber yard in 1895 and the south yard in July 1896 hampered operations for some time.

The disastrous fires did however facilitate some useful changes. Three new berths were constructed, and the joiner's shop, sawmill and mould loft which had been destroyed were now relocated to the junction of Queen's Road and Victoria Road. The company also acquired the boatyard of John McCausland to provide stabling for the horses that were used to supplement the tramway system in moving material around the works. In addition, engine shops and boiler works were extensively re-equipped with the latest American machine tools and housed in extended sheds, an improvement programme costing almost £100,000. At the same time, the Harbour Commissioners embarked on a massive dock extension scheme, which led to an intense dispute with Harland & Wolff over the right to lease land for the construction of a new repair works to capitalise on the new dock. One of the more notable ships constructed during this time was the *Oceanic*, at 17,274 tonnes and 705 ft, the largest vessel in the world at that time and built at a cost of £750,000. Even the Kaiser came to the Queen's Island to see her launch on 14 January, 1899. Harland & Wolff thus ended the 19th century on a high note, with impressive profits and a full order book. However, their success had estranged them from the rest of the industry, and this, together with a refusal to involve the company in the national lockout policy (imposed after a dispute with the engineering unions in 1897) made Harland & Wolff some powerful enemies. Nevertheless, Pirrie's energies as the nominal head of Harland & Wolff, the bold investment of the company and their technical excellence had established the company as the undisputed leader of the shipbuilding industry by the turn of the century.

From 1900 onward, Harland & Wolff were to build an increasingly grand series of liners for a diverse set of clients, whilst continuing to maintain

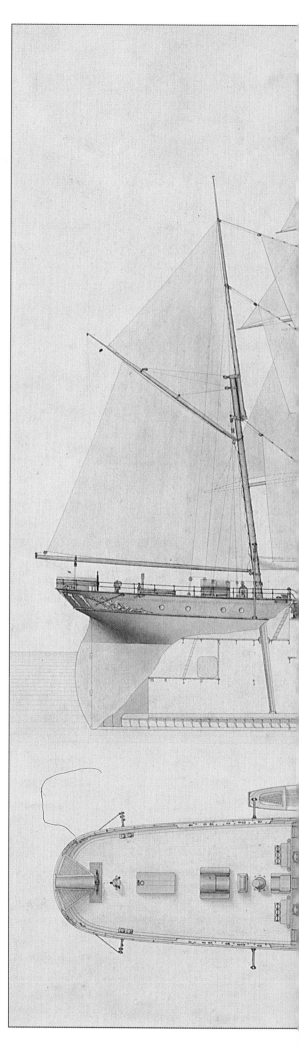

*RIGHT: The history of the* Broughton *plays a very special part in the history of Harland & Wolff because it very nearly caused the closure of the company when the original owner was declared bankrupt. Gustav Schwabe, Wolff's uncle, who introduced the partners to Thomas Henry Ismay, consequently purchased the vessel for use by his recent acquisition — the White Star Line. She was named* Broughton *after Broughton Hall, Gustav Schwabe's Liverpool home.*

financial interests in a number of shipping companies.

When Thomas Ismay, owner of the White Star Line, died in October 1899 ownership of his business passed to his two sons, Bruce and James. White Star were to provide the yard with their most important contracts over the next decade, including that for the *Titanic*. During 1900, the exclusive club of favoured Harland & Wolff clients placed orders for 13 new liners, in addition to the White Star order for the *Cedric* super-liner. The swelling tide of business persuaded Pirrie to invest in yet another programme of improvements. The future of the yard could be in no doubt when the company came to an 'unofficial' arrangement to construct all the ships of J. Pierpont Morgan's newly formed International Mercantile Marine group in February 1902. Morgan's company was financially powerful and aimed to dominate north Atlantic trade at the expense of the Cunard, Hamburg-Amerika and Rotterdam lines. With the order books now full and slipways groaning under the weight of new tonnage, the yard continued expansion of both the gantry systems and the machine shops: the new electrical generating plant next to the boiler shop cost £150,000 alone. Harland & Wolff had little choice but to make these investments since as mainland port facilities and the bigger yards were continually being similarly upgraded.

Slump followed boom yet again with the completion of these orders, and Pirrie was once more forced to revert to established tactics such as building for cost, or even loss, to save the yard. The lack of new orders from I.M.M.

*RIGHT: The building of the* British Queen *heralded yet another innovation for Harland & Wolff. Along with* British King, *the two vessels were the first all-passenger ships to be constructed by the company. They also marked a radical change from the use of iron, the traditional construction material of shipbuilding, and employed steel for the first time in the hull construction.*

*BELOW: The* Lord Downshire *would soon come to represent the end of an era in ocean transport. Constructed in iron, rather than the more modern steel, and built as a sailing vessel as opposed to a steamship, the vessel struggled to operate profitably, and after only ten years in service was laid up.*

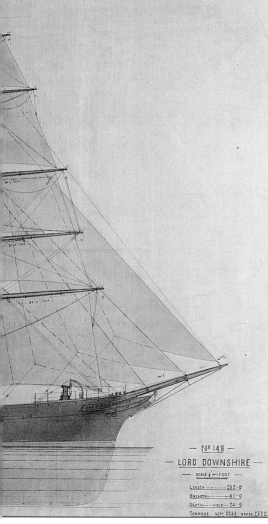

— Nº 148 —
— LORD DOWNSHIRE —
— SCALE ⅛ =1 FOOT —

Length ———— 262·0
Breadth ———— 41·0
Depth — Hold — 24·9
Tonnage nett 2263 gross 2322

in 1904-5 was partly offset by refit and engine orders from the Admiralty. The landslide Liberal victory once again unsettled the political situation in the north of Ireland as Pirrie exerted all his skills as a financier to cover the company's problems and present a brave face. However, the new government no longer needed the support of Irish Nationalists in Parliament and ignored the Home Rule issue. The withdrawal of G. W. Wolff from his post as a principal in 1903 meant that Pirrie had almost autocratic control of Harland & Wolff by the time of his appointment to the peerage in 1906. Pirrie had long been a Liberal supporter and provided much financial support to Liberal candidates in Ulster during the election campaign.

In 1907, Bruce Ismay announced his intention to purchase two giant liners, each of 46,000 tons, to compete with Cunard's *Lusitania* and *Mauretania*, then under construction. Over the next two years extensive alterations were made to the north yard as it was equipped for the construction of *Olympic* and *Titanic*. Admiralty work from Portsmouth and Plymouth also encouraged Pirrie to develop a repair works in Southampton and from 1907, Harland & Wolff had a base on the south coast, to match the one at Liverpool on the Irish Sea. Orders continued to roll in, but were dominated by the £3 million order for *Olympic* and *Titanic* which was confirmed in 1908. Harland & Wolff had weathered the storms that had rocked the shipbuilding industry and had emerged as one of the most powerful and modern shipyards in the world when construction of the *Titanic* began.

However, the invincibility of the yard and the confidence of the men who built the 'unsinkable' liners was to suffer a lasting blow in the coming years.

# WHITE STAR LINE

The history of the *Olympic*, the *Britannic* and the dramatic story of the *Titanic* is inextricably bound up with that of their owners, Morgan's I.M.M. and the White Star Line. The company was founded in Liverpool by Henry Threlfall Wilson in 1845, his first partner in business being a John Pilkington. Initially the line employed traditional sailing ships and concentrated on the Australian trade, carrying goods and emigrants on the outward voyages and returning with wool, minerals, whale oil and other imports from the new colony on the return leg.

In 1857 Pilkington was replaced by a new partner, James Chambers, and six years later the company acquired its first steamship, the 2,033 ton *Royal Standard*, although, like its contemporaries, this vessel also carried sails. In an uncanny portent of things to come, the *Royal Standard* actually suffered a collision with a large iceberg on 4 April, 1864, while proceeding under sail on the return from her maiden voyage to Melbourne. Despite major damage to the masts, spars and rigging, the hull was undamaged and the steam plant subsequently functioned perfectly, enabling the ship to reach Rio de Janeiro for repairs.

While these dramatic events were taking place at sea, equally dramatic events of a different nature were occurring ashore. Wilson and Chambers had attempted to amalgamate the White Star Line with two other shipping companies but the scheme, and another similar flotation, failed amidst charges of illegal share dealings. The line subsequently suffered great financial difficulties and a second steamship had to be sold off before it entered service. A short-lived attempt at a transatlantic service also failed. The com-

*BELOW: The construction of the* Baltic *marked an evolution in the design of merchant vessels. She was one of the first purpose-built passenger liners and a forerunner of things to come, with a long and slim hull form and a new and totally novel design of passenger accommodation, which extended the full width of the ship and almost its entire length. On introduction to service the* Baltic *and her sisters received worldwide acclaim. Such was the fierce nature of the competition for the passenger trade across the Atlantic that Cunard Line immediately contracted Harland to lengthen four of its vessels and to refurbish their internal arrangements to the same standards as the White Star Line's vessels.*

pany was liquidated and its sole remaining assets — consisting of the name, houseflag and the residue of any business goodwill—was sold for the sum of £1,000.

The buyer was Thomas Henry Ismay, a 31-year old shipping entrepreneur with plans to start a transatlantic passenger steamship company of his own. Finance for his scheme was forthcoming from a Liverpool merchant, Gustav Schwabe, who gave his support on the condition that the new line would order its new ships from the Belfast shipbuilders Harland & Wolff, of which his nephew, Gustav Wolff, was the junior partner. Thus the chain of events which would lead to the commissioning and building of the *Titanic* over 40 years later were set irrevocably in motion.

Ismay and a colleague, George Hamilton Fletcher, negotiated with Harland & Wolff over the design and specification of the vessels to be built and by 1869 orders for up to six ships had been placed. Ismay then formed a new company, the Oceanic Steam Navigation Company Limited, to operate the ships under the name and flag of the White Star Line. The first pair were named *Oceanic* and *Atlantic*, starting a tradition of giving the line's ships names ending in '-ic'. The new vessels introduced several modern features which distinguished them from other liners of the time. Although still carrying some sail, they were much slimmer than previous ships with a length to beam ratio of around ten to one, compared to the more standard eight to one, and both had a deep keel to counterbalance the pressures on the sails. Overall length was 420 ft, with a gross registered tonnage of 3,707, and they were powered by two four-cylinder compound reciprocating steam engines that drove them at over 13 knots. More importantly, they could carry 166 saloon class passengers in great luxury, as well as 1,000 in steerage class accommodation which, while lacking the comforts provided for saloon class, was a great improvement on anything which had been provided for this class of passenger previously. The design of the superstructure was rationalised

*ABOVE: The* Celtic *was a further adaptation and improvement on the successful design of the* Baltic. *Again designed to operate on the Liverpool-New York service, the successful 'all inclusive' liner concept was further developed to provide greater public lounge areas, together with a reading and writing room and an exclusive lounge for ladies.*

*FOLLOWING PAGES:* Arabic *and* Coptic *were designed for the White Star transatlantic routes; however, the operations of these two vessels were slightly more unusual than other ships in the fleet. While accommodating the normal mixture of steerage and more affluent passengers, they were also specifically designed to carry another lucrative passenger; one that did not require the various trappings of comfort and who did not complain about the food or service — live cattle, now a major source of income for the shipping lines.*

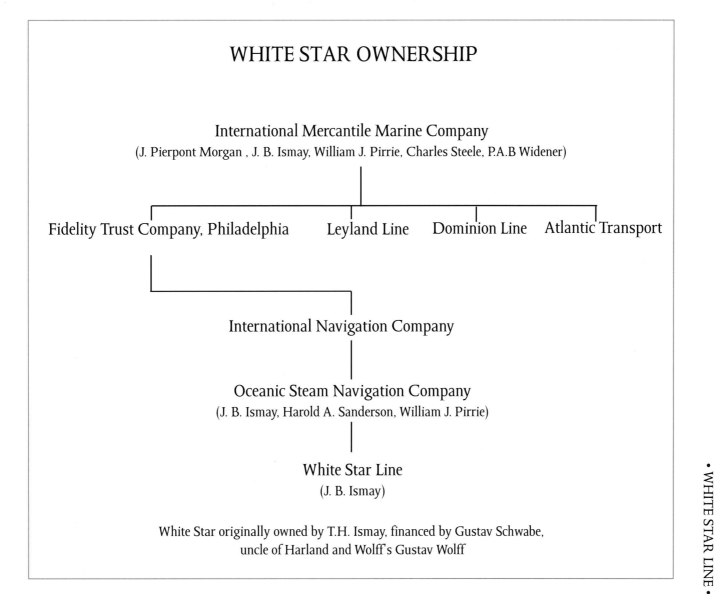

# WHITE STAR OWNERSHIP

**International Mercantile Marine Company**
(J. Pierpont Morgan , J. B. Ismay, William J. Pirrie, Charles Steele, P.A.B Widener)

Fidelity Trust Company, Philadelphia      Leyland Line      Dominion Line      Atlantic Transport

**International Navigation Company**

**Oceanic Steam Navigation Company**
(J. B. Ismay, Harold A. Sanderson, William J. Pirrie)

**White Star Line**
(J. B. Ismay)

White Star originally owned by T.H. Ismay, financed by Gustav Schwabe,
uncle of Harland and Wolff's Gustav Wolff

into a single long deckhouse which replaced the many and varied structures of other ships and innovations such as electrical systems and running water in the cabins were incorporated. In many ways the *Oceanic* could be regarded as the first modern liner and she was imitated extensively.

While the *Oceanic* was being fitted out at Belfast, T. H. Ismay was reorganising his business empire and with an associate, William Imrie, formed Ismay, Imrie and Company to oversee the running of the Oceanic Steam Navigation Company and the White Star Line. Over the next 20 years White Star prospered and became the acknowledged pace setter on the north Atlantic run, while still successfully operating its original Australian routes. This was despite the fact that a major disaster had occurred on 1 April, 1873 when the *Atlantic*, sister ship to the *Oceanic*, was lost after striking Marrs Rock off Halifax, Nova Scotia.

The ship had been battered by a storm which had caused coal consumption to be increased to the extent that her master, Captain James H. Williams, became concerned about *Atlantic*'s ability to reach New York. The ship's course was consequently altered to stop at Halifax and refuel. Due to a major navigational error however, the ship was west of her calculated position and ran aground on rocks near the shore, only 15 miles from her destination. No fewer than 546 people, many of them children, died in this horrif-

*ABOVE: White Star Line ownership*

*FOLLOWING PAGES: Mauretania at Southampton. She was the flagship of the Cunard Line and her acquisition of the Blue Riband in 1907 led to great publicity.*

*LEFT: White Star publicity for the 'Olympic' class.*

ic occurrence which, at the time, was the worst marine accident on record. At the subsequent court of inquiry, one of the incidental causes of the accident was attributed to the fact that the ship did not carry enough coal to complete safely her voyage in circumstances which could reasonably have been foreseen, although the White Star Line disputed this finding. On appeal the Board of Trade ruled that lack of fuel was not a factor in the ship's loss.

Over the years that followed, the White Star Line's safety record was far less than satisfactory, even by the standards of the time when accidental shipping losses were at a much greater level than today. The 6,594 ton *Naronic*, then the world's largest livestock carrier, disappeared without trace on a north Atlantic crossing in 1893; while the liner *Germanic* capsized during a blizzard in New York harbour on 11 February, 1899, because of the weight of snow and ice on her upper works (the ship was subsequently salvaged and put back into service). On 17 March, 1907, the *Suevic* ran aground on Stag Rock near Land's End, Cornwall, when nearing the end of a voyage from Australia, and lost over 200 ft from the forward section of the hull before she was towed away and repaired. The liner *Republic* sank in 1909 after a collision with the liner *Florida* — fortunately, almost all of the passengers and crew were saved due to one of the earliest recorded instances of a radio distress call being successfully transmitted.

In spite of these disasters, the White Star Line pressed on with its premier north Atlantic services, and in 1899 introduced a new liner, regarded by many as the pinnacle of 19th century shipbuilding achievement and certainly one of the most graceful ships ever built. This was the *Oceanic* (the second ship of the name) which, with a length of 705 ft and a 17,274 gross tonnage, was the largest liner of her day and was the first to exceed the length of Isambard Kingdom Brunel's gigantic but ill-fated *Great Eastern*, built for the Cunard Line in 1859. By this time steamships no longer carried auxiliary sails, and the *Oceanic*'s long hull, with its sweeping curves and rounded cruiser stern, was dominated by two tall, widely-spaced and well-propor-

*BELOW: Publicity postcard of the* Titanic.

R.M.S. TITANIC (COPYRIGHT)

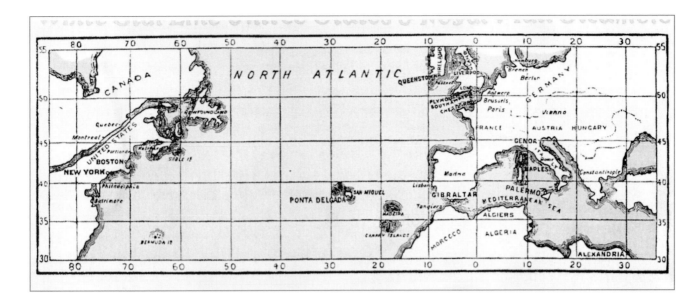

*ABOVE: A White Star map of the north Atlantic.*

*LEFT: More White Star publicity material.*

*BELOW: White Star poster showing Olympic as a troopship, in 'dazzle' camouflage. See original photograph on page 234.*

# WHITE STAR LINE

NEW YORK
PLYMOUTH
CHERBOURG
SOUTHAMPTON

NEW YORK
QUEENSTOWN
LIVERPOOL

BOSTON
QUEENSTOWN
LIVERPOOL

MONTREAL
QUEBEC
LIVERPOOL

NEW YORK
AZORES
MEDITERRANEAN

BOSTON
AZORES
MEDITERRANEAN

## United States & Royal Mail Steamers

WHITE
STAR
LINE

tioned funnels, which gave the ship a unique and pleasing appearance.

Internally, the ship lived up to its external promise. *Oceanic* had accommodation for 410 first class, 300 second and 1,000 third class passengers. The former were carried in luxurious surroundings, including a 400 seat restaurant capped by a 21 ft square atrium dome, with additional light coming from oversize portholes on either side. The library was held to be the finest of its kind aboard any ship. The *Oceanic* was also a fast ship and made many crossings at average speeds in excess of 20 knots, although she was never fast enough to gain the coveted Blue Riband. Instead she was responsible for the start of the White Star Line's traditional policy of excelling in comfort, luxury and standard of service, rather than competing in terms of sheer speed. This much-loved ship remained in service right up to the outbreak of war in 1914, although by then she was overshadowed by much larger ships. *Oceanic* met an unfortunate end in September of that year when she ran aground off the Shetlands while under naval command.

As well as the introduction into service of the *Oceanic*, 1899 also saw the death of White Star's autocratic leader, Thomas Henry Ismay. The task of steering the company's future into the new century fell into the hands of his son, Joseph Bruce Ismay. Between 1901 and 1907 he was responsible for White Star commissioning four new ships: the *Celtic*, *Cedric*, *Baltic* and *Adriatic*, or the 'Big Four' as they were known. Built, as usual, by Harland & Wolff, they were capable of speeds of 16-17 knots and had a tonnage of between 21,000 and 24,000. By now the company precedent had been almost

*ABOVE RIGHT:* Britannic *nears completion on this hand-coloured postcard.*

*BELOW RIGHT:* Olympic *compared with some of the world's tallest structures.*

*BELOW: White Star advert dated 1914.*

54

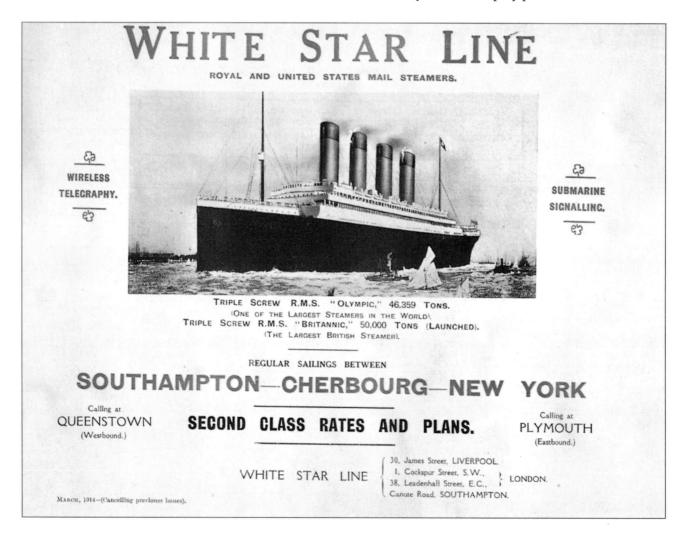

# WHITE STAR LINE.

The White Star Line's famous Triple and Twin Screw Steamers are engaged in services to all parts of the world. Besides possessing Wireless Telegraphy, Bilge Keels and Watertight Compartments, all of which constitute the most modern devices for safety and comfort; there are spacious promenades where deck games and many other such like pleasures may be indulged in. The food, which is of unlimited quantity, is of the best quality obtainable, and the bill of fare is varied daily.

## R.M.S. "MAJESTIC," 56,000 Tons,

# THE WORLD'S LARGEST LINER.

**WHITE STAR LINE**

AMERICAN SERVICES.

**MAJESTIC**
56,000 Tons.
THE WORLD'S
LARGEST LINER.

SOUTHAMPTON—
CHERBOURG—NEW YORK.
LIVERPOOL—
QUEENSTOWN—NEW YORK.
LIVERPOOL—
QUEENSTOWN—BOSTON.

MAJESTIC ... 56,000 Tons
OLYMPIC ... 46,439 „
ADRIATIC 24,541 „
BALTIC ... 23,876 „
CEDRIC ... 21,073 „
CELTIC ... 20,904 „
VEDIC ... 9,332 „

LIVERPOOL—QUEENSTOWN—
PHILADELPHIA.

HAVERFORD 11,635 Tons
PITTSBURGH (Building)

NEW YORK—
BOSTON—MEDITERRANEAN.

ARABIC ... 17,324 Tons
CRETIC ... 12,517 „
CANOPIC ... 12,098 „

**WHITE STAR LINE**

AUSTRALASIAN
SERVICES.
NEW ZEALAND.

ATHENIC ... 12,368 Tons
IONIC ... 12,332 „
CORINTHIC 12,267 „
ZEALANDIC 8,089 „

AUSTRALIAN.

CERAMIC ... 18,421 Tons
SUEVIC ... 12,531 „
RUNIC ... 12,489 „
PERSIC ... 12,042 „
MEDIC ... 12,032 „

**WHITE STAR—
DOMINION LINE**

CANADIAN SERVICE.
LIVERPOOL—
QUEBEC—MONTREAL.
(Summer Service)
LIVERPOOL—
HALIFAX—PORTLAND, Me.
(Winter Service)

MEGANTIC 14,878 Tons
CANADA ... 9,472 „
REGINA ... 16,314 „
RIMOUSKI 9,251 „
DORIC ... 16,000 „
(Building)
LAURENTIC 17,000 „
(Building)

## WHITE STAR LINE. R.M.S. "OLYMPIC"
*COMPARED WITH VARIOUS FAMOUS BUILDINGS.*

56

carved in stone: although the vessels maybe slower than their rivals, they were outfitted to the highest standard of craftsmanship using only the very best materials and equipment available. In short, White Star epitomised the very finest in elegance and style of the Victorian era — an ocean voyage, after all, was to be relished to the fullest extent; they would leave the vulgar pursuit of speed to others, notably the White Star Line's great rival Cunard.

However, when Cunard captured the Blue Riband in 1907 with the introduction of its flagship *Mauretania*, the enormous publicity that the rival line received galled J. B. Ismay. He regarded the attention that Cunard was enjoying as indifference to his beloved White Star Line. Ismay determined that something had to be done to redress the balance and recapture the company's leading position. However, it was still his firm intention to ensure that the name 'White Star Line' would forever be synonymous with the upper end of the transatlantic passenger market, and be renowned for the excellence of the service it provided in the most opulent surroundings possible. Ismay decided that he needed something that would capture the public imagination while embracing White Star's philosophy of minimising operational costs and setting new precedents for transatlantic passenger comfort.

*RIGHT: Publicity material for the 'Olympic' class often included a small sailing vessel to show their size.*

*ABOVE RIGHT: Publicity drawing of the Verandah Café*

*FAR RIGHT: Empire-style first class suite.*

# I.M.M. GROUP

TOP: *J. P. Morgan formed the I.M.M. Group.*

CENTRE: *Lord Pirrie who developed the link between Harland & Wolff and I.M.M.*

ABOVE: *J. Bruce Ismay, head of the Oceanic Steamship Navigation Company.*

While the *Oceanic* was doing much to restore the White Star Line's good name, the company underwent a significant change of ownership when it was purchased in 1902 by the International Mercantile Marine Company (or I.M.M. as it was more commonly known) for the sum of £10 million. I.M.M. was a massive shipping conglomerate constructed by its owner, J. Pierpont Morgan, an American tycoon who had single-handedly built up his business to become the largest private banking house in America. Having achieved this he then diversified into railways, steelmaking and shipping.

Much of the new wealth that America offered was centred in the hands of the trusts and combines where huge capital was beginning to play a major part in the affairs of the shipping industry. One such combine was the Morgan Combine, whose aim was to establish a monopoly of transatlantic travel similar to that enjoyed by others on the American railroads.

Morgan's dream of monopolising the lucrative transatlantic passenger business had begun in 1893 when he bought the Liverpool-based Inman Line to add to his own International Navigation Company of New Jersey, which already owned the American Line and the Belgian Red Star Line. In 1902, Morgan restyled his shipping empire as the International Mercantile Marine Company and went on to take over other concerns, including the British-owned Atlantic Transport, Dominion and Leyland lines. But the jewel in his crown, and the acquisition which made his dreams a reality, was the purchase of the White Star Line.

The line was under the control of J. B. Ismay, who was acting in partnership with his younger brother James as well as William Imrie. Although the Ismay family resisted the take-over, the shareholders were unable to resist the generous offer made by Morgan, to whom money was no object. Faced with a *fait accompli*, Bruce Ismay co-operated with Morgan and not only remained as chief executive of the White Star Line but, in 1904, was appointed as president of the I.M.M. group, a post which he held until his resignation in October 1913, after the sinking of the *Titanic*. However, he had announced this in Jauary 1912, before the *Titanic* was lost. Although the White Star Line was now completely American-owned, its ships still flew the British Red Ensign and continued to be manned by British officers and crews — to all external appearances it operated as a British shipping line.

The purchase of the Oceanic Steam Navigation Company, and with it the White Star Line provided the I.M.M. Group with the means to consolidate three shipping companies — White Star, Red Star and Leyland Lines — under a single operating structure. In purchasing the Oceanic Steam Navigation Company the I.M.M. Group had, at a stroke, achieved its corporate objective: it now had control of three associated, yet diverse, shipping lines and it immediately set about creating a niche and an identity for each. White Star was selected to be the standard bearer for the group and would accordingly focus its corporate attentions on the luxury end of the passenger market.

As mentioned earlier, Bruce Ismay was keen to recapture, as quickly as possible, the prestigious luxury segment of the transatlantic passenger trade. Underwritten by J. Pierpont Morgan's vast wealth, Ismay had in effect almost unlimited funds at his disposal to acquire suitable vessels to accomplish this objective — perhaps the only restriction being imposed on him was the instruction by J. Pierpont Morgan to 'get me the finest vessels afloat.' With I.M.M.'s fortune behind Ismay, there was nothing to stop him achieving his ambition to make the White Star Line the most prestigious and talked about transatlantic line bar none.

Most accounts credit William Pirrie, the thrusting chairman of the Belfast shipbuilders Harland & Wolff, with the original plan to build two (later three) new 45,000 ton luxury liners for the White Star Line. In 1907, at a dinner held at Downshire House, his Belgrave Square mansion, he out-lined to Bruce Ismay the merits of these ships, which would not attempt to surpass Cunard in terms of speed, but would excel in every other aspect, particularly in sheer size and in the standard of accommodation and facilities offered. Ismay had been having similar thoughts and did not take much con-vincing. As they retired to the smoking room for coffee and cigars to discuss further the concept of the 'Olympic' class vessels (as they were to become known), and to draw up a rough design specification, Ismay found himself in excellent spirits. Here he was in the home of his friend Lord Pirrie, chairman of the greatest shipbuilders in the world, who very obviously shared his enthusiasm for these new vessels. He felt secure in his conviction that the

*BELOW: Artist's impression of the B Deck reception area and Grand Staircase.*

White Star Line, under his stewardship, would continue to prosper and expand, and that the construction of these magnificent new vessels would demonstrate to the world man's total control over his environment.

The principal considerations for the vessels were to be safety, comfort and luxury, together with a reasonably fast speed. From the original notes taken by Pirrie at the meeting, the original specification called for the vessels to have three funnels and four masts; however, this plan was soon changed to one of four funnels and two masts. The change of specification was designed to foster an image of grace and power (in the public perception at that time, the number of funnels equated directly to the degree of magnificence of the vessel. The most powerful vessels then in service had four funnels, and so it was decided that the 'Olympic' class must follow this trend). The result was a graceful and balanced profile but, in order to achieve this, the fourth aftmost funnel was to be a dummy, constructed purely for cosmetic purposes.

Immediately upon Pirrie's return to Belfast he called together his usual design team — himself, Thomas Andrews (who was the managing director of the design department and Pirrie's nephew) and Edward Wilding, who was Andrews' deputy and responsible for design calculations. The last member was Alexander M. Carlisle, managing director of the shipyard.

The four began to develop and refine Ismay and Pirrie's initial concepts of the 'Olympic' class of vessels, working them into a realistic and workable design. Ismay insisted that he was kept fully involved in this initial stage of design development and, accordingly, played a major role in the final project specification. Once the basic requirements for the vessels were agreed, the design team could proceed with the complex and difficult task of producing the final hull specification and outline design drawings. These were of vital importance to the various drawing offices that would produce the thousands of illustrations necessary for hull construction.

As mentioned in an earlier chapter, Harland & Wolff had a long-established association with the White Star Line. This was primarily as a result of Lord Pirrie's personal relationship with Ismay and, latterly, J. Pierpont Morgan. Pirrie had joined Harland & Wolff in 1862, becoming a partner in 1874 and eventually rising to chairman in 1896. The White Star Line had commissioned all of its vessels exclusively from Harland & Wolff in this period and it was generally accepted that Pirrie's close personal relationship with Ismay was the decisive factor in this. In addition to this, Lord Pirrie, on behalf of Harland & Wolff, also maintained a financial interest in the I.M.M. Group, which was by now the behind-the-scenes owner of the White Star Line itself. This close inter-personal and business relationship ensured that any prospective shipbuilding throughout the group was, in effect, kept in-house by virtue of the various share dealings within this close association. These share dealings were not in any way illegal or improper, but their existence meant that no other shipyard was afforded the opportunity to compete against Harland & Wolff for I.M.M. Group business.

Harland & Wolff then, was in the fortuitous position of obtaining all orders for White Star or other I.M.M. Group vessels on a cost-plus basis.

ABOVE: *The luxury of the transatlantic liners was legendary.*

This arrangement meant that, however much the cost of the vessel rose because of changes to the specification or increases in material costs, Harland & Wolff would be guaranteed a profit on the contract. The usual profit margin in these contracts was five percent over the actual vessel cost, which would be paid in share stock in the contracting company.

There was another mutual advantage to the special relationship between I.M.M. and Harland & Wolff; as Harland & Wolff could do its best work and make honest recommendations concerning construction without fear of being undercut by a rival, the White Star Line could thus be assured of receiving the very best vessels. This was to be the basis on which the I.M.M. Group would build the three sister ships *Olympic*, *Titanic* and *Gigantic* (later to be named *Britannic*).

And so it happened that the corporate triumvirate of Harland & Wolff, the White Star Line and the behind-the-scenes financial muscle of I.M.M., harnessed their considerable resources and set out to challenge the rest of the world's shipbuilders, operators and owners. The prize was to establish just who was the very biggest — and therefore, the very best.

# THE TRANSLANTIC MARKET

To examine the competition to the White Star Line offered by rival operators it is worth examining the history of the transatlantic shipping route. For almost 400 years, following the early voyages of discovery, the traffic between Europe and America grew steadily, despite many wars involving the United States, Britain, France and Spain. By the early 19th century a substantial trade involving both passengers and cargo had built up: all carried by sailing ships which were completely at the mercy of the elements. A typical crossing could easily take a month or more and any kind of regular timetable was impossible.

The introduction of steam power radically altered the picture, although it was not until around 1840 that the first purpose-designed steam-powered transatlantic liners were built. The White Star Line's greatest rival, the British Cunard Line, founded in 1839, introduced the 1,154 grt *Britannia*, which set off on its maiden transatlantic voyage on 4 July, 1840. The ship could carry up to 115 passengers and took 12 days and 10 hours for the crossing from Liverpool to Halifax. Its reciprocating machinery drove two large paddle wheels, which gave the *Britannia* a speed of 8.5 knots although, like most steamships of the period, a full sailing rig was also carried.

The introduction of steamships to the north Atlantic route had a similar impact to that produced over a century later when jet airliners replaced the old propeller-driven aircraft — passenger demand increased, leading to larger ships which could offer lower fares, thus stimulating even more demand.

The first significant American transatlantic passenger steamship was the *Washington*, which entered service in 1847 and was built with German financial assistance for the increasingly important link between the two countries. At 1,640 grt, she was larger than the *Britannia* and could carry up to 300 passengers in two classes of accommodation. Although slightly slower than the British ship, she was cheaper to operate and undercut Cunard's fares by almost a third. Following *Washington*'s success, the Germans decided to start their own line, setting the scene for the intense competition and rivalry which continued unabated right up to the outbreak of World War I.

In the mid-19th century the American economy was expanding quickly and the Atlantic crossing between Europe and the United States had grown proportionally in importance. In addition to this the Great Irish Famine started an exodus that would eventually see half of Ireland's population leave their homeland. The floodgates were not just open for the Irish famine refugees however: the United States was very keen to increase its population

and consequently its strength as a nation. To achieve this it offered unrestricted freedom of immigration to the citizens of all nations.

The invitation was accepted by the citizens of almost every European country, many of which were racked by war, civil strife, religious persecution or sheer poverty. In their hundreds of thousands people were attracted by the promise of a life of freedom in a vast new country where individual labour and enterprise could bring untold rewards. Continuing tales (some greatly exaggerated) of fortunes made from sensational strikes of gold, silver and other minerals also fed the demand for passage to this brave new world. With the large increase in immigration, trade and social links between the Old and New Worlds, the climate was perfect for the transatlantic passenger markets to boom. The race was on to produce ever larger and faster liners, using the relatively new technology of steam engines pushing iron ships.

By the 1890s this boom in world trade sustained thousands of small ships that travelled to any destination with any cargo. Most shared engine room characteristics along similar lines; a 1,500 hp triple expansion engine and three boilers with their backs in the engine room. Few had electric light — instead using oil lamps at sea and a smoky 'duck' lamp for working in port. Engine controls were simple, with throttle, reversing gear, drains and impulse valves all grouped together with a telegraph nearby. Few of these engines had governors, which meant that watch-keeping required continuous care and attention to prevent overspeed.

PREVIOUS PAGE: *The elegance and luxury of the first class accommodation on board passenger-carrying steamers of the Edwardian era continues to fascinate us today. Here is* Lusitania*'s first class lounge, reminiscent of a London club.*

BELOW: *Cunard's R.M.S.* Lusitania — *like* Titanic *she would meet an untimely end.*

RIGHT: *The Blue Riband was awarded to the fastest passenger ship on the Transatlantic run and was held by Cunard ships for many years. This is a list of the holders of the Blue Riband holders contemporary with the 'Olympic' class.*

## BLUE RIBAND WESTBOUND WINNERS 1889–1925

| 28/8/1889 | *City of Paris* | I&I Line | 5d.19hr.18min. | 20.01kts. |
|---|---|---|---|---|
| 5/8/1891 | *Majestic* | White Star Line | 5d.18hr.8min. | 20.10kts. |
| 19/8/1891 | *Teutonic* | White Star Line | 5d.16hr.31min. | 20.35kts. |
| 27/7/1892 | *City of Paris* | I&I Line | 5d.15hr.53min. | 20.48kts. |
| 18/10/1892 | *City of Paris* | I&I Line | 5d.14hr.24min. | 20.70kts. |
| 23/6/1893 | *Campania* | Cunard Line | 5d.15hr.37min. | 21.12kts. |
| 17/8/1894 | *Campania* | Cunard Line | 5d.9hr.29min. | 21.44kts. |
| 31/8/1894 | *Lucania* | Cunard Line | 5d.8hr.38min. | 21.65kts. |
| 28/9/1894 | *Lucania* | Cunard Line | 5d.7hr.48min. | 21.75kts. |
| 26/10/1894 | *Lucania* | Cunard Line | 5d.7hr.23min. | 21.81kts. |
| 5/4/1898 | *Kaiser Wilhelm der Grosse* | Norddeutscher Lloyd | 5d.20hr | 22.29kts. |
| 12/7/1900 | *Deutschland* | Hamburg Amerika Line | 5d.15hr.46min. | 22.42kts. |
| 1/9/1900 | *Deutschland* | Hamburg Amerika Line | 5d.12hr.29min. | 23.02kts. |
| 1/8/1901 | *Deutschland* | Hamburg Amerika Line | 5d.11hr.46min. | 22.42kts. |
| 16/9/1902 | *Kronprinz Wilhelm* | Norddeutscher Lloyd | 5d.11hr.57min. | 23.09kts. |
| 8/9/1903 | *Deutschland* | Hamburg Amerika Line | 5d.11hr.54min. | 23.15kts. |
| 10/10/1907 | *Lusitania* | Cunard line | 4d.19hr.52min. | 23.99kts. |
| 21/5/1908 | Lusitania | Cunard line | 4d.19hr.52min. | 23.99kts. |
| 10/7/1908 | Lusitania | Cunard line | 4d.16hr.40min. | 25.65kts. |
| 30/9/1909 | Mauretania | Cunard line | 4d.10hr.51min. | 26.06kts. |

Record held until 1929.

ABOVE: Aquitania *at Southampton. Another of Cunard's great liners, she may have been built for speed but that didn't stop her from being luxuriously appointed.*

RIGHT: *First class sleeping and cabin accommodation was particularly luxurious. This is one of* Lusitania's *'suite de luxe'.*

FOLLOWING PAGES: *Another view of* Aquitania; *alongside is the tug* Clausentum.

By the turn of the century the major seafaring nations were striving to seize the lion's share of this lucrative market. The main contenders were the mercantile fleets of Britain and Germany, echoing the massive naval armaments race which was also in progress at the time and which led eventually to war in 1914. The main German operators were North German Lloyd (originally partners in the *Washington*) and the Hamburg-Amerika Line. In 1897, North German launched the world's largest liner to date. This was the four-funnelled 14,300 ton *Kaiser Wilhelm der Grosse* which was 655 ft long. Very soon she also proved that she was also the world's fastest by capturing the prestigious Blue Riband from the Cunard-owned *Lucania* in the September of that year — crossing the Atlantic at an average speed of 22.35 knots. This was a major blow to British pride, which suffered further when Hamburg-Amerika 16,500 ton *Deutschland* became the next holder of the Blue Riband. Other German liners of the period were the 14,900 ton *Kronprinz Wilhelm* and the 19,300 ton *Kaiser Wilhelm II*, both owned by the North German Line. The latter ship became the third German holder of the Blue Riband in 1906 following its introduction to service in 1903. The Fourth ship in this series of world-beating German liners was the 19,300 ton, 707 ft, *Kronprinzessin Cecilie*, which was commissioned in 1907 and could carry up to 1,808 passengers as well as 602 crew. (To digress from the story of *Titanic* and her sisters, it is interesting to relate that the *Kronprinzessin Cecilie* was at sea when war broke out in August 1914. Unable to reach Germany, she repainted her funnels in the White Star Line colours of buff with a black top,

and returned to the then neutral United States where she was initially mistaken for the *Olympic* when she anchored in Bar Harbour, Maine on 4 August. The ship was interned and later taken over by the U.S. Navy before being laid up for many years and finally scrapped in 1940.)

The coveted Blue Riband had now become such a highly prized talisman that the British were determined to recapture it. Already the contention between the two most powerful maritime powers in Europe had led to a rapid increase in liner building. British and German shipyards responded to an insatiable demand for larger ship designs which were pushing the boundaries of naval architecture to the very limit and sometimes beyond.

While this culture of intense competition was good news for the shipyards, it placed a heavy financial burden on the shipping companies who had to pay for the vessels. Some method had to be found to alleviate the enormous drain on the ship owners' resources, in particular those of the Cunard Line, which was at the very vanguard of this battle. The British Government eventually woke up to the fact that its merchant marine fleet, the very lifeblood of the country and its enormous empire, was either being out built by the Germans or taken over by the Americans. The decisive development which finally galvanised the politicians into action was Morgan's purchase of the White Star Line. Under legislation in force at the time, it was illegal to offer direct financial assistance in the funding of merchant vessel construction and therefore a method had to be found to circumvent the law. The solution, like most good ideas, was remarkably simple and

*RIGHT:* Mauretania *was a little longer, a little heavier and, it turned out, a little faster than her sister ship* Lusitania *against whom she would contest the Blue Riband.* Mauretania *would hold the Blue Riband from 1909 until 1929.*

*BELOW: Boat Deck on* Mauretania*'s, where — as on the 'Olympic' class — first class passengers could promenade.*

*BELOW:* Mauretania*'s bridge.*

*More views of* Mauretania's *first class accommodation: the lounge (ABOVE), dining saloon (ABOVE RIGHT) and the smoke room (BELOW RIGHT).*

involved the possibility that merchant vessels could be commandeered by the Royal Navy in time of war. The British government introduced a scheme to provide ship owners with a cost subsidy — to a maximum of 50 percent of the cost of vessel construction. To qualify for this substantial subsidy, ship owners undertook to remain British-owned and all new vessels built under the scheme were required to be constructed to Admiralty standard, in order that they would be suitable for conversion to the armed merchant service if war broke out. In reality, this requirement consisted mainly of a greater than normal thickness of upper deck plating to accommodate the mounting of a naval gun, and additional watertight compartments throughout the hull.

The greatest beneficiary of these subsidies was, of course, the Cunard Line, which was still locked in fierce combat for Atlantic supremacy with the

German national shipping company Hamburg-Amerika. Cunard immediately instituted a rapid expansion program for its fleet of vessels, the orders going to the John Brown and Swan Hunter shipyards.

The result of this commission was two ships which, for different reasons, became household names. The first was the ill-fated *Lusitania*, the subject of a notorious demise — she was sunk without warning by a German U-boat in May 1915 with the loss of 1,195 lives. However, her early career was extremely successful and she quickly rewarded her owners and builders when she regained the Blue Riband for Britain; crossing the Atlantic with an average speed of 23.6 knots on her second westward voyage in late 1907. With a length of 787 ft and a gross tonnage of 31,550, she was easily the world's largest liner as well as the fastest. Her handsome slim lines were complemented by four evenly-spaced raked funnels which gave an air of speed even when she was at anchor. As the crew became familiar with the operation of her machinery — new steam turbines geared to quadruple screws—the ship's performance steadily improved to the extent that average speeds on the transatlantic run rose to 26 knots.

Although the Germans and Americans had no vessels which could make a response to this incredible speed, the second ship of the British pair eventually proved to have the edge in terms of sheer performance. This was the *Mauretania* which, by a very small margin, was longer and heavier than her sister and on her maiden eastbound voyage also showed that she was also slightly faster, making the crossing at an average of 23.69 knots. From then until 1914, the two great Cunarders engaged in friendly rivalry until the *Mauretania* set an average of 26.6 knots in September 1909, a record which was not broken until 1929 by the German liner, the *Bremen*.

Although built for speed, the two Cunard ships did not stint on luxury and could carry 560 first, 475 second and 1,300 third class passengers at fares ranging from over £200 in first to around £20 in steerage — these figures comparing with the sort of money which today's travellers might pay for a crossing by supersonic Concorde or by the cheapest economy air fare respectively. The *Lusitania* and *Mauretania* were set to dominate the British-based transatlantic market in the years up to the First World War.

As an American-owned company, the White Star Line's position had become one of temperance regarding this competition. It had preferred to sit on the sidelines and let the two opponents battle things out between them: that is until the fateful evening when Ismay and Pirrie concocted the 'Olympic' class, the dimensions of which were nothing short of astonishing. They were to be 883 feet in length and 92.5 feet in beam and have a gross tonnage of 45,000 tons. Their competitors, the existing Cunard giants *Lusitania* and *Mauretania*, were some ninety feet shorter, four feet narrower and 14,000 tons lighter. The first two of the three White Star liners planned to compete with the Cunarders were to be constructed side by side and launched within a year or so of one another. These were the vessels which would put the White Star Line right back at the top of the transatlantic trade.

*Left:* Mauretania*'s smoke room.*

# KEY PEOPLE

*ABOVE: Captain E. J. Smith.*

### CAPTAIN EDWARD J. SMITH

Captain Smith was born in 1850, and went to sea at the age of 13. A Staffordshire man, he had an early apprenticeship at sea in the ships of Gibson & Company, and took his master's certificate at twenty five years of age. By 1880 he had joined the White Star Line as a junior officer and later became chief officer of the *Cufic* . He gained his first command in 1887 as captain of the *Celtic*. Just two years later he was involved in a serious incident when the ship then in his command, the *Republic*, ran aground off New York and was embarrassingly stranded for several hours before being refloated. On the same day, three crewmen were killed in a boiler accident. As vessels increased in size and power, Captain Smith changed from one ship to another, and bore the burden of increasing responsibility. In 1890 he again ran a ship aground near Rio de Janeiro, but his career continued and he commanded several troopships during the Boer War, these services resulting in the award of medals and a commission in the Royal Naval Reserve as a commander; a distinction which allowed any merchant ship under his command to fly the Blue Ensign instead of the Red Ensign normally flown by British merchant ships. In 1901 aboard the *Majestic* and again, in 1906, aboard the *Baltic*, his ships experienced serious onboard fires; in November 1909 he again ran aground, this time in the White Star Line's flagship *Adriatic* in the Ambrose Channel near New York. When the *Olympic* entered service in 1911, he continued this amazing record by almost crushing a tug while berthing at New York and he was also in command on both of the occasions when the Olympic was forced to return to Belfast for repairs. Seamen above all men are superstitious and many shook their heads and uttered the private words that, 'Captain Smith has broken his luck'. Nevertheless the company appointed him commodore of the White Star Fleet, and had no hesitation in appointing him to the command of the *Titanic* when she was ready for sea, although some sources indicate that he was due to retire on completion of the return maiden voyage. Smith handed the *Olympic* over to Captain Herbert James Haddock and arrived in Belfast on 1 April to take the new ship to sea for her trials.

Despite the many incidents which had marred his career, Captain Smith was generally well-respected by his fellow professionals — indeed most reports state that he was one of the most popular officers aboard any of the ocean going liners. *Lloyd's Weekly News* gave this, somewhat glowing, profile of the man after the *Titanic* was lost;

'He was the very type of a British sea-captain, quiet, with shrewd, keen eyes beneath his shaggy brows, strong in command, gentle in social conserve, modest as a simple seaman, brave as a lion of unblemished honour'.

Never had any Captain been responsible for the safety of such wealthy passengers as those who joined *Titanic* but his employers had absolute faith in his skill and judgement. He had commanded seventeen White Star Liners in succession and it is only fair to point out that some of the incidents in which he had been involved were not his fault — nevertheless, he seems to have had more than his fair share of problems and fate had more in store for him yet.

*ABOVE: Captain E. J. Smith.*

## LORD WILLIAM J. PIRRIE

William James Pirrie was born on 24 May, 1847, in Quebec. His father, James, had been sent to Canada in 1844 to embark on a career in the timber trade but had died only five years later in 1849. Following the death, William's mother, Eliza Swan Montgomery, brought young William and his sister Eliza to live with their paternal grandfather, Captain Pirrie, who had his home in Ireland, at Conlig, Co. Down. Captain Pirrie showed a keen

*BELOW: Captain E. J. Smith and Lord Pirrie aborad Olympic at Southampton.*

*ABOVE: Lord and Lady Pirrie.*

interest in his grandson's development over the following decade and it was very natural that he should encourage the boy to choose a career connected with ships. In fact, the young William James was to grow up surrounded by relatives who were either involved in trade or ship owning; no less than four different sets of aunts and uncles were either in the shipping business or worked in connected concerns such as commission agents or insurance brokers. However, after his Grandfather's death, on 8 June, 1858, no relative was to have such a controlling influence on Pirrie's early life than his staunch Presbyterian mother.

As a schoolboy at the Royal Belfast Academic Institution young William noted the success of Harland & Wolff, the Belfast shipbuilders, and set about the task of persuading his mother to arrange for him to become their new gentleman apprentice. In June of 1862 he began his apprenticeship at the Queen's Island yard and embarked on his rise up through the managerial ranks. His small frame, meticulously groomed appearance and an ever smiling face, did little to hide the man's enormous energy and piercing intelligence from his employers, and he was rewarded with ever increasing responsibility and larger shares in the firm. In 1894, William Pirrie was elected to the Belfast Corporation and to the Harbour Commissioners — a position that he retained and used well. On Christmas Eve of 1895, Edward Harland died and the following year William James Pirrie assumed the leadership of the firm. It was not long before he was elected as its first chairman and this elevation was soon augmented by a further illustrious position; that of Lord Mayor of Belfast. Pirrie quickly disappointed loyalist opinion by rejecting his political affiliations, proposing some measure of representation for the Nationalist and Labour parties against a strong Tory backdrop. The influence of a Liberal upbringing instilled a growing Liberalism in his office which served to ease sectarian tensions that were brewing at the time. In 1898, at the end of a successful period of office as Lord Mayor, Pirrie was made the first Freeman of Belfast (following as the second in 1899 was Thomas Ismay, in recognition of the contribution he had made to Harland & Wolff and therefore to Belfast). In 1906, with a new Liberal Government in power, he was rapidly made a peer and was bestowed the title of Viscount Pirrie. That year yielded other good fortune when G. W. Wolff retired, selling Pirrie all his shares in the shipyard. This purchase made Harland & Wolff virtually Pirrie's personal fiefdom. He surrounded himself with his so called 'splendid men', who were revered for their technical skill and the devotion of their service. All of them owed their promotions to Pirrie and were far too scared to question his decisions, something he was not only aware of but actually manipulated. William Pirrie had always been adept at understanding political mechanisms and was uninhibited in using them to his own advantage, indeed, Lord Pirrie, as he was now known, guided Harland & Wolff, through both good times and lean times with courage, skill and audacity. When *Titanic* was lost, Pirrie was devastated by the death of his beloved nephew Thomas Andrews: unlike Bruce Ismay and the White Star Line however, Lord Pirrie and Harland & Wolff survived the disaster with their reputations intact.

While on a tour of South America and with his health already failing, Lord Pirrie picked up a chill in Autofagosta, Chile. This sickness rapidly developed into pneumonia but, dogmatic as ever, he persisted with his cruise aboard the *Ebro*. On 7 June, 1924, his vessel reached the Panama Canal and he insisted that he be brought up on deck to take in the views. At 11:30 that evening he died at the age of 78. His embalmed body was shipped home to Belfast on board the Harland & Wolff built *Olympic*. As an indication of his status, the newspaper headlines that day read; 'The Passing of the World's Greatest Shipbuilder'.

Pirrie's autocratic style had been such that none of the 'splendid men' left in his wake had the knowledge or the personality to continue the work at Harland & Wolff effectively. It was also discovered that he had made no provision for his death and many important company secrets had died with him. Pirrie had become a very complex and secretive man — perhaps the turning point was, after all, the death of Andrews onboard *Titanic*, maybe it was following this loss that Lord Pirrie's will for a progressive future at Harland & Wolff after his own death was ultimately lost.

## THOMAS ANDREWS JUNIOR

Thomas Andrews, was born in 1873 in the quiet village of Comber on the outskirts of Belfast and was a member of a long-established and well-known Ulster family which maintained several business interests in property and linen spinning mills throughout Northern Ireland. He was the second son of Thomas and Eliza Morison Andrews, his mother's maiden name being Eliza Morison Pirrie. Eliza was Lord William Pirrie's sister and Thomas Andrews Junior therefore, his nephew. Andrews' father the Rt. Honourable Thomas Andrews was a politician, a career which Thomas' elder brother, John Miller Andrews, was to follow and in which he eventually exceeded, becoming the second Prime Minister of Ireland. In just fifty years the Andrews/Pirrie family had created the biggest rope works, the biggest thread works, the biggest shipyard and the biggest ships in the world and possessed a strong voice in both Irish and British politics.

Andrews joined Harland & Wolff as a premium apprentice in 1899. He quickly proved himself to be a model pupil, gaining the respect of the whole workforce for his technical skill. Often he would work far into the night trying to master the theory of ship design and the techniques of draughtsmanship. In 1894, having completed his apprenticeship, he was immediately appointed as an outside manager and was soon regarded as a brilliant and innovative ship designer, rapidly progressing to a position on the board at Harland & Wolff. Lord Pirrie held the young man in great affection and it was widely assumed that he was grooming Andrews to be his successor. That Lord Pirrie and his wife were childless added weight to the speculation, although Pirrie never committed himself and there is nothing to suggest that he planned to nominate Thomas Andrews as Chairman. In 1908, Thomas Andrews married Helen Reilly Barbour, a relation of the deputy Prime Minister of Ireland.

After the meeting in London with Ismay, Lord Pirrie returned to Belfast and called together his elite band of 'splendid men' to brief them on the magnificent new project upon which they were about to embark. Thomas Andrews was a member of the group by merit of his technical skill. As the managing director of the design department he reported directly to the Rt. Honourable Alexander M. Carlisle the shipyard managing director. Andrews' able deputy Edward Wilding, was responsible for design calculations. These four began to develop and refine Ismay and Pirrie's initial concepts of the 'Olympic' class of vessel though it was Thomas Andrews who was ultimately handed full responsibility for the design of the two sister ships. His deputy, Edward Wilding, while responsible for the general management of the various drawing offices, also held the key role of producing the detailed design calculations necessary for the new vessels, in particular those concerning stability, damage control and safety. Andrews was later to accompany *Titanic* on her maiden voyage in the capacity of builder's representative, travelling with J. B Ismay of the White Star Line. After she struck the iceberg Andrews was summoned to assist Captain Smith in assessing the damage and duly made extremely accurate calculations of how long he thought she would remain afloat. As the stricken ship drew nearer to her

82

death, Thomas Andrews was last seen sat alone in the first class smoking room transfixed by a painting on the wall. Wilding, unfortunately, was to incur the full wrath of Pirrie over the loss of *Titanic* and of Thomas Andrews. As the main witness called to represent Harland & Wolff at the Board of Trade inquiry into the loss of *Titanic*, Wilding presented his evidence in a clear and concise manner. Attendance at the inquiry was particularly trying for him, as he endured hours of detailed questions and theoretical supposition regarding what may have happened during the sinking. A sensitive and quiet man, the ordeal had a traumatic effect on him, made all the more intense by his enduring sorrow at the loss of his colleague Thomas Andrews. Shortly after the inquiry was concluded, with Harland & Wolff exonerated of any blame for the loss of the vessel, Wilding was summoned to see Lord Pirrie in his office whereupon he was summarily dismissed. In fact, he was given just one hour to clear his desk of all personal property and to leave the premises. Mystery surrounds the actual reasons for Wilding's abrupt dismissal — however, it is widely supposed that Pirrie held him personally responsible for the loss of *Titanic* and, consequently, the death of his much-loved nephew. This assumption, if indeed it was true, was grossly unfair to Wilding and his design calculations, especially those regarding the survivability of the vessel in a damaged condition. Pirrie's injustice though, emphatically underlines how much the autocratic chairman thought of his chief designer and nephew, Thomas Andrews.

## JOSEPH BRUCE ISMAY

Joseph Bruce Ismay, or Bruce, as he was commonly referred to, was the son of T. H. Ismay, the founder of the White Star Line. He was born on 12 December, 1862, and was the eldest of Thomas Ismay's three sons. Bower, his youngest brother never joined the family firm, but the second, James, went into management of the family business with his elder brother until it was purchased by I.M.M. Bruce was educated at Harrow and then later privately in Dinard. Accounts tell that he was an excellent sportsman who fully enjoyed the lifestyle that his father's money allowed him, although living up to his father's reputation was

probably something that he never escaped from. He was never a favourite of his father — in fact quite the opposite — and a simple anecdote best depicts their relationship. Having been upon a world tour, Bruce returned to his father's shipping office to learn the family business. On his first day there, having deposited his hat and coat in his father's private room, the latter instructed a subordinate, in front of the staff, to inform the new office boy to leave his hat and coat somewhere else! In spite of such harsh treatment, when his father died in 1899, Bruce Ismay subsequently inherited the White Star Line.

Although Thomas Ismay had relinquished the running of the business to his son when he retired in 1892, behind the scenes he was still very much the driving force and was notified of anything outside the realms of day to day management. Following his father's death however, Bruce assumed complete control of the White Star Line and some accounts attribute the American take-over of the firm just three years later to Bruce's reserved and retiring nature. Others cite that it was a shrewd business move guided behind the scenes by Lord Pirrie of Harland and Wolff. Pirrie had adopted a paternal relationship with Bruce and therefore the White Star Line itself. Indeed, it seems that Bruce Ismay was once again in the shadow of another very autocratic figure who, with his usual political flair, always made sure that he got what was best for Harland & Wolff first, any advantage to Ismay's beloved White Star Line coming a very definite second. Following the fateful dinner engagement with Pirrie, Ismay attended the launch of the *Titanic* and was actively involved at the initial concept stage of the new vessels and also later with fixture specifications. Ismay also provided a critique of *Olympic* when he crossed the Atlantic with her, which was characteristically fastidious, drawing attention to bed springs that were too springy and the lack of cigar holders in first class toilets. While it seems that he was not sufficiently interested in the mechanics of the great liner to join her for her sea trials, he was on board for the ship's maiden voyage occupying the port side first class suite on B Deck, one of the two so-called 'millionaire's suites'.

It is widely known that, when the loss of the *Titanic* became public, Ismay found himself shunned by his friends and society in general because of his actions on the night of the disaster. Ismay survived the sinking after stepping into a departing lifeboat at a time when only women and children were being evacuated. While he always maintained that the deck was clear of any women and children and that there was still ample room in the boat, some witness statements allege that this was not the case. To a great extent Ismay was the architect of his own downfall as, immediately upon being rescued by the *Carpathia*, Ismay requested a private cabin, studiously avoiding all contact with the other survivors. His actions were probably a reaction to the shock of the previous night's events, but when taken together with his abandonment of the *Titanic* they were interpreted as those of a coward. On 30 June, 1913, Bruce Ismay retired as Chairman of I.M.M. and the White Star Line, although he remained an executive until 1916. He died at 74 years of age on 17 October, 1937. However, Bruce Ismay was not the only major figure in the *Titanic* disaster to suffer because of the tragedy.

## JOHN PIERPONT MORGAN

J Pierpont Morgan was an American financier, steel magnate and railway baron.

He had achieved tremendous success in amalgamating different American railway companies and decided that the same measure of prosperity could be achieved with the shipping business. His overriding philosophy was that by placing different shipping lines under one umbrella he could eradicate the price wars that were so bad for business. Without delay, he set about planning, and then creating, an enormous shipping syndicate, one that was to be American owned and which was designed — in the opinion of a contemporary, 'to provide a complete system of transportation from the far and near West over the railway, by lake steamer and over the Atlantic to Europe'. This kind of corporate conglomerate hardly seems revolutionary to modern eyes, but shock waves started to reverberate throughout the world of shipping as rumours became substantiated by fact and Morgan steadily bought up the shares of the different lines needed. The press of the day even coined the phrase 'morganising' to describe other such conglomerate business activity. As Morgan's acquisitions grew it became increasingly obvious to both Lord Pirrie of Harland & Wolff and Bruce Ismay of the White Star Line that, for different reasons, they had no choice but to join Morgan's combine. The name Morgan gave to this vast syndicate was I.M.M. — the International Mercantile Marine Company. Morgan regarded The White Star Line as the standard-bearer of the I.M.M., and took great pride in the construction of the first two 'Olympic' class vessels. It is not widely known that J. Pierpoint Morgan, who was ultimately *Titanic*'s owner, received the news of her sinking with great shock. In fact, he was so devastated by the tragic news that he became a recluse, to all intents and purposes withdrawing from public life. The White Star Line itself never fully recovered from the disaster and much the same could be said of J. Pierpoint Morgan. His health rapidly deteriorated and in March 1913 he died in Rome a broken man.

*ABOVE: J. Pierpont Morgan.*

# BUILDING
# OLYMPIC & TITANIC

In March 1908, the decision was finally made to proceed with the construction of the first two 'Olympic' class vessels. However, the order for *Olympic* and *Titanic,* while being of great value to Harland & Wolff, also presented the company with several major logistical problems. During the initial discussions and, indeed, when the agreement to build the vessels was made, no great thought had been given to exactly where they would be constructed. Obviously, they would be built in Belfast but this presented the first problem. Harland & Wolff shipyard facilities at their main Queen's Island complex did not even have a single slipway capable of accommodating a vessel of this size, let alone two of them. The complex comprised of four individual shipbuilding yards. In order of building capacity; the Musgrave, Queen's, Abercorn and Victoria shipyards. After much debate by the board, it was decided that the best course of action would be to demolish the three existing slipways in the Queen's shipyard and build two larger ones in their place. These slipways were eventually to be allocated the numbers 2 and 3, as during the reconstruction works it was discovered that a smaller slipway, number 1, could be accommodated at an angle of 45 degrees to the larger ones. Pirrie, always mindful of the need to maximise the potential of shipbuilding

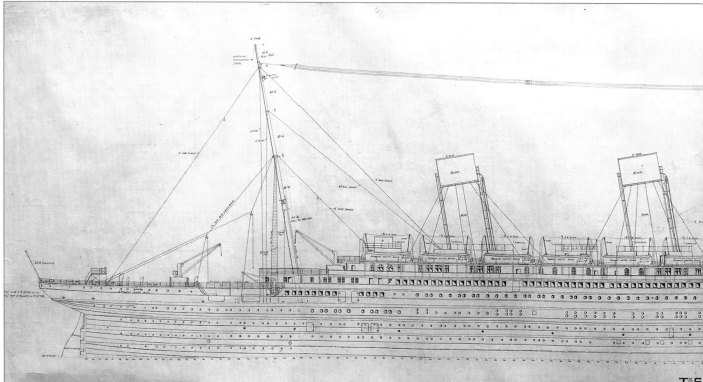

WHITE STAR LINE R.M.S
'OLYMPIC' & TITANIC
THE LARGEST SHIPS IN THE WORLD

capacity, personally championed the construction of this additional slipway against much internal opposition. Such was Pirrie's control over the affairs of Harland & Wolff, that all resistance to his proposal was quickly dispelled and the construction of slipway number 1 commenced. In reality, the additional shipbuilding capacity this slipway provided proved to be of little use and, as a consequence, it rapidly fell into disuse, overshadowed by its two much larger neighbours. Pirrie regarded the reconstruction of the Queen's shipyard as the culmination of his ambition to place Harland & Wolff at the pinnacle of world shipbuilding. He had always regarded other yards, in particular those in Europe, as inferior to British shipyards and was fiercely

*ABOVE: Harland & Wolff's original model of an 'Olympic' class vessel. The Olympic and Titanic were virtually identical, a fact which has led to a great many pictures of Olympic being identified as Titanic.*

*BELOW: Builder's rigging plan for Olympic.*

OLYMPIC."

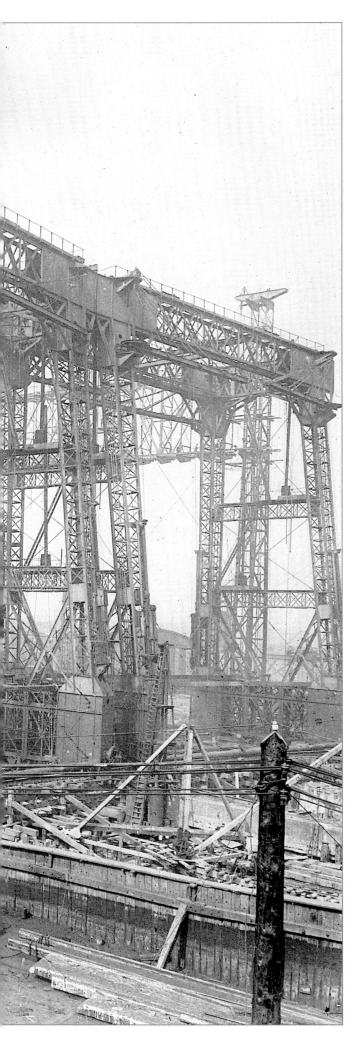

LEFT AND BELOW: *Erection of the Arrol Gantry's primary steelwork on Nos 2 and 3 slips, Queen's Shipyard. Many designs were submitted for consideration, with the order eventually going to Thomas Arrol and Company of Glasgow, who proposed a distinctive latticework design topped by the most powerful cranes possible. The following photographs show the gantry under construction.*

• BUILDING OLYMPIC AND TITANIC •

determined that this position would be maintained. He reasoned that the creation of these new slipways, specifically designed to facilitate the construction of the greatest vessels ever built, would enhance Harland & Wolff's reputation as the world's greatest shipbuilder. Construction of the slipways themselves was not enough to secure this objective; something was missing, something that would demonstrate Harland & Wolff's commitment to be the most technologically advanced and progressive shipbuilder in the world at that time. The answer was provided by what Lord Pirrie came to regard as the jewel in Harland & Wolff's crown. The new slipways would be equipped with the largest and most powerful cranes available. On completion these were not to be just simple cranes but an enormous purpose-built gantry that would dominate the skyline of Belfast. Many designs were submitted for consideration, with the order eventually going to Thomas Arrol and Company of Glasgow, who proposed a distinctive latticework design. Each slipway would be surmounted with its own self-contained and independent gantry situated in tandem with each other. Each massive gantry had an overall length of 840 ft, a width spanning each slipway of 150 ft and an overall operating height of 100 ft. This massive structure was in turn topped by a set of mobile cranes each with a lifting capacity of three tons. In addition to the land works necessary to construct these two enormous structures, the decision was taken to purchase, second-hand, a large floating crane from a German shipyard in order to provide much needed extra lifting capacity at the fitting-out wharf. This giant crane had a maximum lifting capacity of

LEFT AND ABOVE: *Each of the specially constructed slipways was surmounted by its own self-contained and independent gantry situated in tandem with each other. Each massive gantry had an overall length of 840 ft, a width spanning each slipway of 150 ft and an overall operating height of 100 ft. This massive structure was, in turn, topped by a set of mobile cranes each with a lifting capacity of three tons.*

*ABOVE AND RIGHT: Construction continues on the enormous gantry that would dominate the skyline of Belfast.*

250 tons and, being mounted on a large pontoon, provided the company with a mobile heavy lift facility.

The final piece in this grand jigsaw was finally completed when Pirrie, himself a harbour commissioner, persuaded the Belfast Harbour Commissioners to fund the building of a new graving (or dry) dock which would be capable of taking the new vessels on their completion. (Dry docks are properly referred to as 'graving' docks, this term being derived from their rectangular shape, which is similar to that of a human grave). This task was accomplished despite much personal hostility towards Pirrie and his plans from several of his fellow harbour commissioners, who regarded him as bombastic and self-serving because Pirrie regarded the harbour commissioners as subservient to the requirements of Harland & Wolff. This assumption was very probably correct: Pirrie did indeed have power on his side and would not hesitate to wield it whenever he thought necessary. Pirrie had anticipated opposition to his plans and developed a two-part strategy to achieve his aim. The first part was a threat to close Harland & Wolff, the largest employer in the country, if funding for this new dock was refused. Pirrie had earlier bluntly informed the Harbour Commissioners and Belfast City Council that, should support for this new facility be refused, he would have no alternative but to close Harland & Wolff and transfer the business to the mainland. Horrified by this prospect, both bodies agreed to examine various ways in which funding could be found. The second part of the strategy involved Pirrie in considerable political lobbying among his contemporaries

in the House of Lords at Westminster, primarily to ensure that the political will would be in place to provide financial support should a request for assistance be received from Belfast. By employing these methods Pirrie ensured that all opposition to his proposal was swept aside. He was an astute businessman and saw no difficulty in hedging his bets. Construction work began immediately and by spring 1911 the new dock was ready. It was named the Thompson Graving Dock in honour of the then chairman of the Harbour Commissioners.

Lord Pirrie, by virtue of his position as chairman of Harland & Wolff, had the ultimate control over the activities of the company. He was however, a very secretive man and did not readily share with his fellow directors exactly what was going on. Pirrie held such absolute and autonomous control over the company affairs that the precise terms and conditions of any vessel-building contracts or, indeed, the financial position of Harland & Wolff itself, were known only to him. Pirrie insisted on surrounding himself only with people whom he felt could implicitly trust and upon whom he could rely without question. The Rt. Honourable Alexander M. Carlisle headed this privileged group of confidants. Personally appointed by Pirrie as

*BELOW: The tank-top plating is almost complete, in this photograph that shows the plates forming water ballast tanks.*

ABOVE LEFT: *Centre girder and keel plates in position under the Arrol Gantry.*

ABOVE RIGHT: *Central keel girder and hydraulic riveting machine.*

LEFT: *This photograph shows the double bottom internal construction before the tank-top plating went in (compare with photograph on far left).*

*RIGHT: Internal steelwork construction, showing the decks beginning to be formed.*

*FAR RIGHT: These two reproductions are examples of the detailed construction drawings produced for* Titanic. *They show the arrangement of internal supports at Frame 67 on the tank-top.*

*BELOW AND BELOW RIGHT: Framing before plating began. Note the wooden supports and the plates in the foreground.*

Managing Director he was responsible for all shipbuilding operations throughout Harland & Wolff. Reporting directly to Carlisle as Managing Director of the design department and with full responsibility for the design of *Olympic* and *Titanic* was Thomas Andrews.

By July of 1908 the preliminary design work had progressed enough for Harland & Wolff to make a formal proposal to the directors of the Oceanic Steam Navigation Company (White Star's nominal owners), who visited Belfast at the end of that month. They liked what they saw and a formal letter of understanding was exchanged between the two parties. Such was the level of trust between the builders and their customers that no formal contract was ever drawn up. The ships were built on the same 'cost plus' basis which had pertained to all previous orders and a fixed price of £3 million for the pair was agreed (however this agreement did not prevent Harland & Wolff from submitting to White Star a large account for 'extras to contract' upon completion of the vessels). It is notable that Harland & Wolff's financial year actually began on July 1, which meant that, at the start of the new financial year Harland & Wolff found itself graced with an order from White Star to commence the building process for this new class of vessel. Initially, the order called for three vessels, though this was subsequently cut to two, the third to follow at a later date.

The *Olympic* keel was laid down as Number 400 on 16 December, 1908. As the first of her class she attracted enormous interest from the general public, other shipyards and shipping companies in general. Her dimensions

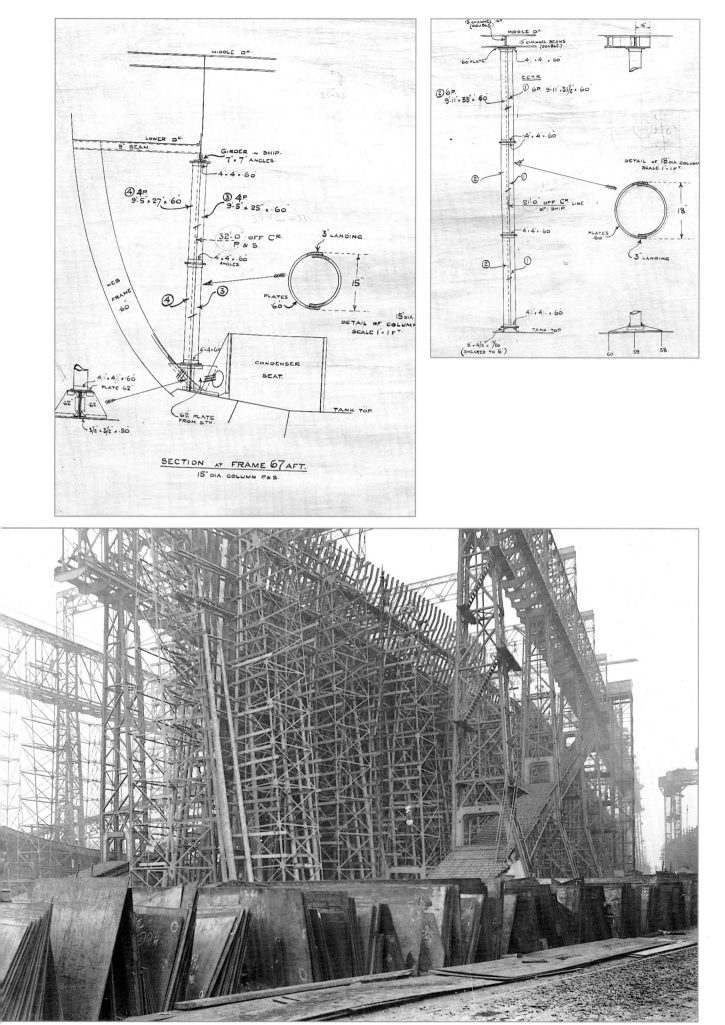

*ABOVE: Lifting sternpost into slipway at stern area.*

*RIGHT: Wooden staging surrounds* Olympic *as she is plated.*

*FAR RIGHT: View of aft framing before the shell plating was erected.*

were to be 882 ft in length, 92 ft in beam with a projected gross registered tonnage of 45,000. When finished, she would be able to accommodate 2,345 passengers with a crew complement of around 860. Her passenger capacity was to be divided between 689 first class, 674 second class and 1,026 third class, each to be billeted in specific areas of the ship. Construction began using the traditional shipbuilding method of keel, frame and shell plating built up in riveted sections. The writer Filson Young described the scene as his mail steamer pulled into Belfast Harbour, and approached the huge gantries of the Harland & Wolff shipyard.

'On the flattest of the mud flats arises a veritable forest of iron. A leafless forest stripped of its leaves and laid bare. But as you glide nearer still you see that the forest is not lifeless nor its branches deserted. From the bottom to the topmost boughs it is crowded with a life that at first seems like that of mites in the interstices of some rotting fabric, and then like birds crowding the branches of the leafless forest, and finally appears as a multitude of pigmy men swarming and toiling amid the skeleton iron structures that are as vast as cathedrals and seem as frail as gossamer.'[1]

On 31 March, 1909, the second keel, Number 401, that of *Titanic*, was laid on the adjacent slipway. Her dimensions were the same as her sister's as was her projected tonnage and work now commenced on the sister ships side-by-side and in an identical fashion. The centre keel girder (or spine) was a hollow box section 5 ft 3 in deep, mounted on a flat keelplate 1.5 in thick. Resting on this keelplate was the keelbar itself, a solid bar of 3 in thick steel, which provided the basic hull strength. Projecting outwards from each side of the keelbar were the tank-top floor plates ready for the first longitudinal

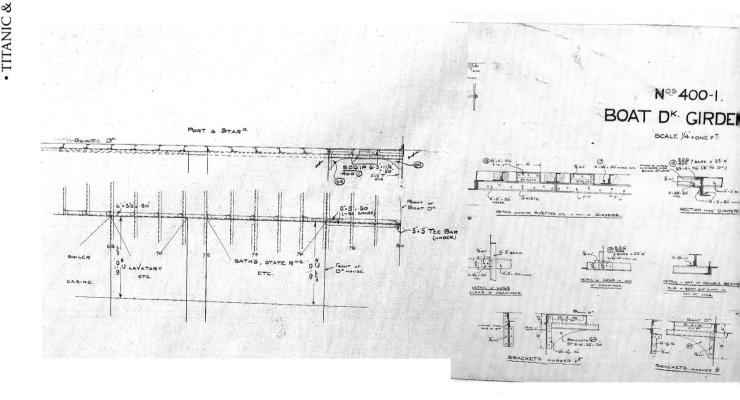

LEFT: *Detail drawing of Boat deck support structure.*

strength girders extending fore and aft along the bottom of the hull. On the two 'Olympic' class ships were placed four of these longitudinal girders on each side between the centre hull casing and the margin plate; however, under the machinery compartment, additional girders were incorporated to provide greater hull strength. Between the margin plate and the turn of the bilge were located the wing or side tanks, which together with the double-bottom tank carried the water ballast for the vessels. The whole of the double bottom was built up in this manner and riveted together using hydraulic power. To facilitate the free flow of ballast water, the floor plates between the girders were provided with lightening holes, producing a honeycomb effect. At intervals along the double bottom the floor plates were of solid construction to form the boundaries of the separate ballast tanks.

Rising up from the double bottom at each side of the hull were the side frames (or ribs) to which the outside shell (or skin) was attached. If we imagine the keel as the spine of a human body, these frames perform an identical function to the ribs in a human skeleton. The frames extended from the double bottom upwards to the base of the Bridge deck, which was the eighth deck from the inner bottom. Each frame had a height of 66 ft and was spaced apart at 3 ft intervals, except at the bow and stern where the frame spacing was 2 ft at the bow and 2 ft 3 in at the stern. The frames were constructed in a channel section, 10 in deep amidships, with angle and reverse bars at the frame end of 45 degrees. In addition to the frames themselves, at frequent intervals in the structure there were heavy web frames for greater strength. Increased strength was also ensured in the machinery spaces by the addition of web frames placed at closer intervals with especially heavy bracket plates connecting the frames to the wing tanks, and wing brackets to provide maximum hull stiffness in heavy seas.

The framing extended past each deck level. Attached to each frame were the deck beams; these were also of 10 in deep channel section up to the lower deck level and of smaller section above this for stability purposes. Each deck beam was located in accordance with the frame spacing and was attached to its respective frames by strong support brackets.

As the hull construction proceeded, transverse (or across) beams were

added and placed at each deck level. These beams were also of a 10 in channel section at the lower deck and, as previously for the deck beams, they were of a smaller section above this deck. Each transverse beam was attached to the side frames by thick bracket plates reinforced with angle bars for additional strength.

To complete the structure, four additional longitudinal girders ran the length of the ship, each girder being constructed of plates with deep angles at the top and bottom. Because of the width of the compartments required in the machinery spaces, these girders were not continuous. To compensate for this, the girders in the engine and turbine compartments were provided with a special cranked (or angled) arrangement. Each of these cranked girders had the equivalent collective sectional area to that of the four main longitudinal girders in the other part of the vessel. Stanchions (upright columns) were

*These photographs show plating in process: on* Titanic's *tank top (FAR LEFT);* Olympic *completed and* Titanic *about to start (BELOW); and* Titanic *nearing completion (LEFT).*

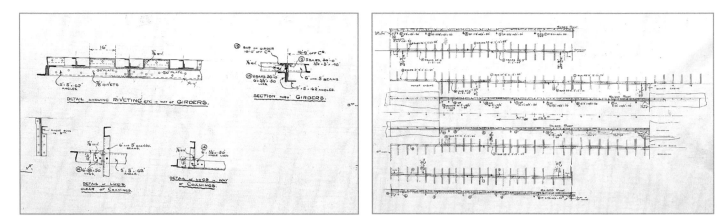

*ABOVE: Detailed construction drawings for the raised roof girders to support the glass roof over the grand staircase — one of the most remarkable interior design features of the class.*

*BELOW RIGHT: Deck plans of Olympic's upper accommodation — Boat and Promenade decks — also showing the two expansion joints. Note these, and all the drawings in this book, are concept drawings, often of Olympic, because shipbuilders in general, and Harland & Wolff was no exception — frequently only had the lead ship of a class photographed or drawn. Titanic would have benefited from a number of FIS (fitted in ship) changes, both on the spot modifications and those stemming from Olympic's sea trials.*

*BELOW AND ABOVE RIGHT: These photographs show a rudder post ready to leave Darlington (BELOW), arriving on site (ABOVE RIGHT), and being put in position at the end of the framework (ABOVE, FAR RIGHT).*

erected and fitted at intervals below these girders up to and including the middle deck (third deck level above the double bottom). Each stanchion was constructed from solid steel columns. Above the third deck level the stanchions were replaced with solid steel pillars of smaller diameter. This unusual arrangement was a design feature incorporated by Thomas Andrews to allow him to place the pillars at more frequent intervals thus providing greater hull strength. The deck plates were also increased in thickness to ensure that hull strength and integrity was maintained throughout the structure. This general description of the internal structure of *Olympic* and *Titanic* indicates the considerable lengths to which Harland & Wolff went in ensuring their hulls had the greatest possible strength. As they were intended to be the largest vessels in the world it was of vital importance that the hull had the maximum degree of stiffness in order for them to operate safely and comfortably in heavy seas. Attached to the immensely strong internal frame were 1 in thick steel plates, each being 30 ft in length by 6 ft wide;

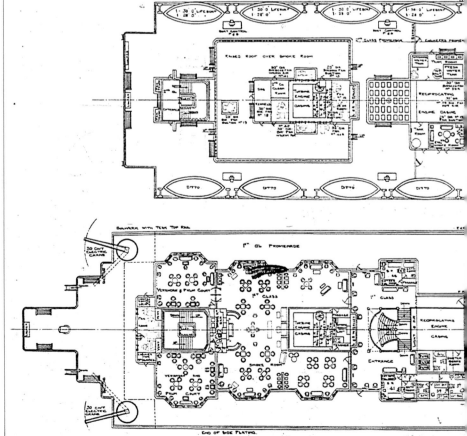

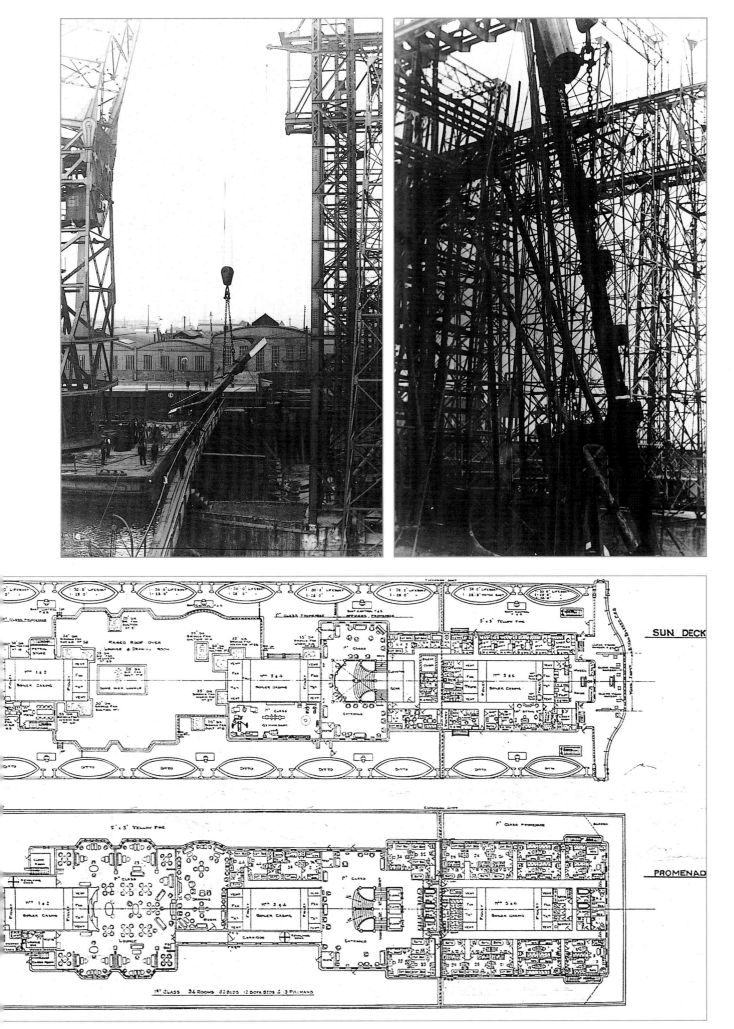

SUN DECK

PROMENAD

SPECIAL MILD STEEL

FAR LEFT: *The rudder at the end of the framework.*

ABOVE: *Stern frame prior to erection of rudder.*

LEFT: *Propeller shaft support arm — boss arm — being lifted into position.*

BELOW: *Port boss arm being lifted into position. Note the connecting plate. This will be attached to the frame for increased solidity.*

*RIGHT: Detail of central propeller aperture on rudder post.*

*ABOVE: Close-up of the central propeller shaft housing after plating. In the background can be seen the port main engine propeller shaft housing and boss arm.*

*ABOVE: Central propeller shaft housing with port and starboard boss arms in place.*

when riveted together, these formed the deck structure. To provide additional strength to the upper part of the hull, the thickness of the deck plating was increased to 1.5 in on the two uppermost decks — the Shelter and Bridge decks.

The side shell plating, (or outer skin) of the vessels, at 1 in thick was also exceptionally heavy for ships of this type; however, as speed was not to be a consideration in the design of the 'Olympic' class, the shell thickness became irrelevant. The shell plates were of identical size to those of the deck plates and these were rectangular in shape, the dimensions being the industry standard for steel plates supplied to shipbuilders by steel manufacturers. Interestingly, modern shipbuilding steel plates, while of vastly different chemical composition to those available in the early 20th century, are still supplied to this standard dimension. The shell for the ships was attached to the internal framing in strips known as strakes along the length of the vessel. Each line of plating, or strake, would be laid together in a system of overlaps or 'joggles', with each strake having an 'in' or 'out' joggle. These overlaps were necessary to provide enough material to rivet the strakes together securely but prevented the ships from having a smooth outer hull. Today shell plates are laid edge-to-edge and welded, thus creating a smooth and efficient hull profile. Finally, the shell plates were triple-riveted at each joint — and this also applied at the turn of the bilge (the curve of the bottom hull). Directly attached at this point of curve was the bilge keel, which was

25 in deep and extended for 295 ft along the length of the vessel amidships. This long bilge keel acted as a damper to reduce rolling in rough sea conditions, and was an early development of the modern day stabiliser.

As mentioned earlier the hulls of both ships were double bottomed. This was the first of two important safety features. Instead of one bottom, two (in between which a man had enough space to walk) were to provide the hull with twice the strength in the event of a collision, although it did not extend above the water line, it was unusual in that it was carried above the bilge instead of stopping short of it. Secondly, the hull was subdivided into 16 watertight compartments by means of 15 one-inch thick bulkheads which extended up through the F deck at the bow and stern and through the E deck in the middle two thirds of the ship. Heavy watertight doors provided communication between the compartments during normal operation. These 'cylinder' doors, as they were known, could be closed in three ways; by means of an electric switch on the bridge, by a lever next to the door and by an automatic trip device which sealed off that compartment in the event of any incoming water. The ships were designed to remain afloat with any two compartments flooded as the worst imagined scenario of a broadside collision would damage no more than two compartments, hence White Star's confidence in its official description;

'[the door]...is held in the open position by a suitable friction clutch, which can be instantly released by means of a powerful electric magnet con-

*ABOVE: A view under the completed hull. The 'joggled' steel plating can be clearly seen.*

*LEFT: Olympic double bottom framing complete prior to installation of plating to complete Tank Top.*

trolled from the captain's bridge, so that in the event of accident, or at any time when it might be considered advisable, the captain can, by simply moving an electric switch, instantly close the doors throughout—practically making the vessel unsinkable.'

Those last few words were quoted a thousand times over, eventually forming the myth that they were indeed totally unsinkable. By now, having had the benefit of a head start, *Olympic* was ahead of *Titanic* towards completion. Internally the ship had been arranged in eight major deck levels designated from A deck, immediately below the open Boat deck, down to G deck, all of which included areas of accommodation for passengers or crew. Below G deck was the Orlop deck, mainly taken up by the machinery spaces but also providing stowage for cargo and stores fore and aft, and at the very lowest level was the Tank Top which rested on the ship's double bottom and provided the base on which the machinery and boilers were mounted. The double bottom itself stowed water tanks for boiler and ballast water.

Apart from the rounded bilges, the hull was almost square for most of the amidships section—a shape which allowed the maximum usable internal space. Below the stern were massive castings to support the propellers and the 78 ft high, 101 ton, rudder. Indeed, everything about the ship was on an epic scale; the anchors were as tall as a house, and the links in the chain were taller than a man, their two piles of cable drag weighing 80 tons each. The massive hulls straddled by the biggest gantry crane in the world, lifting

*BELOW: A photograph showing the* Olympic's *Promenade deck and the windows of the first class reading and writing room.*

HISI8.
RW.

*ABOVE:* Titanic*'s internal construction continues under the gantry.*

*LEFT:* Olympic*'s Promenade deck and the windows of the reading and writing room.*

and positioning the thousands of tons of steel plates and girders that were needed for their construction, dominated the skyline of Belfast. In the *Olympic* alone there were some three million rivets, which accounted for some 1,500 tons of the ship's final displacement, and were driven home at the rate of 200 per day per squad. A squad consisted of four men working from six in the morning until half past five in the evening. The first man (the heater boy) heated the rivet in a coke brazier for three to four minutes, threw it to a catch boy who put the stall of the rivet into a hole through two over-lapping plates. A third man held it in position while a fourth flattened the rivet into the hole. Filson Young writes;

'The seasons passed; the creatures who wrought and clambered among the iron branches, and sang their endless song of labour there, felt the steel chill beneath the frosts of winter, and burning hot beneath the rays of sum-mer, until at last the skeleton within the scaffolding began to take a shape, at the sight of which men held their breaths. It was the shape of a ship, a ship so monstrous and unthinkable that it towered high over the buildings and dwarfed the very mountains beside the water.'3

The power for these vast 'floating cathedrals' was to be derived from 29 boilers housed in six boiler rooms, which were to be arranged in pairs grouped directly below each of the three forward funnels (the boilers and the funnels were amongst the last plant machinery to be fitted soon after

*Olympic* had been launched). Each boiler room was located between two watertight bulkheads, with bunkers capable of holding up to 8,000 tons of coal lining each side of the bulkhead, while the boilers themselves were arranged laterally across the beam of the ship. Immediately aft of the boilers was the compartment containing the main machinery, two reciprocating compound steam engines. The selection of the propulsion machinery had been the result of careful investigation and trials in other ships. The *Lusitania* and *Mauretania* derived their record breaking performance from the use of quadruple screws powered by steam turbines and it might have been expected that Harland & Wolff would follow suit in their new design. However, as speed was not the prime consideration, the designers eventually came up with a compromise which they hoped would give great economy of operation (always a prime consideration with the White Star Line) while providing sufficient power to enable the ship a regular six-day Atlantic crossing to be scheduled in service. The original planned machinery installation consisted of two conventional 15,000 hp four-cylinder triple-expansion reciprocating engines each driving 23 ft 6 in diameter three-bladed propellers. However, the design was subsequently altered to utilise the exhaust steam from these engines which, instead of being vented wastefully up the funnels, was recycled and fed to a Parsons low pressure turbine which was mounted on the ship's centreline. This would produce another 16,000 hp and drive a separate 16 ft 6 in diameter four-bladed propeller. This arrangement was first tested on the White Star liner *Laurentic*, completed in 1909, and showed an outstanding increase in economy and efficiency when compared to the other-

*BELOW:* Olympic *shortly after launch. Following an inspection she will be off to the fitting-out dock.*

*ABOVE:* Britannic *shortly after her launch. Funnels and masts have yet to be added; next stop outfitting.*

*NEXT PAGE:* Harland & Wolff *advertising poster showing the almost constructed* Olympic. *White Star and Harland & Wolff were keen to whet the public appetite and keep interest in the sister ships high.*

wise identical but conventionally powered *Meganatic* built at the same time. It's also worth noting that Harland & Wolff were anxious to gain experience in turbine propulsion, something that had particularly interested Thomas Andrews, the managing director of the design department. Unlike today, when this method of propulsion is commonplace, steam turbine technology was very much in its infancy at the start of the century. By today's standards this turbine was of basic design, capable of ahead-only propulsion and powered by waste steam from the two main reciprocating engines. Running together at the maximum continuous service rating, these three engines produced a normal service speed of 21 knots. However, *Titanic* was capable of emergency (or flank) speed of 23.5 knots. This additional reserve power output was achieved when the engines were run to their maximum revolutions, much the same as 'red lining' a modern motor vehicle. In normal service these operating conditions would have been studiously avoided due to the enormous strain placed on the engine component parts in operating them for extended periods at their maximum limit.

By October 1910 the *Olympic* was ready for launching, this ceremony being carried out on the 20th of that month. Bruce Ismay, rightly proud of what he and Pirrie were achieving together, decided that it would be appropriate, if not advantageous to his own esteem, to invite J. Pierpont Morgan the head of the I.M.M. group to the launch. For the occasion *Olympic* was painted white to ensure that photographers got the best possible, and most imposing, images of this magnificent vessel. However, although the guest list was impressive and included such noteworthy attendees as the Lord

THE ROYAL MAIL TR "OLY

WHITE

BUILT AND ENGINED BY HARLAND

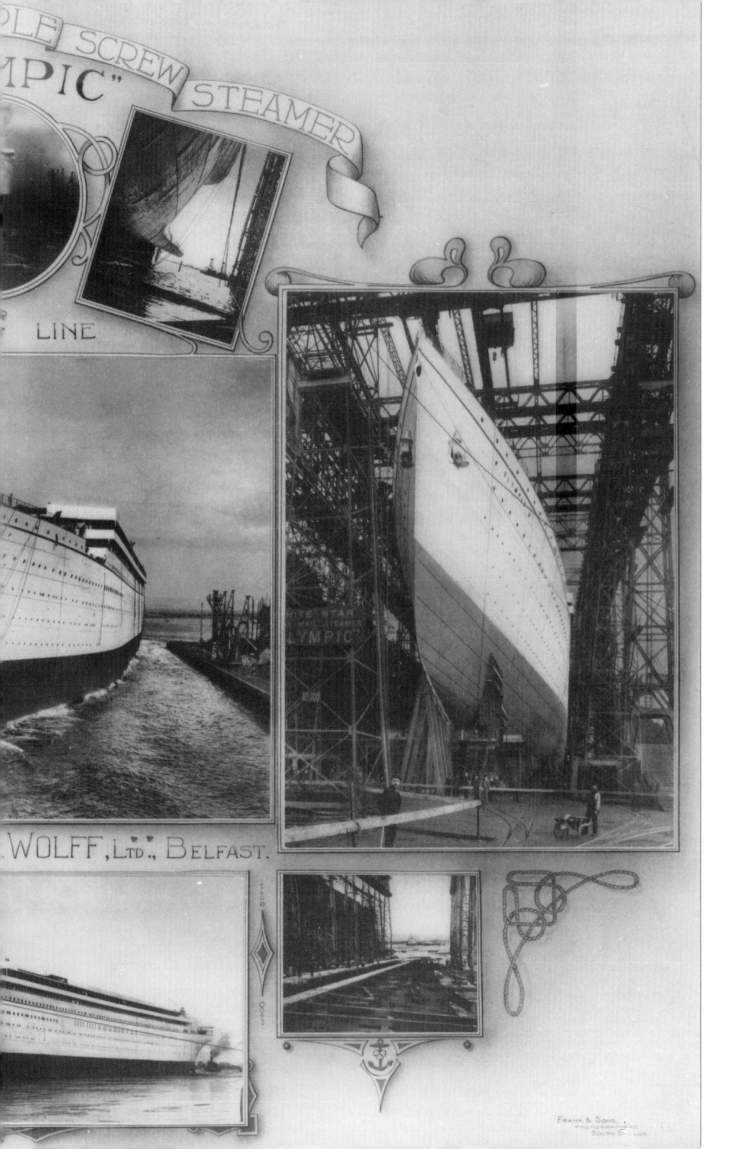

Lieutenant of Ireland, the occasion was somewhat different to the usual launching procedure. Unlike all other shipping lines, White Star Line had adopted a unique policy of not launching their new vessels with any particular ceremony; new vessels were not named at launch nor did they have the traditional champagne bottle smashed over the bow. Like all of her predecessors *Olympic* was simply released from the hydraulic rams holding her on the slipway and allowed to slide into her natural element. The complete launch process lasted a total of 62 seconds and passed without incident . Although stripped of the usual pomp and ceremony, the sheer scale of the spectacle did not go unnoticed, as Filson Young noted;

'Only the waters themselves dared to give the impulse that should set this monster afloat. The waters touched the cradle, and the cradle moved on the ways, carrying the ship down towards the waters. And when the cradle stopped the ship moved on; slowly at first, then with a movement that grew quicker until it increased to the speed of a fast trotting horse, touching the waters, dipping into them, cleaving them, forcing them asunder in waves and ripples that fled astonished to the surrounding shores; finally resting and floating upon them, while thousands of pygmy men who had roosted in the bare iron branches, who had raised the hideous clamour amid which the giant was born, greeted their handiwork, dropped their tools, and raised their hoarse voices in a cheer. The miracle had happened.'4

*RIGHT: Stern, rudder and propeller shaft plating — note the intricate and complex plating surrounding the outer, or wing, propeller shafts.*

*BELOW: Olympic's launch on October 20, 1910, was not a grand affair. It followed White Star tradition and the vessel was simply released from the slipway and allowed to enter its natural element.*

117

*ABOVE: A fine view of* Olympic *in dry dock for hull inspection.*

*BELOW RIGHT: A ticket to the launch of* Titanic. *This event attracted thousands of onlookers but was completed with the same lack of ceremony as that of* Olympic.

After her launch, the hull was moved into the specially built Thompson outfitting wharf where she was completed. At the time of her launch, the ship's hull and main superstructure was complete and the propelling machinery had been installed. All 29 of the boilers were now fitted in the Thompson dock, the four tall funnels were also erected at this point and the masts stepped. In fact only three funnels were required by the ship's steam boilers, the fourth being added for appearance — it actually contained ventilation ducts. Her gross registered tonnage was 45,324 tons and much was already being reported in the press of her fantastic size and magnitude. The ship was talked of at every level of society — Ismay's plan to build vessels that captured the imaginations of the population had certainly come to fruition.

While the *Olympic* was hitting the headlines in 1910, work on the *Titanic* pressed ahead through the winter until she was launched amid great publicity on 31 May, 1911. The weather was fitting for the occasion with clear skies, sunshine and a stiff breeze which blew up the Lough from the south causing the many flags, pennants and ensigns to stand out and add to the air of excitement. The White Star Line capitalised on the event for maximum publicity by arranging for the *Olympic* to sail from Belfast on the same day and the double event drew enormous crowds which filled the shoreline around Belfast Lough and jostled aboard the numerous ferries and pleasure craft that were sailing around the harbour. Lord Pirrie, the Harland & Wolff chairman, and his wife acted as hosts to the V.I.P. guests, who included J. Pierpont Morgan and Bruce Ismay, on a specially erected stand near the bows where they witnessed the speeches and the intricate preparations for the launch. However, as with the launch of her sister there was none of the champagne bottle smashing and other theatrical ceremony.

The building of the R M S *Titanic* marked the construction of the largest man-made moveable object in the world at that time, to ensure a smooth pas-

BELOW: *The forefoot accounted for some 4 ft of the bow of* Titanic, *seen here just prior to launch.*

NEXT PAGE: *The moment of* Titanic's *launch, 31 May 1911, some seven months after her sister* Olympic. *An engineer was unfortunately killed by a falling support during the vessel's journey down the slipway — not the best of omens.*

• TITANIC & HER SISTERS OLYMPIC & BRITANNIC •

*BELOW LEFT: Titanic's stern just before launch*

*BELOW: Titanic immediately after launch.*

*FAR RIGHT: Pumping out the slipway preparatory to Titanic's launch.*

*FAR RIGHT: Hydraulic launch triggers were released to launch the vessel. The release took place upon receipt of a signal from the launch platform — not the lady with the champagne bottle!*

*RIGHT: After launch* Titanic *was moved to the outfitting quay where the funnels, superstructure and internal equipment were put in place.*

*BELOW RIGHT: The vast army of Harland & Wolff workers at the outfitting quay.*

*BELOW:* Titanic *lies completed in Belfast Lough.*

sage down the slipway required 23 tons of tallow, train oil and soft soap to grease the ways for her launch. At 12:05 p.m. two rockets were fired followed by a third five minutes later. At precisely 12:13 p.m., the final order was given and the *Titanic* began her short, 62 second journey down the heavily greased slipway and into the water. Unfortunately the otherwise successful launch was marred by the death of a shipyard worker, James Dobbins, who was fatally injured during the preparations — the unlucky *Titanic* claiming her second life (another worker had been killed during the construction of the hull). Ignorant of this tragedy, the V.I.P.s retired to the Queen's Island yard where Lord Pirrie entertained his guests with an expansive lunch before they boarded the *Olympic* to return to the British mainland.

With celebrations completed, work continued on the immense task of fitting out the *Titanic*. Originally this was scheduled to have been completed by March 1912, with the all-important maiden commercial voyage advertised as departing from Southampton on the 20th of that month. However, this timetable was disrupted when on 5 October, after undergoing temporary repairs at Southampton, the *Olympic* returned to her Belfast birthplace, immediately going into the Thompson dry dock from which the still incomplete *Titanic* had been removed. The repairs took just over six weeks and, to save time, the *Titanic*'s starboard propeller shaft and a number of other components were appropriated. The number of men transferred to her damaged sister in order to carry out the necessary work further drained resources and work on the *Titanic* was at a virtual halt. A new in-service date of 10 April, 1912, was announced and work resumed at full speed as soon as the *Olympic* sailed again at the end of November 1911.

By the following January the *Titanic*'s exterior was virtually complete, with all four funnels in place, although there was still a considerable amount of internal work to be done. By the time of her completion, in almost every respect the *Titanic* and the *Olympic* were absolutely identical, and consequently there are numerous instances of confusion and mistaken identities.

*ABOVE: Internal detailing on* Olympic.

*RIGHT: The German-made floating crane. This giant piece of machinery had a maximum lifting capacity of 250 tons and, being mounted on a large pontoon, provided the outfitting dock with a mobile heavy lift facility as is shown here.*

In fact, a great proportion of postcards and photographs purporting to show the *Titanic*, particularly those which show the interior of the ship and her cabins, actually illustrate her sister ship. It was only in the latter stages of fitting out that an addition was made to the *Titanic* which served to differentiate the two ships: following initial experience with the *Olympic*, a steel frame equipped with sliding windows was fitted to the forward half of the promenades on A Deck to protect passegers from spray and rain. These were intended to provide additional shelter from the weather for first class passengers, although the windows were normally bolted shut and could only be opened with a special spanner. It has been speculated that these glass screens could have impeded access to the lifeboats being lowered from above during *Titanic*'s demise. The vessels' staggering dimensions, and the technological advances in marine engineering that they represented, made possible unprecedented developments in ocean transportation. The two vessels were not only much larger than any other ships previously constructed, but they embodied in the exquisite detail of their internal fittings a microcosm of the Victorian age of elegance and grace. Working upwards, it was not until G deck (the Lower deck) level that there was space for accommodation and this was limited to crew spaces for stokers and greasers forward in the bow, together with a few third class cabins. To aft on this deck were further third class cabins separated from the machinery spaces by the galley stores. The amidships section was entirely given over to the boiler and machinery casings and even at the Middle deck (F) the boiler uptakes and machinery cas-

*ABOVE: Port profile of the Titanic at the outfitting quay, with heavy lift crane in the background.*

*RIGHT: Work on the superstructure during outfitting.*

ings intruded although there was also room for the third class dining saloon, ship's laundry complex, and some crew cabins amidships. Of special interest to passengers were the swimming pool and Turkish baths housed forward on the starboard side, while a squash court, which also occupied part of G deck, was towards the bow. Otherwise F deck echoed the arrangement of housing crew and third class passengers forward and a mix of second and third class passenger accommodation aft. F deck was the first deck to be completely above the waterline and at various points along the ship's side would be found the scuttles covering the coal shutes used for the unpleasant task of coaling ship whilst in harbour.

The Upper (or E) deck was the lowest deck on which it was possible to traverse the whole length of the ship at one level and although pierced by the three boiler uptakes and part of the main engine casing, it contained considerably more accommodation and public spaces than the decks below. In the bow were crew spaces housing seamen and coal trimmers as well as a few third class cabins and toilet facilities while the stern section carried more second and third class cabins. Amidships, the entire starboard side of the ship was taken up with sumptuous first class cabins, while the port side housed the hundreds of stewards and waiters who formed a significant proportion of the total crew. A long straight passageway flanking the port side of the boiler uptakes was known as the 'Scotland Road' and provided access to the crew accommodation, which also included the engineers' mess further aft. Above E deck was the Saloon (D) deck which was the highest continuous deck in the ship and which carried more crew accommodation forward together with an open public area used by third class passengers. In the after section was the second class dining saloon, which straddled the full width of the ship, as well as more accommodation, mostly second class but including a few third class cabins in the extreme stern. In the area below the fore funnel were some 14 first class cabins, but the rest of the amidships section was taken up with the first class reception areas and dining saloon, both of which stretched right across the ship in the area between the first and third funnels,

*ABOVE: Side anchor being taken to the outfitting quay. Again, the child in the picture gives an indication of its enormous size. Each of these anchors weighed 8 tons but they were dwarfed by the massive centre anchor which weighed 50.5 tons.*

*BELOW RIGHT: The centre or bow anchor stowed on its cradle under the bow stem. Each of the links in its chain was as the length of a man.*

while in the region below the fourth funnel were the pantries and galleys serving both first and second class dining saloons. The ship's hospital was also located here on the starboard side.

At Shelter (C) deck level there were breaks fore and aft to allow access to loading hatches which were served by a total of six electric cranes. There was more crew accommodation in the forecastle and under the Poop deck were the third class general and smoke rooms, these passengers also using the open Well deck as their promenade. The rest of the Shelter deck was given over to first class cabins apart from the second class library and sheltered promenade at the after end of the main superstructure section. Throughout the first class areas of the ship were cabins for the many maids and servants who accompanied their masters and mistresses and these people also had their own saloon at this deck level. Above them was the Bridge (B) deck which held yet more first class accommodation, including two opulent suites situated one on either side of the ship abreast of the second funnel: these were universally and rightly known as the 'millionaires' suites.

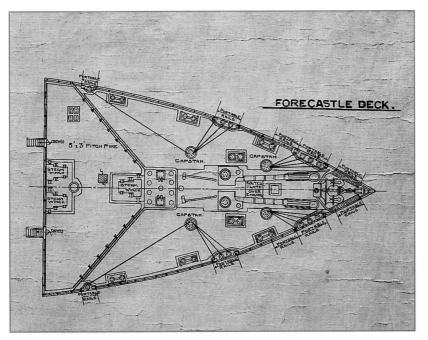

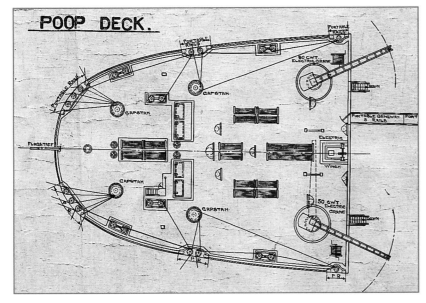

Towards the after end were more first class restaurants including the informal Café Parisien on the starboard side, while the second class smoke room and open promenade was at the after end. The Promenade (A) deck was given over almost entirely to first class amenities including reading and smoking rooms, a large lounge and the Palm Court areas aft. There were extensive areas of open promenade decks, the forward sections of which were protected by the screens mentioned earlier. At the highest level of the ship was the open Boat deck with the bridge and officers' accommodation forward and a gymnasium tucked up against the second funnel. The open areas of deck were used as promenade areas by both first and second class passengers as well as the ship's officers, although some sections were blocked off by the raised roofs over the lounge and smoke rooms below.

Mention of the Boat deck leads to a consideration of the lifeboats carried by the *Titanic*, a matter which raised considerable controversy in the immediate aftermath of the sinking. At the time of the disaster the ship carried a total of 20 lifeboats of which 14 were of a standard design capable of carrying approximately 65 people, two emergency cutters which were permanent-

After launch Titanic *should have been completed by March 1912 but an accident to Olympic saw disruption to* Titanic's *schedule as workers were taken off one to work on the other, and* Titanic's *sea trials were postponed to April. This spread of photographs shows:* Olympic's *Boat deck structures taking shape, 7 February, 1911 (FAR LEFT); another view of* Olympic *with one funnel in place (LEFT);* Titanic *nearing completion (BELOW).*

*ABOVE: Main ship's whistle.*

*RIGHT: Titanic at the Thompson Dry Dock; note the wooden supports at ship's side to prevent movement.*

134

*BELOW: The outfitting quay's access gangway was fitted with wheels to allow for movement caused by the rise and fall of the tide.*

*ABOVE AND BELOW: Three-furnace boilers ready for installation in the boiler rooms. The figure gives scale.*

ly swung out could each carry 40 people and four collapsible 'Engelhardt' lifeboats each capable of carrying 47 people. Readers with a mathematical inclination will have worked out that the total capacity of all available life-craft came to 1,178, a figure well short of the 3,300 passengers and crew which the ship was certified to carry when fully loaded. Scandalous as this might seem, this meagre provision not only complied with, but actually exceeded, the official Board of Trade requirements at the time. There were two reasons for this state of affairs: the first was that, as often happens, government regulations had failed to keep up with the headlong advances in technology so that, by the time that 46,000 grt ships like *Titanic* and *Olympic* were being laid down, the rules were based on the 10,000 grt ships built almost 20 years before. The second was that the philosophy behind the new breed of liners deemed that, even in the worst case, they would take some time to sink, by which time other vessels would be in the vicinity. They would have been summoned by that modern miracle, radio, and the task of the lifeboats would not be to serve as a refuge for those on board but merely to ferry survivors to other ships which had come to the rescue. With this in mind there were more than enough lifebelts (3,560) for all on board but these would be of little use if a survivor had no lifeboat to which he could swim

MAIN BOILERS

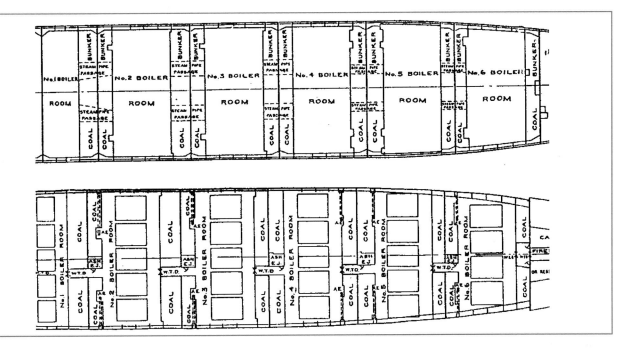

once in the water. The hollow thinking behind this lack of emergency craft was to be sadly exposed on the night of 14 April, 1912.

The ship's statistics were widely known and quoted — thanks to the blanket coverage given to the two new White Star liners in the national, local and technical press of the day. In fact any schoolboy could probably have recited that the hull had a length of 88 2 ft 9 in, a beam of 92 ft 6 in, and a total height from the base of the keel to the top of the navigating bridge deck of 104 ft. In her normal service condition *Titanic* operated on a design load draught of 34 ft 6 in, and although the gross registered tonnage was given as 46,329, the ship actually displaced some 66,000 tons. It is this final statistic which makes her the largest ship of her era with *Olympic* weighing in at 45,324 gross registered tons, over 1,000 tons less. Some sources, including the White Star Line's own advertising material, failed to differentiate between them pronouncing them both as 45,000 gross registered tons. Despite her great size, the *Titanic* was extremely elegant in design, with an almost straight bow, a slightly rising sheerline fore and aft, and a traditional overhanging counter stern. The superstructure decks were continuous and unbroken, while the four funnels were well-proportioned, equally spaced and stylishly raked. A raised forecastle and poop decks left well decks fore and aft, which provided space for the installation of hatches permitting the loading of food and stores. Tall masts were stepped fore and aft to carry the signal halyards and also supporting the aerials required by the powerful Marconi radio equipment which was fitted in the ship — a relatively modern innovation. She was given her final coats of paint, this time in the White Star Line colours—a black hull with red boot topping at the waterline, white superstructure and upper works, a yellow/gold band around the hull at main deck and yellow masts and buff funnels, the latter each capped with a broad black band.

On 1 April, 1912, she was at last ready for her sea trials, although these were delayed until the following day due to adverse weather conditions. Tuesday, 2 April, was therefore the date on which the ship left her birthplace

*ABOVE: The boilers and their casings stretched from the tank-top to the Boat deck where the three working funnels vented their exhaust. This drawing of the Lower deck (TOP), Orlop deck (CENTRE) and tank-top shows the main boiler spaces and how high the casings reached on the lower levels.*

138

*ABOVE: Construction of the boiler flue uptakes. These uptakes carried the combustion gases to the funnels and account for the massive internal space needed above the boiler rooms.*

and moved for the first time under the power of her own engines. At 6:00 a.m. she was hauled from her shipyard berth by a fleet of four tugs and, despite the early hour, there were many spectators as the ship was towed out into Belfast Lough and taken downstream to a point off Carrickfergus.

Here the tugs cast off and *Titanic* pulled out into the open waters of the Irish Sea for a busy program of trials. These included putting to work and testing all of her machinery as well as the steering gear, and making a series of runs at different propeller r.p.m. so that her speed and performance could be related to engine room indications. One important test measured her ability to stop in an emergency and to calculate this the ship was worked up to 20 knots at which point the engines were thrown into reverse and full power applied. The resulting stopping distance was around 850 yards (just under

half a mile), roughly equivalent to three times the length of the ship — a very creditable performance for a 46,329 grt ship. After this the *Titanic* set course to the south and ran for two hours in a straight line before reversing course and heading north again for a similar period. These timed runs were completed at an average speed of 18 knots. With the ship again at a stand-still, the anchors were lowered and raised, and then she returned back to the Belfast Lough where she moored for a few hours while final supplies were taken aboard and non-essential shipyard workers who had accompanied the trials were ferried ashore.

Those present during the day's trials are as follows; the White Star Line had been represented by one of their directors, Harold Sanderson, Harland & Wolff by Lord Pirrie's nephew, Thomas Andrews, and also by Edward

Wilding and a team of nine other specialists known as the guarantee group. As was common practice on such occasions, the latter group would stay aboard the ship at least for the maiden voyage, in order to be on hand to assist with rectifying any faults or problems which might occur. One other important personage who accompanied the initial sea trials, and no idle spectator, was the Board of Trade's representative and surveyor, Francis Carruthers. It was he who, on the return to Belfast at the end of the busy day of trials, signed the *Titanic* 's official certificate of seaworthiness which was necessary before the ship was allowed to carry fare-paying passengers. With this accomplished, Harland & Wolff officially handed the ship over to the White Star Line, Sanderson and Andrews conducting the necessary formalities and exchange of documents. After this was completed, and with the crew at their stations, the *Titanic* slipped from her mooring at just after 8:00 p.m. and sailed out into the Irish Sea, leaving Belfast for ever and setting course for her home port of Southampton where she arrived just before midnight on the night of 3 April. During the 570-mile voyage further trials and tests were carried out and at one point the ship had worked up to 23.25 knots, the fastest speed that she is known to have attained. On arrival at Southampton she was met by five tugs, which skillfully turned her in midstream and then manoeuvred her stern first into Berth 44 at the White Star Dock. The *Titanic* had now arrived!

Quotations
1,2,4 from *Titanic* by Filson Young. (Grant Richards Limited 1912)
3 from Lloyds Weekly News reprinted in 1972 as Great Newspaper Reprinted

141

LEFT: *The boilers were taken on board at the outfitting quay after launch. The giant floating crane, seen lifting a boiler into* Olympic, *had been bought second-hand from a German shipyard and could lift a maximum of 250 tons.*

*TOP AND ABOVE:* Britannic and Titanic *were practically identical. This profile of* Titanic *is prior to installation of Promenade deck plating as shown on* Britannic *profile. At this stage* Titanic *and* Olympic *were often confused with each other.*

*RIGHT: Funnels were taken to the outfitting quay by rail. The figures give a good indication of the sheer size of the equipment for the vessels.*

*Various stages of funnel erection: Funnel arrives at dockside (ABOVE); is lifted into place (RIGHT); and is secured on the Boat Deck (TOP RIGHT).*

*FAR RIGHT: Titanic with the three working funnels. The dummy fourth would be added later.*

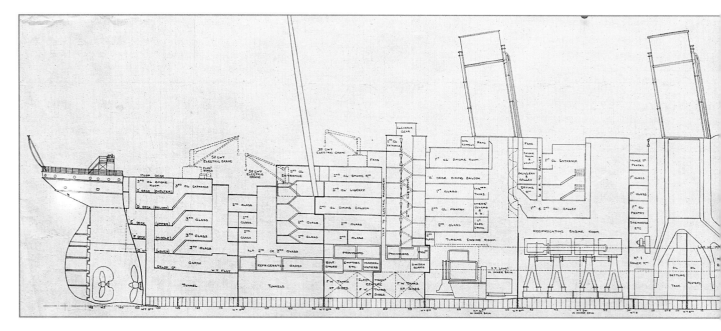

*ABOVE: Internal profile of the Titanic, note in particular the height of the watertight bulkheads, identified here in black.*

*RIGHT: Internal shell framing detail.*

*MIDDLE RIGHT: One of Britannic's self-closing watertight doors. These were patented by 'McFarlane' and used by Harland & Wolff following the loss of the Titanic.*

*FAR RIGHT TOP AND BOTTOM: One of the fifteen watertight doors.*

146

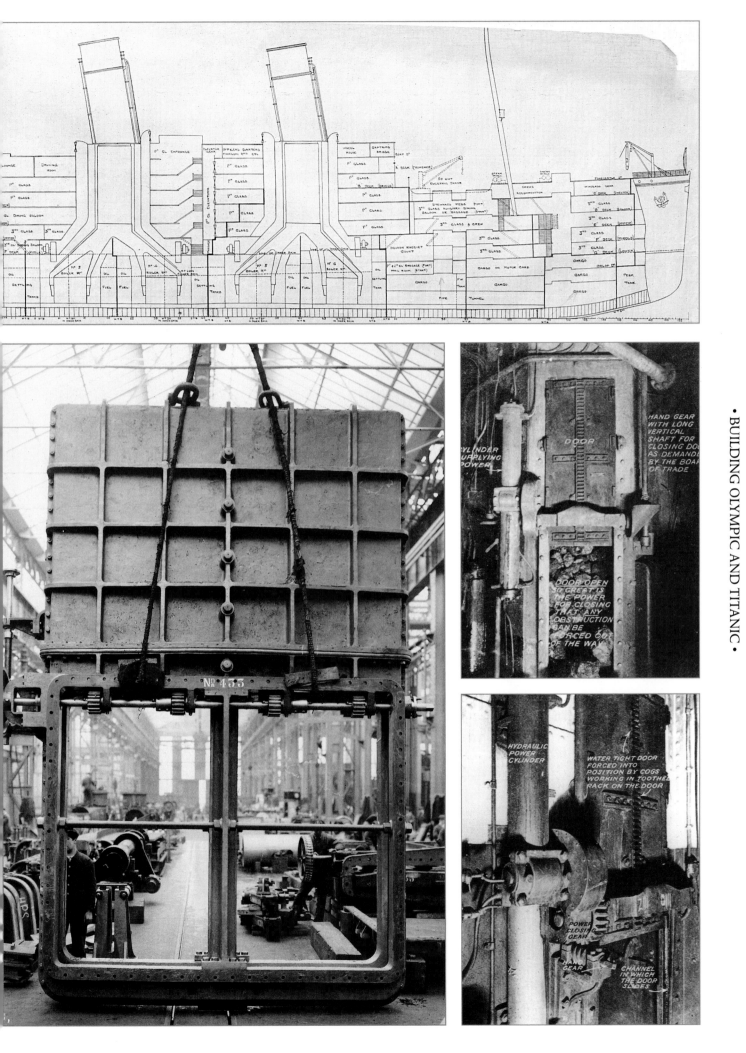

FAR LEFT: *Titanic's starboard tail shaft being fitted just prior to her launch.*

BELOW LEFT: *Shell plating at the bilge area.*

LEFT: *View of stern plating around the propellor shaft area.*

BELOW: *Stern, rudder and propeller shaft plating — note the intricate and complex plating surrounding the outer (wing) propeller shafts.*

FOLLOWING PAGES: *Olympic, side plan (Top Left); deck plan (Bottom Left).*

RIGHT: *Highly detailed elevation and deck plans for the Titanic taken from the original construction plans held by Harland & Wolff. (8 to D deck underside, 7 to E deck underside).*

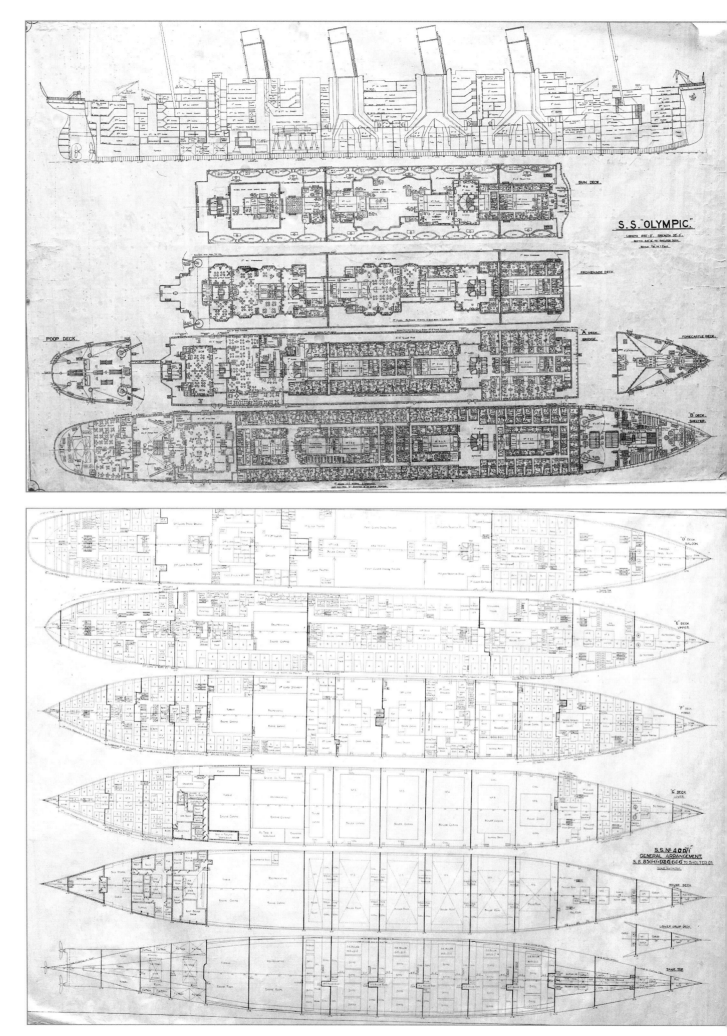

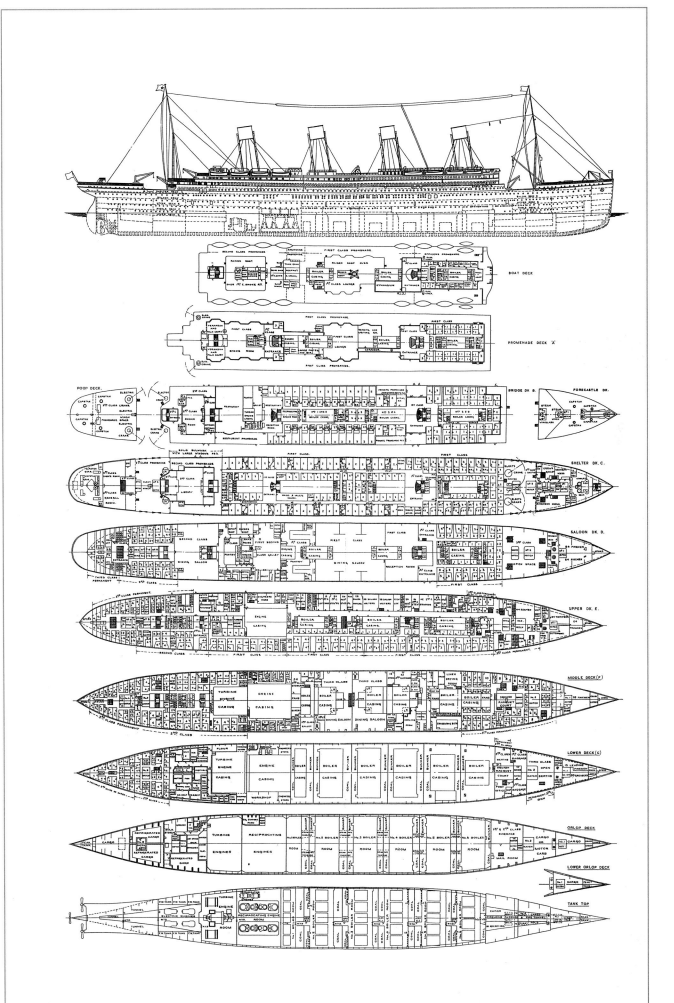

*TOP LEFT: The main companionways and elevators can be seen on this elevation:*
*A — forward, main first class companionway (Boat to Saloon deck)*
*B — aft first class companionway (Promenade to Shelter deck) .*
*C — forward second class companionway (Boat to Middle deck)*
*D — aft second class companionway (Bridge to Middle deck)*
*E — third class companionway (Shelter to Lower deck)*

*FAR LEFT: Titanic's first class grand staircase.*

*ABOVE: Olympic's first class grand staircase was identical to Titanic's with the exception of Olympic's clock which was far less ornate.*

*LEFT: Otis elevator and operating machinery.*

*BELOW LEFT: Another photograph of Titanic's first class grand stairway showing the beautifully carved clock.*

*LEFT AND FAR LEFT: Two more details of Titanic's main, first class, grand staircase.*

*BELOW: Titanic's second class forward staircase ran from the Boat to Middle deck with an elevator in the middle of the two flights of stairs. Here it is seen at B (Bridge) deck where the entrances to the second class smoke room were situated.*

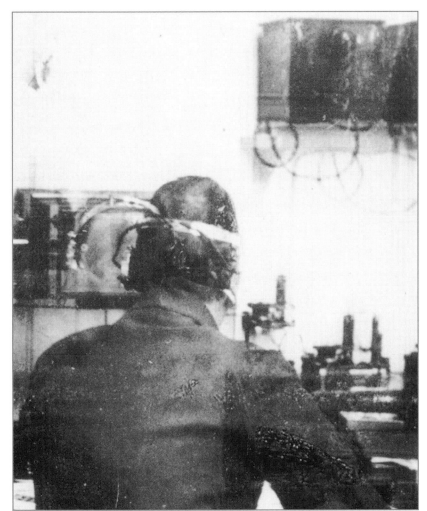

*TOP FAR LEFT: The Bridge of the Olympic showing the helm.*

*BOTTOM FAR LEFT: An operator at work in Olympic's Marconi room.*

*LEFT: Marconi radio operator in his radio room on Titanic's Bridge deck.*

*BELOW LEFT: The compass platform on Titanic's Boat deck. Placed 12 ft above any iron or steel, it was 78 ft from the waterline.*

*BELOW RIGHT: Two views of the starboard wing showing the lifeboat davits.*

*RIGHT: This illustrates the difference between concept drawings and reality: it does not show Andrews' cabin and it also purports to show 18 rather than 16 lifeboats. The two smaller boats actually nested inside two lifeboats. These 'rescue' boats were very small and designed to be used for small scale incidents such as man overboard.*

*FAR RIGHT MIDDLE: Olympic's starboard Boat deck showing details of the second class lifeboat arrangements.*

*FAR RIGHT BOTTOM (LEFT AND RIGHT): Two photographs of ventilation fans which supplied fresh air to passenger and crew accommodation.*

*BELOW: The wide promenade of the Boat deck — Olympic's port side looking aft, showing the compass platform and the clerestory windows above the first class lounge.*

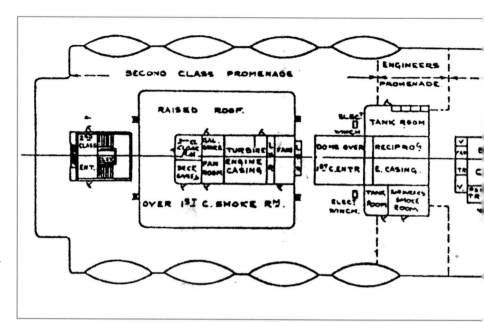

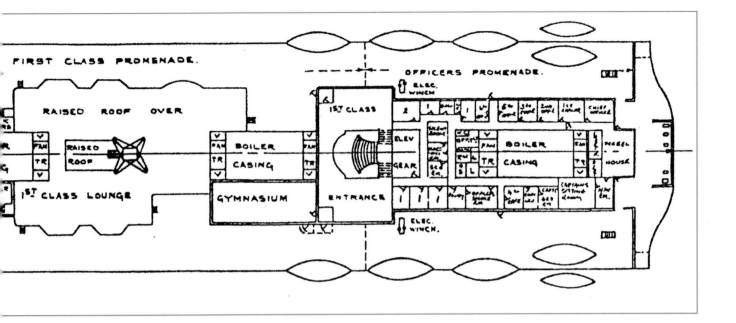

Titanic's gymnasium was situated on the starboard side of the vessel alongside the second funnel. It was lit by a number of large windows
(ABOVE) and contained a variety of modern
apperatus (LEFT AND FAR LEFT). Both of the latter views are looking aft.

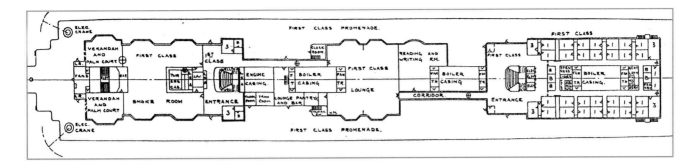

FAR LEFT TOP: *View aft along Olympic's port upper Promenade deck.*

FAR LEFT BOTTOM: *First class reading and writing room onboard the Olympic.*

ABOVE: *Plan of the Promenade (B) deck.*

LEFT: *Olympic's Promenade deck as seen by Father Browne.*

BELOW LEFT: *Another of Father Brown's photographs. This shows Olympic's reading and writing room.*

BELOW: *The port side windows of the first class lounge looking forward to those of the multi-paned reading and writing room bay windows.*

• BUILDING OLYMPIC AND TITANIC •

*ABOVE: Looking down the length of Olympic's starboard Promenade deck. Nearest the camera are the doors leading to the main first class companionway. Titanic's Promenade deck was glazed almost as far as the third funnel.*

*FAR RIGHT TOP AND BOTTOM AND BELOW RIGHT: These three photographs show different aspects of the reading and writing room. It was on the port side of the ship, entered from the corridor running from the main companionway to the Lounge (see drawing RIGHT).*

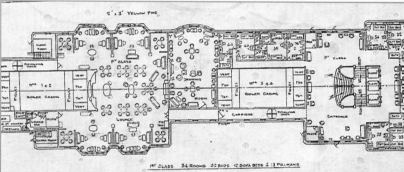

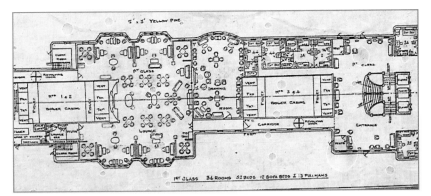

FAR LEFT TOP, BOTTOM AND LEFT: *The first class lounge was situated between the second and third funnels. The photographs show the opulence of the surroundings.*

BELOW: *The windows of the port side of Olympic's smoke room, looking aft to the Palm Court.*

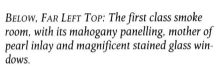

*Left and Bottom Far Left: The trellised Palm Court.*

*Below, Far Left Top: The first class smoke room, with its mahogany panelling, mother of pearl inlay and magnificent stained glass windows.*

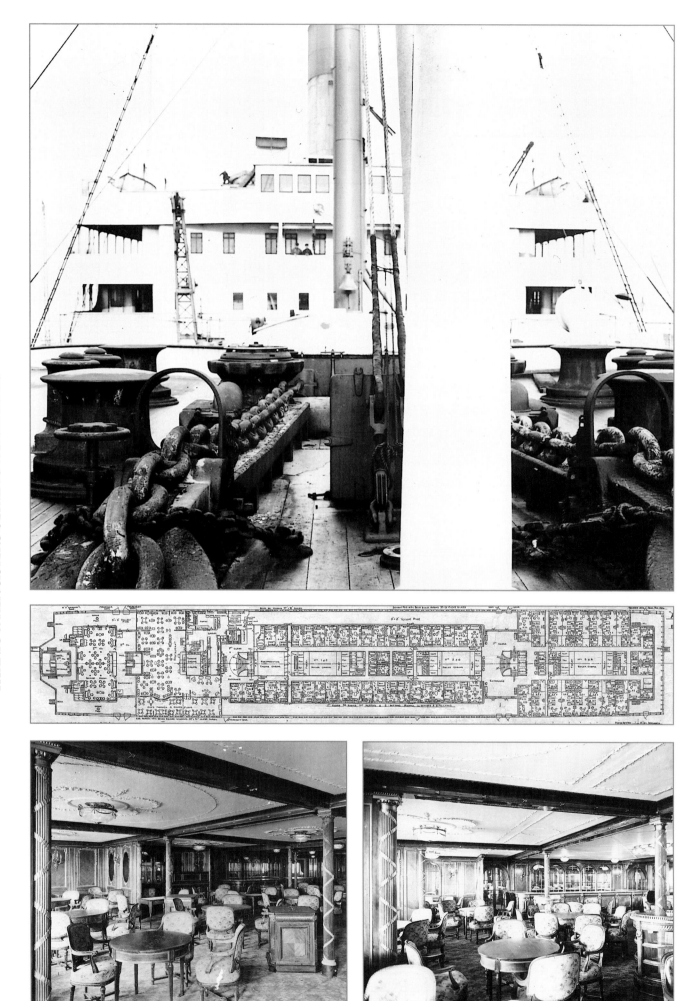

170

*TOP LEFT: View from the Olympic's Forecastle deck looking aft toward the Bridge itself. Note the ship's bell — Titanic's was recovered from the wreck site.*

*BOTTOM LEFT (BOTH PHOTOGRAPHS): The à la carte restaurant was situated aft of the second of the two first class companionways.*

*ABOVE: Olympic's second class smoke room. Olympic's and Titanic's second class accommodation rivalled that of first class on other ships.*

*RIGHT, MIDDLE AND BOTTOM: The Café Parisien was used by younger first class passengers and was a popular place.*

*FAR LEFT: Third class stairway.*

*LEFT: First class passageway.*

*BOTTOM LEFT: Cargo cranes on the after end of the Shelter deck.*

*BELOW LEFT AND RIGHT: Example of a second class bathroom with wash basin and bath; note shower unit at head of bath.*

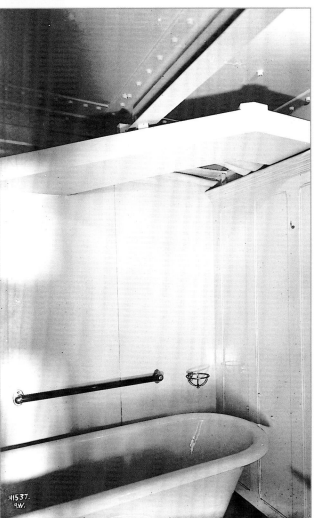

*Illustrated on this page are a number of typical first class cabins .*

*ABOVE:* Titanic's *Suite B59.*

*RIGHT:* Bedroom B60 opening onto a private drawing room.

*BELOW RIGHT: Suite B38 on the* Titanic.

A selection of first class cabins — modern Dutch style in sycamore (Top); old Dutch style (Above); modern Dutch in sycamore and oak (Left and Below).

*RIGHT AND BOTTOM RIGHT: First class Empire style double cabin.*

*BELOW RIGHT: Empire style drawing room.*

*OPPOSITE PAGE: First class parlour suite Louis XVI style sitting room (ABOVE) and bedroom (BELOW).*

• TITANIC & HER SISTERS OLYMPIC & BRITANNIC •

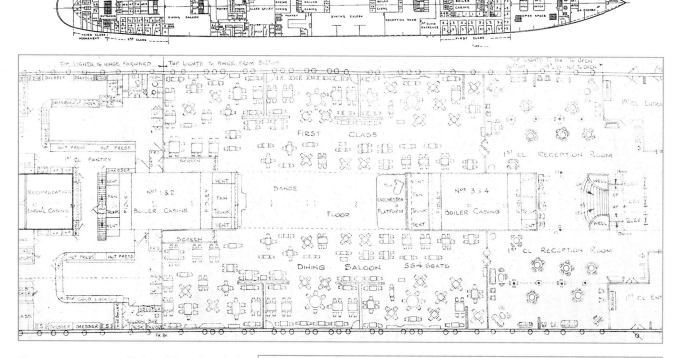

TOP AND ABOVE: *Overall plan of the Saloon deck and detailed layout of the first class reception room and dining saloon.*

RIGHT: *First class dining saloon.*

BELOW RIGHT: *First class reception area that led to the dining room.*

TOP: *The swimming pool was situated on the starboard side of the Middle deck alongside the first boiler casing.*

LEFT: *Crew passageway.*

ABOVE: *Port intermediate cylinder casing.*

LEFT: *Port and Starboard main engines undergoing erection on test bed.*

*ABOVE AND BELOW LEFT: Turbine casing mouldings.*

*FAR LEFT: One of the steam-reciprocating engines under test in the engine works at Belfast.*

*LEFT: Installing the turbine engine.*

*LEFT AND BELOW LEFT: There were four 400kW generating engines on the Titanic, located in the turbine engine room at the aft end of the vessel. They would keep supplying power uintil the final moments.*

*RIGHT: Electric power switchboard.*

*BELOW RIGHT: Accommodation electrical power light switches behind decorative panel.*

# OLYMPIC

In recalling the drama of the *Titanic*'s loss, it is often forgotten that she was one of a class of three ships, the others being the *Olympic* and the *Britannic*. Of these, the latter also had a tragic ending, being lost while acting as a hospital ship during World War I after less than a year in service. However, *Olympic*, first of the class, had a much longer and more successful career and her story impinges on that of the *Titanic* at several points.

The *Olympic* was laid down as Keel Number 400 at Harland & Wolff's Belfast shipyard on 16 December, 1908, while work on the *Titanic*, Keel Number 401, commenced on the adjacent slipway on 31 March, 1909. Work on the two giants progressed rapidly, their massive hulls being straddled by an enormous gantry crane, the largest in the world at that time, which lifted and positioned the thousands of tons of steel plate and girders used in the construction of the ships.

By October 1910 the *Olympic* was ready for launching, this ceremony being carried out on the 20th of that month, after which the hull was moved into the Thompson graving dock which had been specially built to accommodate the new liners while they were fitted out and completed. At the time of her launch, the ship's hull and main superstructure was complete and the propelling machinery had been installed. Subsequently the boilers were installed, no fewer than twenty-nine of them in six separate boiler rooms, after which the four tall funnels were erected and the masts stepped. While all this was going on, a host of joiners, carpenters, plumbers, electricians, and other skilled craftsmen were preparing and fitting out the accommodation for the crew and passengers. Despite the magnitude of the task, the *Olympic* was completed by May 1911, only seven months after launching, and began two days of formal sea trials on 29 May, following which the Board of Trade surveyor issued a certificate of seaworthiness and the ship was ready for service.

The White Star Line milked the occasion for maximum publicity by arranging for the *Olympic* to sail from Belfast on the same day that the *Titanic* was launched (31 May, 1911) and the double event drew enormous crowds, who filled the shoreline around Belfast Lough and jostled aboard the numerous ferries and pleasure craft which plied on trips around the harbour.

On completion of the celebrations, the *Olympic* sailed for Liverpool and, after a brief stay, carried on to Southampton where the White Star Line had established its main terminal for transatlantic services since 1907. The ship's maiden voyage, on 14 June, 1911, was fully booked with travellers eager to sample the world's largest liner. Subsequent to this maiden voyage, under

*RIGHT: Olympic's launch, 20 October, 1910.*

194

*ABOVE RIGHT: Captain E. J. Smith (on right of photograph) and the crew of the* Olympic. *After captaining* Olympic, *Smith would become master of the* Titanic *for its maiden voyage. Much has been made of the problems Smith's vessels encountered —* Olympic's *tussle with* Hawke *and* Titanic's *with an iceberg are the best known.*

*BELOW RIGHT:* Olympic *is prepared for sea trials.*

the command of Captain Edward Smith, she settled into a routine which was based around a three-week cycle. Each cycle started with a seven-day voyage to New York, with calls at Cherbourg and Queenstown (Ireland); then there was a three and a half day turnround, followed by the return voyage calling at Plymouth and Cherbourg before reaching Southampton. A further three and a half days were spent preparing the ship for the next voyage which started each third Wednesday.

This pattern was shared with two other ships, the *Majestic* and *Oceanic*, thus enabling the White Star Line to maintain a weekly return service across the Atlantic. However, this timetable was rudely interrupted on Wednesday, September 20, 1911, when the *Olympic* set off from Southampton for her fifth revenue earning voyage, still under the command of Captain Smith. As she made her stately way down the Solent and headed out to pass around the east end of the Isle of Wight, she worked up to 18 knots nominally under the direction of George Bowyer, a very experienced Trinity House pilot.

Turning to starboard to round the Bramble bank, speed was reduced to 11 knots but the wide radius of her turn surprised the commander of H.M.S. *Hawke*, a rather ancient 7,000 ton cruiser. *Hawke* was unable to take sufficient avoiding action and the two ships collided, the cruiser's steel and concrete bow ram burying itself deep into the starboard quarter of the great liner. Fortunately, nobody was killed and both ships remained afloat, the *Olympic* making it back to Southampton on one engine, despite two major watertight compartments being completely flooded.

This sorry incident resulted in a celebrated legal argument which decided that the fault lay with the *Olympic*. Although the ship was technically under the control of the pilot, the White Star Line was faced with large legal costs as well as the cost of repairing the ship and the losses resulting from the disruption of services. One apparent source of solace was that the ship had survived a major collision (the *Hawke*, after all, was designed to sink enemy ships by ramming them) and had remained afloat and stable despite serious flooding. This seemed to vindicate the design of the 'Olympic' class and helped to lend credence to the myth that they were unsinkable.

After undergoing temporary repairs at Southampton, the *Olympic* returned to her Belfast birthplace, arriving on 5 October, and immediately going into the Thompson dock from which the still incomplete *Titanic* had been removed. The repairs took just over six weeks and, to save time, the *Titanic*'s starboard propeller shaft and a number of other components were appropriated. Eventually, the *Olympic* returned to the transatlantic run on 29 November, 1911, but the work involved in her repairs had a significant effect on the completion date of the *Titanic*, although the latter's entry into service was eventually only delayed by some three weeks.

*Olympic*'s career suffered another setback on 24 February, 1912, when she lost a propeller blade after striking an uncharted obstruction while eastbound over the Grand Banks, some 750 miles off the Newfoundland coast. Once again she returned to Belfast for repairs, spending a week there early in March 1912, and again disrupting work on the *Titanic*. It was during this period that the last photographs of the two ships together were taken. Back

*ABOVE: An early portrait of* Olympic *.*

*RIGHT:* Olympic *manoeuvring in harbour with tugs assisting.*

in service, she was actually at sea and homeward bound from New York on the fateful 13 April, 1912, when her crew learned of the loss of the *Titanic*, but she was too far away to be of any useful assistance.

At the end of the 1912 summer season, after the lessons of the *Titanic* disaster had been absorbed, the *Olympic* was withdrawn from service and returned to Harland & Wolff for what amounted to a major rebuild, costing $1,215,000. The work extended the ship's double bottom upwards on either side to above the waterline and increased the height of the watertight bulkheads. In order to facilitate this work it was necessary to remove the four great funnels and all of the ship's boilers. When they were reinstalled, miles of additional pipework and wiring was also added. Lifeboat capacity was greatly increased by the addition of a further 48 lifeboats, making a total of 68 stowed in a triple row along the length of the Boat Deck, so that there were enough to carry all passengers and crew.

In spite of the complexity of the task, it was completed in time for the *Olympic* to rejoin the White Star fleet and to sail for New York on 2 April, 1913, when she resumed her weekly transatlantic timetable. She proved to be extremely popular, partly because of the fact that she was the *Titanic's* sister ship. Even in those days there was a considerable fascination with the events of that April night and any person or object connected with the tragedy engendered as much interest as they would today. Passenger appeal had also been improved by the addition of extra first class cabins on the Promenade Deck and changes to the restaurant facilities.

By the time that the *Olympic* returned to service, she was no longer the largest liner afloat, this distinction now belonging to the German-owned 52,000-ton *Imperator*, which had been launched at Hamburg only a month after the loss of the *Titanic*. However, the British ship was generally considered the more comfortable and was certainly more stable, the German ship gaining a very unfortunate reputation for rolling heavily with a predictable effect on the stomachs of her poor passengers.

The commercial rivalry between the British and German shipping lines was overtaken in the autumn of 1914 by a more deadly rivalry as war broke out and the *Olympic* was caught up in the traumatic events which followed. When, on 4 August, 1914, Great Britain declared war on Germany, the *Olympic* was heading westbound across the Atlantic to New York. Here the White Star house colours were covered with a uniform coat of naval grey

*ABOVE LEFT: Olympic following the collision with Hawke. This is the wooden patch at the stern covering the damage. It was put on the vessel at Southampton before she moved to Belfast for major repairs. The damage was primarily to the hull (upper, middle and lower hole), the starboard propeller shaft and the bottom of the boat.*

*ABOVE: The hole between the Saloon and Upper decks looking aft.*

*BELOW: The same hole looking forward.*

*ABOVE:* Olympic *following the collision with* Hawke. *Detail of damaged shell plates.*

*ABOVE RIGHT: Part of the upper hole from the inside.*

*BELOW AND BELOW RIGHT: Boss plating (the boss arms held the outer propellers) showing temporary wedging in holes (BELOW) and with the holes open (BELOW RIGHT).*

paint and the ship returned empty at high speed to Liverpool instead of her usual destination of Southampton. For a while a transatlantic service was continued, mainly patronised by Americans wishing to leave Europe as the war started. However, as this traffic eventually declined, it was planned that she would be laid up at Belfast at the end of October 1914.

While homeward bound on what would have been her last commercial voyage of the war, she met with the 2nd Battle Squadron of the Royal Navy off the Scottish coast. This squadron consisted of four 25,000 ton battleships of the 'King George V class', some of the most modern in the Royal Navy, having been completed only twelve months earlier. One of them, H.M.S. *Audacious*, had struck a mine and was seriously damaged. Various small craft were in attendance taking off the crew but the large battleships had left the area fearing a torpedo attack. *Olympic* was ordered to stand by to assist with the evacuation of the crew, eventually taking on board over 600 officers and men from the stricken battleship.

When this had been completed, an attempt was made to take the *Audacious* under tow but this failed as the tow line continually parted due to rough seas and the saga eventually ended late in the evening when the battleship's forward magazines exploded, causing her to roll over and sink. Despite *Olympic*'s great efforts in the rescue, she received little thanks for her work and was sent to Belfast instead of Liverpool where there was considerable delay in allowing her passengers to come ashore in an attempt to prevent the loss of the battleship becoming widely known.

The ethics of keeping a large liner carrying civilian passengers in a area deemed unsafe for well protected battleships might also be queried, but on this occasion, as on others, the *Olympic* appeared to have a much greater share of luck and good fortune than was ever enjoyed by her sister ships.

With the war now in full swing, and demand for civilian transatlantic travel at only a fraction of normal levels, it was not considered economic to retain the *Olympic* in service and she was laid up at Belfast for over ten months until chartered by the British Admiralty for use as troopship. Harland & Wolff then spent four weeks transforming the ship for her new task, taking out many of the peacetime luxury fittings to make room for over 6,000 troops instead of her normal passenger complement of 2,500. Now under the command of Captain Hays, she left Belfast in October 1915, and sailed via Liverpool, Gibraltar and La Spezia to Mudros, where the troops were disembarked to support the Dardenelles and other Middle East campaigns.

At the end of 1915, the decision to withdraw from the Gallipoli peninsula was made: it was completed early in 1916. After this the demand for major troop movements to the Mediterranean lessened and the *Olympic* found herself back at Belfast after only a few voyages. However, one reason for the withdrawal from Gallipoli was to make more troops available for the Western

*BELOW RIGHT: The upper hole looking forward.*

*FAR RIGHT: Starboard propeller showing boss plating holes and propeller damage.*

*BELOW AND BOTTOM: Views of repair work in train on the hole in* Olympic's *bottom plating and the lower hole.*

H162

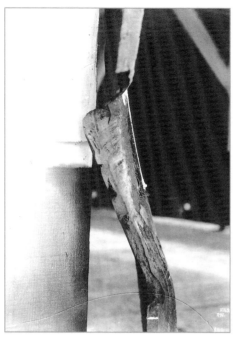

204

*ABOVE AND ABOVE RIGHT: Plate damage.*

*RIGHT: Middle hole looking forward with figure giving scale.*

Front in France and Belgium, and the build up was to be considerably bolstered by the arrival of freshly trained soldiers from the far flung parts of the British Empire. Canada was a major provider of new troops but lacked the means to transport them in any numbers. The *Olympic* was chartered for this task, which began in March 1916, and became a regular series of transatlantic crossings which would occupy her for the remainder of the war.

While being prepared for service the ship was repainted, but this time the normal wartime drab grey was replaced by something altogether more striking. Against a very pale yellow background, the ship was covered with dark blue or black geometric shapes and lines. Known as dazzle paint camouflage, this dramatic pattern was intended to break up the shape of the large hull when viewed from a distance, making it difficult to identify the ship and calculate her course and speed.

These measures were primarily directed at the ever present enemy, German U-boats. As additional protection, it was proposed that the *Olympic* should sail in escorted convoy with other ships but the maximum speed of such a formation would have been about 12 knots and Captain Hays was adamant that the *Olympic*'s greatest chance of survival lay in her inherent high-speed, cruising at 22 knots and presenting a difficult target to any waiting U-boat. Eventually it was agreed that *Olympic*'s transatlantic voyages between Liverpool and Halifax, Canada, would be carried out alone and at high-speed. *Olympic* eventually made no fewer than eleven return crossings in 1916 and continued to carry Canadian troops to Europe for most of 1917

*BELOW: Olympic.*

as well. Her remarkable record of regular safe voyages across the Atlantic earned her the nickname of 'Old Reliable' in naval and military circles and the importance of transporting troops increased substantially from April 1917 following the entry of the United States into the war.

In the end it was the massive build up of fresh American troops into a war-weary Europe that contributed to the turning of the tide and eventual victory in November 1918. However, the *Olympic* continued to ferry Canadian troops until the end of 1917 and it was not until Christmas Day 1917 that she finally arrived back in the familiar surroundings of New York to embark her first load of American soldiers. Thereafter it was back to the old routine as she plied back and forth across the Atlantic, seemingly leading a charmed life. She emerged unscathed although she had been attacked by German submarines on four occasions; fortunately all missed their speeding target.

On 18 May, 1918, *Olympic* had a unique chance for revenge as she approached the Scilly Isles, off the south-west tip of England, at the conclusion of a voyage from New York escorted by four American destroyers. A vigilant lookout in the bow of the liner spotted a German submarine stopped on the surface in the pale light of dawn and alerted the captain on the bridge, who immediately altered course toward the submarine, which was lying just off the starboard bow.

Amazingly the U-boat crew does not seem to have spotted the huge bulk

*continued on page 226*

*RIGHT: Olympic at Queenstown.*

*BELOW: Olympic and Titanic in Belfast in early March 1912, the last time the sisters would be seen together.*

206

*FAR RIGHT: When Olympic was broken up some of her interior work was auctioned. The following pages show rooms and artefacts from a number of locations.*

*RIGHT AND BELOW: Olympic's forward watertight bulkheads were increased in height following the Titanic disaster. These photographs show work being carried out on Olympic.*

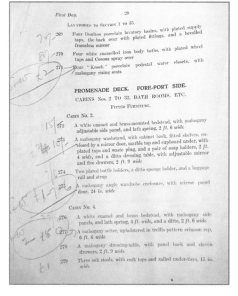

*ABOVE AND TOP: One of the auction documents showing prices for the Promenade deck fore port side cabins.*

*RIGHT: Olympic's luxury produces a stylish board room.*

212

*Much of Olympic's interior would have been produced by Messrs Heaton Tabb & Company, interior designers of Liverpool. The company had offices within most of the major shipbuilders and their work could be found on the Titanic and on many P&O vessels.*

*Next Page: Olympic's smoke room is now at the White Swan Hotel in Alnwick in Northumberland where it is used as a dining room.*

The quality of workmanship is apparent in the detail of Olympic's staterooms.

*ABOVE: The dome — here without glass — above Olympic's main first class stairway was one of the most spectacular sights onboard.*

*RIGHT AND FOLLOWING PAGES: The White Swan in Alnwick boasts many fine examples of Olympic's luxurious interior, including the revolving door from the smoke room.*

ABOVE: *Port side cutaway of* Olympic's *produced by White Star.*

ABOVE RIGHT: *The* Olympic *arrives at Mudros during World War I before it was painted in 'dazzle' camouflage.*

RIGHT: Olympic — *a 1911 portrait .*

*ABOVE: Another 1911 view of Olympic — note the size of the yacht in comparison.*

of the *Olympic* until the liner opened fire with one of the auxiliary six-inch guns fitted for her self-defence. The guns could not depress sufficiently to hit the submarine which frantically got under way and attempted to turn inside the *Olympic*. Captain Hays was quick to react and succeeded in ramming and sinking his quarry. Damage to the *Olympic* was minimal with her stem bent a few feet out of alignment and some dented hull plates. She continued her voyage to Southampton while all on board celebrated this amazing feat, the only recorded instance of a merchant ship sinking an enemy warship in World War I. Some of the American soldiers on board made a collection and paid for a plaque to commemorate the event and this was proudly displayed in one of the lounges.

After this brief moment of excitement, the *Olympic* continued her regular transatlantic crossings and, after the Armistice in November 1918, she was

again chartered by the Canadian government and spent ten months carrying troops back to their home country. It was not until August 1919 that she finally returned to Belfast and a much needed refit to prepare her again for peacetime passenger services.

Earlier that year, while undergoing a routine dry dock inspection, an outer section of the double hull below the waterline amidships was found to have a substantial dent and some sprung plates had allowed water to fill one of the outer compartments. It was almost certain that this damage had been caused by a torpedo hitting the ship some time during the closing stages of the war — fortunately though it had failed to explode.

The contribution of the *Olympic* to the allied war effort is worth recording. Alone she had carried some 66,000 American and Canadian troops to Europe, together with 41,000 civilian passengers and, rather exotically,

12,000 Chinese military construction workers. She was actually part of a four-ship service which also included the British liners *Mauretania* (31,938 tons) and *Aquitania* (45,647 tons), while the American contribution was provided by *Leviathan* (54,282 tons). *Leviathan* , then the largest liner in the world, was originally the German *Vaterland* and was one of several German ships interned in the United States early in the war and subsequently taken over when America entered the war in April 1917.

Although many other vessels were used to transport troops across the Atlantic, these four ships alone carried a substantial proportion. The record for the most troops carried in a single voyage, 10,860, was naturally held by the *Leviathan* but *Olympic* was the British record holder with 6,148, narrowly beating the *Aquitania* with 6,090, while the smaller *Mauretania* managed a maximum of 5,162. During her war service, *Olympic* had steamed no less than 184,000 miles and consumed 347,000 tons of coal.

During her post-war refit the *Olympic* was extensively modernised and her boilers converted to burn oil instead of coal. This resulted in a substantial reduction in the number of stokers required, down from 360 to around 60, and considerably eased the task of refuelling while much improving the ship's operating economics.

The peacetime fittings which had been removed and stored in 1915 were now renovated and brought back on board — the ship once again represented the ultimate in luxury travel. The total cost of this refit was $2,430,000; it appeared to be money well spent, for the ship now embarked on a peaceful career which spanned another fifteen years. For most of this time she was one of the most popular liners on the highly competitive transatlantic run and earned a useful profit for the White Star Line. The 1920s were a boom

*ABOVE RIGHT: Mudros Harbour in 1915 showing* Olympic *in foreground.*

*BELOW RIGHT:* Olympic *and* Aquitania *in the Mediterranean during World War I.*

*BELOW:* Olympic *in dazzle camouflage as a troopship — here seen with U.S. troops on board.*

*ABOVE, ABOVE AND BELOW RIGHT, FOLLOWING PAGES:* Olympic *in 'dazzle' camouflage. This camouflage was designed to break-up the vessel's silhouette and reduce the likelihood of attack by enemy submarines and surface raiders.*

time for sea travel as the horror of the war receded, and there was no competition from the still primitive aeroplane. Many of the rich and famous chose to travel aboard the *Olympic*, including Charlie Chaplin in 1921 and the young Prince of Wales in 1924. In the same year a rather sombre cargo on a return voyage to England was the body of Lord Pirrie, the Harland & Wolff chairman who had been one of the prime instigators in the planning and construction of the *Titanic* and her sisters.

Although the *Olympic* was a great success in the post-war era, the White Star Line was handicapped by the lack of an suitable ship to partner her in a regular weekly service, as was originally intended when the *Titanic* was laid down to follow her into service. A solution was provide by the allocation of the ex-German unfinished liner *Bismarck* as war reparation for the loss of the *Britannic*. Renamed *Majestic*, she was not completed until 1922 and at 56,551 grt she took over the distinction of being the world's largest liner. Together with the *Homeric*, another smaller ex-German ship, these liners formed the backbone of White Star's passenger fleet in 1920s and early 1930s.

As with other shipping lines, White Star was badly hit by the effects of the Wall Street crash in 1929 and the years of depression which followed. In 1930 over one million passengers had crossed the North Atlantic by ship: by 1935 this had slumped to less than half a million. This amount of passengers could not sustain the number of liners and shipping companies then in existence. One of the casualties was the White Star Line itself — in 1934 it was taken over and merged with Cunard. The title Cunard White Star Line was adopted, although this was dropped in the late 1940s and the company reverted to its old name, which is still used today — the Cunard Line. Following the merger the ex-White Star ships were repainted briefly in

*ABOVE: A post-war view of Olympic in 1924. She would serve on the transatlantic routes until retirement in 1935.*

*RIGHT: Olympic as a troopship during World War I. Note the extra lifeboats — 14 hanging from davits on each side—many more on the Boat deck.*

*NEXT PAGE: Olympic in 1933, two years before retirement.*

Cunard colours before being laid up and sold off, partly as a result of the declining passenger traffic and partly to make way for the new breed of super liners represented by the 80,000-ton *Queen Mary* which joined the Cunard fleet in 1936.

Almost immediately after the takeover by Cunard, the *Olympic* was involved in a tragic accident, when she accidentally hit and sank the Nantucket lightship while steaming in thick fog on the approaches to New York on May 15, 1934. The unfortunate lightship, strategically marking the channel through the shoals to the south of Cape Cod, had been narrowly missed before by other ships. The area was notorious for its fogbanks and it was sheer mischance that she was rammed by the massive *Olympic*, which sliced right through her. Seven of the lightship's crew of eleven died in this tragic accident. A subsequent inquiry placed the blame squarely on the *Olympic* and her officers and consequently, the new Cunard White Star company was faced with a bill for $500,000 in damages.

Less than a year later, in April 1935, the *Olympic* was finally retired and laid up at Southampton. Attempts to find another commercial buyer failed and in October of that year she was bought by Metal Industries Limited She left Southampton for the last time on October 11, 1935, to be ignominiously towed to Jarrow, on the River Tyne, for scrapping. It took almost two years to dismantle the *Olympic* completely, much of her metal being melted down and re-used in the naval construction programme of the late 1930s in preparation for another world war.

*BELOW: Olympic in 1922. Many of the rich and famous chose to travel aboard the* Olympic, *including Charlie Chaplin in 1921 and the young Prince of Wales in 1924.*

238

*ABOVE AND RIGHT:* Olympic *in 1929.*

Although she had been stripped of many of her fittings while she lay at Southampton, there was still much of value left aboard when she reached the north-east of England and many parts of the ship found their way into the unlikeliest of places. Some 20 miles north of the River Tyne lies the small Northumberland market town of Alnwick. A thirsty visitor to the town might repair to the old established White Swan Hotel just off the market square. If they did, they would be in for a surprise and a treat for here many of the fixtures and fittings, including mirrors, fireplaces, stained glass windows, light fittings and carved woodwork from the great ship are blended into the decor of the hotel's lounge, hall and dining room.

The *Olympic* lives on, and not only here in Alnwick. Throughout Britain there are reminders, large and small of this great ship. In many cases the provenance of the artefacts has been forgotten until an informed visitor recognises them for what they are — an integral and important part of Britain's great maritime heritage, and a tangible connection with the great events in the lives of the *Olympic* and her tragic sisters.

# TITANIC

The man appointed to command this floating marvel of the age was the White Star Line's commodore, Captain Edward John Smith. However, whilst docked at Southampton, Smith's main preoccupation was not with the passengers or crew, but with a problem which threatened to delay or even prevent the *Titanic* from making her maiden voyage. The timing of the ship's introduction into service coincided with the final stages of a long coal miners' strike, which meant that fuel was in short supply and Southampton was crowded with other ships lying idle in the port as they waited to replenish their bunkers.

The *Titanic* had around 1,880 tons on board when she arrived from Belfast, and picked up more which the *Olympic* had brought across on her previous crossing from the United States. In addition, further supplies were taken from other White Star or I.M.M. owned ships including the *Majestic*, *Oceanic*, *Philadelphia*, *New York* and *St. Louis*. A total of 4,427 tons was gleaned from these sources but records indicate that some 415 tons were burned while in harbour at Southampton to provide a steam supply to the heating system and to generators providing electrical power for various machinery including the cranes. Thus, when the ship finally sailed, she

*BELOW: Titanic at the Belfast outfitting quay with the floating crane in the background. This photograph shows her port side.*

carried only 5,892 tons of coal, sufficient for the planned voyage but less than the 8,000 tons she would normally carry. The task of transferring all this coal was tedious and dirty work and it was the main reason why almost all liners of the time had black hulls. The situation was not helped by the fact that there was a fire in Number 10 bunker on the starboard side of boiler room 6. This had started as the ship left Belfast and was not extinguished until the day before the ship sank. However, this was not quite as alarming as it sounds — bunker fires were common and this one was not near the critical areas damaged by the iceberg, although it has been argued that it eventually weakened the adjacent watertight bulkhead and this may have been one factor which hastened the end of the ship.

When *Titanic* had set sail from Belfast she had been manned by a crew of approximately 120, enough to handle the ship on her short run to Southampton where the rest of the crew would now be signed on. Smith's second-in-command on the *Titanic*'s maiden voyage was Chief Officer Henry Tingle Wilde. Aged 38, Wilde was formerly Chief Officer of the *Olympic* and could reasonably have been expected to have remained aboard that ship in order to assist its new captain on his first voyage. However, for reasons which have never been satisfactorily explained, Wilde was transferred to the *Titanic* at short notice and did not board until the day immediately prior to sailing, 9 April. This appointment caused a reshuffle amongst the deck officers already appointed, and probably some resentment as well. The original Chief Officer, William McMaster Murdoch, was demoted to the position of First Officer, and the same happened to Charles Herbert Lightoller, who now became Second Officer instead of his original

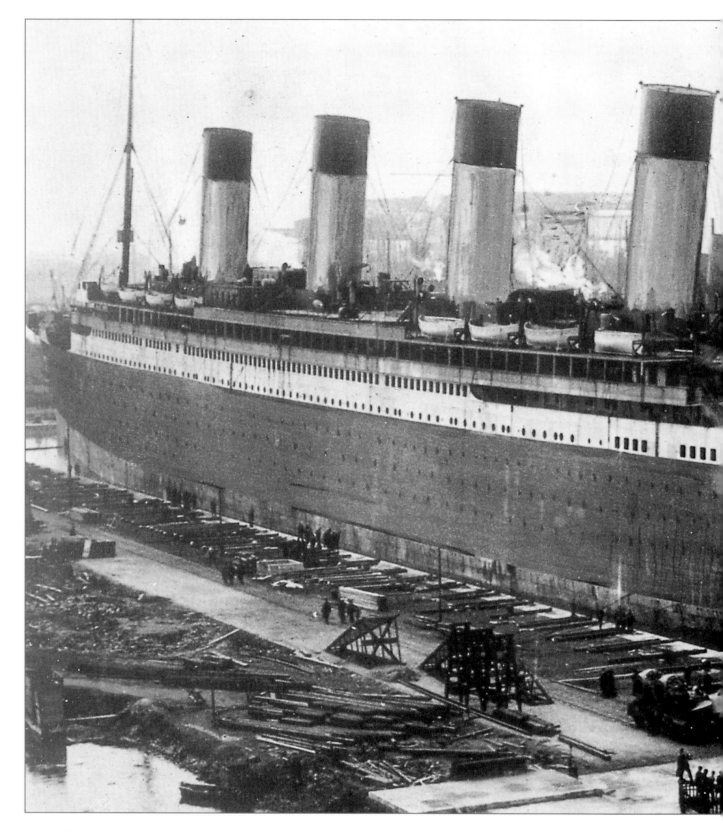

*ABOVE: This picture is taken from a contemporary postcard titled, 'The new White Star liner "Titanic" (45,000 tons) nearing completion; docked in the largest graving dock in the world. Belfast, february 1912.' However, the ship depicted is Olympic. It was not unusual for the Olympic to substitute for her sister in this way as she was far nearer completion at the time.*

appointment as First Officer. The previous Second Officer left the ship as a result of these changes, a chance event for which he must subsequently have been eternally thankful. The remaining four junior deck officers (Pitman, Boxhall, Lowe and Moody in order of seniority) remained unchanged. Whatever the reasons for the last-minute appointment of Chief Officer Wilde, the result was that the ship sailed on her maiden voyage commanded by a group of officers who had had little chance to work together and whose duties had been changed almost on the eve of sailing. With many White Star Line ships laid up because of the coal strike, there was no problem in assem-

bling the rest of the crew, with most of those who signed on having their
homes in the Southampton area. In addition to the crew, there were two
other men on board who would play a very important part in the events
about to unfold. Although wireless equipment had only recently been
introduced aboard ships at sea, its usefulness had been dramatically
illustrated following the collision of the liners *Republic* (a White Star
ship but not that mentioned in the biography of Captain Smith on page
76 ) and *Florida* in 1909. The radio distress message sent out had alerted
other ships, and on that occasion there had been little loss of life.

Consequently, all new ships were being equipped with wireless, although many smaller and older ships remained without. The *Titanic* was provided with a set which had a normal range of around 250 miles, but this could be boosted by atmospheric conditions to significantly greater distances. Power was provided by a five kilowatt generator, and a diesel-powered standby generator and batteries were available as alternative backups. The radio room was incorporated into the bridge superstructure aft at the base of the fore funnel and was manned by two operators who were not employed by the White Star Line, but by the Marconi International Marine Communication Company. Gugliemo Marconi was not only a brilliant inventor, but an astute businessman who realized the importance of his invention and, consequently, kept a personal hold on its deployment and use. The two operators were Jack Phillips and his assistant, Harold Bride, these two continually manning the set while at sea on a six hours on, six hours off, shift pattern.

There was another group to join the ship at Southampton who were not directly employed by White Star, a group which was to earn undying fame in the days to come. They were the eight musicians hired from a Liverpool

*BELOW AND RIGHT: Titanic completed and leaving Belfast Lough for Southampton and her maiden voyage across the Atlantic.*

agency their task would be to entertain the passengers in the various restaurants and saloons. Little did they realize that their final performance would be in the most dramatic circumstances imaginable! At the time of her loss, the *Titanic* was manned by a crew of 892, the majority of which were accommodated on E deck, although 108 firemen were berthed forward under the forecastle and another 140, including more firemen and the third class stewards, were down on F and G decks. The crew accommodation and messing arrangements were completely segregated from the passengers and they had their own passageways and staircases to move through the ship as their duties required.

If finding a full crew had been easy, filling the ship with passengers was a different matter. Normally a prestigious vessel like the *Titanic* could expect to be filled to overflowing on her maiden voyage, but the long running coal strike had disrupted schedules and many would-be travellers had deferred their plans until the situation was resolved. In fact the strike, which had lasted for six weeks, was settled on 6 April, but this was too late to have an effect in time for the *Titanic*'s sailing on 10 April. As she departed from Southampton, only 922 passengers had embarked, although others would join at Cherbourg and Queenstown to bring the final total up to 1,316. This figure was made up of 606 in cabin classes (first and second) and 710 in steerage but was little more than half the 2,436 which the ship could have carried. In the circumstances, it is fortunate that the ship was not fully booked.

The accommodation which had attracted the most publicity would have been the two 'millionaire suites' on B deck. Each consisted of two bedrooms with bathroom and dressing facilities between them and a separate sitting room. The larger of the bedrooms was carpeted, oak-panelled and decorated in the French style. It contained a large double and a single bed, together with various pieces of furniture including a washstand, dressing table and

*ABOVE: Another photograph of* Titanic *steaming away from Belfast.*

*ABOVE RIGHT: A rare view of the completed sisters together —* Titanic *is on the right.*

*BELOW RIGHT: April 1912 —* Titanic *berthed at Southampton.*

sofa. The other bedroom was of similar size and content but was decorated in a different style; the sitting room was expansively fitted out and furnished with a large round table, armchairs and occasional chairs, a writing desk, a coffee stool and, rather incongruously, a fireplace and mantelpiece. Each of these two suites had access to a private verandah equipped with chairs, settees and tables and both had a servant cabin and private pantry immediately adjacent. Also on B deck were 30 parlour suites, which consisted of large cabins containing a double bed and a range of other furniture as well as adjacent washrooms and wardrobes. These were furnished in a variety of decorative styles culled from the stately homes of Europe, including Louis XV and XVI, Adams and Empire styles.

When boarding the ship, the first class passengers immediately came into the impressive entrance hall on B deck where they would be confronted by the 16 ft wide grand staircase which accessed six decks and was over 60 ft high, capped at its upper level by a massive glass dome and also lit by a massive 21-light chandelier. For those passengers unable or unwilling to climb the staircase, there were three electric lifts available. Amidships on A Deck was the reading and writing room, a spacious area decorated in the late Georgian style with white panelled walls and moulded ceilings; the central feature here was a hooded fireplace surmounted by an electric clock. Lower down, on D deck and easily accessible from the grand staircase, was the reception room, extending the whole width of the ship and heavily carpeted with the best quality Axminster; on the wall opposite the stairs was a

specially commissioned French tapestry. If the passengers were hungry, they had a choice of places to eat, ranging from the Grand Dining Saloon, also on D deck, which could seat 550 and was claimed to be the largest compartment aboard any liner in the world, to the à la Carte restaurant and the Café Parisien on B deck. The Grand Saloon was expensively decorated in a mock 17th century Jacobean style, while the à la Carte adopted a more expensive Louis XVI look. Centrally located on the Upper Promenade (A) deck was the smoking room, which was loosely based on English country house of the early Georgian period. As women were not expected to smoke in those days,

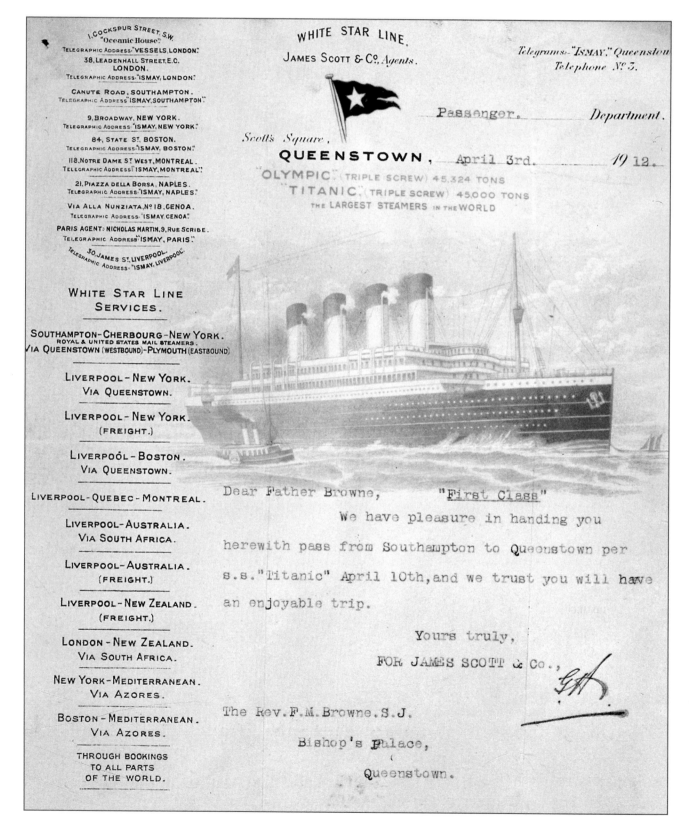

• TITANIC & HER SISTERS OLYMPIC & BRITANNIC •

"Under the Bridge".
Major Butt, President Taft's Aide de Camp is seen in distance.
The boy in middle distance, Master Jack Odell. left Ship at Queenstown.

The forts that "guard" Spithead

The lower promenade Deck. 187 yds long.
In the distance is the R.M.S.P. "Tagus", about to follow the western channel by the "Needles", while the "Titanic" swung to enter the Eastern channel by Cowes + Portsmouth.

this was effectively a gentleman's retreat, rather like the London clubs which they would reluctantly have left behind.

For those with a more energetic turn of mind, there was a novel 32 ft by 13 ft swimming pool which was fully tiled in white and blue. Special periods each day were set aside for female bathers. Even more intriguing was the Turkish and Electric Bath Establishment situated immediately aft of the swimming pool. This was done out in a pastiche of a seventeenth century Arabian style with ornate carvings and original tiling. Hot and temperate sauna rooms were available, together with electric Turkish baths and there was a full staff of attendants and masseuses to ease weary limbs. The customers could also take the opportunity to try out some of the sports facilities on the ship, including the full size squash court, a feature in which the White Star Line publicity placed great store, as it offered a concrete example of how steady and spacious the *Titanic* actually was. A full time professional coach was in attendance and a regular programme of competitions would have been arranged on each voyage. Finally, on the Boat deck, was the gymnasium, which was provided with the latest gadgets in exercise equipment including rowing and weight lifting machines and, perhaps faintly amusing to modern eyes, mechanical horses where passengers could simulate the pleasures of riding on horseback while skimming across the ocean at over 20 knots.

*ABOVE: A facsimile of a page from Father Browne's famous album. Photographs taken by Browne were to feature on the front pages of many of the world's newspapers following the sinking.*

Bruce Ismay, the White Star Line chairman, occupied the port side first class suite on B deck accompanied by his secretary and valet. The richest passenger on board was Colonel John Astor, worth $150 million, who was travelling with his wife, together with an entourage which included a servant, maid and nurse. This party occupied one of the parlour suites on C deck. Second wealthiest was Isidor Straus, a self-made man and co-owner of the famous Macy's store in New York was abroad with his wife and was allegedly worth in excess of $50 million. Other well known or rich travellers included Charles Hays, a Canadian railway mogul, Clarence Moore, Master of the Chevy Chase Hunt, Major Archibald Butt, chief aide to the President of the United States, Henry Harris, a theatrical impresario, and his wife, and a number of American industrialists including John B. Thayer and George D. Widener. The first class passengers could look forward to a week of comfort and opulence which at least equalled, and probably even exceeded anything they were familiar with ashore. Indeed, to these passengers the ship was nothing more than a prestigious five-star floating hotel, complete with all the services and amenities which they would expect from such an establishment.

If the first class passengers were well looked after, those in second class would also have had little to complain about. Although smaller, their cabins were reasonably spacious and normally configured to hold two or four sleeping berths. Each also contained large wardrobes and ingenious foldaway washstands, although none had en suite bath or toilet facilities, these being

*BELOW: Deck plan of the* Titanic *as presented to passengers.*

*ABOVE AND BELOW RIGHT: The passenger trains left from London's Waterloo station for the docks of Southampton; The top picture shows Colonel John Jacob Astor, the wealthiest man on board.*

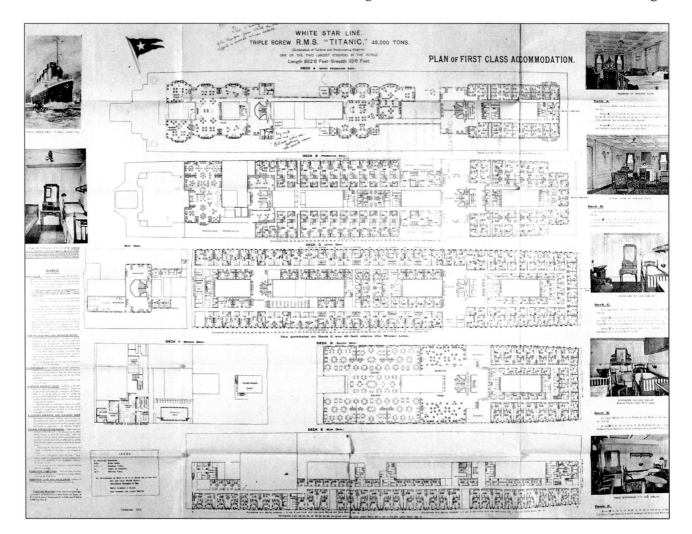

SURVEY OF AN EMIGRANT SHIP.

# Certificate for Clearance.

| Ship's Name and Official Number. (1.) | | Port of Registry, and Tonnage. (2.) | | Name of Master. (3.) | |
|---|---|---|---|---|---|
| Titanic 131428 | | Gross. 46328 | Register. 21831 | E. J. Smith | |
| Port of Departure. (4.) | | Ports of Call. (5.) | | Destination. (6.) | |
| Southampton | | Cherbourg Queenstown | | New York | |

### CABIN PASSENGERS.

| Adults (12 years and upwards). | | | | Children. | | | | Total Cabin Passengers. (15.) | Equal to Adults computed by Part III. M. S. Act, 1894. (16.) |
|---|---|---|---|---|---|---|---|---|---|
| Married. | | Single. | | Between 1 and 12. | | Under 1 Year. | | | |
| Male. (7.) | Female. (8.) | Male. (9.) | Female. (10.) | Male. (11.) | Female. (12.) | Male. (13.) | Female. (14.) | | |
| 52 | 52 | 196 | 101 | 10 | 12 | 4 | . | 427 | 412 |

### STEERAGE PASSENGERS.*

| Adults (12 years and upwards). | | | | Children. | | | | Total Steerage Passengers. (25.) | Equal to Adults computed by Part III. M. S. Act, 1894. (26.) |
|---|---|---|---|---|---|---|---|---|---|
| Married. | | Single. | | Between 1 and 12. | | Under 1 Year. | | | |
| Male. (17.) | Female. (18.) | Male. (19.) | Female. (20.) | Male. (21.) | Female. (22.) | Male. (23.) | Female. (24.) | | |
| 25 | 25 | 315 | 74 | 22 | 28 | 3 | 3 | 495 | 464 |
| 2 | 2 | 50 | 5 | 5 | | | | 113 | 110½ |

### CREW.

| Deck Department. (27.) | Engine Department. (28.) | Stewards' Department. (29.) | Total Crew. (30.) | Equal to Adults computed by Part III. M. S. Act, 1894. (31.) |
|---|---|---|---|---|
| 73 | 325 | 494 | 892 | 892 |

Total Number actually on board, including Crew . . . . . . .

| * Total Number of Statute Adults (as Steerage Passengers), exclusive of the Master, Crew, and Cabin Passengers, which the Ship can legally carry according to space allotted | Clear Space in Sq. Ft. | Number of Beds fitted. |
|---|---|---|
| 1735 | 26992 | 1134 |

I hereby certify that the particulars inserted in the above form are correct. I also certify that all the requirements of the Merchant Shipping Acts relating to emigrant ships, so far as they can be complied with before the departure of the ship, have been complied with, and that the ship is, in my opinion, seaworthy and in safe trim, and in all respects fit for her intended voyage; that she does not carry a greater number of passengers than in the proportion of one statute adult to every five superficial feet of space clear for exercise on deck; and that her passengers and crew are in a fit state to proceed.

Dated at Southampton

this ___ APP 10 1912 ___ day of ___ 19___

M. H. Clarke

Emigration Officer, or Assistant Emigration Officer.

provided in special areas on the centreline of the ship with the cabins mostly grouped along the ship's sides in the after section of the hull. The second class dining saloon on D deck was oak-panelled but was smaller than the first class equivalent, seating only 394 people. Although more simply decorated and furnished, the second class public areas such as the smoking room, library and entrance lobby were spacious and roomy and the passengers would certainly have felt that they had received good value for the money that they had paid. In second class were the eight musicians, who were counted as passengers and not as part of the crew. Other occupants included several families as well as businessmen, teachers, priests, and representatives of many ordinary professions and occupations.

The lot of the third class or steerage passengers was often thought of as arduous, cramped and uncomfortable. While this might have been true on many earlier ships, the builders of the *Titanic* had attempted to provide a much improved style of accommodation in this area. The vast majority of such passengers were emigrants from Europe, intent on starting a new life in America and, in such circumstances, the voyage across the Atlantic was literally a once in a lifetime experience, which the White Star Line did its best to make as pleasant as possible. The public areas were open and spacious, although the decor was simple and straightforward, generally white-painted pine-panelled or plain bulkheads with wooden furniture. Despite this, the meals were still served by stewards and waiters and there was plenty of food available. A typical day's menu lists porridge, fish, eggs, tripe and onions, bread, butter, marmalade, tea and coffee for breakfast; soup, rabbit, bacon, beans, potatoes, biscuits, bread, semolina and apples for lunch; and brawn

*ABOVE: The* Titanic *'special' leaves Waterloo station for the first and last time.*

*LEFT: Titanic's Certificate for Clearance as issued by the Board of Trade on 13 April, 1912, for an emigrant ship. This gives passenger details broken down by age, sex and marital status. The lower paragraph states:*

*'I hereby certify that the particulars inserted in the above form are correct. I also certify that all the requirements of the Merchant Shipping Acts relating to emigrant ships, so far as they can be complied with before the departure of the ship, have been complied with, and that the ship is, in my opinion, seaworthy, in safe trim, and in all respects fit for her intended voyage; that she does not carry a greater number of passengers than in the proportion of one statute adult to every five superficial feet of space clear for exercise on deck; and that her passengers and crew are in a fit state to proceed.*

*'Dated at Southampton this 10th day of April 1912.'*

*This certificate had to be completed by the Emigration Officer at each port from which the emigrant ship took on passengers.*

**ISSUED BY THE BOARD OF TRADE.**

# SURVEY OF AN EMIGRANT SHIP.

# Certificate for Clearance.

**• TITANIC & HER SISTERS OLYMPIC & BRITANNIC •**

| Ship's Name and Official Number. (1.) | Port of Registry, and Tonnage. (2.) | | Name of Master. (3.) |
|---|---|---|---|
| | Gross. | Register. | *E. J. Smith* |
| | *45328* | *24781* | |

| Port of Departure. (4.) | Ports of Call. (5.) | Destination. (6.) |
|---|---|---|
| *Cherbourg* | *Queenstown* | *New York* |

## CABIN PASSENGERS.

| Adults (12 years and upwards). | | | | Children. | | | | Total Cabin Passengers. (15.) | Equal to Adults computed by Part III. M. S. Act, 1894. (16.) |
|---|---|---|---|---|---|---|---|---|---|
| Married. | | Single. | | Between 1 and 12. | | Under 1 Year. | | | |
| Male. (7.) | Female. (8.) | Male. (9.) | Female. (10.) | Male. (11.) | Female. (12.) | Male. (13.) | Female. (14.) | | |
| *29* | *29* | *51* | *58* | *3* | *2* | — | — | *172* | *169 1/2* |

## STEERAGE PASSENGERS.*

| Adults (12 years and upwards). | | | | Children. | | | | Total Steerage Passengers. (25.) | Equal to Adults computed by Part III. M. S. Act, 1894. (26.) |
|---|---|---|---|---|---|---|---|---|---|
| Married. | | Single. | | Between 1 and 12. | | Under 1 Year. | | | |
| Male. (17.) | Female. (18.) | Male. (19.) | Female. (20.) | Male. (21.) | Female. (22.) | Male. (23.) | Female. (24.) | | |
| *4* | *4* | *59* | *18* | *7* | *7* | *3* | — | *102* | *92 1/2* |

## CREW.

| Deck Department. (27.) | Engine Department. (28.) | Stewards' Department. (29.) | Total Crew. (30.) | Equal to Adults computed by Part III. M. S. Act, 1894. (31.) |
|---|---|---|---|---|
| | | | | |

| Total Number actually on board, including Crew . . . . . . | |
|---|---|

| * Total Number of Statute Adults (as Steerage Passengers), exclusive of the Master, Crew, and Cabin Passengers, which the Ship can legally carry according to space allotted | Clear Space in Sq. Ft. | Number of Beds fitted. |
|---|---|---|
| | | |

I hereby certify that the particulars inserted in the above form are correct. I also certify that all the requirements of the Merchant Shipping Acts relating to emigrant ships, so far as they can be complied with before the departure of the ship, have been complied with, and that the ship is, in my opinion, seaworthy, in safe trim, and in all respects fit for her intended voyage; that she does not carry a greater number of passengers than in the proportion of one statute adult to every five superficial feet of space clear for exercise on deck; and that her passengers and crew are in a fit state to proceed.

Dated at *Cherbourg*

this *10th* day of *April* 19 *12*

(238x) (62245) Wt. 30276/150 3000 12-10 W B & L

Emigration Officer, or Assistant Emigration Officer.

beef, cheese, pickles, bread, butter, jam, tea and buns at teatime.

Accommodation was mostly in twin-berth cabins with basic wash facilities. The bunks folded away to give more space in the day and electric lighting was provided. Although rather spartan, they were not uncomfortable and the design was well thought out. The provision of twin-berth cabins for this class of passenger was very unusual at this time, many other ships sleeping steerage passengers in four or eight-berth cabins, or even in communal dormitories. Amongst the third class passengers was a large proportion of Scandinavian families (180 adults and children in total) emigrating to the United States and travelling on the *Titanic* as a result of a concentrated White Star Line marketing campaign in their homeland. Consequently the passenger list included names such as Andersson, Asplund, Hagland, Hansen, Johnsson, Skoog and Svensson. To balance this, there were 183 British passengers in steerage, including John and Annie Sage with no fewer than nine children, the whole family subsequently perish-

RIGHT: *The official document issued on 12 April, 1912, by the Marine Department of the Board of Trade showing that the Titanic was fit to sail. It shows that the inspectors were fully satisfied that she was in good order and condition.*

FAR RIGHT: *The registration document that British ship owners were required by law to complete and deliver to the customs officers of the port to which the vessel was registered. In the Titanic's case, this was Liverpool where the head office of the Oceanic Steam Navigation Company Ltd. was based. In return the customs officers issued a Certificate of Registry, copied also to the Registrar-General of Shipping and Seamen. This gave the ship's unique official number: Titanic's was 131,428.*

*Applicants for registration had to supply full details of the dimensions, tonnage and engine power, plus the names of all the owners of the nominal '64 shares' (which represented 100 percent ownership of the vessel). Interestingly these details differ somewhat to those given in the records at Harland & Wolff.*

*The original Certificate of Registry went down with the Titanic. This is the Registrar-General's copy, hence the faint writing across the certificate stating:*

*'Registry closed 31st May 1912. Vessel wrecked in the Atlantic Ocean 14 April 1912. Certificate of Registry lost with the vessel. Advice received from the registered manager — the form received 3rd June 1912.*

NEXT PAGE: *10 April, 1912. Passengers boarding the Titanic at Southampton Docks.*

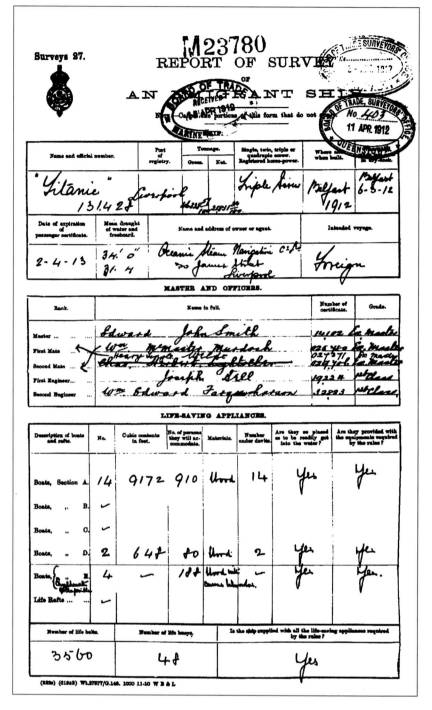

ing in the impending disaster, as did the Goodwin family with its six children.

Examination of the passenger lists has highlighted a fascinating cross-section of travellers, from the very richest men in the world to the poorest migrants seeking a fresh start. Prices for the crossing echo this spectrum of backgrounds; £2 for the cheapest one-way ticket, and up to £870 for the most expensive.

The majority of the second and third class passengers arrived at Southampton just after 9:30 a.m. on Wednesday 10 April, carried there by the London & South Western Railway boat train which had left London's Waterloo station at 7:30 a.m. A second train arrived at 11:00 a.m. bringing the last of the first class and second class passengers. It is easy to imagine the scene as the hundreds of passengers swarmed aboard, the confusion as they searched excitedly for their cabins within the unfamiliar confines of the

# Transcript of Register for Transmission to Registrar-General of Shipping and Seamen.

| Official Number | Name of Ship | No., Date, and Port of Registry |
|---|---|---|
| 131,428 | Titanic | 24 / 1912 Liverpool |

| No., Date, and Port of previous Registry (if any) | New vessel |
|---|---|

| Whether British or Foreign Built | Whether a Sailing or Steam Ship; and if a Steam Ship, how propelled | Where Built | When Built | Name and Address of Builders |
|---|---|---|---|---|
| British | Steamship Triple screw. | Belfast | 1912 | Harland and Wolff Ld, Belfast. |

| | | Feet | Tenths |
|---|---|---|---|
| Number of Decks ... five & two partial | Length from fore part of stem, under the bowsprit, to the aft side of the head of the stern post ... | 852 | 5 |
| Number of Masts ... two | Length at quarter of depth from top of weather deck at side amidships to bottom of keel | 849 | 2 |
| Rigged ... Schooner | Main breadth to outside of plank plating ... | 92 | 5 |
| Stern ... Elliptical | Depth in hold from tonnage deck to ceiling at midships ... | 31 | 6 |
| Build ... Clencher | Depth in hold from upper deck to ceiling at midships, in the case of three decks and upwards ... | 59 | 5.8 |
| Galleries ... | | | |
| Head ... | Depth from top of beam amidships to top of keel ... | 64 | 9.1 |
| Framework and description of vessel ... steel | Depth from top of deck at side amidships to bottom of keel | 65 | 3.3 |
| Number of Bulkheads ... fifteen | Round of beam ... | | 2.5 |
| Number of water ballast tanks seventeen and their capacity in tons ... 5026 | Length of engine room, if any ... | | |

*Registry closed 31 May 1912 Vessel wrecked in the Atlantic Ocean 14th April 1912. Certificate destroyed ... with the vessel ... of the ... Manager ... Form 20 Received 3 June 1912.*

## PARTICULARS OF DISPLACEMENT.

Total to quarter the depth from weather deck at side amidships 70,480 Tons. Ditto per inch immersion at same depth 150 Tons.

## PARTICULARS OF PROPELLING ENGINES, &c. (if any).

| No. of sets of Engines | Description of Engines | Whether British or Foreign made | When made | Name and address of makers | Reciprocating Engines No. and Diameter of Cylinders in each set. | Length of Stroke | Rotary Engines No. of Cylinders in each set. | N.H.P. / I.H.P. Speed of Ship. |
|---|---|---|---|---|---|---|---|---|
| Two reciprocating and one Turbine | Four cylinder triple expansion inverted vertical direct acting surface condensing and turbine | British | 1912 | Harland & Wolff Ld | 1-84" / 2-97" | | one | 6906 / 50,000 21 Knots |

| No. of Shafts | Description of Boilers | | | | | | | |
|---|---|---|---|---|---|---|---|---|
| Three | Number twenty nine Iron or Steel steel Loaded Pressure 215 lbs □/□ | British | 1912 | 3 Belfast | | | | |

## PARTICULARS OF TONNAGE.

| GROSS TONNAGE. | No. of Tons | DEDUCTIONS ALLOWED. | No. of Tons |
|---|---|---|---|
| Under Tonnage Deck ... | 17,870.66 | On account of space required for propelling power ... | 21,687.68 |
| Space or spaces between Decks lower upper middle | 14,142.81 | On account of spaces occupied by Seamen or Apprentices, and appropriated to their use, and kept free from Goods or Stores of every kind, not being the personal property of the Crew ... These spaces are the following, viz.:— In lower middle upper and saloon tween decks poop forecastle bridge and round houses | 2628.96 |
| Turret or Trunk ... | | | |
| Forecastle ... | 270.39 | | |
| Bridge space ... | 3633.45 | | |
| Poop or Break ... | 294.21 | | |
| Side Houses ... | | | |
| Deck Houses ... | 5702.89 | | |
| Chart House ... | | | |
| Spaces for machinery, and light, and air, under Section 78 (2) of the Merchant Shipping Act, 1894 | 1184.16 | Deductions under Section 79 of the Merchant Shipping Act, 1894, and Section 54 of the Merchant Shipping Act, 1906, as follows:— | |
| Excess of Hatchways ... | | Cubic Metres. Fore peak water ballast tank 44.43 After " 30.95 Master's Accommodation " 21.98 Boatswain's Stores 78.00 Chart Room 6.23 | 148.89 |
| **Gross Tonnage** ... | 46,328.57 / 131,109.88 | | |
| Deductions, as per Contra ... | 24,497.23 / 69,327.16 | Total ... | 24,497.23 |
| **Register Tonnage** ... | 21,831.34 / 61,782.69 | | |

NOTE.—1. The tonnage of the engine room spaces below the upper deck is 11,209.94 tons, and the tonnage of the total spaces framed in above the upper deck for propelling machinery and for light and air is 1184.16 tons.

NOTE.—2. The undermentioned spaces above the upper deck are not included in the cubical contents forming the ship's register tonnage: Open space in front of poop 16 feet long = 65.24 Tons Open space abaft 2nd class smoke room 6 ft long = 15... Open space on Promenade deck abreast windows, port side - 198 feet long = 343.24 Tons. Open " " " " " Starbd " 198 " - 377.24 "

| Name of Master | | Certificate of { Service No. / Competency No. |
|---|---|---|

Names, Residence, and Description of the Owners, and Number of Sixty-fourth Shares held by each ... viz.:

Oceanic Steam Navigation Company Limited having its principal place of business at 30 James Street Liverpool } Sixty four Shares

Harold Arthur Sanderson 30 James Street, Liverpool designated Manager

Advice received 25th day of March 1912

Under the seal of the owning Company

| Dated 25th March 1912 | W. H. Tymms | Registrar. |
|---|---|---|

NOTE.—Registrars in the Colonies are requested to distinguish...

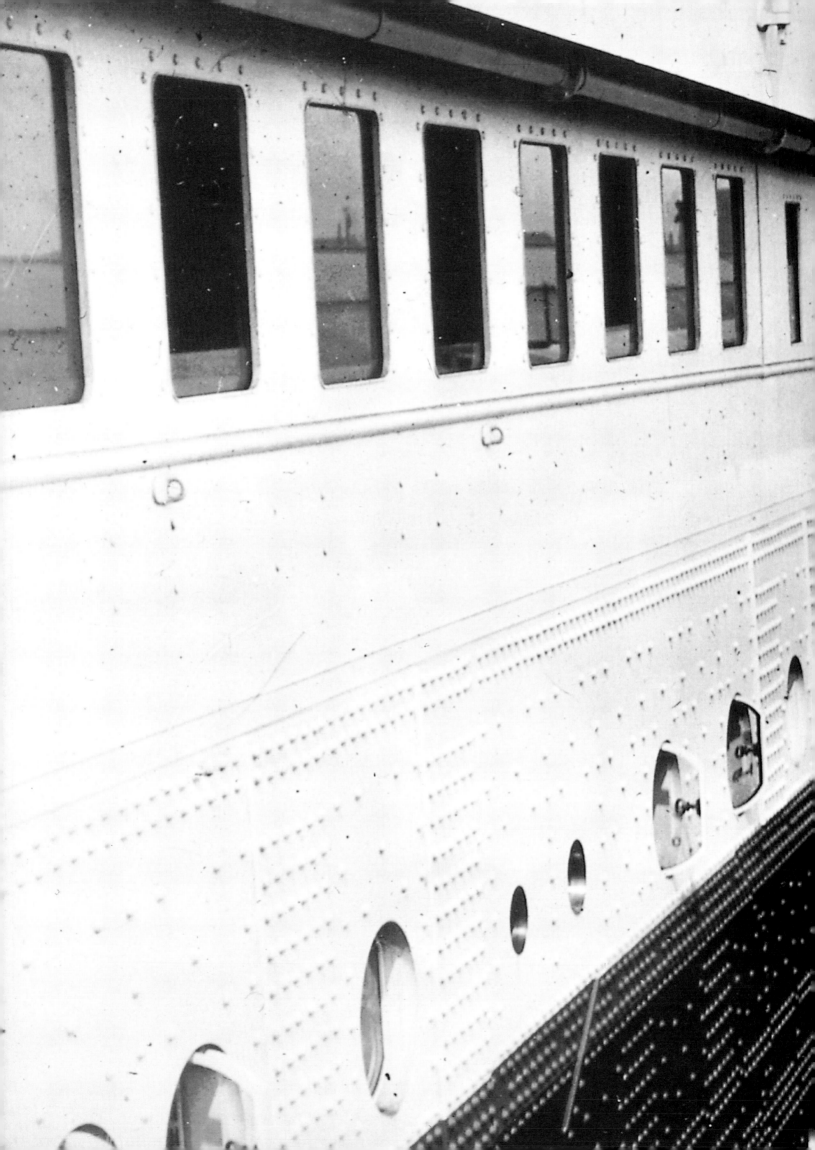

*BELOW: A letter written by the Reverend John Harper on 2 April 1912 informing friends that his passage on the* Lusitania *had been cancelled. The crucial part of the letter reads:*

*'I am to be in Walworth — God willing — after all this weekend as I received instructions this morning that my steamer the* Lusitania *cannot sail on Saturday; and as the steamer that goes in her place is a slow one I have decided to wait till next Wednesday.'*

*Next Wednesday was* Titanic's *sailing day and his decision sadly proved fatal as Reverend Harper would go down with the ship.*

*ABOVE RIGHT: The tugs* Neptune *and* Hector *ease* Titanic *away from the quay,*

*BELOW RIGHT: In this photograph the stern of the* New York *can be clearly seen blocking* Titanic's *path. Also shown is* Titanic's *Forecastle deck, which now rests intact on the ocean floor complete with all the fixtures visible here.*

ship, baggage being carried aboard and littering the lobbies, stewards frantically trying to restore some form of order and the general buzz of activity as the ship prepared to sail. The ship's officers had already spent the previous few days ensuring that everything was ready but, even as the passengers were boarding, the local Board of Trade inspector, Captain Maurice Harvey Clarke, was making his final check that all was well before certifying that the ship was safe to proceed. Despite a rigorous inspection, which included requiring the crew to operate and lower two of the ship's lifeboats, he did not notice, or was not advised of, the bunker fire raging below. While the inspector signed the final documents, the White Star Line marine superintendent at Southampton, Captain Benjamin Steele, received the formal Captain's Report from Captain Smith, stating that the ship was loaded and ready for sea and confirming that the engines and boilers were in good order and that all charts and sailing directions were up to date. As the midday sailing time approached, the officials took their leave and all gangways except one were landed. Already aboard was the pilot, George Bowyer, who had been piloting the *Olympic* when she collided with H.M.S. *Hawke*, and his red and white striped flag flew at the masthead.

On the stroke of 12 noon, Captain Smith gave the order to sound the ship's horns and the traditional triple blast echoed across Southampton. As the last gangway was being swung away, six stokers and firemen who had been patronizing some of the nearby public houses came running up: it was too late and Sixth Officer Moody allowed the gangway to be landed. The

*ABOVE: Looking aft from the starboard Boat deck can be seen three ships whose voyages were cancelled due to their coal being transferred to the* Titanic. *They are the* St. Louis, *the* Philadelphia *and the* Majestic.

*FAR RIGHT:* Titanic *raises her anchor.*

*RIGHT: As she leaves Southampton dock, friends and relatives on shore wave the travellers off.*

263

missing men's places were taken by standby men already embarked for such an eventually. On the bow, Chief Officer Wilde and Second Officer Lightoller confirmed that all was ready, while First Officer Murdoch did likewise at the stern, their reports being passed to the bridge where Captain Smith ordered the lines cast off.

As the thick hawsers splashed into the water and the *Titanic* was freed from the land, the same five tugs which had brought her into the dock now gently edged her out into the main channel and turned her bow downstream. The crowd of sightseers and well wishers on the quayside saw the tugs cast off and move clear as the ship's telegraph rang down to start the ship's propellers turning. At first just stemming the incoming tide, the *Titanic* then began to gather speed and move down Southampton water, turning to port as she came around the end of the docks complex where two liners were moored, the *Oceanic* alongside the quay with the *New York*, berthed on her outboard side. This situation arose due to the number of ships in Southampton as a result of the coal strike and meant that the deep channel which the *Titanic* was obliged to follow was slightly obstructed. By the time that she passed the two moored ships, the *Titanic* was travelling fast enough to generate a suction force (known as the canal effect) on the *New York* to the extent that her after mooring lines parted under the strain and her stern began to drift out into the path of the *Titanic*. Only prompt action by the master of tug *Vulcan*, who managed to get a line aboard the *New York* and steady the swinging stern, prevented a collision, although quick action

*FAR LEFT: A tug pushes the New York safely out of the Titanic's path. In the background can be seen another White Star liner, Oceanic. Both of these ships had once been considered to be among the biggest liners in the world but are obviously tiny in comparison to the passing Titanic.*

*LEFT: This photograph shows clearly the stern of the New York and how narrowly the two ships avoided a collision.*

*RIGHT: A Father Browne photograph taken over the starboard railing. In the distance can be seen one of the small emergency cutters (boat number 1) swung out over the side of the ship. This is the boat that would carry Sir Cosmo and Lady Duff-Gordon among its few escaping passengers.*

*BELOW: A view from the port side of* Titanic, *looking aft. The ship is steaming away from Portsmouth.*

aboard the *Titanic* also helped as 'Full Astern' was ordered and the starboard anchor was lowered to the waterline, ready to act as a brake if required. As the *Titanic* slowed and then reversed, the gap between the two ships was a matter of feet and, once past, the *New York* drifted out into the main channel as tugs fought to control her. Eventually the situation was restored and, with the *New York* now moored in midstream, the *Titanic* was again able to proceed after a delay of nearly an hour — not an auspicious start and an incident that profoundly effected one passenger. Mrs. Harris, wife of an American impresario, found herself suddenly addressed by a stranger: 'This is a bad omen,' he told her, adding, 'Do you love life?'

She replied simply, 'I love it.' 'Then get off this ship at Cherbourg. That's what I'm going to do.'

However, once under way, things settled down and after disembarking the pilot onto the Nab Light Vessel, the *Titanic* turned south and set course for her short run across the English Channel to Cherbourg.

While the passengers set about finding their way about the ship and had their tea, *Titanic* proceeded toward the French coast. It was at this time that it was discovered that the binoculars which were normally provided for the lookouts were missing. It seems that there were some, but they had gone missing during the officer reshuffle at Southampton. As the sun sank toward the western horizon the coast of France came into sight. Although the port of Cherbourg had no dock or jetty large enough to accommodate liners, its geographical position on the northern French coast made it an ideal stopping off

Outside the Solent

The pilot boat coming to take the pilot

Card given me by

Mr. T. W. McCawley,
Physical Educator.

THE GYMNASIUM,
R.M.S. TITANIC,
WHITE STAR LINE.

From without.

From within.

FAR LEFT: *The curving wake left by the* Titanic *indicates that a meandering course was being set in order to test the ship's compass. In the foreground is the head of the cargo crane.*

LEFT: Titanic's *first sunrise. Father Browne took this photograph near Land's End, Cornwall while the ship was sailing from Cherbourg to Queenstown. The time was about 6:45 a.m. on 11 April.*

BELOW LEFT: *Another page from Father Browne's album.*

point for vessels about to cross the Atlantic. The White Star Line had commissioned two specially built tenders, the *Nomadic* and *Traffic*, for the specific purpose of ferrying passengers, baggage, cargo and mail out to its own ships making weekly calls. The former conveyed first and second class passengers, while the latter carried the third class passengers and other items. In other respects the process of embarkation echoed that at Southampton, with all the passengers arriving in a special boat train, the 'Train Transatlantique', which was scheduled to leave Paris at 9:40 a.m. and arrived at Cherbourg's Gare Maritime at around 3:45 p.m. Normally they would transfer directly to the waiting tenders and be taken immediately to their ship, which should have just anchored after the short crossing from Southampton. On 10 April, these arrangements had been thrown out of gear by the *Titanic*'s delay at Southampton and consequently the 274 passengers had had to wait aboard the tenders or in the railway station until the liner arrived just after 6:00 p.m.

It was a mixed group of travellers who waited patiently for the great ship to appear. There were 142 first class passengers including Mrs. Charlotte Drake Cardeza and her son. Together with a valet, maid and no fewer than 14 trunks and three crates they booked into the grand suite on B deck, accommodation which had cost them a total of £890 ($4,350). Another well known party was Sir Cosmo and Lady Duff-Gordon, together with the latter's secretary. In an attempt to remain relatively incognito, the Duff-Gordons had booked themselves using the surname Morgan, also the

surname of the owner of I.M.M. and the White Star Line, J. Pierpont Morgan. Whether there was any significance in this choice of alias remains one of the *Titanic*'s many coincidences and unsolved mysteries. Also joining at Cherbourg was Benjamin Guggenheim, a member of a dynasty which had made its money from mining, metal dealing and industrial machinery. He became the second wealthiest aboard with interests worth some $100 million. Among the 30 second class passengers was a well-known contemporary marine artist, Samuel Ward Stanton, and the rather grandly titled Baron Alfred von Drachstedt. The latter made a great fuss about what he considered to be the poor standard of the second class accommodation and succeeded in being upgraded to first class after paying part of the fare difference. Although he subsequently survived the sinking, it transpired at the later inquiry that he was no 'Baron' at all, just plain Mr. Alfred Nournay. The new third class passengers were a very mixed bunch who came from a wide variety of Balkan and Middle East countries and had already had an arduous journey across the Mediterranean to Marseilles and then by rail through France to join the boat train from Paris. For them the delay at Cherbourg must have seemed interminable and they were, no doubt, heartily relieved to be settled aboard.

The *Titanic* dropped anchor in the roadstead at Cherbourg just after 6:30 p.m., as the sun was setting. She remained for only an hour and a half, embarking passengers from the tenders but also dropping off 13 first class and seven second class passengers whose journey, fortunately for them,

ABOVE: *Queenstown from offshore. When approaching the Irish coast,* Titanic *would have flown a red and white signal flag indicating that the captain required a pilot.* Titanic *was guided to the port of Queenstown by John Whelan who joined the ship earlier off Roche's Point.*

LEFT: *Porters awaiting employment in the harbour at Queenstown.*

TOP: *A picture taken from on board the tender* America. Titanic *steams gracefully into Queenstown, flags flying from her stern and masts.*

ABOVE: *The two tenders,* Ireland *and* America.

RIGHT: *Sightseeing third class passengers crowd* Titanic's *stern as the tender,* America, *approaches. This photograph also shows the small figure of a dirty stoker at the top of the aft funnel — he had climbed the inside of the dummy funnel for a good view of the Irish port. A few superstitious passengers took his black appearance to be a bad omen; from below he looked like a spectre of death.*

terminated at Cherbourg (presumably the mystery stranger was the first to disembark). As the daylight faded, the massive ship rode quietly at anchor with all of her lights blazing, creating an image which was captured on film and was remembered by local people for many years afterwards. Just before 8:00 p.m., a triple blast from the horns alerted the town to the fact that the ship was about to sail and minutes later the anchor was aweigh. *Titanic* turned under her own power and edged slowly out of the harbour before gathering speed and setting off westward into the night. While the passengers dined and then slept through their first night aboard, the ship rounded Land's End and turned north-west to cross the St. George's Channel before arriving off Queenstown (currently known as Cobh) on the south coast of Ireland at 11:30 a.m. the next day. Here the *Titanic* anchored some two miles offshore and a further group of passengers was ferried out from the jetty at the Queenstown railway station by the tenders *America* and *Ireland*. Of the 120 people who came aboard, all but seven were destined for third class, the others being second class passengers. 1,385 sacks of mail were loaded, while only seven passengers officially disembarked, one of them subsequently

proving to be of the utmost interest to researchers and historians looking into the story of the *Titanic*. This was Frances Browne, a teacher and a student priest, whose subsequent value lay in the camera and exposed photographic plates which he took with him. A keen amateur photographer, Browne had taken an extensive series of photographs of the ship, mostly in the second class areas where he had travelled, and also took several photographs as he disembarked including the last known photograph of the captain, posed looking down from the lofty heights of his bridge. A photographer of the local paper, the *Cork Examiner*, also took many photographs at this time and the two collections today form a major and valuable archive relating to the *Titanic* story. Unbeknown to anybody else aboard the liner, the tenders speeding back to the shore as the anchor was raised included one deserting crewman, a 24-year old stoker named John Coffey. As he gave his home address as Queenstown when he signed on, it is generally thought that he had planned from the start to jump ship at Queenstown as a way of getting a free ride home. If this was the case, then his plan had an even happier outcome than he could have imagined at the time. However, nobody aboard the *Titanic* gave any thought to the missing stoker as the anchor was brought inboard for the last time and the great propellers began to turn yet again after a rest of only two hours.

With smoke rising from her funnels as the firemen and trimmers sweated below to stoke up the boilers, the ship's head turned to the west and she gradually worked up to her cruising speed. As the land faded astern, a lone piper struck up on the third class promenade deck aft and played the sentimental air 'Erin's Lament'. The piper was Eugene Daly, who had entertained his fellow passengers as they had come out in the tender and now played a farewell to the homeland that he never expected to see again, although, of course, he had no inkling of what lay ahead and in fact actually survived the sinking.

While the ship lay off Queenstown, the White Star Line chairman, Bruce Ismay, is reported to have had a long discussion with Chief Engineer Joseph Bell. While there were no witnesses to this conversation, Ismay himself subsequently admitted of an intention to run the ship at full speed on the Monday or Tuesday (15 or 16 April) given suitable weather conditions. In fact the weather was remarkably pleasant for the time of the year with only light winds, clear skies and very little swell. Certainly the latter was not enough to worry a ship the size of the *Titanic* and several passengers' accounts of this stage of the voyage attest to the steadiness of the ship.

As she cruised 45 miles off the southern Irish coast, the lookouts once again repeated their request for binoculars. About tea time the circular tower

*BELOW: Confusion aboard the crowded tender allowed the stoker, John Coffey, to desert, hidden beneath a pile of mail bags. It seems that he had joined the crew at Southampton in order to procure a free trip to his home in Queenstown.*

*RIGHT: Passengers disembarking the tender, their journey on board the* Titanic *over.*

274

*ABOVE AND ABOVE RIGHT: The two captains of the White Star tenders at Queenstown.*

*RIGHT: Passengers disembarking the tender at the White Star Wharf.*

of the Fastnet light was sighted but by dinner time the coast had disappeared into the darkness. All classes now settled into the routine of the voyage and took advantage of the various facilities on offer; although there was little in the way of formally organized activities such as one might find on a cruise ship today. Most people were quite happy to relax in the saloons and lounges, passing the time between the meals which formed the highpoints of the day. Breakfast was available between 8:30 and 10:30 a.m., lunch was served from 1:00 to 2:30 p.m. and dinner between 6:00 and 7:30 p.m. Mealtimes were signalled by the ship's bugler, P. Fletcher, whose vibrant musical cadences called the passengers to their various dining saloons: 532 seated at once in first class, 394 in second and 473 in third. Even with these figures, two sittings would normally have been necessary to allow a full passenger load to dine. However, the fact that the *Titanic* was little more than half full on this voyage meant that all could be accommodated in one sitting, especially as those first class passengers who did not wish to be tied to set mealtimes could eat in the à la Carte restaurant at any time between 8:00 a.m. and 11 p.m. In fact these passengers could, if they so wished, elect to take all their meals in this establishment and were granted a rebate of $15 or $25 if they exercised this option, in recognition of the fact that they would pay separately for such meals. First class passengers could also use the swimming pool, Turkish and electric baths, the squash court and the gymnasium in order to work up an appetite or to work off the effects of a meal; tickets for these various establishments were available from the

purser's inquiry office on C deck. For the less energetic, particularly in second and third class where the facilities were less lavish, the traditional shipboard occupations of reading, playing cards, attending concerts and dances, and just resting or sleeping were the order of the day.

While the passengers relaxed, the crew busied themselves with the ship's routine. At their head was the grand figure of Captain Smith, who made his rounds of inspection every day at 10:30 a.m., following a daily meeting at 10:00 a.m. with the various heads of department. This was ordained by the White Star Line regulations and was meticulously carried out: the captain, dressed in full uniform with medals, made his way through all parts of the ship including the public areas of all three classes, the dining rooms and galleys, the bakery, the hospital, workshops and stores until, finally, he worked his way down to machinery spaces where he was met and escorted by the chief engineer. With his inspection of the ship complete, Captain Smith would return to the bridge where he would call the attention of his officers to any points arising from his tour of the ship and would update himself on the ship's progress, poring over the charts and checking the ship's position. He might also have received and read the various radio messages directed to the ship or himself, or checked over general messages broadcast by other vessels within range. In this respect the work of the radio operators, Bride and Philips, was absolutely vital, as wireless communications became essential to the everyday running of the ship rather than an interesting novelty. Many of the messages would be social in nature: various ships which the *Titanic*

*ABOVE: Illegal traders took many risks to market their wares on board the wealthy liners.*

*ABOVE LEFT: Disembarking passengers aboard the tender bid a sad farewell to the* Titanic.

*BELOW LEFT: In the first decades of this century immigration to the United States was in full swing and many of those boarding* Titanic *at Queenstown would have been anticipating the start of a new life in the land of opportunity. This photograph shows the eye examination of emigrants coming on board. These people would be checked again at New York and, if found to be carrying a disease, would be turned away. White Star would subsequently have to carry the cost of their return journey so took precautions to ensure that this did not happen.*

OPPOSITE PAGE ABOVE AND BELOW: *Crewmen loading the enormous amount of transatlantic mail that came aboard at Queenstown. A total of 1,385 sacks were brought over on the tenders.*

ABOVE: *Another in this series of Father Browne photographs shows passengers on board one of the tenders: 113 third class passengers and seven second class joined Titanic at this port. Among those that left was Frank Browne, taking with him pictures that would soon become internationally famous.*

LEFT: *Passengers queue to board.*

passed making traditional greetings and offering sentiments of congratulations and good wishes to the stately liner on her maiden voyage.

The ship was indeed performing well at this point. With the steam from the boilers turning the propellers at 70, later increased to 75, revolutions per minute, the ship sliced through the light seas building up to a steady 21.5 knots throughout the Thursday evening and Friday morning, to record a distance run in the 24 hours to noon of 386 miles. In the next 24 hours she logged 519 miles, the greater distance reflecting that the previous day's figure had commenced from a standing start at Queenstown. Speed was increased slightly on Saturday and Sunday as the last of the ship's 24 main boilers was fired up and 546 miles were covered up to noon on 14 April, for an average of 22.5 knots.

During the fateful Sunday, preparations were under way to light up the five auxiliary boilers with the possible intention of a maximum speed run on the Monday. The modest increase in speed and the associated activity led many passengers to speculate that the *Titanic* was going to make an attempt on the Blue Riband record for an Atlantic crossing, which was then held by the *Mauretania*. Such speculation was totally misinformed as there was no way that the *Titanic* could match the smaller, but much more powerful, Cunard rival, which had notched up over 27 knots on its record breaking run in 1907. However, it was entirely possible that Ismay and Smith had decided to take the opportunity offered by the good weather to see if the *Titanic* could beat her sister ship's best speed of 22.75 knots whilst in service trim. If any such attempt was to be made, it would have to be of relatively brief duration as there was not enough coal on board to sustain maximum speed for the remainder of the crossing.

As well as recording the speed, Captain Smith and his navigating officers would have regularly checked on the ship's position in order to ensure that she was keeping to her planned course. This followed a standard summer westbound route known as the Outward Southern Track, which had been agreed by all the major shipping companies in 1899. From the Fastnet Rock off the south coast of Ireland she followed a great circle route to position 42°N, 47°W, and thereafter by great circle or thumb line to the Nantucket

Light Vessel. For the purposes of this agreement, summertime was defined as 15 January to 15 August. This route was generally far enough south to be clear of any danger of ice, and there had only been three occasions since 1898 when any significant ice had affected shipping following the prescribed track. However, the winter of 1912 had been exceptionally mild in northern latitudes, causing large ice floes and even whole sheets of pack ice to break away from the Arctic icecap and drift southward towards the shipping lanes.

By one of those geophysical quirks which often cause freak conditions, the normally warm Gulf Stream which flows eastward across the Atlantic to northern Europe was sited further south than was normal, a factor which allowed the ice to drift yet further south than would normally be the case and right across the track followed by the *Titanic* and many other ships. Indeed, on the very day that the *Titanic* left Southampton, the French liner *Niagara* reported that she was stopped and damaged following a collision with ice at 44°07'N, 50°40'W. This was over 100 miles north of the *Titanic*'s planned course but, nevertheless, gave an early warning of possible hazards. As the great ship set off from Queenstown, other reports were being transmitted by at least 20 ships at various times over the period 11-14 April. By no means all of these reached the *Titanic* but there is irrefutable evidence that enough were picked up to ensure that Captain Smith was well aware of the potential danger.

The first of these reports to be received on the fateful Sunday came from the Cunard-owned *Caronia* (Captain Barr), eastbound from New York, which transmitted a warning by wireless at 9:00 a.m. specifically addressed to the *Titanic*. This read, 'Captain, Titanic. Westbound steamers report bergs, growlers and field ice in 42 degrees North from 49 degrees to 51 degrees West, April 12. Compliments, Barr.' This lay right on the *Titanic*'s track and could not have been clearer. A copy was delivered personally to Captain Smith who had it posted on the bridge after noting its contents. A further report, originating from the Greek ship *Athinai*, reported icebergs

*ABOVE: The position where* Titanic *dropped her anchor off Roche's Point, Cork Harbour.*

*ABOVE LEFT: Deepwater Quay and the White Star tenders* Ireland *and* America.

*BELOW LEFT: The 'plucky little Countess'. Standing in front of lifeboat number 8, which she would later row from the sinking* Titanic, *the Countess of Rothes watches the tender as it passe the ship to starboard.*

and large quantities of field ice at 41°51'N, 49°52'W. This message was relayed by the White Star Line ship *Baltic* and was received in the *Titanic's* wireless office at 1:42 p.m. By this time, the passengers who had been enjoying the spring sunshine on the *Titanic's* promenade decks were beginning to retire to their various lounges and cabins as the air temperature was becoming noticeably colder. The *Baltic's* message was taken to the bridge and then passed on to Captain Smith who was lunching with J. Bruce Ismay. After reading it, he passed it on to Ismay, remarking that the ship might soon encounter ice itself. Ismay apparently retained the message for several hours, showing it to several other passengers, before it was finally retrieved and posted on the bridge at around 7:15 p.m. in the evening. Much has been made of the fact that Ismay kept the message, and it has been suggested that he did so deliberately for reasons best known to himself, perhaps fearing that it would prevent the high speed run planned for the following day. Whether such motives were present is really immaterial, as there were many other warnings which were quite sufficient to ensure that both captain and crew were aware of the potential dangers looming ahead that night.

In fact another was received within minutes, this time from the German liner *Amerika*, which reported two large icebergs at 41°27'N, 50°8'W. However, this was not addressed to the *Titanic* but to the U.S. Navy Office in Washington D.C. and the radio operators merely filed it for onward transmission when the ship came in range of the radio station at Cape Race, Newfoundland, later that evening. There is no evidence that it was ever passed on to Captain Smith or any other officer. Another message was picked up at 7:30 p.m. from the Leyland Line ship *Californian* reporting three large icebergs south of her position at 42°3'N, 49°9'W. Again this message was not addressed to the *Titanic* but on this occasion the radio operator on duty, Bride, subsequently stated that he passed it on to an unnamed officer. Yet another message came in, addressed to the *Titanic* and other ships, at 9:40 p.m. from a ship named the *Mesaba*, reporting pack ice, icebergs and field ice in an area bounded by 42°N to 41°25'N and 49° to 50°30'W, totally

*ABOVE: The* Titanic *steams slowly away from Ireland, toward the open sea and her doom. As she leaves the harbour, piper Eugene Daly salutes his receding homeland with the dirge 'Erin's Lament'. She leaves behing Frank Browne and his invaluable photographic record.*

*LEFT: The view from the tender,* America *as she closes with the* Titanic. *This photograph shows Captain Smith leaning over the starboard bridge wing, as well as third and first class passengers. The lifeboat is emergency cutter number 2.*

Card given me by

Mr. T. W. McCawley,

Physical Educator.

THE GYMNASIUM,
R.M.S. TITANIC,
WHITE STAR LINE.

*ABOVE RIGHT: Among Father Browne's souvenirs was this card, from the gymnasium instructor of the* Titanic.

*RIGHT: The gentle giant, American novelist, Jacques Futrelle outside the gymnasium on the Boat deck. He was later to urge his wife into a lifeboat before going bravely to his death.*

*BELOW: Gymnasium instructor T. W. McCawley poses for Frank Browne in a rowing machine. He attempted to keep passengers calm by inviting them to use the gym equipment.*

*NEXT PAGE: Looking up to the aft end of the Boat deck — a second class promenade area — from the first class only Promenade deck.*

straddling the spot where the *Titanic* eventually went down. Unfortunately, there is no definite evidence that this message ever reached the bridge, although, as it was directly addressed, it certainly should have.

One message which was acknowledged and must have been brought to the attention of the bridge was from a British cargo ship, the S.S. *Rappahannock*, which reported that she had just passed through a heavy icefield and had observed several icebergs. Although the message did not say so, this ship had actually suffered some damage to her steering from the ice. The interesting point about this exchange, which occurred at 10:30 p.m., was that it was not transmitted by radio but by visual signal lamp, indicating clearly that the *Titanic* was now very close to the icefield. Less than half an hour later the *Californian* began to transmit a message directly to the *Titanic*

stating that she was stopped and completely surrounded by ice, but this message interfered with transmissions to Cape Race from the larger ship, whose operator curtly ordered the *Californian* to stop transmitting.

Earlier in the day, Captain Smith had ordered that a planned change of course at 47°W should be delayed for 30 minutes with the result that the ship subsequently ran some ten miles south of what would have been her original course. His reasons for this order will never be known, although if it was intended to keep the ship clear of the icefields reported ahead, it was not the major alteration which would have been expected in the circumstances.

At 7:15 p.m., Murdoch said to a lamp trimmer, 'Hemming, when you go forward get the fire scuttle hatch closed. There is a glow left from that, and as we are in vicinity of ice I want everything dark before the bridge.' As the evening was drawing on, the temperature was dropping steadily, from 6°C at 7:00 p.m. to 4°C only half an hour later, and only 0.5°C (barely above freezing) at 9:00 p.m. With the dropping temperature and conscious of the possibility of ice ahead, First Officer Murdoch ordered an iceberg watch to be set with two lookouts in the crow's nest on the foremast. Various officers had made their own estimates of when the reported icefield might be encountered, these varying between 9:30 p.m. and 11:00 p.m., though by this stage nobody seriously doubted that there was a definite hazard ahead.

During the early part of the evening Captain Smith had been dining with a party in the à la Carte restaurant but left at 8:50 p.m. and went up to the bridge where he spoke to Second Officer Lightoller, by then officer of the watch. Already Lightoller had noted the dropping temperature and had advised the ship's carpenter, J. Maxwell, and the chief engineer that they should respectively check the fresh water and boiler water tanks in the ship's bottom as there was a danger of their contents freezing. When the captain came to the bridge, he was updated with the situation and the measures so far ordered — during the next 20 minutes the conversation touched on the extremely unusual calm weather being experienced and the difficulties of spotting icebergs in such conditions, particularly as there was no moon that night (although the sky was clear and stars could be seen). Despite the topic, no specific mention was made of the warnings already received and at around 9:20 p.m. Captain Smith retired to his sea cabin, immediately abaft the bridge on the starboard side, leaving instructions that he was to be called, saying, 'If it becomes at all doubtful, let me know. I will be just inside'. Although not specifically stated, Lightoller understood this to mean that the captain was to be called if ice was sighted, again confirming that everybody was alert for such a possibility.

After the captain had gone, Lightoller passed an order to the lookouts in the crow's nest to keep 'a sharp lookout for ice, particularly small ice and growlers' and asked that this reminder be passed on to their reliefs, Frederick Fleet and Reginald Lee, when they took over at 10:00 p.m. Lightoller himself was relieved by First Officer Murdoch at 9:30 p.m. The entries in the ship's log at this point show that the ship was making a steady 22.5 knots and that the air temperature was right on freezing (0°C). Whatever precautions had been considered necessary in view of the

*ABOVE AND RIGHT: Two photographs of Father Browne's bedroom, cabin number A37. The photograph above is out of focus and was destined to be thrown away before the liner sank.*

*NEXT PAGE: One of Browne's favourite photographs, he called it 'The Children's Playground'. It was taken on the Saloon deck at about midday on 11 April.*

approaching icefield, a reduction in speed was obviously not given serious consideration. As the ship sped on through the still night, the sea temperature dropped even further to half a degree below freezing (salt water, of course, freezes at a lower temperature than fresh water). Although not realised at the time, subsequent metallurgical tests on samples taken from the wreck suggest that it may have been exactly at this temperature that the *Titanic*'s steel plates were at their most brittle and therefore most vulnerable to impact damage.

High up ahead of the bridge, the two lookouts were probably concentrating as much on keeping warm as they were on trying to peer into the darkness ahead. Although there was no wind, the ship's speed would have been enough to send a bitingly cold draught though the rigging and the lookout's eyes would have been streaming in the chill air. As was mentioned earlier, they had no binoculars, and how much this affected their ability to do their job proficiently that night can only be speculated upon, though it is doubtless that it did not help matters. At 9:45 p.m., Lightoller told the Sixth Officer to warn the men in the crow's nest to keep an especially sharp lookout for ice until daybreak, particularly small ice and growlers (icebergs less than 15 ft tall and 50 ft long). After acknowledging the order Jewell turned to his mate Symons and murmured: 'It is very cold here'. Symons replied, 'Yes; by the smell of it there's ice about.' Shortly after 11:30 p.m., less than half an hour before they were due to be relieved, the lookouts noticed an area of low lying mist ahead and the air became damp, adding to their discomfort. Silence descended as the two men peered intently ahead. Suddenly, without a word, Fleet tensed, leaned forward for a brief second and then reached across to give three sharp tugs on the lanyard which rang the 16-inch high brass bell suspended above the crow's nest. As the sharp tones rang out, Fleet frantically grabbed the telephone linked directly to the bridge and twirled the ringer handle. Alerted by the warning bell, Sixth Officer James Moody picked up his receiver and heard the fatal message.

'Iceberg Right Ahead!'

As the *Titanic* sped through the darkness towards its doom, the majority of the passengers and crew had not the slightest inkling that they were in any danger at all. The lowering temperatures had long since driven the passengers off the promenade decks into the warmth of the saloons and cabins. Many had joined together to form their own groups and parties at dinner, one of which included the captain, and afterwards had dispersed to the smoke rooms, lounges and their own cabins. In the second class dining saloon, the Reverend E. C. Carter had organized a hymn service, attended by over a hundred passengers, which started at 8:00 p.m. and lasted until after 10:00 p.m. By 11:30 p.m., just before the impact, most of the passengers had followed the captain's example and had retired to bed, leaving only a few stalwarts finishing their nightcaps and smoking a last cigar in the almost deserted smoking rooms and lounges.

On the bridge, the calm routine of the night was shattered by the warning bell from the crow's nest and Fleet's dramatic telephone call, although Sixth Officer Moody did not forget his manners as he thanked the lookout

for his report before calling across to First Officer Murdoch, 'Iceberg right ahead!'

Murdoch's reactions were creditably instantaneous. Leaping forward he grabbed the handles of the engine telegraph and rang down, 'Stop', followed by, 'Full Astern'. At the same time he ordered the helmsman, Quartermaster Robert Hitchens, to turn the wheel 'Hard-a-starboard'. The order was obeyed promptly, Hitchens spinning the wheel as far as it would go, causing the ship to begin swinging to port (the apparent discrepancy between the helm order and the direction of the turn results from the system of orders in common use at that time which dated back to the days when ships were steered by a tiller, and pushing it to starboard resulted in a turn to port and vice versa (this system survived until the more logical current system was made standard in 1928). As the ship began to turn, Murdoch pressed the bell switch which warned all in the lower compartments that the watertight doors were about to close automatically, holding it down for 10 seconds before operating the lever to actuate the closure.

Despite the prompt reaction of all involved, the ship had only veered some 20 degrees to port when the collision occurred. The interval between the first sighting and the impact was later estimated to have been a little over 30 seconds, only enough time for the ship to cover some 500 yd and far too short to allow any successful avoiding action to be taken. Although a head-on collision had been averted, the starboard side of the *Titanic*'s hull crashed into the great mass of solid ice which then scraped relentlessly along the brittle underwater plating, leaving a trail of damage estimated at 300 ft long. In places it had gashed open the hull to a width of a few inches; in some points the hole was probably as little as half an inch wide. It was enough.

On the bridge, Fourth Officer Boxhall arrived just as the collision occurred, having been due to take over watch a few minutes later. Almost immediately he was joined by the captain who had heard the warnings and felt the impact.

'What have we struck?' he asked the first officer anxiously. Murdoch quickly made his report, confirming that they had hit an iceberg and detailing the actions he had already taken. Both officers strode out onto the bridge wing to look aft for the iceberg and on re-entering the bridge the captain told Boxhall to inspect the forward area of the hull below decks and to report back as soon as possible. He moved the engine telegraphs to 'Half Ahead', but then rang down 'Stop', shortly afterwards. The *Titanic* slowed and then stopped dead in the water.

While the deck officers were uncertain as to the extent of the damage, if any, some of the stokers, firemen, trimmers and engineers unfortunate enough to have been on duty in the machinery spaces at the time had no doubts as to the seriousness of the situation. In the forward boiler room (No. 6), only two stokers and an engineer got out before the water began to rise and the watertight doors were closed. However, in the engine rooms further aft, the collision was only felt as a bump or a jar although the noise of the iceberg scrapping along the side was heard. In the ensuing 15 minutes, Fourth Officer Boxhall made a quick tour of inspection in the forward hull and discovered that the Orlop deck was flooded forward of No. 4 watertight bulkhead and, although he saw no water on F deck, he was informed by the postal clerks that water was rising in the post office on the deck below.

Returning quickly to the bridge he informed the captain of his findings and was then ordered to establish the ship's position so that it could be included in any subsequent wireless messages. Boxhall poured over the charts and calculated a dead reckoning position based on his own stellar observation at 7:30 p.m., updated with the ship's subsequent course and an estimate of its speed. Working under pressure, he quickly reported that the *Titanic* lay stopped at 41°46´N, 50°14´W, a position which became enshrined in maritime lore but was subsequently proved to be incorrect by a few vital miles, causing misunderstanding and controversy for decades afterwards.

While Boxhall worked at the chart table, Captain Smith went below to see things for himself and was accompanied by Thomas Andrews, who probably knew as much as anybody about the ship and her construction. The latter did not take long to reach the unpalatable conclusion that the ship was mortally damaged and estimated that it would sink in an hour and a half, or two hours at the outside, a remarkably accurate assessment in the circumstances. One can only guess at how both men must have felt as the realization dawned upon them.

The main problem was the fact that the No. 6 boiler room was holed and that all the bow watertight compartments were also holed or filling. In this situation, it was only a matter of time before the bow sank low enough for

*RIGHT: A typical first class luncheon menu aboard the* Titanic. *This was scheduled to be the fare on 14 April.*

*BELOW: One of the very few photographs taken of the first class dining room.*

**R.M.S. "TITANIC**

APRIL 14, 1912.

# LUNCHEON.

CONSOMMÉ FERMIER          COCKIE LEEKIE

FILLETS OF BRILL

EGG À L'ARGENTEUIL

CHICKEN À LA MARYLAND

CORNED BEEF, VEGETABLES, DUMPLINGS

## FROM THE GRILL.

GRILLED MUTTON CHOPS

MASHED, FRIED & BAKED JACKET POTATOES

CUSTARD PUDDING

APPLE MERINGUE          PASTRY

## BUFFET.

SALMON MAYONNAISE          POTTED SHRIMPS

NORWEGIAN ANCHOVIES          SOUSED HERRINGS

PLAIN & SMOKED SARDINES

ROAST BEEF

ROUND OF SPICED BEEF

VEAL & HAM PIE

VIRGINIA & CUMBERLAND HAM

BOLOGNA SAUSAGE          BRAWN

GALANTINE OF CHICKEN

CORNED OX TONGUE

LETTUCE          BEETROOT          TOMATOES

## CHEESE.

CHESHIRE, STILTON, GORGONZOLA, EDAM,
CAMEMBERT, ROQUEFORT, ST. IVEL.
CHEDDAR

*Iced draught Munich Lager Beer 3d. & 6d. a Tankard.*

water to lap over the top of the next watertight bulkhead, which only extend-ed to E deck, and into No. 5 boiler room. When this happened, the ship would settle even lower in the water and the other compartments would then flood in turn at successively shorter intervals. On his return to the bridge, a grim-faced captain ordered the crew to be mustered, the lifeboats uncovered, and the radio operators to begin transmitting a distress message using an approximate position, and this was first received at Cape Race and by at least two ships (*Mount Temple* and *Provence*) at 12:15 a.m.

Once armed with Boxhall's new estimated position, accurate or not, the captain personally went to the radio room and ensured that it was included in all subsequent transmissions, beginning at 12:25 a.m. The message, sent in Morse code, took the form of the *Titanic*'s calling code, 'M.G.Y.', then the letters 'C.Q.', which meant that it was addressed to 'all ships', followed by the letter 'D', indicating distress or danger. The resulting three letter group was often held to mean 'Come Quick, Danger', but in fact the letters had no significance other than as outlined above. In 1908 the famous S.O.S. signal had been introduced, this being easier to send in Morse code as it consisted of three dots, three dashes and three dots, but it was still not in common use by 1912. Later in the evening, Bride and Phillips started using the S.O.S. code instead of 'C.Q.D.', one of the first times that it had been used in an emergency.

As the officers and crew were roused and assembled, they were ordered to inform the passengers and direct them to assemble on the Boat deck. This

*LEFT: Olympic's reading and writing room on A deck. The huge 10 ft windows overlooked the promenade.*

*BELOW: Passengers on A deck aft, braving the inclement weather.*

• TITANIC & HER SISTERS OLYMPIC & BRITANNIC •

*ABOVE: A Father Browne photograph taken at Queenstown where port officials demanded a lifeboat drill and also inspected life-jackets and other safety equipment.*

turned out to be an extremely difficult task as there was no tannoy or public address system and the stewards and crew had to go round all the cabins, waking those many occupants who had not been disturbed by the collision and urge them to put on their lifejackets and find their way up to the boats on the boat deck. This task was not made any easier by the cacophony of noise on the upper decks caused by steam escaping through safety valves as the main engines were closed down, this noise also caused problems for the radio operators in their cabin at the base of the fore funnel where they could barely hear the high pitched Morse signals being transmitted. At first, most passengers were not unduly concerned, refusing to believe that such a fine ship could be in any imminent danger. Indeed, many first class passengers formed an orderly queue at the purser's office on C deck where they withdrew jewelry and other valuable items deposited for safe keeping during the voyage. Others took no immediate action to dress themselves in warm clothing or to find their lifejackets, assuming that all would be well in the end. Those passengers who did heed the warning slowly made their way up to the Boat deck and, for the most part, formed patient groups waiting to embark. In the meantime, the ship's musicians, led by Lancashireman Wallace Hartley, assembled in the first class lounge on A deck and began playing a

succession of popular ragtime tunes. Although intended to help calm the passengers, their actions perhaps succeeded too well as the melodies sounding out into the chill night air lent an air of unreality to the proceedings.

Chief Officer Wilde ordered the second officer to see to the preparation of the lifeboats. Lightoller made a round of the Boat deck, assigning crew members to work the lowering mechanism and ensuring that each boat was uncovered and made ready for loading, although he too had difficulty due to the noise, most orders being passed on by hand signals. He quickly checked boats 4, 6 and 8 immediately abaft the bridge on the port side and then moved aft along the Boat deck to where boats 10, 12, 14 and 16 were stowed, before working his way forward along the starboard side past boats 15, 13, 11 and 9 and then to 7, 5 and 3 back by the bridge. Boats 1 and 2, the emergency cutters, were already swung out, and work began to prepare the collapsible Englehardt boats for use if required.

By 12:25 a.m. Captain Smith had accepted that his ship was lost and that a lifeboat evacuation was the only remaining course. Realizing that there were nowhere near enough lifeboat places for all on board, he ordered that only women and children should be loaded at first. Lightoller then ordered the lifeboats to be swung out and personally supervised the loading

*RIGHT: a solitary figure walks aft on Titanic's Promenade deck. This is popularly believed to be Captain Smith. However, it is more likely that the captain would have been on the bridge with the pilot as the ship had not yet reached open water.*

of boats on the port side, while First Officer Murdoch looked after the starboard side. The plan was to load and lower the forward boat on each side, numbers 4 and 5, and then work progressively aft, lowering each boat in turn as they filled. However, progress was slow, partly due to the crew's unfamiliarity with the equipment and the drills to be used — they had been given virtually no training or exercise in such skills up to the time of the sinking. In addition, the officers appeared not to have been briefed on the capacities of the boats and allowed many to be lowered away only half full under the mistaken impression that they could not be safely lowered when filled to capacity. Another problem was caused by the screens fitted to the forward section of the promenades on A deck which prevented passengers boarding boats lowered from the Boat deck just above, as was intended. There was some delay before the tool to undo the screen windows was found, by which time some of the boats had already been lowered.

Because of these and other problems, it was not until 12:45 a.m. that the first lifeboat was finally lowered into the freezing water. This was number 7 from the port side which was considerably less than half full, carrying a around 30 people against its certified capacity of 65. The occupants included three crewmen, and around 13 female and 19 male passengers, a reflection on the lack of urgency pertaining at that time, as the male passengers would only have been allowed to board if no women and children had been waiting. Next in the water was lifeboat number 5 under the command of Third Officer Pitman. Although between 36 and 41 survivors were on board this craft, it was still nowhere near full. The launch of this boat had been accompanied by some drama as J. Bruce Ismay appeared and attempted to take charge, blustering out improbable orders to passengers and crew alike. He was quickly put in his place by Fifth Officer Lowe and disappeared out of sight. Pitman took charge of the two boats as they rowed away from the ship and subsequently played an unedifying part in the drama, later refusing to return and pick up more survivors from the water as the ship sank. On a more amusing note (with hindsight), one of the women passengers suffered two broken ribs when Dr. H. Frauenthal and his brother, observing that the boat which already contained his wife also had many empty berths, leapt into it as it was being lowered and landed heavily on the unfortunate Mrs. Annie Stengel. Despite this unfortunate incident, all happily survived to tell the tale.

On the port side, Lightoller finally managed to get lifeboat number 6 away at around 12:55 a.m. with about 27 people on board (it is difficult accurately to determine the actual numbers in each boat as witnesses' accounts varied tremendously and no official count was made at the time the lifeboats were first picked up). Most of these were women apart from two crew members and two male passengers, one of whom was a Major Arthur Peuchen, an amateur yachtsman who had volunteered to assist in the handling of the boat. In the event, the crew members proved to be of little use and it was left to the women to do most of the rowing. Significantly, as the boat was about to be lowered, Captain Smith ordered Quartermaster Hitchens, who was in charge of the boat, to make way for another ship

whose lights could be seen some five miles away off the *Titanic*'s starboard bow. This was the first of many sightings of one (or possibly more) unidentified vessels in the vicinity and whose existence, or otherwise, became the subject of much speculation and investigation in the aftermath of the sinking.

For various reasons, partly because Murdoch was slightly less strict about the interpretation of the women and children first order and partly because of difficulties caused by the fact that the ship was listing slightly to starboard, the boats on this side were generally got away more quickly. Next away was lifeboat number 3 which contained around 40 people, including many male passengers and approximately 15 crew as, apparently, there were no more women or children in the vicinity when it was ready to be lowered. An attempt was made to load more passengers from A deck as it was lowered, but this was frustrated by the locked windows of the promenade screens. With the three full size forward starboard lifeboats away, Murdoch and Lowe moved forward and attempted to launch the number 1 cutter. This was achieved with some difficulty; it did not enter the water until around 1:10 a.m. and only carried a dozen people, despite having a capacity of 40. The occupants were mostly crew but also included Sir Cosmo and Lady Duff-Gordon and their secretary. Sir Cosmo subsequently achieved some notoriety as there is no doubt that he actually paid the crew members five pounds each, although the reason for doing so was hotly debated. Some alleged that he bribed the men to row away from the ship, ignoring the cries

*BELOW: A deck, immediately below the bridge. The picture shows Major Archibald Butt, aide to President Taft, in the distance. He was to show extreme coolness during the disaster by organising a card game and later helping women into the boats. Sadly, he was lost with the ship.*

ABOVE: *Steerage passengers, recently embarked at Queenstown, taking the air on deck.*

for help of others, so that the lifeboat would not be overloaded or dragged down when the ship sank, he stoutly maintained that the payment was in gratitude for the assistance of the crew and to cover the cost of their personal losses.

Whatever the truth, the story is typical of the many personal dramas which make the tale of the *Titanic* so endlessly fascinating. The seaman in charge of this boat, George Symons, was also one of many witnesses who reported seeing the lights of another ship and started to head towards it, although in this case he reported the lights as being on the *Titanic's* port bow.

Meanwhile, on the port side of the Boat deck, Chief Officer Wilde joined Lightoller and they succeeded in getting lifeboat number 8 away with around four crewmen and 24 women aboard. Captain Smith again instructed the crew to row for a ship whose lights he thought he could see in the distance, but before the boat was lowered another drama was played out when Mrs. Ida Straus refused to leave her husband who, despite urgings to the contrary by other passengers and crew in view of his old age, refused all offers to be allowed to break the women and children first rule. This brave, but needless, stance resulted in both being drowned when the ship finally sank. The undoubted hero, or more correctly, heroine, of this boat was Lady Lucy-Noel Martha, Countess of Rothes, who steadfastly took turns at rowing and steering as well as comforting some of the other women who had lost their husbands.

Back on the starboard side, Murdoch and Moody got boat number 9 away at around 1:20 a.m. with 46 people aboard, the highest total so far and including eight crewmen and many male passengers. Again, occupants thought that they saw the lights of a ship and attempted to row towards them, but with no success. Almost simultaneously, boat number 10 was lowered on the port side; this was less well loaded with four crew members, 28 women and children, together with nine male passengers, two of whom had slipped aboard while the officers in charge of embarkation were distracted.

As the urgency of the situation began to dawn on all concerned, the later boats tended to be filled to much nearer their nominal capacity and boat 11, lowered away from the starboard side at around 1:25 a.m., was one of the most crowded, one estimate putting the total on board at 70 people, mostly women. Almost at the same time, lifeboat 12 was launched on the port side but contained only 26 to 28 passengers and two crew, several male passengers having been denied access. With these two boats in the water, exactly half of the available lifeboats had been launched and work continued apace to get the rest filled up and lowered away. But it was not only on the boat-decks that significant incidents and drama occurred.

While most of the officers were busily engaged in supervising the preparation and lowering of the boats, Fourth Officer Boxhall remained on the bridge and was ordered by the captain to begin firing pyrotechnics known as socket signals, to attract the attention of a vessel whose lights were seen by all on the bridge. The socket signals were fired from a mortar attached to the

*Below: Titanic's first class bedroom B64.*

ABOVE: *Titanic's reading and writing room was very similar to that aboard her sister, Olympic (page 298).*

LEFT: *Alfred Samuel Allsop, saloon steward, was aged 34 when he died aboard the* Titanic.

bridge rail, and each rose up to 800 ft into the air before exploding into a dozen slow falling brilliant white lights. The first was fired at 12:45 a.m. and a total of eight was eventually fired at roughly five-minute intervals, the last at around 1:20 a.m. However, the mystery vessel, estimated to have been some five or six miles away, appeared not to respond to the signals and slowly turned to starboard. It was last observed heading away off the *Titanic's* port bow. Attempts to signal the vessel by means of the powerful Morse signal lamp also met with no response. The identity of this vessel, if it actually existed, is one of the many mysteries of this fateful night; what is certain is that the distress signals were seen by another more distant vessel, the *Californian,* which lay stopped in the icefield somewhere between eight and 19 miles north of the *Titanic.* The actions of this ship and her commander, Captain Stanley Lord, became the centre of much controversy and speculation in the aftermath of the sinking and Lord was accused of virtually ignoring the drama supposedly unfolding before his very eyes.

While these various scenes were being enacted on the bridge and Boat decks, activity below was varied and stories from surviving witnesses are necessarily fragmented. Often told is the cool example of a Colonel Gracie who, on recognizing Frederick Wright the professional squash player, calmly requested that his booking for Monday morning be cancelled! In the third class saloons, many of the Catholic Irish emigrants came together and recited their rosary as they awaited their fate. There were undoubted cases of both passengers and crew helping themselves to gin or brandy, or whatever they could lay their hands on, and drinking whole bottles to blot out what was happening but, on the whole, such instances were uncommon, and most passengers queued stoically for the boats or else waited patiently in the saloons, still perhaps hoping that the ship would not really sink. However, down below, events were moving quickly to seal the vessel's fate. In No. 5 boiler room a few firemen and engineers remained to man the pumps in an attempt to stop the compartment flooding, but at around 12:45 a.m., the bulkhead between 5 and 6 boiler rooms gave way and the whole compartment was flooded within seconds. Only one occupant, Leading Stoker Fred Barrett, managed to escape; all the others were drowned. It has been suggested that the collapsing bulkhead could have been damaged by the bunker fire which was burning when the ship left Belfast.

Up on deck, the work of filling and lowering the boats continued. Following the experiences of those already described was boat number 14 from the port side. This is believed to have contained 42-45 people, about 14 of them women, and was under the command of Fifth Officer Lowe who had been ordered to take charge by the chief officer. Once in the water, Lowe had the boat rowed away from the ship and gathered a number of other boats together. He then transferred most of the passengers out of his boat with the intention of rowing back and picking up more survivors, although by the time he was ready to carry out this plan, there were few left alive in the bitterly cold water to be rescued.

On the starboard side, boats 13 and 15 were launched one after the other both with around 65 people aboard. As the first of these entered the water

ABOVE: *Icebergs photographed in the vicinity of the* Titanic's *demise.*

and drifted slightly sternwards while still attached to the falls, the second boat was almost lowered on top of it, disaster only being averted when those seaman lowering the boat heard screams from below and stopped its descent. In fact boat 15 was one of the few to carry significant numbers of third class passengers, who otherwise had proportionately fewer survivors than amongst first or second class passengers. Subsequent inquiries looked at this point in some detail and it was accepted that there were no physical obstacles to prevent third class passengers accessing the Boat deck but that it would have been difficult for many of them to have found their way around the unfamiliar parts of the ship in the circumstances. With the first class accommodation just below the Boat deck, it was obviously much easier for these passengers to reach the lifeboats, although there were many examples of crew members going below and making efforts to guide other passengers up from the lower decks.

By now the ship was well down by the bows and had taken a slight list. Nevertheless boat 16, the last of the standard lifeboats on the starboard side, was launched without trouble, carrying some 40 passengers and crew. First Officer Murdoch then went forward and began to prepare boat C, one of the collapsible boats, for launching. This had a flat wooden bottom and canvas side which could be raised and rigged to give a freeboard of around three feet. The launch of this boat was not without excitement and Murdoch at one stage fired his pistol into the air in order to hold back a group of men who tried to rush aboard. When it finally got away, estimates of the numbers aboard varied from a wildly exaggerated 70 to a more generally accepted figure of 43, many of whom were women passengers from third class. The most controversial occupant was J. Bruce Ismay, the White Star Line chairman who subsequently stated that he stepped aboard only because there were no other passengers waiting in the vicinity, while other witnesses claimed that he pushed through a crowd of men in order to force himself aboard. Whatever the truth, the poor man was subsequently vilified by unsympathetic commentators who obviously thought that he should have followed the example of the captain and gone down with the ship, although what would have been achieved by such a sacrifice is open to question.

Boat 2, one of the emergency cutters, was launched at 1:45 a.m. and was under the command of hard working Fourth Officer Boxhall, who had the presence of mind to equip himself with some green signal rockets so that, subsequently, his was the first boat to be located and picked up. There were only 18 in the cutter and it was eventually followed by lifeboat number 4, the last of the standard boats, at 1:55 a.m. The launch of this had been one of the many dramas of the night — it was one of the first to be prepared and had been lowered, on Lightoller's instructions, to A deck level so that passengers could board. Unfortunately he had forgotten about the locked screens and had it hauled up again, before it was once more lowered back and efforts made to undo the screens. While all this was going on, a most orderly and genteel queue of first class women passengers, together with their children and maids, waited patiently on the promenade. By the time that the boat was ready for loading, the ship's list had carried it away from the side and a cable was used to pull it in close enough for the women to step across. Eventually some 30 were safely aboard, and these were later joined by four crewman (and one stowaway). Observing that the boat was still not full, the multimillionaire Colonel Astor asked Lightoller if he might join his wife in the lifeboat but permission was refused. Forever the gentleman, Astor did not argue and stood back as his young bride disappeared into the darkness below. He did not survive.

Finally, attention turned to collapsible boat D, which was lowered from davits on the port side and was virtually full with around 22 people on board. As it was launched, at 2:05 a.m, *Titanic*'s forecastle was almost completely submerged, water was lapping around B deck further aft and the ship's stern was noticeably beginning to lift out of the sea. The only boats remaining now were the two collapsibles, A and B, on the roof of the officers' accommodation at the base of the fore funnel. As officers and crew members struggled to release these, the ship began to sink rapidly beneath them and both floated off as a tide of water washed around and over the bridge. Neither of them was properly rigged and boat B ended up inverted. Nevertheless some 30 men managed to climb onto the upturned hull while around 20 swam to boat A which had enough buoyancy to float, even though the canvas screens had not been erected.

The *Titanic* was now in its final death throes, but still the various dramas were being acted out. Although the captain had relieved them of their duties some time earlier, the two radio operators stayed at their posts until the last possible moment, Phillips still trying to transmit up to 2:17 a.m., only minutes before the ship sank. Benjamin Guggenheim, one of the richest passengers, watched the women and children get away in the boats and then retired with his valet to his cabin, reappearing later in full evening dress saying that he was prepared to go down like a gentleman. On the after deck, Catholic priest Thomas Byles was hearing confessions, while in the first class saloon a foursome made up of Major Archie Butt and three friends played cards until well after two o'clock. Thomas Andrews, of Harland & Wolff, sat in the first class smoking room staring at a painting on the wall and was not seen again. On the bridge, the captain was at his post as it was engulfed by the rising sea and, all the time, the ship's musicians played on although, as the bow began to slip under the waves, they stopped the cheerful ragtime music which had lent such an air of unreality to the occasion and struck up with a traditional hymn, 'Nearer, My God, to Thee'. Several survivors attest that their last piece was another hymn, 'Autumn', but the former was known to be a favourite of the bandleader, Hartley, and is the most probable rendition to have been played at this poignant moment.

As the bow went under, the ship began to tilt down rapidly, the stern rising into the air, spilling people into the sea. At the same moment, the ship's lights suddenly went out after having burned brightly throughout the night thanks to the efforts of a dedicated band of engineers who had kept up enough steam to drive the generators. As the ship was dragged down by its flooded forward section, the hull rose almost vertically, the fore funnel breaking off and falling amongst swimmers in the water. *Titanic* hung in this position for several seconds before starting the plunge to the ocean floor over 12,000 ft below, the stern breaking off at the aft expansion joint during the journey to the seabed. As the mighty vessel finally went down, it was accompanied by a rising crescendo of noise as she broke in two, furniture and fittings crashed about inside, coal shifted in the bunkers and hot boilers split and exploded on contact with the ice-cold water. But, suddenly, all was silent and the ship had disappeared forever, taking with it over 1,000 people and leaving others drowning in its ice-cold wake. All that was left were the lifeboats, bobbing in the gradually settling waves, floating in a scene of Arctic desolation lit only by the stars in the clear sky above. The time was 2:20 a.m., 2 hours and 40 minutes from the time that the iceberg ripped into the *Titanic*'s hull.

Much of the controversy surrounding the sinking of the *Titanic* focused on the actions of other ships in the vicinity at the time. Mention has already been made of lights seen by both passengers and crew, but the vessel concerned has never been positively identified, if indeed there actually was a ship so close and the lights observed were not stars — a mistake made on many other occasions, even by experienced observers. One possible candidate was the 506 grt Norwegian sailing barque *Samson*, whose chief officer made a sworn statement in 1962 shortly before his death. He stated that he had seen the *Titanic*'s distress rockets but that the barque had altered course and sailed away as she had previously been engaged in an illegal sealing expedition off the Canadian coast and feared that the rockets were a signal to heave to so that she could be boarded and inspected. While this story could be true, there was no other corroborative evidence and official records showed the ship to be in Icelandic waters at the time. It is known that a Massachusetts fishing schooner, the *Dorothy Baird*, was somewhere near the scene of the sinking but it cannot be established that she was actually within visual range on the night in question. Neither of these vessels carried a radio and their small size would have limited the number of survivors which they could have rescued even if they had realized what was going on.

The ship which was caught up in the backlash of public opinion and the widespread desire to find a scapegoat was the cargo liner *Californian* and

ABOVE: *Latitude 41° 46'N and longitude 50° 14'W, the place where the* Titanic *sank.*

her unfortunate captain, Stanley Lord. This 6,223 grt steamer had been launched in 1901 and was owned by the Leyland Line, itself one of many taken over by International Mercantile Marine who also owned the White Star Line and the *Titanic* herself. She had sailed from Liverpool on 5 April, 1912, carrying a general cargo to Boston, and by noon on the fateful 14 April was at position 42°05'N, 47°25'W. In view of the ice warnings received by his radio operator, Captain Lord had decided to alter course to pass slightly south of his originally planned route. Despite this, large icebergs were spotted at 6:30 p.m., still to the south of the ship, and this information was passed by radio to another Leyland ship, the *Antillian*, at 7:30 p.m. The *Californian*'s radio operator (Cyril Evans) subsequently established that this signal had also been picked up by the *Titanic*. Concerned about the proximity of the icefield, Lord stationed himself on the bridge and doubled his lookouts. At around 10:15 p.m. he ordered the ship to stop when a glow in the darkness ahead was interpreted as a possible icefield and decided to heave to for the night, the position being recorded in the log as 42°05'N, 50°7'W. If Boxhall's estimate of the *Titanic*'s position was correct, then the *Californian* had stopped at a point just under 20 miles north-northeast from where the tragedy was to occur.

At around 10:30 p.m., the masthead lights of a ship approaching from the east were seen and Lord checked with his wireless operator to see if he was aware of any other ships in the vicinity. On being told that the only known vessel was the *Titanic*, he ordered Evans to advise the latter that the *Californian* was stationary in an icefield although, as we have seen, this message was brushed aside by the recipient's operators. Having been on continuous duty since 7:00 a.m. that morning, Evans shut down his radio

RIGHT: *A cross-section of the ship showing the double bottom, and an impression of the damage caused by the iceberg.*

NEXT PAGE: *Survivors watch helplessly from the lifeboats as the White Star Line's proudest achievement, the* Titanic, *plunges beneath the waves.*

and went off duty shortly after this exchange as there was no requirement at that time that ships should maintain a continuous listening watch. An hour later, the other vessel appeared to be passing some five miles to the south and Third Officer Groves attempted to establish contact by signal lamp, but no answer was forthcoming. Over half an hour later, just after midnight, Second Officer Stone thought that he saw the lights of another ship, this time heading east, but again no contact was established. Shortly afterwards Captain Lord retired to the chart room for a rest, leaving orders that he was to be called if anything unusual occurred. Between 12:45 a.m. and 1:15 a.m., Stone observed what he took to be signal rockets in the distance, in line with the vessel which he had previously seen and which now appeared to be stationary, although his report indicated that he did not consider that the lights actually came from the vessel which he could see. After observing the rockets he called down the voicepipe to the captain who requested to be kept informed of any developments. Subsequently, James Gibson, a young cadet, was sent down to report that more rockets had been fired and that the previously stationary vessel had now disappeared. However, Lord does not seem to have been fully awake and the cadet was obviously apprehensive at disturbing his stern captain, and retired after an inconclusive exchange. This version of events, as told by the officers on the bridge, was slightly at variance with evidence subsequently given by a fireman, Ernest Gill, who claimed that he had come on deck at midnight after four hours on duty below and saw a very large steamer passing about ten miles away off the starboard side. He then went below but returned to the deck 30 minutes later when he saw two white rockets within the space of a few minutes, again off to starboard. He did not notify the bridge of these sightings, nor did he see any Morse lamp signals from the other ship nor hear any noises, such as the concussion from the exploding rockets.

And so the night passed, the officers and crew of the *Californian* blissfully unaware of the drama which had actually occurred only a few miles away. However, when daylight came, Captain Lord returned to the bridge in order see if passage through the ice was possible. His attention was drawn to a four-masted vessel with a yellow funnel off to the south-southeast and it was thought that this might have been the one which had fired rockets during the night. Concerned that the vessel might require assistance, Lord roused his radio operator and ordered him to attempt to raise the other ship. As Evans tuned his equipment and transmitted a standard 'C.Q.' message, he was startled to receive a reply from the *Frankfurt*, a 7,431 grt German liner, asking if they were aware that the *Titanic* had struck an iceberg and sunk during the night. This was followed by confirmation from the *Virginian*, a 10,757 grt British ship, which also passed the all-important position of the sinking. Lord and his chief officer plotted this on their charts, realizing as they did so that they were very close to the sinking and possibly able to assist with the search for survivors. The captain immediately ordered the ship to get underway, the time being now around 5:30 a.m., and pushed cautiously though the ice at 6 knots before reaching open water on the west side and pushing southward at the *Californian's* maximum speed of 13 knots.

THE BUCKLED PLATES

BILGE KEEL

FIRST CLASS STATE ROOMS

POST MAIL ROOM

DOUBLE BOTTOM

KEEL

ICE PENETRATING THE DOUBLE BOTTOM

*RIGHT: A photograph of two Marconi wireless operators aboard the* Adriatic, Titanic's *heroic Jack Phillips stands to the left. He was lost while still attempting to send the distress signal. So absorbed was he in his task that he did not notice Harold Bride fit him with a life-jacket.*

*BELOW: Harold Bride, the junior radio operator, photographed at his post by Father Brown. He was fortunate enough to cling to an overturned lifeboat after swimming away from the sinking ship at the last minute. Later he volunteered to help send the messages of other survivors from the* Carpathia *although he was injured and had to be carried to his post.*

After another hour she passed the Canadian Pacific liner *Mount Temple* which lay stopped at the reported position of the sinking although there was no wreckage or survivors to be seen. Continuing southward, the *Californian* eventually sighted the Cunard liner *Carpathia* to the southeast, on the other side of the icefield, and learned by wireless that the latter was at the actual position of the sinking and was even then picking up survivors. The two ships eventually came together at 8:30 a.m., indicating that the *Californian* must have been at least 25 miles from the scene when the *Titanic* sank.

Although Captain Lord subsequently became something of a scapegoat, his was not the only ship which might have been within visual range of the *Titanic* during the night at the time of the sinking. The 6,661 grt Canadian Pacific liner *Mount Temple* under the command of Captain James Moore was sailing from Antwerp to New York and was approximately 49 miles south-west when it picked up the *Titanic's* first distress signals at around 12:15 a.m. Captain Moore immediately altered course to the northeast but shortly after 3:00 a.m. he began to encounter ice and subsequently put his engines in reverse and turned hard to port in order to avoid a collision with a schooner sighted just ahead. After this incident he continued cautiously forward, stopping occasionally, before reaching the reported position of the *Titanic* at 4:30 a.m. No wreckage or lifeboats were seen, and the captain later stated that no signals or rockets had been observed during the night, although an unidentified tramp steamer had been observed on a similar course for some time. When daylight came, he continued searching until approximately 9:00 a.m., when he became aware that the survivors had been rescued. It will be remembered that the *Mount Temple* was sighted by the *Californian* as she headed towards the area of the sinking during the early hours of the 15th, which would indicate that the *Mount Temple* had actually been much closer to the sinking than the latter. Despite her captain's assertions, at least two people (one passenger and one ship's officer) on the Mount Temple made statements to the effect that the *Titanic's* lights and signals had indeed been sighted but that the *Mount Temple* stood off and made

*RIGHT: The first radio message received at 11.45pm by the SS Birma of the Russian East Asiatic SS Co. The message begs for help after hitting the iceberg. Titanic gives her position as Lat 41°46'N, Long 50°14'W.*
*The Birma was about 100 miles southwest of Titanic when her radio operator received this distress call from M.Y.G. — Titanic's call sign.*

*BELOW RIGHT: After asking for further information the radio operator on Birma received this desperate communication from Titanic at about 1.40am: 'We are sinking fast passengers being put into boats.'*

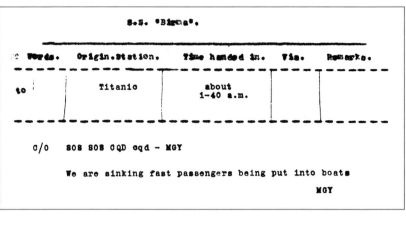

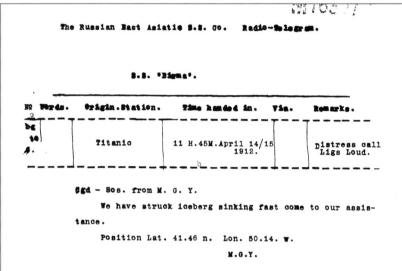

no attempt to move closer until well after daybreak. For some reason, the account and actions of Captain Moore were never seriously challenged and he avoided the destructive publicity directed at Captain Lord.

In contrast to the relatively quiet night passed by the *Californian* and *Mount Temple*, the *Carpathia* had been a shining example of efficiency and properly directed action which had resulted in her being the only ship to arrive in time to pick up the living survivors. The credit for this rested entirely with her captain, Arthur Rostron, who had joined the Cunard Line in 1895 and rose to his first command in 1907, taking over the 13,603 grt *Carpathia* in January 1912. This ship had left New York at noon on 11 April, 1912, with 743 passengers (fortunately only a fraction of her designed accommodation for around 2,200), bound for Gibraltar and then on to other Mediterranean ports. On the fateful Sunday the *Carpathia*'s only radio operator, 21-year old Harold Cottam, had been on duty continuously since 7:00 a.m. that morning and, as midnight approached, he was preparing to close down his radio and retire to bed. While undressing he kept his headphones on, listening out for a reply to an earlier communication which he had addressed to the liner *Parisian* although this was not forthcoming. While he waited, he idly retuned to the Cape Cod frequency and heard several messages addressed to the *Titanic* which he noted down with the intention of passing them on when the opportunity occurred. He then continued his preparations for bed when, on an impulse, he decided to see if he could raise the liner himself. The time was almost 12:30 a.m.

*Above:* Titanic's lifeboats. there were just 20 in all — 14 standard, two emergency clippers and four collapsible.

His message to the *Titanic* was phrased in the jargon favoured by radio operators of the day. Using the *Carpathia's* callsign 'M.P.A.', he started tapping his Morse key.

'I say, Old Man, do you know there is a batch of messages coming through for you from M.C.C. (code for Cape Cod)?'

Even before he had finished, the *Titanic* broke in with an electrifying message of her own: 'M.G.Y. (Titanic), Come at once. We have struck an iceberg. It's C.Q.D., Old Man. Position 41°46'N, 50°14'W'.

Cottam quickly ascertained that this was a genuine message and dashed, half-dressed, to the bridge to report the exchange to the first officer who immediately conducted him down to the captain's cabin where Rostron had just retired for the night. Instantly wide awake, the latter rushed up to the chart room and quickly determined that his ship was some 58 miles southeast of the *Titanic's* reported position. His subsequent actions were those of a professional master mariner who knew his trade inside out and needed no prompting to do what was necessary. As the *Carpathia* swung round onto a course of 308° to close the *Titanic*, he ordered the ship's 18 lifeboats to be prepared and swung out while the chief engineer was asked to raise maximum steam, shutting down much ancillary machinery and heating systems in order to ensure that no steam was wasted. As a result of some Herculean efforts by the stokers, the *Carpathia* eventually worked up to a speed of 17.5 knots, a speed that does not sound particularly impressive until it is realized that the ship's designed maximum speed under favourable conditions was only 14.5 knots! As the hull quivered and vibrated under this extra strain, the entire crew was briefed to prepare to receive survivors, but not before every man was served with a hot drink to fortify them for the work ahead. Passengers were asked to remain calm and keep to their cabins so as not to hinder the crew as they cleared spaces, piled up blankets and made the boats ready. Hot soup and drinks were prepared and arrangements made to accommodate the people from the *Titanic* as they came aboard, while the three doctors aboard were alerted and made their own preparations. Lights were rigged to illuminate the ship's side and ladders; lines and tackle were made ready to gather survivors from the lifeboats. Barrels of oil were made available so that rough waters could, if necessary, be calmed to assist the lifeboats coming alongside.

As the *Carpathia* tore through the night, additional lookouts were posted and all eyes strained forward in the darkness. Meanwhile, Cottam was back at his post in the radio room listening to the *Titanic*'s increasingly desperate radio transmissions, each of which was relayed to his captain by a steward acting as a messenger. The last one which he recorded was received at 1:45 a.m., stating 'Engine Room full up to the boilers'. Only 45 minutes later a green flare was sighted in the distance far ahead. This, it transpired, had been fired by Boxhall from lifeboat number 2. Rostron ordered rockets to be fired at 15-minute intervals so that any survivors would know that rescue was approaching although it was almost another hour before the *Carpathia* reached the reported position of the sinking, and at that time no boats or

*RIGHT: An illustration prepared for a London newspaper showing the distance that the lifeboats had to travel down the side of the ship as compared to an office building.*

*BELOW: The first lifeboat to be picked up by the* Carpathia — *number 14, commanded by Fifth Officer Lowe.*

"A" DECK
70 feet above
the water

"B" DECK
from which many
of the women were
taken into the boats

*RIGHT: Boat number 6 contained too few men to man the boat, so Lightoller sent down the falls an amateur yachtsman, Major Peuchen, to aid the boat. Molly Brown was also aboard.*

*FAR RIGHT: The efficient crew of the Carpathia take survivors on board.*

*BELOW: Collapsible boat D holding 25 people, including the lucky Mr. Hoyt who swam in the dark to be pulled aboard the boat containing his wife. The boat was commanded by the highest ranking officer to escape the sinking, Second Officer Lightoller.*

*ABOVE AND ABOVE RIGHT: More boats are found and brought alongside.*

*RIGHT: As Lowe approaches in boat 14, he lowers the sail to reveal that he has a collapsible boat in tow.*

wreckage had been spotted. However, there were occasional glimpses of green lights low in the water ahead and these eventually turned out to be those of the lifeboats. At 4:00 a.m., just before dawn broke, Captain Rostron order the engines to 'Stop' and the *Carpathia* drifted to a halt only a few hundred yards from Boxhall's boat. Ten minutes later it lay under the *Carpathia*'s starboard side and the work of getting the 25 occupants aboard began. Boxhall himself, still suffering from exposure to the cold and from shock, was taken to the bridge where he was able to give a brief account of what had happened, confirming to the disbelieving listeners that the *Titanic* had indeed been lost.

As the thin daylight began to illuminate the scene, the scale and nature of the catastrophe slowly became apparent. The *Titanic*'s lifeboats with their pitiful survivors rode the barely disturbed sea, while the whole area was strewn with icebergs of all shapes and sizes, the largest towering more than 200 ft above the water. Fortunately the calm conditions meant that the lifeboats had mostly remained together, being contained within an area of four or five square miles. Even so, the task of manoeuvering a large ship amongst the icefloes without crushing or overturning the small boats was extremely difficult and taxed Captain Rostron's skills to the limit. The painstaking task of recovering survivors took several hours and it was not until 8:00 a.m. that the last boat was located and brought alongside. This was number 12, which by now contained more than 70 people, as survivors from the overturned collapsible B had been transferred to it as well as few

from collapsible D. The last to come aboard the *Carpathia*, at 8:30 a.m., was the exhausted Second Officer Lightoller, now the senior surviving officer from the *Titanic*. It was none too soon, as already the calm weather which had characterised the night was beginning to break and the sea was being whipped up by a freshening wind, making the rescue of the last survivors a difficult business. Rostron ordered the *Titanic's* lifeboats to be hoisted aboard (13 were recovered in this way), and handed over the search for further survivors to Captain Lord in the *Californian*, which had now arrived on the scene.

Before leaving the area, a brief but emotional service for those lost in the disaster was held in the *Carpathia's* first class saloon as the ship passed over the spot where the *Titanic* was assumed to have sunk. By 8:50 a.m. the ship was underway, returning to New York to land the survivors. However, it took the Cunard ship several hours to get free of the great icepack which had been the cause of the tragedy. The heart-rending task of counting and identifying the survivors then began, the eventual tally reaching 705 (201 first class, 118 second class and 179 third class passengers, together with 207 crew). While there is no doubt that Captain Rostron had saved all who were alive in the boats when he reached the area, it nevertheless began to dawn on all involved that more than twice this number must have perished when the ship went down. Most of the surviving passengers were women and their grief as they began to realize that they had lost their husbands or fathers or other relatives was heart-breaking to see. The crew and passengers of the *Carpathia* rallied round to do what they could for all the survivors, regardless of their class or status.

## The Lifeboats

*Titanic's* lifeboats were situated on the Boat deck, where they sat on wooden chocks that were hinged to the deck. The forwardmost boat on the port and starboard side, the smaller 'rescue boats', were kept swung out. *Titanic* carried 20 lifeboats on her maiden voyage — fourteen standard wooden boats, capacity 65 persons (boats 3 through 16 were of the standard type); two rescue cutters, capacity 40 persons (Boats 1 and 2 were of this type); four collapsible 'Englehardt' boats, capacity 47 persons. These had a wooden slat bottom like an ordinary lifeboat, but the sides were canvas that could be raised and lowered to allow compact stowage. Boats A through D were collapsibles.

In total these 20 boats would hold 1,178 people. When *Titanic* left Queenstown *en route* to New York, she carried 2,208 souls. *Titanic's* wooden lifeboats were manufactured by Murray's Boats Limited of Glasgow, Scotland and were supplied by White Star to Harland & Wolff. The lifeboat davits were specially designed and manufactured for the *Olympic* and *Titanic* by the Welin Davit and Engineering Company Ltd, London, England. The only survivor of the Harland & Wolff engineering party on board was Alfred Cunningham, an apprentice fitter aged 17. Originally reported as dead, he was found alive but badly injured in New York, among those rescued by the *Carpathia*. *Titanic's* other 'life-saving' features includ-

LEFT: Titanic's *boats were drained of water and hoisted aboard the* Carpathia.

ABOVE: Captain Arthur H. Rostron of the Carpathia. *Following the heroic rescue a special medal was forged by the U.S congress in honour of his actions.*

*ABOVE, ABOVE RIGHT AND RIGHT: Various photographs of the crew of the* Carpathia. *So grateful were the survivors of the* Titanic *that they organised a collection which amounted to some £15,000.*

ed 3,500 lifebelts and forty-eight life rings. These last two measures were useless in the freezing water.

### Boat 1

Containing only a dozen people, this was the least filled of the lifeboats. At about ship's time 1:10 a.m. it was lowered from starboard on the order of First Officer Murdoch who was assisted by Fifth Officer Lowe.

### Boat 2

Chief Officer Wilde ordered the launching of boat two at 1:45 a.m. 28 escaped on it.

### Boat 3

Boat 3 held between 38 to 40 people including 26 male passengers, and 13 male crew members, ten of whom were firemen. The men were given space as no willing women could be found by First Officer Murdoch who ordered the launch at 1:00 a.m.

### Boat 4

Second Officer Lightoller ordered the launch of boat number 4 at 1:55 a.m. At first it contained some 30 people though not enough crew to man it effectively, the sole crew member being Storekeeper Foley. However, Foley was soon joined in the lifeboat by Quartermaster Perkiss and Able Seaman McCarthy, who descended from the *Titanic* by the falls. Perkiss, who took command of the boat, had originally been told by Lightoller to row the boat to the aft gangway doors where he was to collect more passengers. However, these doors remained closed and, while waiting at the gangway, the only

*ABOVE AND RIGHT: Crewmen from the* Carpathia.

additional people to join the lifeboat were Greasers Ranger and Scott who were attempting to reach boat 16 which was being lowered nearby. Ranger dropped accidentally into boat 4, and Scott, having fallen into the water, was dragged to safety. As these few crew were unable to pull the boat away from the scene quickly, it later managed to pick up seven swimming crew members due to its proximity to the sinking *Titanic*: of these, six lost consciousness, and two of them died during the night.

## Boat 5

At 12:55 a.m. First Officer Murdoch ordered the launch of boat 5; he was aided by Fifth Officer Lowe. Between 36 and 41 people made their escape on this lifeboat; of these, half were male.

## Boat 6

Boat 6 was ordered lowered from the port side of the ship at 12:55 a.m. by Second Officer Lightoller, who was helped by Sixth Officer Moody. It contained only 26 people including only two crewmen. Realising that this was insufficient to man the craft, Lightoller sent down the falls an amateur yachtsman, Major Peuchen, to aid the boat. One member of the crew, Hitchens, would later have his conduct criticized by the survivors of boat 6.

## Boat 7

The first lifeboat to leave the *Titanic*. Lowered at 12:45 a.m. by First Officer Murdoch and Fifth Officer Lowe. It carried about 32 people including three crew, 13 female and 19 male passengers.

## Boat 8

Second Officer Lightoller ordered the launch of boat 8 at 1:15 a.m. Of the 28 on board, Ellen Bird, a maid, was helped to its safety by her mistress, first class passenger Ida Straus who, having seen to her employee's survival, immediately returned to the *Titanic* and her husband. Captain Smith also helped the launch of this boat and, noticing that it was undermanned, ordered two additional crew members to aid its departure.

## Boat 9

With the assistance of Sixth Officer Moody, First Officer Murdoch ordered boat 9 into the water at 1:20 a.m. It is believed that the boat held 45 or 46 survivors.

## Boat 10

At 1:20 a.m boat 10 was lowered by Second Officer Lightoller with the assistance of Sixth Officer Moody. Records of this boat are sketchy but it is thought to have had around 30 people on board.

## Boat 11

Boat 11 contained between 55 and 60 survivors; of these, most were stewards, stewardesses and second class women and children. It was ordered lowered at 1:25 a.m. by First Officer Murdoch and assisted into the water by Sixth Officer Moody. Quartermaster Humphreys and Seaman Brice joined the boat via the falls after it was realized that there were no sailors on board.

Boat 12

Boat 12 escaped the *Titanic* with between 28 and 30 survivors. Of these, two were crew and about 25 were women from second class. The boat was lowered at 1:25 a.m. by Second Officer Lightoller who was assisted by Fifth Officer Lowe.

Boat 13

Boat 13 was lowered at 1:30 a.m. by the order of Sixth Officer Moody. It had about 65 people on board.

Boat 14

Fifth Officer Lowe ordered the launch of boat 14 at 1:45 a.m.; it is thought that he was assisted by Chief Officer Wilde. Two male passengers were among the up to 45 people on board as the boat was lowered. One of these, Charles Williams, was selected by Lowe to aid in the rowing of the boat. However, the other, thought to be Edward Ryan, joined with a towel wrapped around his head to imitate a shawl.

### Boat 15

At 1:35 a.m., soon after boat 13 was lowered, First Officer Murdoch, aided by Sixth Officer Moody, ordered the launch of boat 15. However, the previous boat continued to drift, attatched to *Titanic* by the falls, directly below. Shouts from boat 13 were apparently unheard and the crew were pressed to cut the lines and move away in time to avoid additional tragedy. About 65 people were on board.

### Boat 16

Master-at-Arms Bailey commanded this boat, having been ordered down the falls by Sixth Officer Moody. It was launched at 1:35 a.m. and initially was manned only by two seaman, a steward and a fireman. It carried in the region of 40 people to safety.

### Collapsible Boat A

This boat eventually held 12 survivors, although there were eight dead aboard when it was discovered by Officer Lowe in the morning following the disaster. Originally stored on the starboard side of the roof of the officers' quarters, it was dropped to the Boat deck and attached to the falls from which boat 1 and Collapsible C had been launched.

As loading was about to commence, however, the forward end of the Boat deck disappeared below the water, and, while still attatched to the davits the boat began to drift away. The falls were quickly cut by Saloon Steward Edward Brown and another man who jumped onto the boat, though at this point a wave had swamped the boat and washed others who had managed to climb aboard into the sea. In such extreme conditions 20 finally managed to clamber into the boat but, after a night of standing or sitting in the freezing water, hypothermia had taken those eight before Officer Lowe managed to transfer the living to his lifeboat.

### Collapsible Boat B

In the region of 30 men miraculously reached safety on this unlucky boat. As it was being unloaded from storage on the port side of the roof of the officers' quarters it was mishandled and dropped down to the Boat deck where it landed upside down. While men struggled to heave it to the davits, a wave produced by the sinking bridge washed it and those working on it overboard.

Now capsized in the water, another wave, this time caused by the collapsing forward funnel, washed it clear of the ship. During the night the fortunate 30 managed to swim to its relative safety, though, as their weight caused it to settle deeper into the water, many more were turned away to perish in the freezing water.

### Collapsible Boat C

Chief Officer Wilde and First Officer Murdoch ordered this boat to be lowered at 1:40 a.m. It carried  around 40 people to safety, inluding the president of the White Star Line, J. Bruce Ismay, whose survival would later cause much controversy. It is claimed that during its dramatic launch, the collapsible was rushed by several men, causing an officer, possibly Murdoch, to fire three warning rounds from his revolver. The only recorded and confirmed shots were fired by Fifth Officer Lowe along the side of the vessel at approximately 1:30 a.m. Lowe fired three shots to quell the panic surrounding the launch of lifeboat Number 4 — while this deterred most of the men who fled back onto the deck, four Chinese sailors managed to conceal themselves among the women and escaped the sinking *Titanic*.

## Collapsible Boat D

This boat was launched by Second Officer Lightoller at 2:05 a.m., shortly before the *Titanic* slipped beneath the waves. Initially it held around 20 people, including five crewmen and one male stowaway. However, three others managed to find their way onto it; two passengers who jumped in, and a Mr Hoyt, who jumped into the water after seeing his wife safely on board and swam in the dark to where he guessed that the boat might be passing. Luckily his guess proved correct and he was pulled on board.

*LEFT: An illustration by Frenchman Henry Laros of the imagined fate of the* Titanic, *lying on the seabed under pack ice.*

# AFTERMATH

GRIM WIRELESS MESSAGE FROM
SCENE OF DISASTER
From the cable ship *Mackay-Bennett*
which was hurried to the scene of the
disaster to bring in any dead bodies
that could be found, the following
wireless message was received in
New York on 25 April:

'Bodies are numerous in latitude
41°35' North, longitude 48°37' West,
extending many miles both east and
west. Mailships should give this
region a wide berth.

'The medical opinion is that death
has been instantaneous in all the
cases owing to the pressure when
the bodies were drawn down in the
vortex. We have been drifting in a
dense fog since noon yesterday, and
the total number of bodies picked up
is 205.

'We brought away all the embalm-
ing fluid in Halifax, which is enough
for 70. With a week's fine weather we
think we should pretty well clear up
the relics of the disaster.

'In my opinion the majority of the
bodies will never come to the surface.'

*RIGHT: The* Daily Sketch *of 18 April, 1912, used
two of Father Browne's photographs on the front
page in a world exclusive. For impact, or in
error, both were printed the wrong way round!
(See Chapter 8, pages 294/295 and 304.)*

News of *Titanic*'s collision was soon relayed around the world. At first the
message was garbled: thus the *Evening Star*'s headline announced; 'All saved
from *Titanic* after collision'. Indeed the owners of the White Star Line — The
International Mercantile Marine company — even issued a statement to the
effect that they were absolutely certain that the *Titanic* was able to with-
stand any damage. This mood of optimism was not to last. On board
*Carpathia* was Bruce Ismay who, at Rostron's suggestion, composed a message to be sent to his company's offices in New York advising them of the
sinking. It was dispatched during the morning of the 15th and read:

'Deeply regret to advise you *Titanic* sank this morning after collision
with iceberg, resulting in serious loss of life. Full particulars later, Ismay.'

This was addressed to P. A. Franklin, the American vice president of I.M.M.
On the morning of 16 April, the White Star Line sent the British Board of
Trade a brief statement which included the number of passengers picked up.
Later that day Prime Minister Asquith addressed a sombre House of
Commons:

'I am afraid we must brace ourselves to confront one of those terrible
events in the order of providence which baffle foresight, which appall the
imagination, and which make us feel the inadequacy of words to do justice to
what we feel'.

In New York the mood of optimism had persisted since until about six
o'clock in the evening when the *Olympic* sent a widely intercepted message
to White Star saying that only 675 people had been picked up — this was
later amended to 705 making the official death toll 1,503 souls. Soon the
White Star Line offices were besieged by an anxious and frantic crowd
eagerly awaiting news. Back on board *Carpathia* preparations were made to
transmit the long list of survivors' names but the task proved too great for
Cottam, the *Carpathia*'s radio operator, who had now been on continuous
duty for over 24 hours and was on the point of collapse. Fortunately, one of
the *Titanic*'s operators, Harold Bride, had been picked up and, although suffering from frostbite and exposure, he gamely volunteered to assist and was
carried up to the radio room where he spent the rest of the voyage transmitting the names of survivors. However, Captain Rostron placed him and
Cottam under strict orders to divulge no further details, much to the conster-
nation of the world's press; they would have to wait until the *Carpathia*
docked for further news. While still aboard the *Carpathia*, survivors from

# DAILY SKETCH.

No. 970—THURSDAY, APRIL 18, 1912.     THE PREMIER PICTURE PAPER.     (Registered as a Newspaper)  ONE HALFPENNY.

## FIRST UNCLOUDED HOURS OF TITANIC'S FATAL VOYAGE.

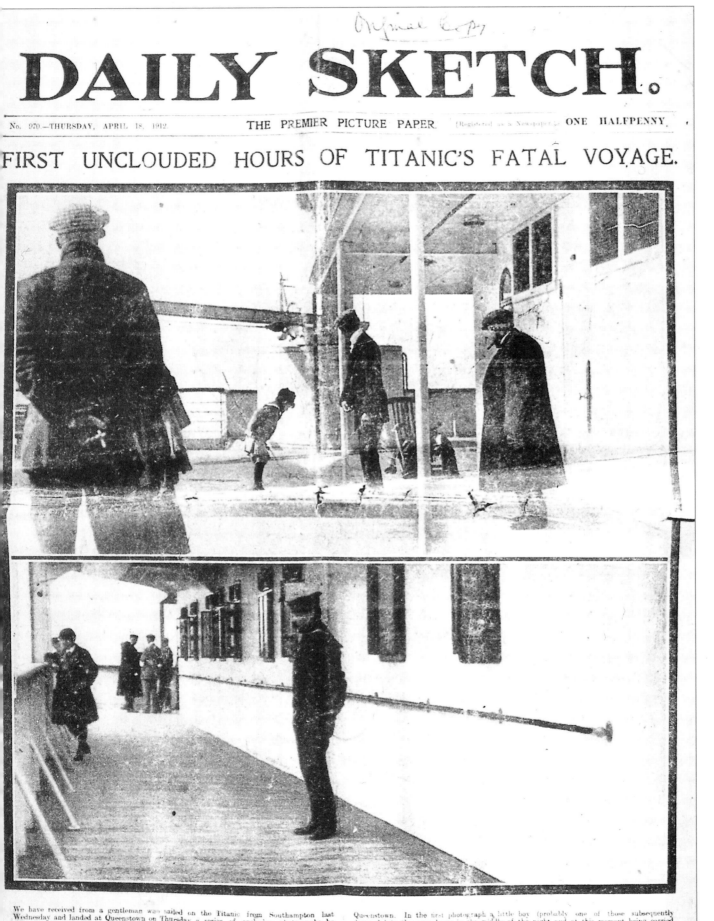

We have received from a gentleman who sailed on the Titanic from Southampton last Wednesday and landed at Queenstown on Thursday a series of exclusive photographs he secured on the trip, which have a pathetic interest in view of the terrible fate which awaited the great liner and those on board less than four days after our contributor came ashore at Queenstown, under the bridge as the Titanic Queenstown. In the first photograph a little boy (probably one of those subsequently dropped into the open boats in the middle of the night and at this moment being carried to New York on board the Carpathia) is seen spinning his top on the saloon deck on Thursday morning, whilst men now buried in the Atlantic look on. The second snapshot steamed out to sea down the Solent.

RIGHT: *More photographs of* Titanic *inside the* Daily Sketch *of 18 April, 1912.*

BELOW RIGHT: *Queenstown in mourning, with the flags at half mast on 19 April, 1912. Tenders* Ireland *and* America *are moored on the right.*

the *Titanic* organized a committee to raise a fund to express their gratitude and this later amounted to some $15,000 which was used to provide a distribution of cash to all members of the *Carpathia*'s crew. On the night of 18 April, an enormous crowd lined the streets of New York. Their excitement had reached fever pitch. As the *Carpathia* entered New York Harbour she was besieged by tugs laden with clamouring reporters. As she berthed at Cunard's Pier 54, Marconi (by whose invention so many lives had been saved) came aboard with a reporter from the New York Times. The subsequent interview with Bride, the *Titanic*'s junior radio operator was published later that night in the New York Times. This 'exclusive' represented one of the most important and controversial scoops of all time. It also established two enduring *Titanic* legends concerning the heroism of Chief Wireless Operator Phillips, in continuing to send out messages and the bravery of the ship's orchestra in continuing to play even as the *Titanic* went down:

'The way the band kept playing was a noble thing. When I was floating out on the sea with my lifebelt on, it was still on deck playing 'Autumn'. How they ever did it I cannot imagine. That and the way Phillips kept sending after the Captain told him his life was his own, and to look out for himself, are two things that stood out in my mind over all the rest.'

Over the days that followed, many remarkable stories were to unfold of miraculous escapes and tragic endings; how Captain Smith was alleged to have rescued a child from the icy waters then swam back to die with his ship. Another that stands out especially, and certainly most bizarrely, was the account given by crew members of the discovery of six Chinese on board the *Carpathia*. Presumably stowaways, they were found hidden beneath seats in *Titanic*'s lifeboats. Two of their companions had been crushed to death by the weight of passengers sitting above them. In England the reporting of the disaster tended to be less anecdotal: 'The *Titanic* like some monstrous syren, had by her beauty and ease, by her splendour and confidence, lured to the sea men and women to whom life itself seemed subservient and obedient'. wrote the *Daily Mail* in London.  However, the landing of the *Titanic*'s survivors in New York, and the ensuing American and British hearings were by no means the end of the story. In fact they were merely the opening pages in a narrative which has steadfastly refused to die and has become part of 20th century legend — with fact and fiction so completely intertwined that it is difficult to tell one from the other. As the scale of the tragedy became apparent, moving and grief-ridden memorial services were held in New York, London and Belfast. Perhaps the most poignant was at St. Mary's church in Southampton, only a short distance from the berth in Southampton docks from whence the *Titanic* had set off on its ill-fated voyage. The town was devastated as many of the 685 crew lost when the ship went down had had their homes and families in the area. In order to raise money for them, and for the families of the 818 passengers also lost, fund-raising concerts, performances and other events were held not only in the United Kingdom and America, but in Canada, New Zealand, Australia and many other parts of

## THE VOYAGE OF DISASTER: EXCLUSIVE PHOTOGRAPHS BY PASSENGER WHO LEFT THE DOOMED TITANIC AT QUEENSTOWN.

The Titanic dropping the Southampton pilot off Portsmouth last Wednesday. He was taken ashore by an Isle of Wight boat. In the distance are the Channel forts. This photograph was taken from the upper promenade deck. — The last photograph of the fast liner, the Titanic leaving Queenstown Harbour on Thursday morning after taking on board the mails. The decks are crowded with passengers waving a "Good-bye to Southampton." — A photograph taken from the top deck of the Titanic cast off and commenced her first and last voyage.

### BUSINESS HELD UP BY THE ECLIPSE OF THE SUN.     EVERYBODY SUN-GAZING AT NOON YESTERDAY.

Everybody passed in their daily occupations to view the eclipse of the sun. Londoners took it quite comfortably by accepting the invitation to make their observations from Selfridge's roof garden. Below is a photograph of children looking at the eclipse under the shadow of the dome at Greenwich Observatory. — Taking a photograph at the West Kensington Observatory at the moment of the greatest illumination. Photographs of the eclipse at 11.40 noon and 12.50. — The eclipse, which commenced at 10.34 a.m. and ended at 1.31 p.m., photographed over the Houses of Parliament. — The sad way and the new—a naval officer using a sextant alongside a man gazing through smoked glass. Below is Mr. Hawks examining the radiator at the Scientific Society's Observatory at Hampstead Heath. — A motor-car party provided with glasses on Hampstead Heath. At adjournment at the Law Courts where judge, jury and counsel go outside to view the eclipse. — Dailysketch Photograph.

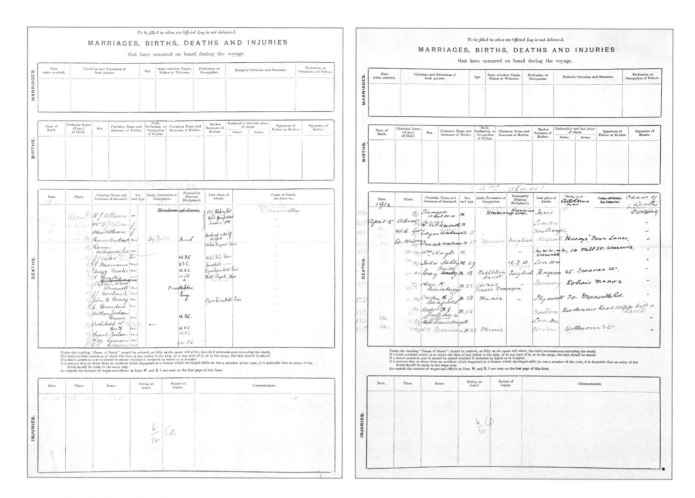

ABOVE: *The death certificate for passengers travelling first class. In the first column is the date of the disaster April 15, 1912, the second column gives the place as about 41°16' Lat 50°14' Long. The third column starts the alphabetical list of passengers who died; the next gives their sex (almost exclusively men), the following completed column gives nationality, then address, and finally cause of death — in every case by drowning although the more likely reason for most would have been hypothermia.*

ABOVE RIGHT: *The death certificate for travellers in second class. The details are much the same as for first class, but this time some ages are given.*

RIGHT: *The death certificate for travellers in third class. Note the number of Scandinavians; 62 percent of third class passengers were drowned while 62 percent of first class passengers were saved.*

the world which had been affected in some way or other. On both sides of the Atlantic memorials were erected to honour those who died and fittingly, among the very first of these were examples at Liverpool, Boston and New York dedicated to the brave musicians who kept playing until the very end and who perished to a man. One of the survivors, Jack Thayer, wrote of the pre-*Titanic* era: 'the world had an even tenor to its ways . . . the disaster was the event which not only made the world rub its eyes and awake, but woke it with a start.' To his own complete disbelief, man had overreached himself.

There were to be two full scale inquiries, one in Britain held under the auspices of the Board of Trade and the other in America under the chairmanship of Senator William Smith. At first the British authorities resented the idea that the Americans had any right to carry out an inquiry as it concerned a British-registered ship, owned by a British Company, flying the British flag and manned by a British crew. However, the Americans gave little credence to such niceties, pointing out that the White Star Line was in fact itself owned by an American company and that the *Titanic* went down with a number of prominent American citizens on board. Indeed the news was so shocking to the American Senate and people that, even before the survivors had reached New York, an official announcement from Washington proclaimed that a special sub-committee was to be set up by the Senate to inquire into the circumstances of the disaster. The man appointed to head the inquiry was Senator William Smith. Senator Smith saw himself as the standard bearer for the common man, fighting in the face of the commercial trusts and cartels of the American subcontinent — such as I.M.M. Although ignorant of nautical matters he made a virtue of this, stating that, 'energy is

To be filled in when an Official Log is not delivered.

# MARRIAGES, BIRTHS, DEATHS AND INJURIES

that have occurred on board during the voyage.

| | Date when married. | Christian and Surnames of both parties. | Age. | State whether Single, Widow or Widower. | Profession or Occupation. | Father's Christian and Surname. | Profession Occupation of |
|---|---|---|---|---|---|---|---|
| **MARRIAGES.** | | | | | | | |

| | Date of Birth. | Christian Name (if any) of Child. | Sex. | Christian Name and Surname of Father. | Rank, Profession or Occupation of Father. | Christian Name and Surname of Mother. | Maiden Surname of Mother. | Nationality and last place of abode. Father. | Nationality and last place of abode. Mother. | Signature of Father or Mother. | Signatur Maste |
|---|---|---|---|---|---|---|---|---|---|---|---|
| **BIRTHS.** | | | | | | | | | | | |

## THIRD CLASS.

| | Date. 1912 | Place. | Christian Name and Surname of deceased. | Sex and Age. | Rank, Profession or Occupation. | Nationality (Stating Birthplace). | Last place of Abode. | Address | Cause of Death. See footnotes. Cause Death |
|---|---|---|---|---|---|---|---|---|---|
| | | | | | PASSENGERS. ~~Members of Crew.~~ | | | | Supposed |
| 291 | April 15 | About | Anthony Abbing | m 42 | Blacksmith | U.S.A. | Southampton | | Drowned |
| 292 | do. | 41.16 Lat | Eugene Abbott | m 13 | Scholar | " | London | Salvation Army London | " |
| 293 | do. | 50.14 Long | Rossmore Abbott | m 16 | Jeweller | " | " | | " |
| 294 | do. | | Maurits Adahl | m 30 | Labourer | Sweden | Copenhagen | | " |
| | | | Adams | m | Farm Labr. | English | Yeovil | Hyatt Cottage Winton Church Rd Bournemouth | " |
| | | | Johanna Ahlin | F. 40 | Wife | Sweden | Gothenburg | | |
| | | | Ali Ahmed | m 24 | Labr. | Syria | Buenos Ayres | 10. Belverdere Place Kitchener Rd Gt. Yarmouth | " |
| | | | William Alexander | m 23 | Labr. | England | Gt. Yarmouth | | " |
| | | | Ilmari Alhomaki | m 20 | Labr. | Finland | Finland | | " |
| | | | William Ali | m 25 | Labr. | Syria | Buenos Ayres | | " |
| | | | William Allen | m 35 | Tool-maker | England | Birmingham | c/o F. Hunt 78 Queens Rd Erdington | " |
| | | | Owen George Allum | m 18 | Gardener | " | London | 22. Oswald Rd Southall | " |
| | | | Amin Saad | m 30 | Farm Labr. | Syria | Syria | | " |
| | | | Albert Andersen | m 33 | Engineer | Norway | Bergen. | | " |
| | | | Thor. Anderson | m 20 | Labr. | Norway | Christiania | | " |

Under the heading "Cause of Death" should be entered, as fully as the space will allow, the chief circumstances attending the death.
If a fatal accident occurs at or about the time of any injury to the ship, or to any part of it, or to the cargo, the fact should be stated.
If a death occurs in port it should be stated whether it occurred on board or in hospital.
If a seaman dies on shore from an accident which happened or a disease which developed while he was a member of the crew, it is desirable that an entry of the death should be made in the same way.
As regards the account of wages and effects on form W. and E. 1 see note on the first page of this form.

| | Date. | Place. | Name. | Rating on board. | Nature of Injury. | Circumstances. |
|---|---|---|---|---|---|---|
| **INJURIES.** | | | | | | |

# STATEMENT BY COMMITTEE OF SURVIVORS

*When the* Carpathia *arrived at New York, the following statement, drawn up by a committee of the surviving passengers of the* Titanic *was handed to the press:-*

We the undersigned surviving passengers of the *Titanic*, in order to forestall any sensational and exaggerated statements, deem it our duty to give to the Press a statement of the facts which have come to our knowledge, and which we believe to be true.

On Sunday, April 14, 1912, at about 11.40 on a cold, star-lit night, the ship struck an iceberg, which had been reported to the bridge by the look-out, but not early enough to avoid collision. Steps were taken to ascertain the damage and save the passengers and ship. Orders were given to put on lifebelts, the boats were lowered, and the usual distress signals were sent out by wireless telegraphy, and rockets were fired at intervals.

Fortunately, a wireless message was received by the *Carpathia* about midnight. She arrived on the scene of the disaster about 4 a.m. on Monday. The officers and crew of the *Carpathia* had been preparing all night for the rescue work, and for the comfort of the survivors. These were received on board with the most touching care and kindness, every attention being given to all, irrespective of class. Passengers, officers, and crew gladly gave up their state rooms, clothing, and comforts for our benefit; all honour to them.

The English Board of Trade passengers certificate on board the *Titanic* allowed for a total of approximately 3,500. The same certificate called for lifeboat accommodation for approximately 950, in the following boats:- Fourteen large lifeboats, two smaller boats, and four collapsible boats. Life preservers were accessible in apparently sufficient number for all on board. The approximate number of passengers carried at the time of the collision was:

First class 330; Second class 320; Third class 750 Total 1,400: Officers and crew 940 Total 2, 340

Of the foregoing about the following number were rescued by the *Carpathia*:-

First class 210; Second class 125; Third class 200;

Officers 4; Seaman 39; Stewards 95; Firemen 71; Total of crew 210

A total of about 775

The number saved was about about 80 percent of the maximum capacity of the lifeboats. We feel it our duty to call the attention of the public to what we consider the inadequate supply of lifesaving appliances provided for modern passenger steamships, and recommend that immediate steps be taken to compel passenger steamers to carry sufficient boats to accommodate the maximum number of people carried on board.

The following facts were observed, and should be considered in this connection:

In addition to the insufficiency of lifeboats, rafts, etc. there was a lack of trained seamen to man the same (stokers, stewards, etc. are not efficient boat handlers). There were not enough officers to carry out the emergency orders on the bridge and to superintend the launching and control of the lifeboats, and there was an absence of searchlights. The Board of Trade rules allow for entirely too many people in each boat to permit the same to be properly handled.

On the *Titanic* the boat deck was about 75 ft above water, and consequently the passengers were required to embark before the lowering of the boats, thus endangering the operation and preventing the taking on of the maximum number the boats would hold.

The boats at all times to be properly equipped with provisions, water, lamps, compasses. lights, etc. Life-saving boat drills should be more frequent and thoroughly carried out, and officers should be armed at boat-drill.

A greater reduction in speed in fog and ice, as the damage if a collision actually occurs is liable to be less.

In conclusion, we suggest that an international conference should be called, and we recommend the passage of identical laws providing for the safety of all at sea. We urge the United States Government to take the initiative as soon as possible.

*THIS PAGE: The survivors return.* Carpathia *arrived in New York late in the evening of Thursday, 18 April and the eyes of the world began to focus on the survivors and their stories. The crew — except for the four officers and 30 others subpoenaed for the American Inquiry — were transferred immediately to the* Lapland, *a Red Star Line vessel, and returned to Plymouth where they were questioned before being allowed to return to their loved ones. While this interrogation was going on, they were housed in (BELOW LEFT) Plymouth Dockyard.*

RIGHT: 'Eclipse for the World's Leviathan' — The Graphic's view of the tragedy. The morse code messages relate to distress signals sent out from Titanic after she hit the iceberg. The CQD emergency message would have been prefaced by Titanic's calling code, MGY. While many think CQD meant 'Come Quick Danger', much as SOS is taken to mean 'Save Our Souls', in fact the letters have no more significance than that CQ meant the message was addressed to all ships and the D meant danger. In fact radio operators Bride and Phillips started using SOS later in the evening, one of the first times it had been used in an emergency.

often more desirable than learning'. Energetic he was indeed; a prominent politician with an eye on the main chance, who saw the disaster as an opportunity to make a name for himself, to the extent that the official inquiry was conducted almost entirely by himself — and in the full blaze of publicity — although nominally the committee did include six other senators. Smith issued subpoenas to prevent the owner, four officers and over 30 of the crew of Titanic from leaving America until they had made 'certain explanations to the American people'. This compounded the crew's misery as the cash-strapped White Star Line had stopped their wages from the moment that the ship sank. Although this was standard practice at the time, its application in these circumstances seemed particularly harsh.

The hearings, which took place over 17 days between 19 April, and 25 May, in New York and Washington, elicited much significant information which was still fresh in the minds of the many witnesses called. In fact there were no fewer than 82 witnesses, both passengers and crew. The inquiry concentrated in detail of the circumstances of the disaster and the behavior of certain passengers and crew. As they worked their way through the last moments before she struck ice, to the time she took to finally go under, eyewitness reports provided chilling reminders of what had occurred that night in the Atlantic. Tales of cowardice, heroism, terror and devotion were about to capture the public imagination and be the subject of debate in every office, factory and home.

One eyewitness testified; 'Sailors tried to force Mrs. Straus into a boat. She was an old lady but she clung to her husband with great strength. As they tried again to separate her she said simply, 'We have lived together for forty years and we will not part now'. The crew were also expected to recount in detail anything they could remember about striking the ice and Titanic's evacuation, 'At one time, while we were waiting for rescue in the boats, every time we moved our oars they would strike a corpse', uttered another survivor. As the old rule of the sea of 'women and children first' had been applied as rigorously as possible, any men who had survived were quizzed thoroughly on the exact means of their escape. Bruce Ismay was one such man, and he told his particular story of how a half empty lifeboat was being lowered from the deck he was on. Seeing that there were no women or children in the vicinity, he jumped in it. The public did not find Mr. Ismay's account wholly satisfying and even if they believed it, many felt that he should have gone down with the ship. In addition to discussing how he had made his escape, Bruce Ismay was given a grilling as Smith attempted to prove negligence on the part of I.M.M., the White Star Line's owners. (A transcript of Ismay's testimony to the Senate hearing is given at the end of this chapter.)

The ship's officers were scrutinized most closely, quickly becoming key witnesses. It was important to establish just how male survivors — especially crew — had made their exit. If fellow crew members were prepared to stay dutifully at their posts or act solely for the benefit of others, then there had to be some kind of justice.

Of vital importance was the testimony of the lookouts and the radio oper-

# ECLIPSE—FOR THE WORLD'S LEVIATHAN
## THE LOSS OF THE TITANIC AMID THE NORTH ATLANTIC ICE

WHAT THE TITANIC LOOKED LIKE INSIDE—A SECTION OF THE VESSEL SPECIALLY DRAWN FOR THIS JOURNAL BY G. F. MORRELL

**SUNK** THE MARCONI-IST    COL. J. J. ASTOR

THE KITCHEN OF THE VESSEL

MR. D. W. MARVIN    MR. W. T. STEAD

**C Q D**

SKY   **ECLIPSE** (in progress)   APRIL 17

> Man that is Mortal pits his Brain
> 'Gainst Time and Space;
> Yet is not Master of the Main—
> His proud Leviathan lies Slain
> Athwart Cape Race.
>
> J.M.B.

SEA    **ECLIPSE**    APRIL 15

SKY   **ECLIPSE** (maximum)   APRIL 17

Eclipse! That is the note of this week by sea and sky; and in an age more mystery-loving than ours the two darkening facts would undoubtedly have been regarded as interdependent. But while an eclipse of the sun has occurred before, there has never been anything in the history of wrecks to equal the eclipse of the good ship Titanic on her maiden voyage to New York. Laden with 2358 human beings—1455 passengers and 903 of a crew—the monster —she was 50,000 tons—set out gaily from Southampton on Wednesday week; and then most of us forgot all about her, just as we cease to remember that the sun rises daily. Then when we were all asleep—most of us with the certainty of rising again—a dread signal flashed out from a spot 400 miles south of Cape Race—

"S.O.S.," "Save our souls." It reached Cape Race at about 10.25 on Sunday evening (which was about 2 o'clock on Monday morning with us), and told in a blur that the Titanic had struck an iceberg and was sinking. Even at the moment of going to press we know few details of the disaster, for the Carpathia, which reached the fatal spot at daybreak on Monday, had not reached New York until we had printed off these pages. But bad news travels quickly, even in an ice-strewn sea, and it was not long before we learned that only 868, or about a third of the human freight on the ship, had been rescued, the vessel with the rest going to the bottom, two miles below. The tragedy is intensified by the fact that 1500 doomed beings were kept in suspense for four hours waiting for help that never came.

SAVED—TWO BRIDES : Mrs. Astor and Mrs. Marvin.

THE LIFEBOATS OF THE VESSEL

**S O S**

THE MARCONI DANGER SIGNAL, "S.O.S." WHICH REPLACED THE OLD SIGNAL, "C.Q.D."

MR. BRUCE ISMAY    SIR C. DUFF-GORDON

THE SPACE WHICH THE TITANIC WOULD HAVE FILLED IF SHE HAD BEEN PLACED ACROSS TRAFALGAR SQUARE (with the stern in the White Star office in Cockspur Street).

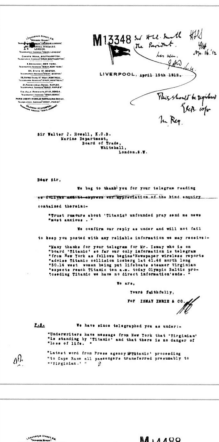

ator and although nothing specific seems to have been gleaned from the former, the latter's role would lead to the suggestion of 24 hour manning of the wireless in future. Also of significance at the American inquiry were the three witnesses from the *Californian*, including Captain Lord who gave a factual account of the night's happenings from his point of view, while his fireman, Barrett, repeated his statement that he had seen a large ship and rockets being fired close to his own ship. In addition the radio operator, Cyril Evans, said that his captain had been informed three times about the rockets. The ordeal was far from over for Captain Lord, who would also be asked to appear in London at the British inquiry soon after.

As well as noting the bravery of the band and the Marconi operators, the inquiry looked at the fatalities amongst the engineers. 'The engineering department consisted of 327 men. Of these, 72 survived but including not a single one of the engineering officers'. The above is a quote taken from the American inquiry, and presumably much was made of the valour and professionalism which those men displayed to make the fatalities so high in that particular department. There were not just a few lights burning to help make evacuation possible, as remarks of the witnesses confirmed the sheer extent of the illumination (although the devotion of the engineers was commended at the time, even by King George the V of England, it seems that very little has been said in the following eight decades).

The committee's final report and recommendations were published on 28 May, 1912, only three days after the proceedings had ended. As well as setting out a narrative of the event, they also spotlighted the lack of lifeboat capacity together with the problems experienced in loading and lowering them. There was detailed discussion of the various wireless messages sent, and a considerable number of recommendations. These ranged widely from obvious improvements in the provision and equipping of lifeboats, through regulations to be applied to the manning and operation of maritime radio stations, to rules for the use of pyrotechnics at sea and substantial improvements in the design and construction of commercial vessels. The report also highlighted in favourable terms, the actions of Captain Rostron — Senator Smith subsequently asked that legislation be enacted to allow the striking of a commemorative medal which would be presented to the Captain by the President of the United States. However, the report also contained criticism of the professional conduct of Captain Smith who was held to have acted negligently in proceeding at speed through a known icefield. Senator Smith remarked; 'Captain Smith knew the sea and his clear eye had often guided his ship through dangerous paths. Overconfidence seems to have dulled the faculties usually so alert'. The British government itself did not escape censure, and was lambasted for failing to ensure that adequate provision was made for a potential disaster on this scale. To British eyes, the Americans were brash and erratic and did not know how to conduct a 'formal' investigation — as might be expected, the results of their inquiry were not received with the greatest of pleasure in the United Kingdom. However, one finding was eventually echoed and accepted at the subsequent British inquiry. This concerned Captain Lord of the *Californian* who was roundly condemned for

his apparent inactivity on the night and was held to have been grossly negligent. It was strongly hinted that, if he had heeded what were assumed to have been unambiguous distress signals from the *Titanic*, his ship could have reached the scene before the liner sank and he could have rescued far more people than were actually in the lifeboats.

The British inquiry was more technical and in many ways a more weighty affair. The 'Formal Investigation into the loss of the Steamship Titanic', by The British Board of Trade began on 2 May, 1912, while the American inquiry was still in progress. It was held, rather incongruously, in the drill hall of the London Scottish Regiment, not far from Buckingham Palace and was under the direction of Lord Mersey, otherwise known as Mr. Justice Bingham, Baron Mersey of Toxteth (Lancashire). Other members of the board of inquiry, known as assessors, included experts in naval architecture and marine engineering as well as professional seamen. The Board of Trade was represented by a formidable selection of the legal profession led by the Attorney General himself, Sir Rufus Isaacs Q.C., while other legal worthies represented various interested parties including the White Star Line, the National Seamen's and Firemen's Union, the *Californian*'s owners and crew, and the passengers. Notorious survivors, Sir Cosmo and Lady Duff-Gordon had their own legal representatives. The inquiry took the form of 26 questions presented by Sir Rufus Isaacs, to which the proceedings would attempt to establish answers. Most of these covered predictable matters such as the design and construction of the vessels, the events leading up to the tragedy and the aftermath of the sinking. The most controversial ques-

ABOVE: *Following the* Titanic *tragedy, firemen on* Olympic *went on strike at the end of April 1912, refusing to sail. The reasons given were that they felt the collapsible boats were not seaworthy, and that many of the crew were not up to scratch; however, there were also inter-union problems that may have contributed. In the end 53 men were arrested and tried on the charge of mutiny: they are seen here waiting on the steps of Portsmouth Town Hall. The court found them guilty in early May but they went unpunished. The* Daily Sketch *of Monday 6 May, 1912, reported Sir Thomas Bramsdon Chairman of the Bench, as saying that the* Titanic *disaster was in the minds of the defendants, and that the men had done what on any other occasion they would not have done.*

ABOVE LEFT: *White Star letter sent to Father Browne on 4 March, 1913*

CENTRE LEFT: *The first message to the Marine Board of Trade from the White Star Line reassures the Board that there is no loss of life from* Titanic *and that all passengers are presumed safe on the* Virginian.

BELOW LEFT: *A second communication from the White Star Line to the Board of Trade correcting the previous day's telegram and admitting to the dreadful news that* Titanic *had sunk with great loss of life.*

*ABOVE: Survivors arriving in England. At centre is Fifth Officer Harold Godfrey Lowe, who struggled manfully to get the lifeboats launched from the Boat deck. It was Lowe who fired shots to dissuade passengers from jumping into Boat 14 as it was lowered, and who later supervised boats 4, 10, 14 and collapsible D once they were in the water.*

tion turned out to be Number 24 which as originally framed, read as follows:

'What was the cause of the loss of the *Titanic* and of the loss of lives which thereby ensued or occurred? Was the construction of the vessel and its arrangement such as to make it difficult for any class of passenger or any portion of the crew to take full advantage of the existing provisions for safety?'

This question, or rather two as written, which was already loaded with enough implications and innuendo was altered during the course of the inquiry at the instigation of the Attorney General by the insertion of a further query which read;

'What vessels had the opportunity of rendering assistance to the *Titanic*, and, if any, how was it that assistance did not reach the *Titanic* before the steamship *Carpathia* arrived.'

This was squarely aimed at Captain Lord of the *Californian*, who was grilled at some length by the Attorney General, while the somewhat conflicting evidence of other officers and crew members was to be selectively handled in the final report. However, Lord was not the only person who caused more than usual public interest in what otherwise became a lengthy, technical, and, ultimately, rather boring affair. The occupants of lifeboat number 1 had included the wealthy Sir Cosmo Duff-Gordon and his society wife and fashion entrepreneur, Lady Lucy Duff-Gordon. On the fifth day of the proceedings, Leading Fireman Charles Hendrickson, who had been assigned to this boat, stated that he had wanted to go back and rescue screaming survivors in the water but that the Duff-Gordons had prevented him, even though the boat was less than half full. He also confirmed that he and the other crew members in the boat had each received a cheque for £5 from Sir Cosmo before the *Carpathia* reached New York. Subsequently, no less than one and a half days of the inquiry's expensive time was spent exploring every little idiosyncrasy of this drama and Sir Cosmo himself was called to give his account, which was basically that he had given the money in recognition that the seaman had lost everything and out of sheer gratitude for surviving. He denied that he or his wife had obstructed any attempt to rescue other survivors but admitted that no such attempt had actually been made. Much of London's polite society turned out to see how the Duff-Gordons would fare but otherwise public interest waned as the inquiry dragged on. Not that there was a shortage of interesting witnesses although, unlike the American hearing, no passengers except the Duff-Gordons were called to give evidence. The surviving ship's officers, Lightoller, Pitman, Boxhall and Lowe, were all put through the mill with Lightoller himself answering no fewer than 1,600 questions.

Representing Harland & Wolff was the naval architect Edward Wilding. The prompt, totally correct, actions of First Officer Murdoch on being told of the iceberg ahead have already been recounted. However, Wilding, revealed that if the *Titanic* had maintained its course and speed and hit the iceberg

*BELOW: Survivors are transferred to a Great Western Railway tender to be taken ashore at Plymouth.*

*LEFT: A requiem mass was held in St. Colman's Cathedral, Queenstown, on 22 April, 1922. Presiding was Father Browne's uncle, Bishop Robert Browne.*

head on, she would not have sunk although there would have been considerable damage to the bow section and around 200 casualties, (mostly amongst crew members and third class passengers accommodated in that part of the ship). Of course, nobody seriously suggested that Murdoch should have acted other than he did but, if the lookouts had not sighted the iceberg until a few seconds later, it might have changed the outcome. Ismay and Sanderson, White Star Line directors, did their best to convince the inquiry that the *Titanic* complied with all regulations and that the former had not influenced Captain Smith's actions in any way. While condemning the prevalent practice of continuing at speed into an area known to contain ice, the Board exonerated White Star since their regulations governing navigational practice cautioned against such conduct. Independent witnesses included the noted explorer, Sir Ernest Shackelton, who gave his expert opinion on the characteristics of icepacks and icebergs and an assessment of how likely it was that a particular icefloe would be seen under various conditions. The closing days of the hearing were occupied with the testimony of various technical witnesses, including some significant statements from respected mariners who confirmed that it was not accepted practice at the time for ships to slow down when ice was known to be in the vicinity. The Inquiry made a note that despite the disaster, sea travel appeared to be extremely safe and the point was made that in the previous 20 years there had been an estimated 32,000 Atlantic crossings in which a total of only 148 people had died as a result of marine accidents.

After the last witness had appeared on 21 June, 1912, a further eight days were occupied with submissions and statements by counsels for the various interested parties and it was not until 3 July, after 36 arduous working days, that the official inquiry was ended. Lord Mersey presented his final report on 30 July, and it contained no surprises. In fact, considering the nature and scale of the tragedy, it was remarkably restrained. It found that the basic cause was that the *Titanic* was being navigated at excessive speed in view of the conditions but, nevertheless, did not find Captain Smith to have been negligent in this respect. For his part Lord Mersey 'hoped that the last has been heard of the practice. What was a mistake in the case of *Titanic* would, without doubt, be negligence in any similar case in the future'. There was criticism of the arrangements for manning the lifeboats and the Board of Trade was castigated for not ensuring that its regulations had kept pace with technological progress. Both Bruce Ismay and Sir Cosmo Duff-Gordon were found not to have acted improperly and, once again, Captain Rostron of the *Carpathia* was praised for his actions. However the Board did arrive at a conclusion which differs radically from the modern day interpretation of how *Titanic* actually went down; the evidence of eye witnesses was, as usual, conflicting. Some say that she slid under, intact, at about 45 degrees. Others said that the stern levelled off before she sank. Whilst not conclusive the British Board of Trade accepted that she sank in one piece;

'Her stern was gradually rising out of the water, the propellers were clear

*continued page 356*

*A fine tribute to the engineers and boiler room staff of the* Titanic, *the 'black squad', who stood to their posts in the bowels of the ship, to the last, was paid by Lord Charles Beresford in a letter to* The Times. *He wrote:*

'In the late appalling disaster to the *Titanic*, perhaps the greatest in maritime history, attention has rightly been called to the bravery, resolution, and chivalrous gallantry of Captain Smith, the officers, seamen, band and passengers, who were true to the spirit of manly duty of the English speaking races in a sudden and terrible emergency.

'Many comments have been justly made regarding the heroism on deck, but nothing has been said of the heroism below.

'I respectfully submit that unintentionally the dauntless heroism of those employed in the engine and boiler room (such as the carpenter and his crew), have been passed over without comment.

'Nothing can exceed the heroism of the captain, officers, and seamen of the ship; but officers and seamen are the first to offer a whole-hearted tribute of unbounded admiration to those working below, as they well know how often the real grit and courage of the officers and men of these departments is called upon in moments of emergency.

'It is stated that the lights were burning until a few minutes before the ship took her final plunge.

'This proves that the officers and men below remained at their posts when they must have known that death — the most terrible and painful that it is possible to conceive — awaited them at any minute, either by the bursting of a steampipe or water rising in a compartment.

'It is certain that those working below must have known the awful danger the ship was in long before anybody else, but they remained at their posts, resolving to die sooner than come on deck and create a panic of attempting to save themselves.

'Those below must have heard the muffled sound of the ice tearing through the ship's side.

'Within ten minutes or a little more they knew that the pumps would not check the rising water, yet for over two hours they remained at their posts, as was evinced by the lights burning and the few of them who were saved being picked up after the ship went down.

'That so many people were saved was due to the fact that those working below remained at their posts working the dynamos and kept the lights burning, and never came on deck to state what had really happened.

'Again and again the indomitable pluck and discipline of those who work below in the engine and boiler room is illustrated when some disaster of the sea occurs, but on no occasion have these traits been more brilliantly shown.

'It should be remembered that those below work in confined spaces, watertight doors closed, often in intolerable heat, with a roar of machinery making orders difficult to understand.

'A man will face death with greater equanimity on deck than working below under the incidents I have mentioned.

'Working below really requires more fortitude or pluck.

'All honour and respect to those men whose names will be recorded on the roll of fame for gallantry in a sudden and unlooked-for disaster. But I am sure the survivors of this shocking catastrophe will agree with me in placing those who worked below on "The right of the line".

'At the time of the disaster, says *The Times*, the first watch in the engine-room was on duty, the second watch was off duty, and the third watch was asleep. When the alarm was sent round every man on board ship, from captain to boy, would be called to take up his allotted station. The engine-room staff ordinarily take part in boat drill. The fact that none of the engineers was saved is attributed to the circumstance that they would all be required at their stations below, not only in the engine-rooms and stokeholds, but looking to the auxiliary machinery, the water-tight bulkheads, and other matters which are under the control of the chief engineer. Until released from duty, which could only be at the last moment, it is unlikely that any one of the them would be able to go up to the higher decks. This would not apply, at all events in the same degree, to the case of the stokers, and those stokers who were off duty below would, no doubt, take their part with the seamen in getting away the boats. These men, therefore, would have an opportunity to attempt to save themselves when the ship made her final plunge. The names of at least two stokers appear in the list of the saved.'

'One who has served as a chief engineer of an ocean liner and has had experience in some of the largest steamships said that the tribute led by Lord Charles Beresford to the engineers of the *Titanic* was fully deserved. The work of the engineering staff in the modern vessel was essentially of a character involving great personal risk at all times and a minimum of personal recognition.

'None would ever know', he added — 'for not a soul emerged from the engine room' — what happened during the last hours of the vessel's existence. From his experience of other, and happily less serious, accidents, he conjectured that, in accordance with practice, when the collision occurred, every one of the engineers off duty hurried to the engine room and there, down in the bowels of the ship, remained until the awful moment when the hulk rose for its final plunge into the depths. From the outset the engineers could have been under no misconceptions as to the extent of the damage to the vessel, though probably they were, for the most part, firmly of the opinion that the vessel was practically unsinkable. They kept the lights in operation and, equally important, kept up the power for the wireless system. Water was probably pouring in beyond all possibility of their doing any good with the pumps, and the boiler rooms were doubtless first flooded. The magnitude of the disaster must have been early evident to the engineers, and escape would not have been impossible, but that would have meant shirking their duty. Only those who had served in the engine room could form any idea of the terrible incidents which probably preceded the final disappearance of the vessel. The devotion of her engineering staff was beyond praise.'

NEXT PAGE: *Children putting money into a collection box in aid of the victims of the disaster, outside the Mansion House, London.*

*Unsurprisingly, there was much debate after the disaster about the number of lifeboats* Titanic *carried and the Board of Trade rules that pertained to lifeboats. The immediate result of this was that the transatlantic liners took on extra boats as is shown in the photographs of* Lusitania *(ABOVE RIGHT) and* Baltic *(CENTRE RIGHT). Also examined were motorised lifeboats — which would have made saving people in the water easier, Seen here is a 28 ft boat planned for use on* Aquitania *on builder's trials. A more fanciful notion was provided by* The Graphic *— detachable decks which could be converted into rafts (ABOVE).*

out of the water. The ship did not break in two: and she did eventually attain the perpendicular, when the second funnel from aft about reached the water. There were no lights burning then, though they kept alight practically until the last'.

With the aide of modern science and technology the final moments of *Titanic* are now generally believed to be as follows. At 2:18 a.m., the ship broke in two, almost instantly rupturing the lines through which steam was still flowing to the generator engines. The lights go out, and any men remaining in the reciprocating engine room meet their fate at that moment. At 2:20 a.m. the broken off stern plunges beneath the surface, following the bow section which had sunk a minute or two earlier.

Although the inquiry was by no means a court of law, it effectively found Captain Lord of the *Californian* guilty of gross negligence and implied that he was directly responsible for the loss of the many souls which it was alleged that he could have rescued. Despite their differences of style and tone the two enquiries had reached similar basic conclusions. The American inquiry strongly criticized the insufficient number of lifeboats, whereas the British felt this obscured the real fundamental design shortcoming; there was a fatal flaw in the design of the compartments formed by the watertight bulkheads: they were not, in themselves, independently watertight. There was no covering watertight deck to cap them (as was included in the contemporary Cunard liners, *Lusitania* and *Mauretania*). The effect of this was that water actually filled a compartment to above the top of the watertight bulkhead, and then flowed into the adjoining compartment and flooded that one in turn. The two inquiries differed most widely in their conclusions surrounding the Titanic's master, the British exonerating Smith, the Americans attributing blame to his judgment which they felt amounted to negligence. Both inquiries agreed that once the ship had been damaged nothing could have been done to save her. However, more of her passengers could have been saved had the crew been better acquainted with the launching and manning of the lifeboats. Recommendations were made for 24 hour wireless operations on board liners, for more frequent lifeboat drills, and for the steering of a more southerly route across the Atlantic. (In 1913 the first International Convention for Safety at Sea met in London. All the above safety measures were agreed with the addition of the deployment of international ice patrols for the north Atlantic shipping lanes.)

And that was the end of the inquiries. Many factors brought about the end of the ship but the undeniable truth was that man had placed too much faith in his own invention until, finally, he had deluded himself. Perhaps the Bishop of Winchester was right when he referred to the *Titanic* as a 'monument to human presumption'.

However, the end of the official inquiries by no means marked the end of legal activity. Indeed it was only the start as companies and individuals sought damages and compensation from the White Star Line for the loss of relatives, goods, and cargo. They had, of necessity, awaited the outcome of the official inquiries before proceeding with their own cases: had the White

Star Line or its servants or agents been found plainly negligent in the discharge of their responsibilities, then the way would have been clear for all concerned to press ahead with their claims for massive damages. As it was, neither inquiry made a clear-cut assignment of responsibility and it therefore appeared unlikely that claimants in the United Kingdom would receive anything beyond the meagre allowances under the Merchant Shipping Act. In America, several major claims were filed and these were considered by the Southern District Court for the State of New York, the total involved being in the region of almost $17 million. The White Star Line contested these claims and brought a counter suit to American courts in which it sought to limit its liabilities to the salvage value of the *Titanic*'s assets, as permitted under American law. These consisted of the value of the 13 lifeboats recovered by the *Carpathia*, together with pre-paid freight charges and revenue from passenger tickets, which together came to $97,772. However, it was eventually ruled that British law would stand in this instance and the battle between the legal representatives of the claimants and those of White Star intensified. The hearing of these cases dragged on for some time, and probably would have continued for longer had it not been for the outbreak of the First World War which forced attention onto other issues. In the end the lawyers for the various parties agreed on a settlement under which the sum of $663,000 was

*Right: Statement of Claim*
*The scramble to deny responsibility for the loss of the* Titanic *was carried out at the highest levels in both London and Washington, at the end of which no general compensation was paid out. Tickets issued by the White Star Line for* Titanic *were not in line with Board of Trade requirements but they still held good in the courts. On the back, each ticket stated that the owners would not be liable for any loss or damage caused by the negligent navigation of the vessel by the company or its servants. This document is the written judgement on the claim brought in the High Court of Justice between Thomas Ryan, the father of a victim, and the Oceanic Steam Navigation Company Ltd (otherwise known as the White Star Line). Patrick Ryan and James Moran both drowned in the disaster and their families united to sue the owners for negligence based on the findings of the Commission of Enquiry. The judge awarded in favour of the plaintiffs. The company appealed but the verdict was upheld.*

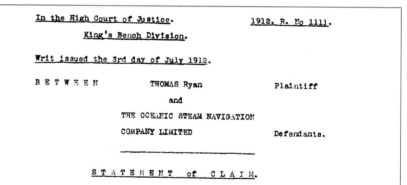

In the High Court of Justice.                1912. R. No 1111.
          King's Bench Division.

Writ issued the 3rd day of July 1912.

B E T W E E N          THOMAS Ryan          Plaintiff
                          and
              THE OCEANIC STEAM NAVIGATION
              COMPANY LIMITED               Defendants.
              _____

              S T A T E M E N T   of   C L A I M.

          The Plaintiff brings this action for the benefit of himself the father of Patrick Ryan deceased he having suffered damage from the Defendants' negligence in carrying the said Patrick Ryan on their Steamship "Titanic" on a voyage from Queenstown to New York hereby the said Patrick Ryan was drowned in consequence of the said ship colliding with an Iceberg and foundering in the North Atlantic Ocean on the 15th April 1912.
              Particulars of negligence.
          The negligence of the Defendants servants consisted in this that they navigated the said Ship at an excessive speed and at an improper speed in view of the conditions then prevailing namely the exceptional darkness of the night the hazy condition of the atmosphere the absence of wind and movement of the sea at and immediately preceding the time of the collision and of the presence of icebergs and fields of ice in the course of the said vessel: that while knowing of the presence of the said ice they failed to alter their course or to diminish their speed so as to avoid the same and failed to provide a sufficient and proper look-out therefor and to supply look-out men with Binoculars: that no adequate lifeboat accommodation was provided on the said Ship having regard to the number of passengers and crew she

paid to the claimants, to be distributed on a pro rata basis, and the proceedings were formally closed on 28 July, 1916.

THE TESTIMONY OF J. BRUCE ISMAY

On Friday, 19 April, 1912, J. Bruce Ismay was called before the Subcommittee of the Committee on Commerce, of the United States Senate, which sat 'to investigate the loss of the steamship *Titanic*.' The exchanges were published in the committee's report. This is an extract from that report:

The subcommittee met at 10:30 a.m.
Present: Senator William Alden Smith, chairman, and Senator Francis G. Newlands.
Present also: Mr George Uhler, Supervising Inspector General, Steamboat-Inspection Service, Department of Commerce and Labor; Mr. J. Bruce Ismay, general manager of the International Mercantile Marine Company; Charles C. Burlingham, Esq., and J. Parker Kirlin, Esq., representing the White Star Line; Emerson E. Parvin, Esq., secretary International Mercantile Marine Company; Guglielmo Marconi, president of the Marconi Wireless Telegraph Company; Hon. John W. Griggs, representing the Marconi Wireless Telegraph Company, and others.

Senator SMITH. For the purpose of executing the command and direction of the Senate of the United States, the inquiry which we contemplate will now begin. The resolution is as follows:

IN THE SENATE OF THE UNITED STATES
17 April, 1912

Resolved, That the Committee on Commerce, or a subcommittee thereof, is hereby authorized and directed to investigate the causes leading to the wreck of the White Star liner *Titanic*, with its attendant loss of life so shocking to the civilized world.

Resolved further, That said committee or a subcommittee thereof is hereby empowered to summon witnesses, send for persons and papers, to administer oaths, and to take such testimony as may be necessary to determine the responsibility therefor, with a view to such legislation as may be necessary to prevent, as far as possible, any repetition of such a disaster.

Resolved further, That the committee shall inquire particularly into the number of life boats, life rafts, and life preservers, and other equipment for the protection of the passengers and crew; the number of persons aboard the *Titanic*, whether passenger or crew, and whether adequate inspections were made of such vessel, in view of the large number of American passengers travelling over a route commonly regarded as dangerous from icebergs; and whether it is feasible for Congress to take steps looking to an international agreement to secure the protection of sea traffic, including regulation of the size of ships and designation of routes.

Resolved further, That in the report of said committee it shall recommend

# In the High Court of Justice

KING'S BENCH DIVISION.

1912, R, No. 1111

BETWEEN

Thomas Ryan

Plaintiff,

AND

Oceanic Steam Navigation
Company Limited

Defendants

I CERTIFY that this action was tried before The Honourable M: Justice
Bailhache

and a Special Jury of the County of Middlesex,
on the 20ᵗʰ, 23ʳᵈ 24ᵗʰ, 25ᵗʰ & 26ᵗʰ days of June 1913.

On the question of negligence
THE JURY FOUND answers to the following questions :—
1. Was the navigation of the Titanic negligent in respect
of (A) look out ? Ans: No (B) Speed ? Ans: Yes.
2. Was the marconigram from the Mesaba communicated
in due course to some responsible officer of the
Titanic ? Ans: Not evidence sufficient.
On the question of contract the jury found answers to the
~~The Jury found that Judgment should be entered for the~~ following question:—
1. Did the Defendants do what was reasonably sufficient
to give Moran notice of the conditions having regard
to Moran's condition in life ? Ans: No.
2. Did the Defendants do what was reasonably sufficient
to give Ryan notice of the conditions having regard to
Ryan's condition in life ? Ans: No.
and by consent assessed the damages at £100 —
The Judge directed that Judgment should be entered

(over)

360

(22,225). Wt.34,764—1440. 2500. 3/10. A.&E.W.

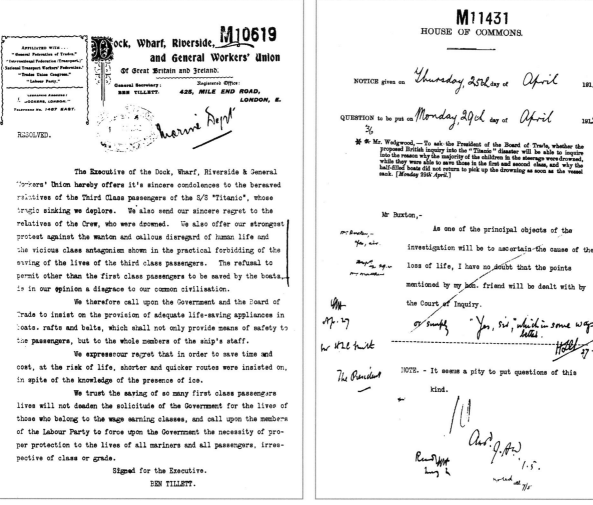

**Dock, Wharf, Riverside, M10619 and General Workers' Union**
**Of Great Britain and Ireland.**

AFFILIATED WITH...
"General Federation of Trades."
"International Federation (Transport)."
National Transport Workers' Federation.
"Trades Union Congress."
"Labour Party."

TELEGRAPHIC ADDRESS:
"DOCKERS, LONDON."
TELEPHONE No. 1467 EAST.

General Secretary: BEN TILLETT.

Registered Office: 425, MILE END ROAD, LONDON, E.

RESOLVED.

The Executive of the Dock, Wharf, Riverside & General Workers' Union hereby offers it's sincere condolences to the bereaved relatives of the Third Class passengers of the S/S "Titanic", whose tragic sinking we deplore. We also send our sincere regret to the relatives of the Crew, who were drowned. We also offer our strongest protest against the wanton and callous disregard of human life and the vicious class antagonism shown in the practical forbidding of the saving of the lives of the third class passengers. The refusal to permit other than the first class passengers to be saved by the boats, is in our opinion a disgrace to our common civilisation.

We therefore call upon the Government and the Board of Trade to insist on the provision of adequate life-saving appliances in boats. rafts and belts, which shall not only provide means of safety to the passengers, but to the whole members of the ship's staff.

We express our regret that in order to save time and cost, at the risk of life, shorter and quicker routes were insisted on, in spite of the knowledge of the presence of ice.

We trust the saving of so many first class passengers lives will not deaden the solicitude of the Government for the lives of those who belong to the wage earning classes, and call upon the members of the Labour Party to force upon the Government the necessity of proper protection to the lives of all mariners and all passengers, irrespective of class or grade.

Signed for the Executive.
BEN TILLETT.

**M11431**
HOUSE OF COMMONS.

NOTICE given on Thursday, 25th day of April 1912

QUESTION to be put on Monday, 29th day of April 1912

36

Mr. Wedgwood, — To ask the President of the Board of Trade, whether the proposed British inquiry into the "Titanic" disaster will be able to inquire into the reason why the majority of the children in the steerage were drowned, while they were able to save those in the first and second class, and why the half-filled boats did not return to pick up the drowning as soon as the vessel sank. [*Monday 29th April.*]

Mr Buxton,-

As one of the principal objects of the investigation will be to ascertain the cause of the loss of life, I have no doubt that the points mentioned by my hon. friend will be dealt with by the Court of Inquiry.

NOTE. - It seems a pity to put questions of this kind.

---

such legislation as it shall deem expedient; and the expenses incurred by this investigation shall be paid from the contingent fund of the Senate upon vouchers to be approved by the chairman of said committee.

Attest:

CHARLES G. BENNETT, Secretary.

By H.M. ROSE, Assistant Secretary.

I will ask Mr J. Bruce Ismay to come forward and take the stand.

Mr J. Bruce Ismay, being duly sworn by the chairman, testified as follows:

Senator SMITH. Mr Ismay, for the purpose of simplifying this hearing, I will ask you a few preliminary questions.

First state your full name, please.

Mr. ISMAY. Joseph Bruce Ismay.

Senator SMITH. And your place of residence?

Mr. ISMAY. Liverpool.

Senator SMITH. And your age?

Mr. ISMAY. I shall be 50 on the 12th of December.

Senator SMITH. And your occupation?

Mr. ISMAY. Ship owner.

Senator SMITH. Are you an officer of the White Star Line?

Mr. ISMAY. I am.

Senator SMITH. In what capacity.

*ABOVE LEFT: Union and employer relations at this time were not good and the Titanic disaster only made matters worse as this letter shows. At the heart of this is the indisputable fact that more people were rescued from first and second class than from the third class and crew. This is ascribed to class prejudice by Ben Tillett, one of the leaders of the Dock, Wharf, Riverside and General Workers' Union.*

*ABOVE: This question was put by Josiah Wedgwood, the Liberal M.P. for Newcastle-under-Lyme to the President of the Board of Trade. In it he asks why more children died in third class than in the rest of the ship.*

*LEFT: The writ between Thomas Ryan and the Oceanic Steam Navigation Company Ltd. The particulars of the negligence were:
'. . .that they navigated the said Ship at an . . . improper speed in view of the conditions then prevailing namely the exceptional darkness of the night, the hazy condition of the atmosphere the absence of wind and movement of the sea at . . . the time of the collision and of the presence of icebergs and fields of ice in the course of the said vessel . . . and failed to provide a sufficient . . . look-out therefore and to supply look-out men with Binoculars: that no adequate lifeboat accommodation was provided on the said Ship having regard to the number of passengers and crew she was then carrying: and that the Defendants failed to have the said crew sufficiently drilled . . . for the work of manning filling and launching such lifeboats as were provided . . .'*

*ABOVE: J. Bruce Ismay.*

Mr. ISMAY. Managing director.

Senator SMITH. As such officer were you officially designated to make the trial trip of the *Titanic*?

Mr. ISMAY. No.

Senator SMITH. Were you a voluntary passenger?

Mr. ISMAY. A voluntary passenger; yes.

Senator SMITH. Where did you board the ship?

Mr. ISMAY. At Southampton.

Senator SMITH. At what time?

Mr. ISMAY. I think it was at 9:30 in the morning.

Senator SMITH. Of what day?

Mr. ISMAY. The 10th of April.

Senator SMITH. The port of destination was New York?

Mr. ISMAY. New York.

Senator SMITH. Will you kindly tell the committee the circumstances surrounding your voyage, and, as succinctly as possible, beginning with your going aboard the vessel at Liverpool, your place on the ship on the voyage, together with any circumstances you feel would be helpful to us in this inquiry?

Mr. ISMAY. In the first place. I would like to express my sincere grief at this deplorable catastrophe.

I understand that you gentlemen have been appointed as a committee of the Senate to inquire into the circumstances. So far as we are concerned, we welcome it. We court the fullest inquiry. We have nothing to conceal; nothing to hide. The ship was built in Belfast. She was the latest thing in the art of shipbuilding; absolutely no money was spared in her construction. She was not built by contract. She was simply built on a commission.

She left Belfast, as far as I can remember — I am not absolutely clear about these dates — I think it was the on the 1st of April.

She underwent her trials, which were entirely satisfactory. She then proceeded to Southampton, arriving there on wednesday.

Senator SMITH. Will you describe the trials she went through?

Mr. ISMAY. I was not present.

She arrived at Southampton on wednesday, the 3rd, I think, and sailed on wednesday, the 10th. She left Southampton at 12 o'clock.

She arrived in Cherbourg that evening, having run over at 68 revolutions.

We left Cherbourg and proceeded to Queenstown. We arrived there, I think, about midday on Thursday.

We ran from Cherbourg to Queenstown at 70 revolutions.

After embarking the mails and passengers, we proceeded at 70 revolutions. I am not absolutely clear what the first day's run was, whether it was 464 miles or 484 miles.

The second day the number of revolutions was increased to 75, and I think we ran for 546 or 549 miles.

The weather during this time was absolutely fine, with the exception, I think, of about 10 minutes fog one evening.

The accident took place on sunday night. What the exact time was I do not know. I was in bed myself, asleep, when the accident happened.

The ship sank, I am told, at 2:20.

That, sir, I think is all I can tell you.

I understand it has been stated that ship was going at full speed. The ship never had been at full speed. The full speed of the ship is 78 revolutions. She works up to 80. So far as I am aware, she never exceeded 75 revolutions. She had not all her boilers on. None of the single-ended boilers were on.

It was our intention, if we had fine weather on Monday afternoon or Tuesday, to drive the ship at full speed. That, owing to the unfortunate catastrophe, never eventuated.

Senator SMITH. Will you describe what you did after the impact or collision?

Mr. ISMAY. I presume the impact awakened me. I lay in bed for a moment or two afterwards, not realizing, probably, what had happened. Eventually I got up and walked along the passageway and met one of the stewards, and said, 'What has happened?' He said, 'I do not know, sir'.

I then went back into my room, put my coat on, and went up on the bridge, where I found Captain Smith. I asked him what had happened, and he said, 'We have struck ice'. I said, 'Do you think the ship is seriously damaged?' He said, 'I am afraid she is'.

I then went down below, I think it was where I met Mr. Bell, the chief engineer, who was in the main companionway. I asked if he thought the ship was seriously damaged, and he said he thought she was, but was quite satisfied the pumps would keep her afloat.

I think I went back onto the bridge. I heard the order given to get the boats out. I walked along to the starboard side of the ship where I met one of the officers. I told him to get the boats out.

Senator SMITH. What officer?

Mr. ISMAY. That I could not remember, sir.

I assisted, as best I could, getting the boats out and putting the women and children into the boats.

I stood upon that deck practically until I left the ship in the starboard collapsible boat, which is the last boat to leave the ship, so far as I know. More than that I do not know.

Senator SMITH. Did the captain remain on the bridge?

Mr. ISMAY. That I could not tell you, sir.

Senator SMITH. Did you leave him on the bridge?

Mr. ISMAY. Yes, sir.

Senator SMITH. And the next statement of the chief engineer was what?

Mr. ISMAY. To the same effect.

Senator SMITH. To the same effect?

Mr. ISMAY. Yes.

Senator SMITH. Did you have any talk with any officer other than the captain or the chief engineer and the steward that you met?

Mr. ISMAY. Not that I remember.

Senator SMITH. Did the officers seem to know the serious character of this collision?

*Alfred Fernand Omont on his oath saith as follows*

*I am a cotton agent at Havre. I joined the Titanic at Cherbourg on the 10th April as a 1st class passenger . . .*

*On Sunday the 14th April so far as I know there was no boat drill — I am practically sure.*

*The captain was in the Saloon at dinner on . . . 14th April . . . Monsieur Marechal remarked to me that the Captain was with a party and seemed very happy and very confident in his boat. Then we went and played Bridge in the 'Café Parisien'. We played on until about 11.40pm and then there was a shock. I have crossed the Atlantic 13 times, and the shock was not a great one, and I thought it was caused by a wave. After a few minutes I asked the waiter to put down the port-hole, and he did so, and we saw nothing. When the shock had happened, we saw something white through the port-holes, and we saw water on the ports . . .*

*About a minute after the waiter had opened the port holes we all left the café . . . We waited a very long time, and everybody told us there was nothing at all. About 12.30 we saw the Captain and the 1st officer going up to the bridge. All around about 50 or 60 women and men were waiting anxiously to know what was happening. The Captain came down . . . and he said 'You had better put your life-preservers on, as a precaution.' Then I went down to my cabin, a few floors down, and I put my life-belt on. Then I went up to the boat deck, and it was deadly cold. I came back to my own cabin, took off my life-belt and put on my overcoat. Then I came up, and put on again my life-belt. I was then on the boat deck. I saw them get*

Mr. ISMAY. That I could not tell, sir, because I had no conversation with them.

Senator SMITH. Did any officer say to you that it evidently was not serious?

Mr. ISMAY. No, sir.

Senator SMITH. All the officers with whom you talked expressed the same fear, saying that it was serious?

Mr. ISMAY. I did not speak to any of them, sir.

Senator SMITH. Except the captain?

Mr. ISMAY. Except the captain and the chief engineer. I have already stated that I had spoken to them; but to no other officer that I remember.

Senator SMITH. You went to the bridge immediately after you had returned to your room?

Mr. ISMAY. After I had put on my coat I went up to the bridge.

Senator SMITH. And you found the captain there?

Mr. ISMAY. The captain was there.

Senator SMITH. In what part of the ship were your quarters?

Mr. ISMAY. My quarters were on B deck, just aft of the main companion-way.

Senator SMITH. I wish you would describe just where that was.

Mr. ISMAY. The sun deck is the upper deck of all. Then we have what we call the A deck, which is the next deck, and then the B deck.

Senator SMITH. The second passenger deck?

Mr. ISMAY. We carry very few passengers on A deck. I think we have a diagram here that will show you these decks. Here it is, and there is the room I was occupying (indicating on diagram).

Senator SMITH. What is the number of that room?

Mr. ISMAY. B-52 is the room I had.

Senator SMITH. You had the suite?

Mr. ISMAY. I had the suite; I was sleeping in that room (indicating on diagram), as a matter of fact.

Senator SMITH. Do you know whether there were any passengers on that deck?

Mr. ISMAY. I have no idea, sir.

Senator SMITH. You say that the trip was a voluntary trip on your part?

Mr. ISMAY. Absolutely.

Senator SMITH. For the purpose of viewing this ship in action, or did you have some business in New York?

Mr. ISMAY. I had no business to bring me to New York at all. I simply came in the natural course of events, as one is apt to, in the case of a new ship, to see how she works, and with the idea of seeing how we could improve on her for the next ship we are building.

Senator SMITH. Was the inspector or builder on board?

Mr. ISMAY. There was a representative of the builders on board.

Senator SMITH. Who was he?

Mr. ISMAY. Mr. Thomas Andrews.

Senator SMITH. In what capacity was he?

Mr. ISMAY. I do not quite follow you.

Senator SMITH. What was the occasion for his coming to make this trial trip?

Mr. ISMAY. As a representative of the builders, to see that everything was working satisfactorily, and also to see how he could improve the next ship.

Senator SMITH. Was he a man of large experience?

Mr. ISMAY. Yes.

Senator SMITH. Had he had part in the construction of this ship himself?

Mr. ISMAY. Yes.

Senator SMITH. Was he among the survivors?

Mr. ISMAY. Unfortunately, no.

Senator SMITH. How old a man was he?

Mr. ISMAY. It is difficult to judge a man's age, as you know, but I should think he was perhaps 42 or 43 years of age. He may have been less. I really could not say.

Senator SMITH. Then, you were the only executive officer aboard representing your company, aside from the ship's customary compliment of officers?

Mr. ISMAY. Yes, sir.

Senator SMITH. Did you have occasion to consult with the captain about the movement of the ship?

Mr. ISMAY. Never.

Senator SMITH. Did he consult you about it?

Mr. ISMAY. Never. Perhaps I am wrong in saying that. I should also like to say this: I do not know that it was quite a matter of consulting him about it, or of his consulting me about it, but what we had arranged to do was that we would not attempt to arrive in New York at the lightship before 5 o'clock on wednesday morning.

Senator SMITH. That was the understanding?

Mr. ISMAY. Yes. But that was arranged before we left Queenstown.

Senator SMITH. Was it supposed that you could reach New York at that time without putting the ship to its full running capacity?

Mr. ISMAY. Oh, yes. sir. There was nothing to be gained by arriving at New York any earlier than that.

Senator SMITH. You spoke of the revolutions on the early part of the voyage.

Mr. ISMAY. Yes, sir.

Senator SMITH. Those were increased as the distance was increased?

Mr. ISMAY. The *Titanic* being a new ship, we were gradually working her up. When you bring out a new ship you naturally do not start her running at full speed until you get everything working smoothly and satisfactorily down below.

Senator SMITH. Did I understand you to say that she exceeded 70 revolutions?

Mr. ISMAY. Yes, sir; she was going 75 revolutions on tuesday.

Senator SMITH. On tuesday?

Mr. ISMAY. No; I am wrong — on saturday. I am mixed up as to the days.

Senator SMITH. The day before the accident?

Mr. ISMAY. The day before the accident. That, of course, is nothing near her

*down some boats. While I was still on the boat deck, a boat was let down. The 1st officer saw me and asked me if I wanted to get in. Some of the passengers shouted to me not to get in as they had such confidence in the ship. I saw that the sea was very calm, and on calm reason I thought it better to jump into the boat and see what would happen. I jumped two or three yards, and landed in the boat anyhow. We were 29 in the boat. the boat could not have held more than 30 in any case. I personally consider and state that the idea of putting sixty people in a boat or on a raft is ridiculous. I have a photograph in my possession which shows how ridiculous it is to attempt to put 50 or 60 persons in one of these boats or rafts. I consider it a monstrosity to state that one could put 60 persons in a boat in safety.*

*When we were being lowered, about 125yds from the sea, a man put one rope much lower than the other one and we nearly went over. Then we went down and touched water . . .*

*When we were in the water we started to row away from the ship. I was rowing. We had about 22 women on board . . . We rowed up to about 150 yards from the ship. We saw the ship sink gradually . . .*

*We had no lights in our lifeboat, no compass, no chart, but we had a small cask of water, and I heard that we had a small box of biscuits. After the ship had gone down and before, we saw a light far off, about eight or ten miles. Everyone thought it was another ship . . . We saw it plainly. We all cheered up, thinking we were going to be saved; we saw it gradually disappear.*

*We thought it was either a sailing boat that could not move on account of the very calm weather, or else an optical illusion . . .*

*Then we waited until dawn: then the Carpathia came up. We were royally treated on board the Carpathia Any man who was saved by the Carpathia will always have in his own mind the faces of the captian and officers. I know personally how much the captain of the Carpathia had at heart to save the Titanic .*

*One of the lookout men was in our boat. He told us that he had seen the iceberg about three minutes before the shock. I am no sailor, but if he did so, we must take into consideration that the ship was going 20 mph at least, ie, he saw the iceberg at 1,760 yards (and advised it) before meeting it.*

*I consider as a passenger, that two people knew that the icebergs were around us — these two are the head of the company and the Captain — I ask, how is it that neither of those two said a word for the safety of the passengers? We passengers always consider that we have to deliver our own safety to the captain, and therefore have a right to know if our life is properly looked after, and if in case of records for speed we have to risk it for the benefit of companies.*

*After the disaster, the captain and officers behaved like gentlemen.*

full speed.

Senator SMITH. During the voyage, do you know, of your own knowledge, of your proximity to icebergs?

Mr. ISMAY. Did I know that we were near icebergs?

Senator SMITH. Yes.

Mr. ISMAY. No, sir; I did not. I know ice had been reported.

Senator SMITH. Ice had been reported?

Mr. ISMAY. Yes.

Senator SMITH. Did you personally see any icebergs, or any large volume of ice?

Mr. ISMAY. No; not until after the accident.

Senator SMITH. Not until after the wreck?

Mr. ISMAY. I had never seen an iceberg in my life before.

Senator SMITH. You never saw one before.

Mr. ISMAY. No, sir.

Senator SMITH. Had you ever been on this so-called northern route before?

Mr. ISMAY. We were on the southern route, sir.

Senator SMITH. On this Newfoundland route?

Mr. ISMAY. We were on the long southern route; not on the northern route.

Senator SMITH. You were not on the extreme northern route?

Mr. ISMAY. We were on the extreme southern route for the westbound ships.

Senator SMITH. What was the longitude and latitude of this ship? Do you know?

Mr. ISMAY. That I could not tell you; I am not a sailor.

Senator SMITH. Were you cognizant of your proximity to icebergs at all on saturday?

Mr. ISMAY. On saturday? No, sir.

Senator SMITH. Do you know anything about a wireless message from the *Amerika* to the *Titanic*.

Mr. ISMAY. No, sir.

Senator SMITH. Saying that the *Amerika* had encountered ice in that latitude?

Mr. ISMAY. No, sir.

Senator SMITH. Were you aware of the proximity of icebergs on sunday?

Mr. ISMAY. On sunday? No; I did not know on sunday. I knew that we would be in the ice region that night sometime.

Senator SMITH. That you would be, or were?

Mr. ISMAY. That we would be in the ice region on sunday night.

Senator SMITH. Did you have any consultation with the captain regarding the matter.

Mr. ISMAY. Absolutely none.

Senator SMITH. Or with any other officer of the ship?

Mr. ISMAY. With no officer at all, sir. It was absolutely out of my province. I am not a navigator. I was simply a passenger on board the ship.

Senator SMITH. Did you know anything about the working of the wireless service on this ship?

Mr. ISMAY. In what way? We had wireless on the ship.

ABOVE: 'Britannia Mourns'. Sand models on Bournemouth beach.

Senator SMITH. Had you taken any unusual precaution to have a reserve power for this wireless?

Mr. ISMAY. I believe there was, but I have no knowledge of that myself.

Senator SMITH. Do you know how long the wireless continued to operate after the blow or collision?

Mr. ISMAY. No, sir; I do not.

Senator SMITH. Did you, at any time, see the operator of the wireless?

Mr. ISMAY. I did not.

Senator SMITH. Were you outside on the deck, or on any deck, when the order was given to lower the lifeboats?

Mr. ISMAY. I heard Captain Smith give the order when I was on the bridge.

Senator SMITH. You heard the captain give the order?

Mr. ISMAY. Yes, sir.

Senator SMITH. Will you tell us what he said?

Mr. ISMAY. It is very difficult for me to remember exactly what he said, sir.

Senator SMITH. As nearly as you can.

Mr. ISMAY. I know I heard him give the order to lower the boats. I think that is all he said. I think he simply turned around and gave the order.

Senator SMITH. Was there anything else said, as to how they should be manned or occupied?

Mr. ISMAY. No, sir; not that I heard. As soon as I heard him give the order to lower the boats, I left the bridge.

Senator SMITH. You left the bridge?

Mr. ISMAY. Yes.

Senator SMITH. Did you see any of the boats lowered?

Mr. ISMAY. Yes, sir.

Senator SMITH. How many?

Mr. ISMAY. Certainly three.

Senator SMITH. Will you tell us, if you can, how they were lowered?

Mr. ISMAY. They were swung out, people were put into the boats from the deck, and then they were simply lowered away down to the water.

Senator SMITH. Were these lifeboats on the various decks?

Mr. ISMAY. They were all on one deck.

Senator SMITH. On what deck?

Mr. ISMAY. On the sun deck; the deck above this (indicating on diagram). I do not think it is shown on this plan.

Senator SMITH. That is, the second deck above yours?

Mr. ISMAY. On this deck here, on the big plan (indicating).

Senator SMITH. On the sun deck?

Mr. ISMAY. Yes; on what we call the sun deck or the boat deck.

Senator SMITH. They were on the boat deck, which would be the upper deck of all?

Mr. ISMAY. The upper deck of all, yes.

Senator SMITH. Was there any order or supervision exercised by the officers of the ship in loading these lifeboats?

Mr. ISMAY. Yes, sir.

Senator SMITH. I wish you would tell us just what that was.

Mr. ISMAY. That I could not say. I could only speak from what I saw for myself.

Senator SMITH. That is all I wish you to do.

Mr. ISMAY. The boats that were lowered where I was were in charge of the officers and were filled and lowered away.

Senator SMITH. They first put men into the boats for the purpose of controlling them?

Mr. ISMAY. We put in some of the ship's people.

Senator SMITH. Some of the ship's people?

Mr. ISMAY. Yes.

Senator SMITH. How many?

Mr. ISMAY. That I could not say.

Senator SMITH. About how many?

Mr. ISMAY. I could not say.

Senator SMITH. About three or four?

Mr. ISMAY. The officer who was there will be able to give you that information, sir. My own statement would be simply guesswork. His statement would be reliable.

Senator SMITH. In the boat in which you left the ship how many men were on board?

Mr. ISMAY. Four.

Senator SMITH. Besides yourself?

Mr. ISMAY. I thought you meant the crew.

Senator SMITH. I did mean the crew.

Mr. ISMAY. There were four of the crew.

Senator SMITH. What position did these men occupy?

Mr. ISMAY. I do not know, sir.

Senator SMITH. Were any of them officers?

Mr. ISMAY. No.

Senator SMITH. Or seamen?

Mr. ISMAY. I believe one was a quartermaster.

Senator SMITH. One was a quartermaster?

Mr. ISMAY. I believe so, but I do not know.

Senator SMITH. You saw three of the boats lowered yourself?

Mr. ISMAY. Yes.

Senator SMITH. And three of them loaded?

Mr. ISMAY. Yes.

Senator SMITH. As they were loaded, was any order given as to how they should be loaded?

Mr. ISMAY. No.

Senator SMITH. How did it happen that the women were first put aboard these lifeboats?

Mr. ISMAY. The natural order would be women and children first.

Senator SMITH. Was that the order?

Mr. ISMAY. Oh, yes.

Senator SMITH. That was followed?

Mr. ISMAY. As far as practicable.

Senator SMITH. So far as you observed?

Mr. ISMAY. So far as I observed.

Senator SMITH. And were all the women and children accommodated in these lifeboats?

Mr. ISMAY. I could not tell you, sir.

Senator SMITH. How many passengers were in the lifeboat in which you left the ship?

Mr. ISMAY. I should think about forty-five.

Senator SMITH. Forty-five?

Mr. ISMAY. That is my recollection.

Senator SMITH. Was that its full capacity?

Mr. ISMAY. Practically.

Senator SMITH. How about the other two boats?

Mr. ISMAY. The other three, I should think, were fairly loaded up.

Senator SMITH. The three besides the one you were in?

Mr. ISMAY. Yes.

Senator SMITH. They were fairly well filled?

Mr. ISMAY. Yes.

Senator SMITH. Was there any struggle or jostling?

Mr. ISMAY. I saw none.

Senator SMITH. Or any attempts by men to get into the boats?

Mr. ISMAY. I saw none.

Senator SMITH. Were these women passengers designated as they went into the lifeboat?

Mr. ISMAY. No, sir.

Senator SMITH. Those that were nearest the lifeboat were taken in?

Mr. ISMAY. We simply picked the women out and put them in the boat as fast as we could.

Senator SMITH. You picked them from among the throng?

Mr. ISMAY. We took the first ones that were there and put them in the lifeboats. I was there myself and put a great many in.

Senator SMITH. Were children shown the same consideration as the women?

Mr. ISMAY. Absolutely.

Senator SMITH. Did you see any lifeboat without its complement of oarsmen?

Mr. ISMAY. I did not.

Senator SMITH. Did you see the first lifeboat lowered?

Mr. ISMAY. That I could not answer, sir. I saw the first lifeboat lowered on the starboard side. What was going on on the port side I have no knowledge of.

Senator SMITH. It has been intimated, Mr. Ismay, that the first lifeboat did not contain the necessary number of men to man it.

Mr. ISMAY. As to that I have no knowledge, sir.

Senator SMITH. And that women were obliged to row the boat.

Mr. HUGHES. That is the second lifeboat, Senator.

Senator SMITH. The second lifeboat; and that women were obliged to row that boat from 10:30 o'clock at night until 7:30 o'clock the next morning.

Mr. ISMAY. The accident did not take place until 11:30 o'clock.

Senator SMITH. Well, from after 11.30 o'clock at night until between 6 and 7 o'clock the next morning.

Mr. ISMAY. Of that I have no knowledge.

Senator SMITH. Until the *Carpathia* overtook them. You have no knowledge of that?

Mr. ISMAY. Absolutely none, sir.

Senator SMITH. So far as your observation went, would you say that was not so?

Mr. ISMAY. I would not say either yes or no; but I did not see it.

Senator SMITH. When you first went on to the deck, you were only partially clothed?

Mr. ISMAY. That is all, sir.

Senator SMITH. And, as I understand, you went as far as to encounter an officer or steward?

Mr. ISMAY. Yes, sir.

Senator SMITH. And then returned?

Mr. ISMAY. That is right.

Senator SMITH. How long were you on the ship after the collision occurred?

Mr. ISMAY. That is a very difficult question to answer, sir. Practically until the time — almost until she sank.

Senator SMITH. How long did it take to lower and load a lifeboat?

Mr. ISMAY. I could not answer that.

Senator SMITH. Can you approximate it?

Mr. ISMAY. It is not possible for me to judge the time. I could not answer that.

Senator SMITH. Were you on the *Titanic* an hour after the collision occurred?

Mr. ISMAY. Oh, yes.

Senator SMITH. How much longer?

Mr. ISMAY. I should think it was an hour and a quarter.

Senator SMITH. An hour and a quarter?

Mr. ISMAY. I should think that was it; perhaps longer.

Senator SMITH. Did you, during this time, see any of the passengers that you knew?

Mr. ISMAY. I really do not remember; I saw a great many passengers, but I do not think I paid very much attention to who they were. I do not remember recognizing any of them.

Senator SMITH. Did you know Charles M. Hayes?

Mr. ISMAY. No, sir.

Senator SMITH. Did you know of the presence of other Americans and Canadians of prominence?

Mr. ISMAY. No, sir; I knew Mr Hayes was on board the ship.

Senator SMITH. You knew he was on the ship?

Mr. ISMAY. Yes, I have known him for some years.

Senator SMITH. But you did not see him after the accident occurred?

Mr. ISMAY. I never saw him after the accident; no.

Senator SMITH. And he is unaccounted for?

Mr. ISMAY. Yes, sir.

Senator SMITH. He was not among the saved?

Mr. ISMAY. No, sir.

Senator SMITH. What were the circumstances, Mr. Ismay, of your departure from the ship?

Mr. ISMAY. In what way?

Senator SMITH. Did the last boat that you went on leave the ship from some point near where you were?

Mr. ISMAY. I was immediately opposite the lifeboat when she left.

Senator SMITH. Immediately opposite?

Mr. ISMAY. Yes.

Senator SMITH. What were the circumstances of your departure from the ship?

Mr. ISMAY. The boat was there. There was a certain number of men in the boat, and the officer called out asking if there were any more women, and there was no response, and there were no passengers left on the deck.

Senator SMITH. There were no passengers left on the deck?

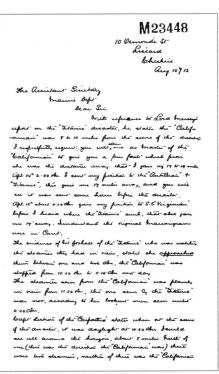

*ABOVE: Stanley Lord, Captain of the SS Carpathia, was vilified for his failure to come to the aid of Titanic, something both inquiries — particularly the British one — said that he could have done. Lord always protested otherwise and was never allowed to answer the accusations. In this letter to the Board of Trade he denies the allegations and asks to put his side of the story — which included details of a steamship that passed by him that was not Titanic. He wasn't allowed to, effectively found guilty although he wasn't on trial, and was forced to resign by his employers. The mystery vessel, it was alleged, was in fact Titanic. Subsequent research, and the discovery of the wreck site, tend to show that Lord was telling the truth. Particularly telling is the evidence of Henrik Naess, First Officer on the Samson, which was in the area poaching seals for their skins. The Samson's crew, fearing a coastguard cutter, fled the area and only later realised that they had been within ten miles of Titanic.*

*RIGHT: Twenty years on — the front page of the* Daily Express *of December 15, 1932, recalls the tragedy in 'new' pictures. In fact, many of them are by Father Browne.*

Mr. ISMAY. No, sir; and as the boat was in the act of being lowered away, I got into it.

Senator SMITH. At that time the *Titanic* was sinking?

Mr. ISMAY. She was sinking.

Senator SMITH. Where did this ship collide? Was it a side blow?

Mr. ISMAY. I have no knowledge, myself. I can only state what I have been told, that she hit the iceberg somewhere between the breakwater and the bridge.

Senator SMITH. State that again.

Mr. ISMAY. Between the breakwater and the bridge.

Senator SMITH. On the starboard side?

Mr. ISMAY. Yes.

Senator SMITH. Did you see any of the men passengers on that ship with life preservers on?

Mr. ISMAY. Nearly all the passengers had life preservers on.

Senator SMITH. All that you saw?

Mr. ISMAY. All that I saw had life preservers on.

Senator SMITH. All of them that you saw?

Mr. ISMAY. Yes; as far as I can remember.

Senator SMITH. Naturally, you would remember that if you saw it? When you entered the lifeboat yourself, you say there were no passengers on that part of the ship?

Mr. ISMAY. None.

Senator SMITH. Did you, at any time, see any struggle among the men to get into these boats?

Mr. ISMAY. No.

Senator SMITH. Was there any attempt, as this boat was being lowered past the other decks, to have you take on more passengers?

Mr. ISMAY. None, sir. There were no passengers there to take on.

Senator SMITH. Before you boarded the lifeboat, did you see any of the passengers jump into the sea?

Mr. ISMAY. I did not.

Senator SMITH. After you had taken the lifeboat did you see any of the passengers or crew with life-saving apparatus on them in the sea?

Mr. ISMAY. No, sir.

Senator SMITH. What course was taken by the lifeboat in which you were after leaving the ship?

Mr. ISMAY. We saw a light some distance off to which we attempted to pull and which we thought was a ship.

Senator SMITH. Can you give the direction of it?

Mr. ISMAY. I could not give that.

Senator SMITH. But you saw a light?

Mr. ISMAY. Yes, sir.

Senator SMITH. And you attempted to pull this boat toward it?

Mr. ISMAY. Yes, sir.

Senator SMITH. How long were you in the open sea in this lifeboat?

Mr. ISMAY. I should think about four hours.

Senator SMITH. Were there any other lifeboats in that vicinity?

Mr. ISMAY. Yes.

Senator SMITH. How many?

Mr. ISMAY. That I could not answer. I know there was one, because we hailed her. She had a light, and we hailed her, but got no answer from her.

Senator SMITH. You got no answer?

Mr. ISMAY. No, sir.

Senator SMITH. Did you see any rafts in the open sea?

Mr. ISMAY. No, sir; none.

Senator SMITH. Were there any other rafts on the *Titanic* that could have been utilized?

Mr. ISMAY. I believe not.

Senator SMITH. Were all of the lifeboats of one type?

Mr. ISMAY. No; there were four that are called collapsible boats.

Senator SMITH. What were the others?

Mr. ISMAY. Ordinary wooden boats.

Senator SMITH. How many were there?

Mr. ISMAY. I think there were 20 altogether.

Senator SMITH. Including both designs?

Mr. ISMAY. Yes. Sixteen wooden boats and four collapsible boats, I think. I am not absolutely certain.

Senator SMITH. When you reached the *Carpathia*, was your lifeboat taken aboard the *Carpathia*?

Mr. ISMAY. That I do not know, sir.

Senator SMITH. Did you see any other lifeboats taken aboard the *Carpathia*?

Mr. ISMAY. I did not.

Senator SMITH. What the method of getting you aboard the *Carpathia*?

Mr. ISMAY. We simply walked up a Jacob's ladder.

Senator SMITH. What was the condition of the sea at that time?

Mr. ISMAY. There was a little ripple on it, nothing more.

Senator SMITH. Do you know whether all the lifeboats that left the *Titanic* were accounted for?

Mr. ISMAY. I believe so. I do not know that of my own knowledge.

Senator SMITH. I think it has been suggested that two of them were engulfed.

Mr. ISMAY. Of that I know nothing.

Senator SMITH. You would know if that were true, would you not?

Mr. ISMAY. I have had no consultation with anybody since the accident with the exception of one officer.

Senator SMITH. Who was that?

Mr. ISMAY. Mr. Lightoller. I have spoken to no member of the crew or anybody since in regard of the accident.

Senator SMITH. What was Mr. Lightoller's position?

Mr. ISMAY. He was the second officer of the *Titanic*.

Senator SMITH. How many officers of the ship's crew were saved?

Mr. ISMAY. I am told four.

Senator SMITH. Can you give their names?

Mr. ISMAY. I can not.

Senator SMITH. Or their occupation?

Mr. ISMAY. I could not. The only one I knew was Mr. Lightoller, who was the second officer.

Senator SMITH. I understand they are here.

Mr. ISMAY. I believe so; I do not know.

Senator SMITH. Mr. Ismay, what can you say about the sinking and disappearance of the ship? Can you describe the manner in which she went down?

Mr. ISMAY. I did not see her go down.

Senator SMITH. You did not see her go down?

Mr. ISMAY. No, sir.

Senator SMITH. How far were you from the ship?

Mr. ISMAY. I do not know how far we were away? I was sitting with my back to the ship. I was rowing all the time I was in the boat. We were pulling away.

Senator SMITH. You were rowing?

Mr. ISMAY. Yes; I did not wish to see her go down.

Senator SMITH. You did not care to see her go down?

Mr. ISMAY. No. I am glad I did not.

Senator SMITH. When you last saw her, were there indications that she had broken in two?

Mr. ISMAY. No, sir.

Senator SMITH. When did you last see her?

Mr. ISMAY. I really could not say. It might have been ten minutes after we left her. It is impossible for me to give any judgement of the time. I could not do it.

Senator SMITH. Was there much apparent confusion on board when you saw her last?

Mr. ISMAY. I did not look to see, sir. My back was turned to her. I looked around once only, to see her red light – her green light, rather.

Senator SMITH. You never saw the captain again after you left him on the bridge?

Mr. ISMAY. No, sir.

Senator SMITH. Did you have any message from him?

Mr. ISMAY. Nothing.

Senator SMITH. Do you know how many wireless operators there were on board the ship?

Mr. ISMAY. I do not; but I presume there were two. There is always one on watch.

Senator SMITH. Do you know whether they survived?

Mr. ISMAY. I am told one of them did, but I do not know whether it is true or not. I really have not asked.

Senator SMITH. Were any of this crew enlisted men in the English Navy?

Mr. ISMAY. I do not know, sir. The ship's articles will show that.

Senator SMITH. Can you tell us anything about the inspection, and the certificate that was made and issued before sailing?

Mr. ISMAY. The ship receives a Board of Trade passenger certificate; other-

NEXT PAGE: *The tragedy illustrated in* The Sphere.

"The Titanic looked enormous"

Boat Deck clear of boats

"The bows & bridge completely under water"

Floating Ice

"Sea calm as a pond"

wise she would not be allowed to carry passengers.

Senator SMITH. Do you know whether that was done?

Mr. ISMAY. You could not sail your ship without it; you could not get your clearance.

Senator SMITH. Do you know whether this ship was equipped with its full complement of lifeboats?

Mr. ISMAY. If she had not been, she could not have sailed. She would not have received her passenger certificate; therefore she must have been fully equipped.

Senator SMITH. Do you know whether these lifeboats were the lifeboats that were planned for the *Titanic*?

Mr. ISMAY. I do not quite understand what you mean, sir. I do not think lifeboats are ever built for the ship. Lifeboats are built to have a certain cubic capacity.

Senator SMITH. I understand that; but I mean whether these lifeboats were completed for the ship coincident with the completion of the ship, or whether the lifeboats, or any of them, were borrowed from the other ships of the White Star Line.

Mr. ISMAY. They certainly would not be borrowed from any other ship.

Senator SMITH. Do you recollect whether the lifeboat in which you left the ship was marked with the name *Titanic* on the boat or on the oars?

Mr. ISMAY. I have no idea. I presume oars would be marked. I do not know whether the boat was marked or not. She was a collapsible boat.

Senator SMITH. Can you recollect whether that was so?

Mr. ISMAY. I did not look to see whether the oars were marked. It would be a natural precaution to take?

Senator SMITH. Mr. Ismay, do you know about the boiler construction of the *Titanic*?

Mr. ISMAY. No, sir; I do not.

May I suggest, gentlemen, if you wish any information in regard to the construction of the ship, in any manner, shape, or form, that I shall be only to pleased to arrange for one of the Harland & Wolff's people to come here and give you all the information you require; the plans and everything.

Senator SMITH. We are much obliged to you. There has been some suggestion by passengers who left the ship in lifeboats, that an explosion took place after this collision. Have you any knowledge on that point?

Mr. ISMAY. Absolutely none.

Senator SMITH. Do you think you would have known about that if it had occurred?

Mr. ISMAY. Yes; I should. Do you mean to say before the ship went down?

Senator SMITH. Yes.

Mr. ISMAY. Absolutely.

Senator SMITH. Mr. Ismay, do you know anything about the action of the amidship turbine; the number of revolutions?

Mr. ISMAY. No.

Mr. UHLER. The reciprocating engines, you say, were going at 75 or 72 revolutions at one time?

Mr. ISMAY. Yes.

Mr. UHLER. Have you any knowledge as to how many revolutions the amidship turbine was making?

Mr. ISMAY. No, sir. Those are all technical questions which can be answered by others, if you desire.

Senator NEWLANDS. What speed would 75 revolutions indicate?

Mr. ISMAY. I should think about 21 knots.

Senator NEWLANDS. What is that in miles?

Mr. ISMAY. It is in the ratio of 11 to 13; about 26 miles, I think.

Senator NEWLANDS. Mr. Ismay, did you have anything to do with the selection of the men who accompanied you in the last boat?

Mr. ISMAY. No, sir.

Senator NEWLANDS. How were they designated?

Mr. ISMAY. I presume by the officer who was in the charge of the boat.

Senator NEWLANDS. Who was that?

Mr. ISMAY. Mr. Weyl.

Senator NEWLANDS. And he was what officer?

Mr. ISMAY. Chief officer.

Senator NEWLANDS. Was that done by lot or by selection?

Mr. ISMAY. I think these men were allotted certain posts.

Senator NEWLANDS. Indiscriminately?

Mr. ISMAY. No; I fancy at the time they had what they called, I think, the boat's crew list. That is all arranged beforehand.

Senator SMITH. Can you describe those rafts?

Mr. ISMAY. There were none on board the ship.

Senator SMITH. Did you see any rafts actually in service?

Mr. ISMAY. No, sir.

Senator SMITH. Is it customary for the White Star Line to carry rafts?

Mr. ISMAY. I believe in the olden days we carried rafts.

Senator SMITH. Recently that has not been done?

Mr. ISMAY. Not in the recent ships; no, sir.

Senator SMITH. Why?

Mr. ISMAY. I presume because they are not considered suitable.

Senator SMITH. Do you know what water capacity there was on that ship?

Mr. ISMAY. I do not, sir.

Senator SMITH. I mean, when she was stove in, what was the capacity of the water-tight bulkheads?

Mr. ISMAY. I beg your pardon, sir. I misunderstood your question. The ship was especially constructed to float with two compartments full of water.

Senator SMITH. She was constructed to float with two compartments full of water?

Mr. ISMAY. The ship was specially constructed so that she would float with any two compartments full of water. I think I am right in saying that there are very few ships — perhaps I had better not say that, but I will continue, now that I have begun it — I believe there are very few ships to-day of which the same can be said.

When we built the *Titanic* we had that especially in mind. If this ship had hit the iceberg stem on, in all human probability she would have been here to-day.

Senator SMITH. If she had hit the iceberg head on, in all probability she would be here now?

Mr. ISMAY. I say in all human probability that ship would have been afloat to-day.

Senator NEWLANDS. How did the ship strike the iceberg?

Mr. ISMAY. From information I have received, I think she struck the iceberg a glancing blow between the end of the forecastle and the captain's bridge, just aft of the foremast, sir.

Senator SMITH. I understood you to say a little while ago that you were rowing, with your back to the ship. If you were rowing and going away from the ship, you would naturally be facing the ship, would you not?

Mr. ISMAY. No; in these boats some row facing the bow of the boat and some facing the stern. I was seated with my back to the man who was steering, so that I was facing away from the ship.

Senator SMITH. You have stated that the ship was specially constructed so that she could float with two compartments filled with water?

Mr. ISMAY. Yes.

Senator SMITH. Is it your idea, then, that there were no two compartments left entire?

Mr. ISMAY. That I cannot answer, sir. I am convinced that more than two compartments were filled. As I tried to explain to you last night, I think the ship's bilge was ripped open.

Senator NEWLANDS. The ship had 16 compartments?

Mr. ISMAY. I could not answer that, sir.

Senator NEWLANDS. Approximately?

Mr. ISMAY. Approximately. That information is absolutely at your disposal. Our shipbuilders will give it to you accurately.

Senator NEWLANDS. She was so built that if any two of these compartments should be filled with water she would still float?

Mr. ISMAY. Yes, sir; if any two of the largest compartments were filled with water she would still float.

Senator SMITH. Mr. Ismay, what time did you dine on Sunday evening?

Mr. ISMAY. At 7:30.

Senator SMITH. With whom?

Mr. ISMAY. With the doctor.

Senator SMITH. Did the captain dine with you?

Mr. ISMAY. He did not, sir.

Senator SMITH. When you went to the bridge after this collision, was there any ice on the decks?

Mr. ISMAY. I saw no ice at all, and no icebergs at all until daylight monday morning.

Senator SMITH. Do you know whether any people were injured or killed from ice that came onto the decks?

Mr. ISMAY. I do not, sir. I heard ice had been found on the decks, but it is only hearsay.

Senator SMITH. I think I have asked you, but in case it appears that I have not, I will ask again: Mr. Ismay. Were all of the women and children saved?

Mr. ISMAY. I am afraid not, sir.

Senator SMITH. What proportion were saved?

Mr. ISMAY. I have no idea. I have not asked. Since the accident I have made very few enquiries of any sort.

Senator SMITH. Did any of the collapsible boats sink, to your knowledge, after leaving the ship?

Mr. ISMAY. No, sir.

Senator NEWLANDS. What was the full equipment of lifeboats for a ship of this size?

Mr. ISMAY. I could not tell you that, sir. That is covered by the Board of Trade regulations. She may have exceeded the Board of Trade regulations, for all I know. I could not answer that question. Anyhow, she had sufficient boats to obtain her passenger certificate, and therefore she must have been fully boated, according to the requirements of the English Board of Trade, which I understand are accepted by this country. Is not that so, General?

Mr UHLER. Yes.

Senator SMITH. Mr. Ismay, did you in any manner attempt to influence or interfere with the wireless communication between the *Carpathia* and other stations?

Mr. ISMAY. No, sir. I think the captain of the *Carpathia* is here, and he will probably tell you that I was never out of my room from the time I got on board the *Carpathia* until the ship docked here last night. I never moved out of the room.

Senator SMITH. How were you dressed? Were you completely dressed when you went into the lifeboat?

Mr. ISMAY. I had a suit of pajamas on, a pair of slippers, a suit of clothes, and an overcoat.

Senator SMITH. How many men, officers and crew, were there on this boat?

Mr. ISMAY. There were no officers.

Senator SMITH. I mean the officers of the ship.

Mr. ISMAY. How many officers were there on the ship?

Senator SMITH. Yes; and how many in the crew?

Mr. ISMAY. I think there were seven officers on the ship.

Senator SMITH. And how many in the crew?

Mr. ISMAY. I do not know the full number of the crew. There were seven officers —or nine officers; there are always three officers on watch.

Senator SMITH. And how many men were in the lifeboat with you?

Mr. ISMAY. Oh, I could not tell. I suppose nine or ten.

Senator SMITH. Do you know who they were?

Mr. ISMAY. I do not. Mr. Carter, a passenger, was one. I do not know who the others were; third class passengers, I think. In fact, all the people on the boat, as far as I could see, were third class passengers.

Senator SMITH. Did they all survive, and were they all taken aboard the *Carpathia*?

Mr. ISMAY. They all survived, yes.

*ABOVE: A letter sent by Sir Edward Grey from the British Embassy in Washington to London reporting on the findings of the Senate Committee into the* Titanic *disaster. The head of the investigation was William Alden Smith, Senator for Michigan, he was empowered to look into the matter despite* Titanic *being a British ship, because the White Star Line was owned by an American trust, the International Mercantile Marine Co. This in turn meant that they could be sued under American law, if negligence could be proved. Senator Smith's motives are questionable but he did point the finger of blame at the Board of Trade inspector for hurrying his inspection during* Titanic's *trials, at Captain Smith for ignoring the presence of ice on her route, to the actions of the captain of the Californian, and the inadequate number, boarding and launching of the lifeboats. The letter quotes the final remarks that Senator Smith would make in his speech to the Senate on the disaster, '. . .we shall leave to the honest judgement of England its painstaking chastisement of the Board of Trade to whose laxity of regulation and hasty inspection the world is largely indebted for this awful fatality.'*

*Right: The Titanic memorial in Belfast when it stood in that part of Donegall Square which housed, ironically, the Ocean Accident and Guarantee Company.*

*Below Right: The front page of the U.S. Senate report.*

Senator SMITH. You have indicated your willingness to supply the committee with any data or information that may be necessary regarding the construction and equipment of this vessel?

Mr. ISMAY. Any information or any data the committee may wish is absolutely at their disposal.

Senator SMITH. And you have indicated your willingness to meet our full committee?

Mr. ISMAY. At any time you wish, sir.

Senator SMITH. And I suppose that includes the surviving officers?

Mr. ISMAY. Certainly, sir. Anybody that you wish is entirely at your disposal.

Senator SMITH. What are your own immediate plans?

Mr. ISMAY. I understand that depends on you.

Senator SMITH. I thank you . . . for responding so readily this morning, and for your statements; and I am going to ask you to hold yourself subject to our wishes during the balance of the day.

For the convenience of the captain of the *Carpathia* I am going to call him at this time.

Mr. ISMAY. I am entirely at your disposal at any time, sir.

# 'TITANIC" DISASTER

## HEARING

#### BEFORE A

## SUBCOMMITTEE OF THE COMMITTEE ON COMMERCE UNITED STATES SENATE

### SIXTY-SECOND CONGRESS
#### SECOND SESSION

#### PURSUANT TO

# S. RES. 283

### DIRECTING THE COMMITTEE ON COMMERCE TO INVESTIGATE THE CAUSES LEADING TO THE WRECK OF THE WHITE STAR LINER "TITANIC"

## PART 15

### DIGEST OF TESTIMONY

Printed for the use of the Committee on Commerce

# BRITANNIC

The third and last of the White Star super liners was the *Britannic*. Like the *Titanic*, this ship also had an unfortunate ending. When the new class of liners was first mooted in 1907, the original plan had been for two ships to be laid down with the possibility of a third ship being ordered at a later date. This option was exercised in 1911 and Harland & Wolff began work on Hull Number 433 later that year.

In the aftermath of the *Titanic* sinking, all work was halted pending the outcome of the various inquiries. As a result, several major changes were made to the design and these were able to be incorporated when work

*BELOW: Britannic — yard number 433 — under the Arrol Gantry in the berth previously occupied by Olympic.*

restarted. The most significant change was to incorporate a full double skin up to the top of the watertight bulkheads: this increased overall beam by two feet. In addition, the existing double bottom was increased in depth from five to six feet and was subdivided longitudinally (i.e. along the length of the hull) by six massive girder bulkheads. This was designed to restrict flooding in the event of the ship receiving damage similar to that which had caused the loss of the *Titanic*. Another major modification was the extension of watertight bulkheads to higher deck levels than had previously been the case. No fewer than five were taken up to B deck level, where they effectively isolated parts of the previously sacrosanct first class accommodation. The remaining twelve came up to E deck.

Combined with new arrangements for closing the watertight doors and pumping out flooded compartments, it was calculated that the ship could survive with up to six compartments flooded, compared with the four which had been the design standard for the *Titanic*. Other modifications visible externally included the strengthening of the hull amidships by means of

*ABOVE AND RIGHT: Britannic's framing and plating underway. The double bottom, increased lifeboat provision and other modifications theoretically made this ship safer than her sister but in practice Britannic went down more quickly than Titanic. The photographs RIGHT show Britannic fully framed with foreward tank-top installed.*

extra riveting and the provision of much larger lifeboat davits with a corresponding increase in lifeboat size and capacity. Originally it was intended that the *Britannic* would be fitted out with eight new gantry-type davits, each capable of handling and launching six large lifeboats stacked between the arms of the gantry. Each gantry was independently electrically powered and was fitted with a lighting system to assist launching at night. In addition, where gaps between the funnels permitted, the gantries could reach across the ship and pick and launch lifeboats from the opposite side in conditions where a list made it difficult to lower boats. Due to the urgent need to get the ship into service, she did not receive the full complement of gantry davits and only five were fitted, four abreast the after funnel and one on the starboard side abreast of the fore funnel, The remaining lifeboats were stowed on conventional Welin davits.

Taken together, if these improvements had been incorporated in the original design, it is probable that the *Titanic* would not have sunk after her fateful impact with the iceberg. Even if she had, then the lifeboat arrangements would have ensured the survival of most of the passengers and crew. As usual, hindsight is a wonderful thing.

There was also another change, which was less obvious to most observers. Although not officially confirmed, it is generally thought that the provisional name allocated to Hull Number 433 was *Gigantic*. This would have conformed with the naming of the other ships, emphasising the overall impression of size and stateliness. However, the loss of *Titanic* had demon-

RIGHT: *Hydraulic riveting machine in operation on the centre plate as Britannic is built on number 2 berth just before World War I.*

H.1919.
R.WELCH.

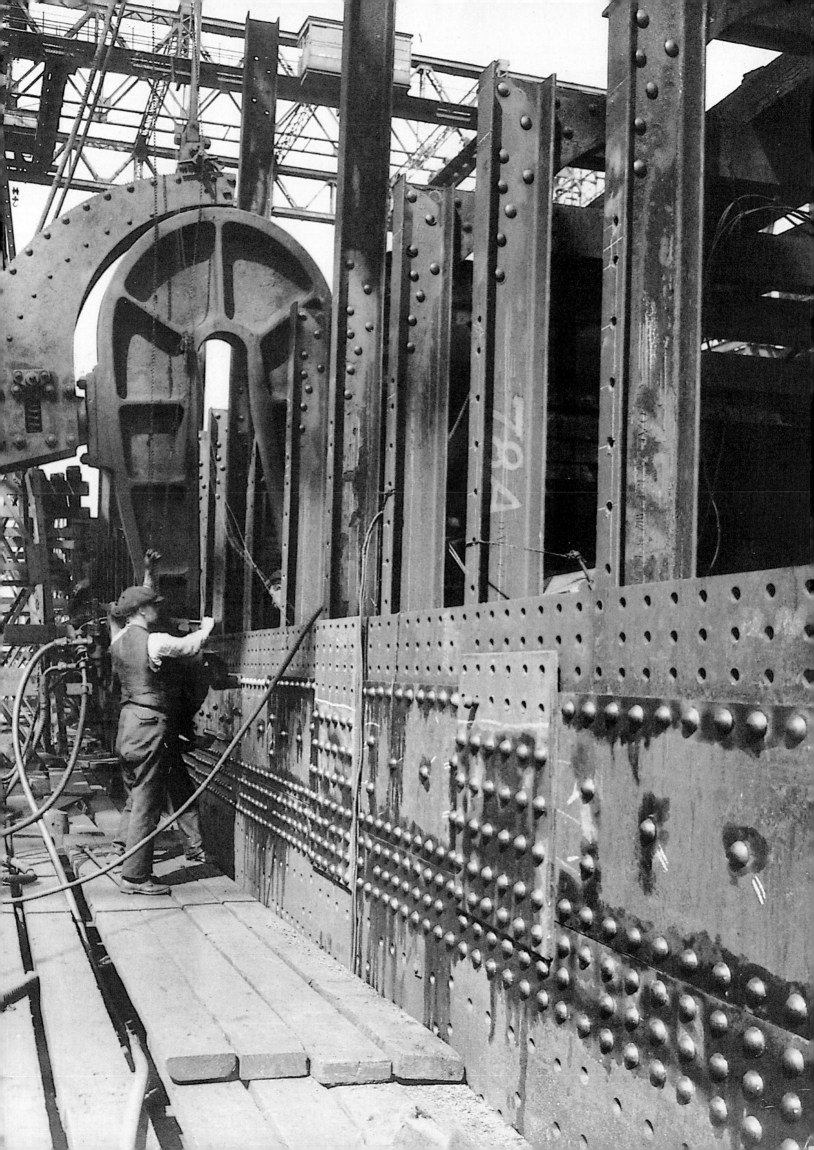

*ABOVE AND RIGHT:* Britannic is under staging prior to hull plating. *Having been laid down soon after* Titanic's *completion, she was launched on 26 February, 1914.*

strated that this was tempting fate and so the name finally chosen was *Britannic*.

In terms of gross registered tonnage, which is based on internal space, the *Britannic* was the largest of the three sister ships at 48,158 tons, while the physical dimensions were also slightly greater. The length overall was 903 feet, the beam 94 feet. The delay caused by the redesign meant that the *Britannic* was not launched until 26 February, 1914, at which time it was planned that the ship would start regular transatlantic services between Southampton and New York in the spring of 1915.

The outbreak of World War I in August 1914 caused these plans to be abandoned, and the fitting out of the ship was further delayed as Harland & Wolff concentrated on other work. Eventually it was decided to use the *Britannic* as a hospital ship and her internal compartments were fitted out for this purpose, although she was not officially requisitioned by the Admiralty until 13 November, 1915, when the work was almost complete.

WATER TIGHT
BULKHEAD.
G.

OUTER

W.F.

W.F.

OR "INNER-SKIN" PLATING

As a hospital ship she could accommodate approximately 3,300 casualties (actual figures given vary between 3,069 and 3,309) together with a medical staff consisting of 52 officers and doctors, 101 nurses, and 336 orderlies. In addition, the ship's crew was made up of another 675 men and women. The fortunate doctors and senior medical staff occupied the first class staterooms, while other staff were allocated various second and third class cabins. The first class dining room was used as an intensive care ward with the adjacent grand reception room converted into an operating theatre. Most of the wounded were accommodated in the various public rooms and spaces on the upper deck which had been converted into massive dormitories, convenient for access to the lifeboats should need arise.

On completion of the final fitting out work at Belfast, the *Britannic* carried out brief sea trials and arrived at Liverpool on 12 December, 1915, having being accompanied by a heavy escort for the short crossing of the Irish Sea. Here she was immediately commissioned as His Majesty's Hospital Ship (H.M.H.S.) *Britannic* and was placed under the command of Captain

*BELOW: The internal steel works showing deck constructions. This photograph gives a clear indication of the width of the vessel and the height between the decks.*

Charles A. Bartlett, a White Star officer who had been the company's marine superintendent at Belfast while the ship was under construction. Instead of the White Star company livery, His Majesty's latest acquisition was painted in the universally recognised hospital ship colours, an all white hull and superstructure, buff coloured funnels and mast, a broad green stripe running the full length of the hull broken only by three prominent red cross markings on either side. Two large red crosses on either side of the upper superstructure could be illuminated at night and a string of green lights ran around the full length of the promenade deck.

On 23 December, 1915, she sailed from Liverpool on her maiden voyage, heading for the Mediterranean where she would be employed on the so-called Dardenelles service alongside her sister ship *Olympic* and the Cunarders *Mauretania* and *Aquitania*. Another liner, the Dutch *Statendam*, would later join them at Mudros on the Greek isle of Lemnos in the Aegean Sea. Mudros was a collection point for casualties, not only from the Dardenelles and Gallipoli campaign, but also from other campaigns in

Macedonia, Mesopotamia and Palestine — there was no shortage of work for the five ships.

After leaving Liverpool, the *Britannic* reached Naples on 28 December, staying for a day to take on coal, before proceeding to Mudros which she reached on 31 December. The start of 1916 saw her lying offshore as a flotilla of small boats and tenders ferried out the casualties. It took four days to embark a full load of 3,300 sick and wounded, before she set sail again bound for Southampton, which was reached on 9 January. Here a series of hospital trains jostled into the dockside station to carry away the wounded to hospitals in London and southern England.

*Britannic*'s second voyage took her back to the Mediterranean, but only as far as Naples where she embarked another load of wounded and returned to Southampton on 9 February. A repeat trip to Naples followed, by which time the backlog of casualties was overwhelming hospitals ashore and the ship spent four weeks anchored off the Isle of White acting as a floating hospital. Eventually she was released from naval service and returned to Belfast on 6 June, 1916, where she was to be refitted for her original role as a mail and passenger ship for the transatlantic service.

However, this reprieve was short-lived, and she was again requisitioned and was back in Southampton on 28 August, leaving there on 24 September, with a Voluntary Aid Detachment aboard. The V.A.D. was destined for Malta, although they stayed aboard while the ship coaled at Naples before disembarking at Mudros on 3 October. During the stay at Mudros a food

*RIGHT AND BELOW: Two views of the construction of* Britannic's *internal steelwork. Note the holes to allow for the boiler uptakes: exhaust gasses will leave by the three working funnels.*

*ABOVE: Another view of* Britannic's *decking.*

*RIGHT:* Britannic *nears launch — plating and painting are complete. Photograph shows the boss arm and shafting before the addition of the propeller.*

poisoning outbreak laid low many crew members on board, but the ship was eventually able to return to Southampton with another load of sick and wounded soldiers, reaching her home port on 11 October.

Almost immediately she sailed for yet another Naples–Mudros–Southampton trip, returning with another 3,000 wounded, who required no fewer than 15 hospital trains. During this voyage the *Britannic* had sailed in some severe weather but had emerged relatively undamaged, unlike the *Aquitania*, which had been in company with *Britannic* and had to be laid up for repairs. The resulting shortage of hospital ship capacity meant that the *Britannic* set sail again for Naples after only the briefest of rests, leaving Southampton on 12 November, 1916, and arriving in Naples five days later to take on coal. Again, fierce storms set in and she was not able to continue towards Mudros until monday, 20 November.

The route from Naples to Mudros, situated in the northern part of the Aegean Sea, took the *Britannic* through the Messina strait between Sicily and the toe of Italy, and then eastward across the Mediterranean to round the southern extremity of the Greek mainland by Cape Matapan. From here the ship turned north-east and began threading its way through the numerous islands which littered the Aegean, intending to pass just south of the port of Piraeus and then between the large islands of Andros and Euboea to the east of Athens. To reach this position it was first necessary to pass close Kea island, some 20 miles off the Athenian shore. This route was used by many ships entering the Aegean from the central Mediterranean and the fact was

not lost on the German Navy who patrolled many of the routes used by allied naval vessels and troopships, including the Kea Channel.

At the end of October the submarine *U-73* had been operating in this area under the command of Kapitänleutnant Gustav Siess. This boat was one of a class of ten U-boats built specifically for the mine laying role: they subsequently earned the grim nickname 'Children of Sorrow'. They could stow a total of 32 mines, which were laid through two special discharge tubes in the stern. In addition they carried two single 19.7 in tubes for conventional torpedoes. After observing allied shipping movements, Kapitänleutnant Siess decided to lay a barrage of twelve mines across the Kea channel, arranged in two lines of six across the main shipping lane.

All this, of course, was unknown to those aboard the *Britannic* as she headed into the Aegean on the morning of Tuesday, 21 November, 1916. In contrast to the earlier storms, the weather was now idyllic and several accounts mentioned how exceptionally calm the sea was as the sun climbed strongly into the eastern sky, promising the sort of day which modern cruise passengers pay good money to enjoy. In 1916 the crew and medical staff were going through their normal routine, many still enjoying a leisurely breakfast, taking advantage of the fact that there were no sick or wounded on board to demand their attention.

*BELOW, RIGHT AND NEXT PAGE: Britannic ready for launch.*

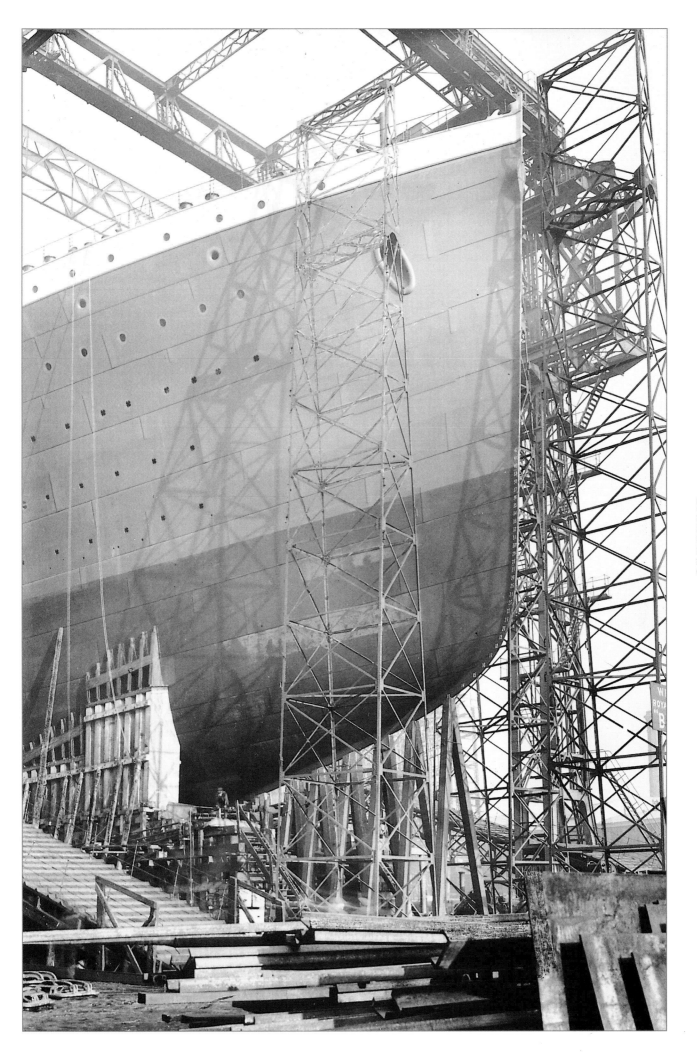

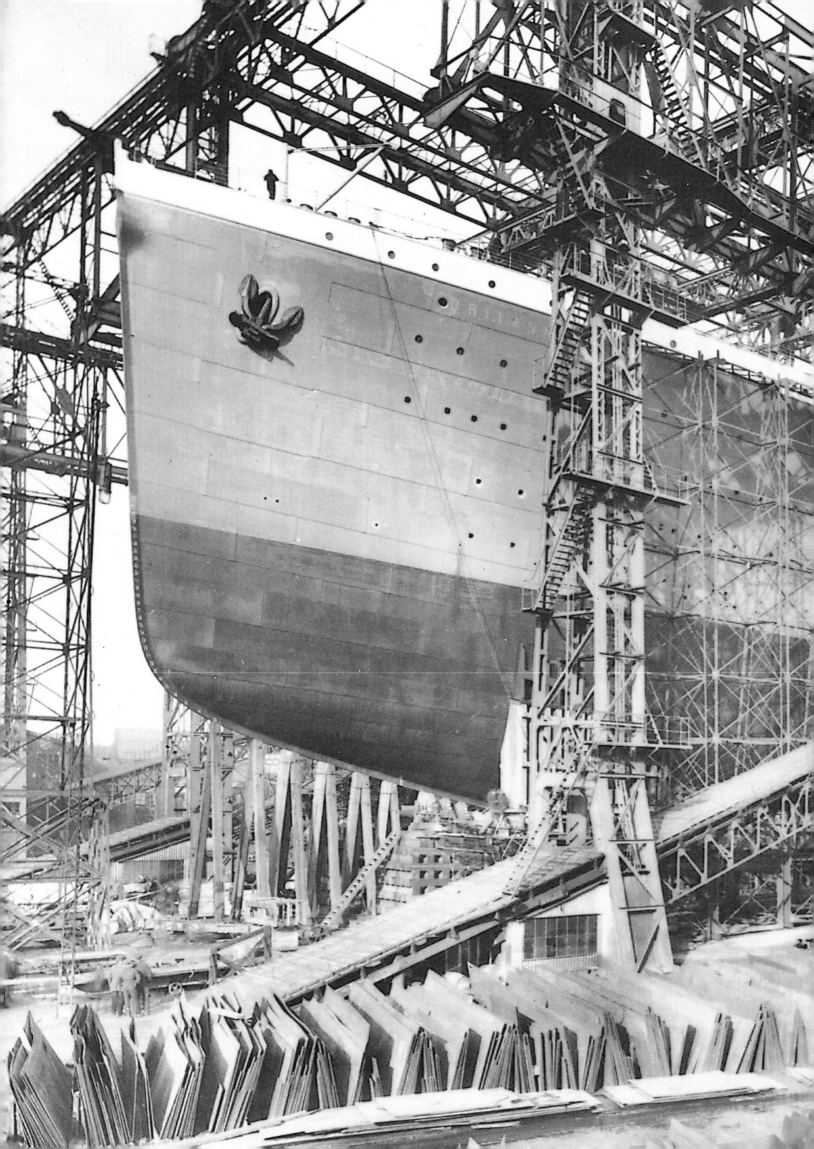

*THIS PAGE:* Britannic's launch took place on 26 February, 1914. The ship was launched down the slipway (*RIGHT*) by hydraulic rams. She would not be completed until December 1915, as the start of World War I led to Admiralty orders for Harland & Wolff, including the conversion of a number of cargo liners into dummy battleships in order to deceive the enemy about the strength of the Grand Fleet and the provision of a number of monitors — 13 were delivered to the Admiralty between 29 May and 4 November, 1915. *ABOVE* is a view of the forward launching cradle and underside of the bow.

At 8:00 a.m. a routine change of watch was under way, and this involved the opening of several watertight doors so that crew could move around the ship to their posts. This routine was suddenly interrupted by an explosion forward, the reverberations of which were felt in varying degrees throughout the ship. The *Britannic* had struck one of the mines laid a few days before by *U-73* and was seriously damaged although, in an echo of the *Titanic* tragedy, this was not immediately apparent to all on board. However, those close to the point of impact, near the starboard bow, needed no convincing. On the bridge, Captain Bartlett recognised what had happened and immediately set in motion the drills to contain the damage. Orders were given to close all watertight doors, a radio distress call was sent out and the lifeboats were made ready for launching.

*LEFT AND BELOW LEFT:* Machinery testing. Unlike the majority of builders, Harland & Wolff tried to install as much machinery as possible into their vessels before their launch to reduce outfitting time and improve on completion dates. The top picture shows the stern post and rudder head on the lathe while the bottom photograph is of the propeller plumber (thrust block) with forced lubrication.

*BELOW:* Britannic's *launch was controlled from the bow platform.*

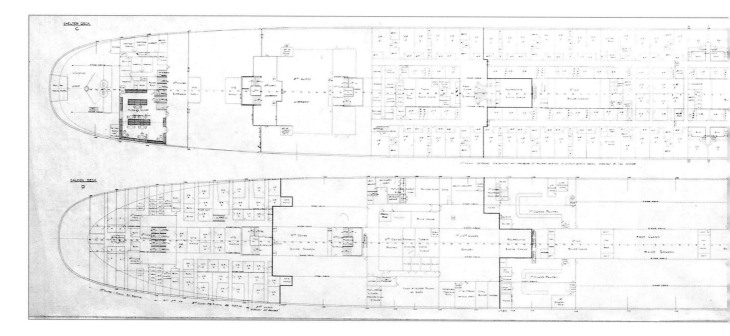

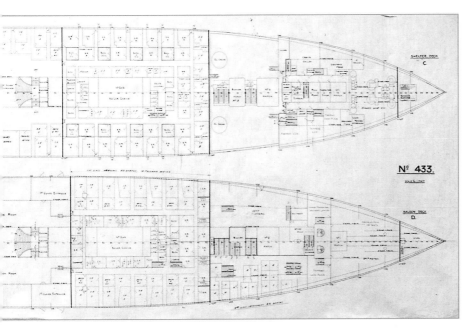

*LEFT: Builder's plans of Britannic's Promenade and Bridge decks.*

*BELOW AND BELOW LEFT: Britannic's main crank shaft prior to machining.*

Amidships, the nurses and doctors sat in silence, wondering what was happening — some even carried on eating their breakfast. When the ship's siren eventually sounded the alarm signal, they were ordered to assemble at their stations on the Boat deck and an orderly and disciplined evacuation of the cabin spaces began. There was little or no sense of panic, and many staff and crew took time to go and collect baggage or personal possessions from their cabin. Perhaps not surprisingly, some of the White Star employees aboard had also been on the *Titanic* when it sank and one of these was Violet Jessop who was now a volunteer nurse. Despite being aware of the explosion forward, she continued preparing a breakfast for sick colleague and took it to her cabin before helping her up to the Boat deck. She then went back to her own cabin to collect her belongings before finally joining the others at the boats which were still waiting to be launched.

Up on the bridge, Captain Bartlett initially had every hope that the ship could be saved. The mine should, at worst, have affected two compartments and there should have been adequate reserve buoyancy. In fact, by a twist of fate, the damage was much more severe. The mine had exploded on the starboard side of the bow and had seriously damaged the bulkhead between the second and third cargo holds, as well as opening up an extensive area of hull plating with the result that the forward four watertight compartments rapidly flooded. The explosion had also damaged the watertight door, which should have closed the passageway leading aft to boiler room Number 6, and this also began to flood.

*Far Left and Left:* Britannic's engines were the same as her sisters' — four-cylinder, triple expansion-steam reciprocating engines to drive the outer propellers and a steam turbine (the casing of which is seen *Below*) driving the central one. The photograph on the far left shows the machining of the turbine rotor prior to installation of the blades.

This should have been the total extent of the damage and if the flooding had been confined to these areas the ship would still have floated. Orders to close the watertight doors should have ensured this state of affairs but unfortunately a critical door between boiler rooms 6 and 5 did not fully close and water began pouring through into the next boiler space. This now meant that the ships six forward compartments were flooding rapidly and the situation was now critical. Whether the ship would have continued to float in these circumstances was a nicely balanced question but two factors intervened to seal the ship's fate. In view of the warm weather several of the portholes on E and F deck had been left open and as the ships began to go down by the head, water poured in through these. Considering that the ship was on active service in a war zone, this should not have been permitted and the watertight integrity of the ship should have been better administered. However , despite being a requisitioned ship, the crew were civilians at heart and the habits of a lifetime could not be changed overnight.

The other factor which contributed to the sinking of the ship was the understandable decision by the captain to attempt to beach the ship in the shallow waters close to the nearby island of Kea. Giving the necessary helm orders, he rang down for full speed and the ship began rushing towards the tantalisingly close shallows. Almost as soon as the ship gathered way, more water began rushing into the damaged compartments and the list to starboard began to increase alarmingly. Captain Bartlett realised the futility of this effort and immediately rang down to stop engines and prepared to have

*More photographs of Britannic's machinery being built and tested prior to insertion. ABOVE is the turbine rotor.*

*TOP LEFT: Installing condenser tubes on a starboard steam condenser.*

*BELOW LEFT: Starboard intermediate propeller shaft.*

the lifeboats lowered when the ship came to rest. It was at this point that an unfortunate tragedy occurred resulting in thirty unnecessary deaths. Miraculously, nobody had been killed or injured in the original explosion and the lower decks had been quickly evacuated, again without loss. However, as the ship now slowed down and stopped, two lifeboats on the port side were lowered without permission and were sucked under the stern where the giant propellers were still turning. Both craft were wrecked and the casualties occurred at this time, with another forty survivors being injured. One of these was the indefatigable Violet Jessop who sustained a fractured skull in the impact but was subsequently rescued by another lifeboat.

Meanwhile, the other boats were being loaded and readied for launching, mostly in good order but there were some reports of a lack of discipline amongst some of the more inexperienced members of the crew. This was firmly handled by the ship's officers but one of the poop deck boats was half filled and lowered without orders by a group of firemen, although they did subsequently return and assist in picking up other survivors in the water. The military staff, including many female nurses conducted themselves with dignity and the remaining lifeboats were lowered away without serious problems except that few contained any trained seaman and the oars and tillers were taken by whoever was available. The evacuation of the ship was conducted without further casualties and eventually some 1,066 survivors stood

*ABOVE:* Britannic'*s engines being fitted in the engine room.*

*LEFT: One of six steam condensers.*

414

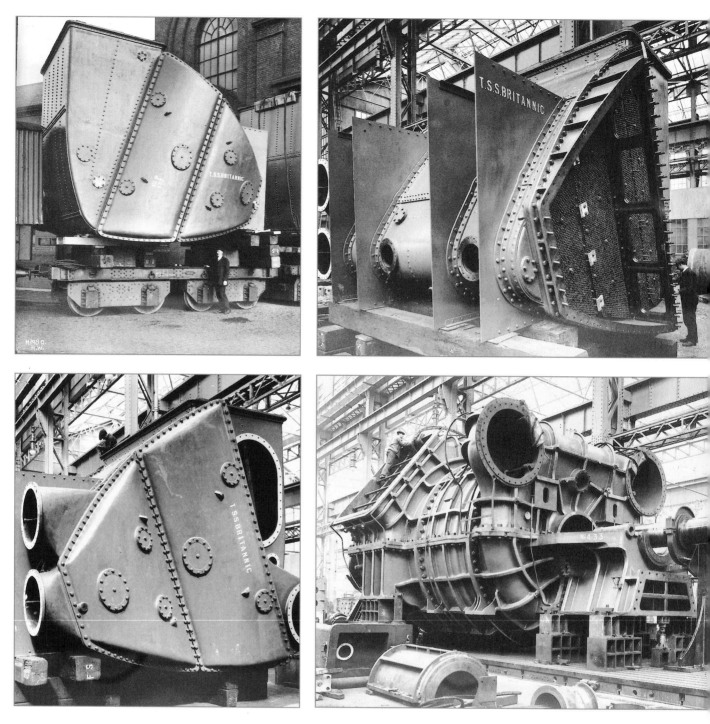

TOP LEFT AND RIGHT AND ABOVE LEFT: *Britannic's massive steam condensers.*

ABOVE RIGHT: *Steam Turbine engine.*

TOP FAR RIGHT: *A young boy giving scale to the steam shaft turbine casing.*

TOP FURTHEST RIGHT: *Turbine fan blades.*

RIGHT: *Steam stearing engines with spurs and bevel gearing.*

NEXT PAGE: *Boilers (LEFT, ABOVE AND BELOW) and funnels (RIGHT) were put in place within the vessels while they were at the outfitting dock.*

off, watching the last moments of the great ship from their lifeboats. By this time the bow was completely submerged and it was sinking fast. The last boat to leave contained the ship's purser and Major Priestly, the commander of the medical staff who had stayed until the last moment ensuring that all the doctors, nurses and orderlies had been accounted for. In the best traditions of the merchant marine, Captain Bartlett was the last man to leave, stepping off the starboard bridge wing into the rising water and swimming to a nearby collapsible liferaft.

As the water poured into the engine rooms the funnels belched out clouds of smoke and steam and then collapsed, the ship tilted down with an increasingly steep angle and then slipped rapidly below the waves, the stern and rudder being the last to disappear from view. As the ship went down there was a series of reports and explosions as the scalded boilers burst open — then all was silent. The time was 9:07 a.m., only 55 minutes from the initial

*RIGHT AND BELOW RIGHT: H.M.H.S. (Hospital Ship) Britannic sporting green and white livery. She was requisitioned for service as a hospital ship by the Admiralty in October 1915 and again in May 1916. In between she had been a troopship.*

*BELOW: Britannic's 34 ft motor lifeboat built by Maynard on sub-contract from Thornycroft.*

*PREVIOUS PAGE: Cunard Line vessel Aquitania in hospital ship livery, note the similarity in profile and appearance to Brittanic.*

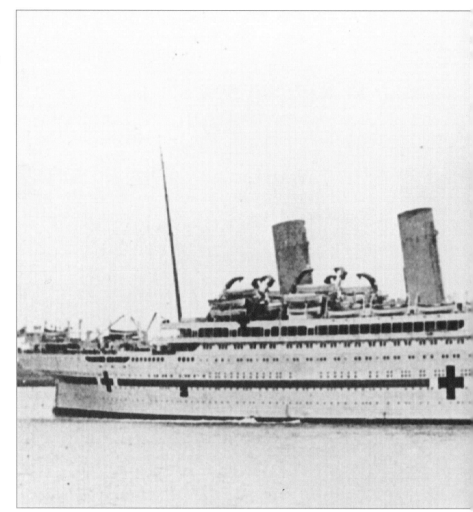

contact with the mine and less than half the time the *Titanic* had taken to sink some four years earlier. Fortunately for the *Britannic's* survivors, conditions were totally different from that cold April night in the Atlantic. This time there was more than enough lifeboat capacity and the survivors floated safely in no fewer than 35 boats. For those few who had actually had to swim, the Mediterranean water was relatively warm, even in November and, most important of all, help was close at hand. The sinking had occurred just off the island of Kea and, if necessary, the boats could probably have been rowed ashore. However, there were several Royal Navy ships in the vicinity as well as local fishing boats. First on the scene was the auxiliary merchant

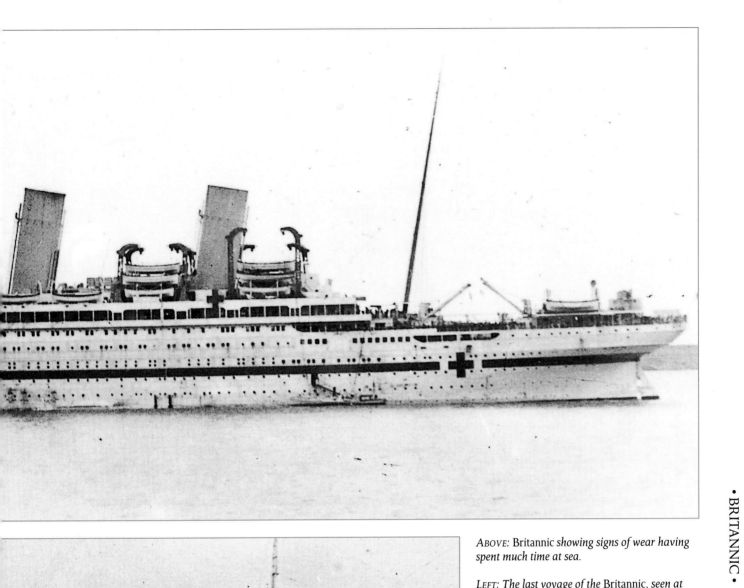

*ABOVE:* Britannic *showing signs of wear having spent much time at sea.*

*LEFT: The last voyage of the* Britannic, *seen at Mudros with the British flagship,* Lord Nelson.

*Left:* Britannic *arriving at Southampton at the end of another trip from the Mediterranean.*

426

cruiser H.M.S. *Heroic*, itself a converted small liner, which had picked up the *Britannic*'s radio distress call. She was quickly joined by a Greek fishing boat and the destroyer H.M.S. *Scourge*. Together these ships picked up approximately 700 survivors and a little before noon anther destroyer, H.M.S. *Foxhound* arrived and picked up another 339. Most of the survivors were taken initially to the port of Piraeus where they were accommodated aboard other British and French ships or ashore in hotels.

As might be expected, a court of inquiry was quickly set up to determine the cause of the loss. This was conducted by the naval authorities and the facts were quickly established so that the proceedings were relatively short and did not carry out any significant technical evaluation. The fact that the loss of life had been mercifully small when horrendous casualties were being daily reported from the military fronts meant that there was little public pressure. The inquiry's report concluded that the probable cause of the sinking was contact with a mine although the possibility that it might have been a torpedo from a submarine was not excluded. However, there was no evidence to support the latter hypothesis although the deliberate sinking of a clearly marked hospital ship would have been a major propaganda blow to the Germans had this been the case. More to the point, and not really explained, was why the ship sank after striking the mine. The modified design should, in theory, have been capable of surviving such damage but actually sank very quickly even though many smaller vessels routinely survived single explosions from mines and torpedoes. There was some speculation that there may have been secondary explosions of military stores on board or from wrecked boilers. Even sabotage was mooted but, at the end of the day, it appeared that the open portholes together with possible lapses in

*BELOW AND RIGHT: Britannic loading stores from the Galeka at Mudros, 1916.*

watertight integrity had made the fatal difference. The *Britannic* was thus left with the dubious distinction of being the largest ship of any nation to be sunk during the First World War.

As with the *Titanic*, this was not quite the end of the story. The ship lay in a well charted channel with a depth of just over 100 metres. She was thus not difficult to locate when the underwater technology of the last quarter of the 20th century was employed in exploring historic wrecks. The first to carry out a properly mounted expedition was the pioneer underwater explorer, Jacques Cousteau, in 1976. He was only able to obtain poor quality TV pictures but found the ship lying on her starboard side with the bow twisted at an angle, He also claimed that the evidence showed the possibility of a secondary explosion causing a large hole forward. In 1995, a much more sophisticated operation was mounted under the direction of Robert Ballard who had previously located the wreck of the *Titanic* in 1986. This time he used a small U.S. Navy nuclear powered submarine together with two

BELOW: Britannic *arriving at Mudros, 3 October, 1916, just a few weeks before her loss to a mine. Note the numerous additional lifeboats and the improved davits.*

remotely controlled underwater vehicles. In addition to this the latest 3D computer imaging techniques were used to build up a complete picture of the ship. Apart from the funnels, which had broken off as the ship sank and lay close by, the ship was relatively intact and Ballard was able to confirm the existence of the large hole near the bow reported by Cousteau. However, investigation tended to show that this had been caused by a combination of the mine impact and subsequent stressing and fracturing as the ship filled with water and sank.

Thus the third of the great White Star sister ships now lies at peace having performed valuable work for her country but never carrying a fare paying passenger. At least she had saved many lives in her short career and her final demise was, fortunately, not accompanied by the massive death toll experienced by the *Titanic* although the story could well have been so different if the ship had been proceeding from Mudros with 3,000 sick and wounded aboard.

NEXT PAGE: *Survivors from the* Britannic — *they did not have to enter freezing seas and there was adequate provision of lifeboats but the story could have been so different if a full complement of wounded had been aboard.*

# THE WRECK

*RIGHT:* Titanic*'s bow.*

Whilst the arguments raged ashore, the wreck of the *Titanic* lay at a depth of 12,500 ft in the middle of the Atlantic Ocean. Tentative plans to salvage the ship were laid in the immediate aftermath but these came to naught and, given the technology of the time, had little chance of success. With the outbreak of war in August 1914, the *Titanic* story began to fade from prominence as other great ships became victims of the conflict. When the lives lost in these and hundreds of other sinkings was added to the millions killed in the armageddon of the fighting on land, the scale of the *Titanic*'s losses, perhaps understandably, began to dwindle in public memory although, of course, not in the thoughts of the families of those directly affected.

In the years between the wars, there was not generally the time, money or technology to attempt any salvage of the vessel although this did not stop exaggerated rumours of great treasures buried within the wreck, this being enough to cause a few hopefuls to come forward with wildly impractical schemes. By the early 1950s there was a definite reawakening of interest in the *Titanic* and the possibility of locating and salvaging at least part of the wreck. One British salvage company, Rosdon Beasley Limited, actually spent a week in the vicinity of the sinking using a technique of recording sound waves from undersea explosions in an unsuccessful attempt to locate the wreck. Schemes to locate the wreck began to proliferate following the post-war success of underwater exploration methods and the development during the cold war period of high frequency scanning sonars which provided very detailed images of the seabed. By the late 1970s a number of groups had been set up, including an alliance between Walt Disney Productions and the *National Geographic* magazine, which was intended to produce a film based on the story of the sinking and the subsequent rediscovery of the wreck.

In Britain, there was Seawise & Titanic Salvage Limited, a company financed by Sir James Goldsmith, which deployed considerable technical expertise although its expedition, planned for the summer of 1980, did not come to fruition. It was left to a Texan oil millionaire, Jack Grimm, to make the first realistic attempts to find the *Titanic* during the course of no fewer than three expeditions in the early 1980s. In July and August 1980, he teamed up with scientists from the Scripps Institute of Oceanography in California and the Lamont-Doherty Geological Observatory, part of New York's Columbia University, and searched an area in mid-Atlantic aboard the research ship *H. J. W. Fay*. Altogether 14 potential targets were located, but none were positively identified as being the actual wreck. In the following year he spent another ten days aboard the research vessel *Gyre* searching an area slightly south of that covered in the previous year but then, as

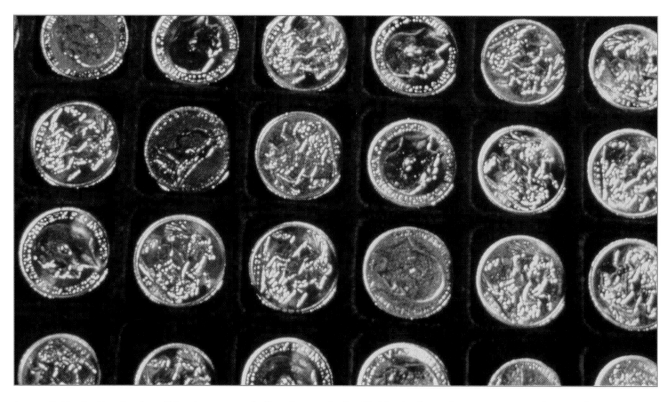

*ABOVE: Gold coins found on board* Titanic.

*RIGHT: A salvaged mooring bollard.*

*BELOW: The purser's safe.*

*NEXT PAGE: The starboard propeller.*

434

before, he was bedevilled by bad weather. However, in the very last sweep, a prototype undersea video system was deployed and it was only when the signals were being decoded whilst on the voyage home that an object swam into view which Grimm subsequently claimed was undoubtedly one of the Titanic's propellers. None of the scientists who accompanied him were prepared to substantiate this claim and a subsequent Grimm expedition in 1983 failed to add anything further to the search.

In the meantime the Scripps Institute co-operated with the Massachusetts Woods Hole Oceanographic Institute to carry out a preliminary expedition in 1981 under the auspices of the U.S. Office of Naval Research, although this was more a test of new equipment than a serious attempt to find the *Titanic*. In 1985 the Woods Hole Institute teamed up with the Institute Français de Recherches pour l'Exploitation des Mers (I.F.R.E.M.E.R., the French Institute for Research and Exploitation of the Seas) to launch an expedition under the joint leadership of Dr. Robert Ballard and Jean-Louis Michel from the U.S. and French institutes respectively.

The first stage of the search was carried out between 9 July and 7 August by the French vessel *Le Surôit* using S.A.R., a deep towed sideways scanning high resolution sonar which swept 1,000 yard wide swathes as it was towed backwards and forwards across the designated search area. This area had been carefully planned and took into account the results of Grimm's searches together with a calculation of all the factors which might have affected the accuracy of Boxhall's calculations on the night of the sinking. Consequently the *Le Surôit* concentrated on an area covering 150 square miles mainly to the south and east of 41°46'N and 50°14'W, the position which the fourth officer had plotted at the time. Again bad weather intervened and nothing was found by the time that the vessel had to depart, being needed for tasks elsewhere.

The second phase of the operation began on 22 August, when the U.S. Navy research vessel *Knoor* arrived to carry on the search with Ballard and Michel aboard, these scientists having transferred from the French ship. The main pieces of American equipment were their unmanned computerised submersibles called *Angus* and *Argo*, which had capabilities of operating at depths of 20,000 ft. *Argo* was a submersible sled towed by a steel-armoured coaxial cable, that carried not only forward-looking and sideways scanning sonar, but also some highly sophisticated real time video cameras which could transmit high quality images via fibre optic cable to the control cabin aboard the ship. *Angus* was an earlier, inferior model which was later used for determining the overall layout of the ship due to its lack of real-time feedback although it was useful as it was a superior still photography platform. Their first task was to investigate the sonar targets and 'propeller' located by the Grimm expeditions, and all these were quickly eliminated from the search which then moved to the areas not already covered by the French activity. For days on end *Argo* was towed back and forth across the Atlantic seabed until, as the operating team struggled to stay awake in the early hours of 1 September, a number of obviously man-made objects suddenly started to appear on their screens. This was immediately followed by a shout from the sonar operator that he had a contact ahead of the *Argo*. The ship's cook was sent to fetch Robert Ballard who rushed into the control room just after a large round object had swum into view — it was the face of a ship's boiler! The control room erupted into whoops and cheers of celebration, Ballard later reflected, 'suddenly it hit me in the stomach'. Fortunately, Ballard had the presence of mind to order the *Argo* to be raised a 100 ft or so away from the seabed in order to prevent it being damaged or lost by actually hitting the side of the *Titanic*'s great hull. As the *Knoor* paused after the initial six minute pass over of the newly found wreck, realisation dawned that it was now nearly 2:00 a.m., almost to the hour the time that the *Titanic* had gone down. A sombre mood broke into the celebrations and, led by Ballard, many of the crew went and stood silently on the quarter-deck, lost in thoughts of what had happened in that very spot over 73 years earlier. Then it was back to work — the *Titanic* had been found at last!

Time was now short, as the *Knoor* could only remain on station for a few more days and operations were affected by worsening weather which made the launch and retrieval of the *Argo* a dangerous business. Nevertheless, a second run was made over the wreck, this time closer than the last passing at only a few feet above the wreck. Some confusion set in after the third run, when the *Argo* reached the position where the stern half of the *Titanic*'s hull should have been; the video images faded into a disorientating mass of twisted wreckage. It appeared that the hull had broken into two separate sections, the break occurring in the region of the third funnel. The team established that the ship lay upright although all four funnels had collapsed, and the forward section was reasonably intact although there was some damage to the forward port side caused when the ship hit the bottom. The foremast had collapsed across the bow and there was a large hole where the forefunnel had fallen away as the ship's bow plunged under the surface. As the wind and

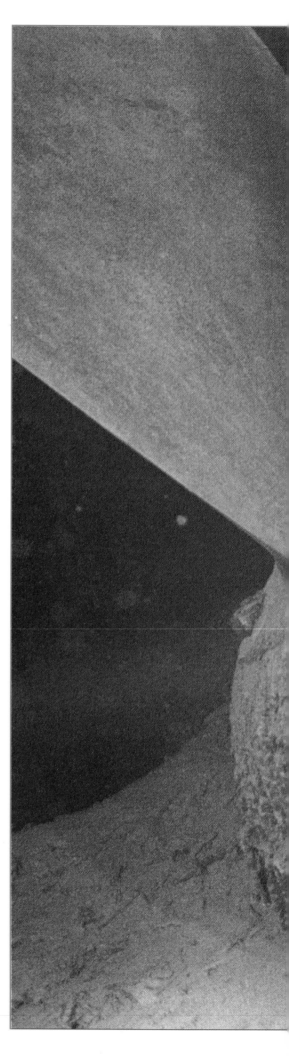

438

seas began to rise, *Argo*'s sister *Angus* was sent down to collect still shots of the wreck. In all she made six passes over the *Titanic* and, when the film was developed, Ballard's team found themselves examining a sombre collection of the Edwardian era, strewn across the ocean floor near the wreck - a silver platter here, a chamber pot there, not to mention numerous unopened bottles of wine. Although good quality images of the whole forward section were obtained, there was not enough time to survey the stern section before the *Knoor* set course for home on the morning 4 September, 1984.

Nevertheless, the expedition had been a resounding success, with news of the achievement leaking out even as the *Knoor* sailed for home. In fact, none of the scientists, or their parent organisations, had foreseen the tremendous media interest which the finding of the *Titanic* would stimulate and they were surprised to find helicopters flying out to the ship in order to gather copies of films and video tapes for transmission across the world. When the *Knoor* eventually reached Wood's Hole on 9 September, it was met by an umbrella of aircraft and helicopters, while the normally quiet haven was packed with sightseeing and official craft. The dockside was covered with cheering crowds and news cameras, aerials and satellite dishes littered the whole area.

As the scientists stepped ashore, they were taken immediately to a massive press conference where they briefly told of the great team effort and cutting edge technology which had made the discovery possible. Other media occasions followed and later, in Washington D.C., Dr. Ballard ended one of these proceedings with the following thoughtful statement.

'The Titanic itself lies in 13,000 ft of water on a gently sloping alpine like countryside overlooking a small canyon below. Its bow faces north and the ship sits upright on the bottom. Its mighty stacks point upward.

'There is no light at this great depth and little light can be found. It is quiet and peaceful and a fitting place for the remains of this greatest of sea tragedies to rest.

'May it forever remain that way and may God bless these found souls'.

Unfortunately these well expressed, noble sentiments would be almost impossible to apply, as the very finding of the wreck had thrown the whole story of the *Titanic* firmly into the public eye and several individuals came forward with schemes to raise the ship or at least to salvage major sections with the idea of using them for commercial museums and other schemes. In an effort to prevent random and possibly damaging salvage attempts on the hull, the United States enacted legislation in 1986 in the form of the *Titanic* Memorial Act, although whether this had any standing in international law was open to debate.

In 1986 Ballard led a further expedition to the now precisely known location of the wreck but this time it was an all-American effort due to a disagreement with I.F.R.E.M.E.R. over the film and video rights from the previous year. A new research vessel, *Atlantis II*, was made available, and the towed *Argo* platform was replaced by a three-man deep-diving submersible called *Alvin* belonging to the U.S. Navy, which substantially funded the expedition as a means of testing various undersea equipment and techniques

440

in a project which pushed the boundaries of achievement in this field. *Alvin* had been adapted to carry a small self-propelled camera-equipped device named *Jason Junior* which was powered and controlled through a 250 ft long umbilical cable linking it to the submersible. This carried high definition video and film cameras, as well as the necessary lighting system. Using this combination it would be possible for scientists to see the wreck at first hand, while *Jason Junior* could actually be manoeuvred inside the hull to visit cabins, passageways and machinery spaces. If it worked, the results would be fascinating and there was an air of eager anticipation as the first dive was made on 13 July, 1986.

This time the weather was kind and sea conditions were calm. As the wreck had been accurately pinpointed the previous year, *Alvin* was able to be steered directly towards it but, as it came into sight, the dive had to be abandoned due to a technical fault. On the second dive, Ballard and his co-pilot Ralph Hollis found themselves confronting for the first time the huge, sharp profile of the *Titanic*'s bow with the anchors still in position. Rivers of rust oozed from the hull on to the ocean bed where she was firmly lodged. For Ballard this was both an exciting and a comforting sight, since it was clear that any attempt to raise the hull would be well nigh impossible; after studying the bow further, *Alvin* and its crew moved aft toward the bridge.

The third dive started well until an unexpectedly strong current caused the planned initial deployment of *Jason Junior* to be cancelled. However, the fourth dive was completely successful and *Jason Junior* was steered through the great hole left by the missing forefunnel and passed down into B deck, allowing the first views inside the ship for 74 years. The scientists had been apprehensive at the possibility of coming across gruesome human remains but in the event none were seen, time and the sea having completely erased any traces, although items of clothing were often found where their wearers had died. Over the next few dives *Jason Junior* was attached to *Alvin*'s underside from where it was deployed to explore deep inside the *Titanic*.

With the confidence gained from experience, *Jason Junior* explored the Boat deck, the crow's nest, the bridge, descended the grand staircase (once the very hub of the ship) and even went into the purser's office, tugging at the safe handle to see if it would open (it didn't!). Ballard and the other scientists were ecstatic; *Jason Junior* was sending back spellbinding images of the ship's interior. Almost three quarters of a mile behind the bow section, was a field of debris which had been carried away by the current as the doomed ship broke up and sank to the bottom. On one dive, *Alvin* and *Jason Junior* roamed over this area where thousands of artefacts such as plates, crockery, pots, pans, heaters, and other cabin fittings could be plainly seen, as could huge piles of coal shed from the ship's bunkers.

Dive eight concentrated on the stern section which lay about 600 metres behind the bow section and was in much worse shape, most of the decks having collapsed onto each other. In other dives some attempt was made to view the damage caused by the collision with the iceberg but this part of the hull was completely buried and could not be seen. In all, Alvin made 11 manned dives, completing its program on 24 July, 1986 when *Atlantis II* set

*ABOVE: A pursur's bag.*

course back to Wood's Hole, arriving home on 28 July. The extraordinary pictures obtained by this expedition were again made available for television viewing and also featured in several books, notably Ballard's own account of the expeditions which was first published in 1987. The discoveries yielded a much better understanding of the dramatic circumstances that brought about the end of the ship, through the use of post operation analysis of photographs brought back from the wreck sites which would provide useful information for ship designers and historians alike. On that bitterly cold night in April 1912, all the world knew was that *Titanic* hit an iceberg which stabbed a 300 ft gash along her starboard side below the water line. Six of her 16 watertight compartments had flooded (but that had been enough. As the water levels rose above the watertight compartments, the ship took on too much weight and sank bow first).

Ballard and Michel's dives found no gash at all (instead they deduced that her riveted plates had been forced apart by the impact with the iceberg and this had caused her demise. The 300 ft slice down her side had existed only in the popular imagination. The journey to the ocean bed had caused catastrophic damage to the ship. Ballard concluded that the hull had failed on the surface while protruding some 200-300 ft on the perpendicular (the unsupported length, hanging out of the water is uncertain but this estimate is corroborated by sketches made soon after, from survivors memories). She had sunk in two pieces and now lay on the bottom of the ocean in three big pieces, the bow and stern some 1,800 ft apart.

'Ballard is clearly right in suggesting that the break occurred well above the sea bed to account for the separation of the two main portions. The fore end, which flooded slowly on the surface, is generally in good shape. The after end is grossly distorted with sides pushed in and decks collapsed. Failure would start with shearing of rivets but if the pressure did not equalise quickly, more dramatic failure, even implosion, would result.'

This theory of violent pressure equalisation seems to account for the collapsed decks in the stern section, and it is there that most of the bodies of the passengers and crew who had been unable to board the lifeboats would be. Ballard describes his feelings about exploring this part of the wreck; 'The stern was the hardest place to work emotionally because it was frozen terror. It was not as enjoyable to work in because you knew what final tragedy was played out on that stern section. The appearance of it just looked violent, it looked destructive and torn.' While Ballard had painstakingly ensured that nothing aboard the *Titanic* was disturbed or retrieved, his erstwhile French colleagues were less scrupulous and the millionaire Jack Grimm negotiated a joint expedition with I.F.R.E.M.E.R. with the intention of recovering artefacts from the wreck. In the event, Grimm was not involved in the final consortium, which married several American business interests with I.F.R.E.M.E.R. and other French agencies. Reaching the area of the *Titanic* wreck on 22 July, 1987, aboard the support vessel *Nadir*, the American-backed French team used equipment very similar to that used by Ballard the year before. This consisted of the manned submersible *Nautile* which deployed *Robin*, a remotely operated mechanical probe. During a period of just over seven weeks, the team made no less than 32 dives and recovered around 1,800 objects, which ranged from small items such as plates, to many of the ship's fittings including masthead lights, a telegraph from the bridge, and much more. Many of these items were exhibited in Paris and subsequently part of the collection toured Scandinavia in 1991 and 1992 (many of the families travelling on the Titanic had originated from this part of the

*BELOW: Some examples of the beautiful silver-ware brought up from the wreck.*

world; as an 'emigrant' ship, she was carrying many people to a new life in the New World). Now that the precise location of the *Titanic* was known, it became a magnet for other exploration groups eager to test their capabilities and technology on the famous shipwreck of all time.

In 1991 a film company made a series of dives using equipment chartered from Russian sources. Using the high quality IMAX® process intended for projection on to wide, wraparound, screens giving audiences a sense of participation in the events they were seeing, a series of absolutely stunning images were obtained and made into a feature film entitled *Titanica*. In 1992 a company called Marex-Titanic Inc., backed yet again by Jack Grimm among others, raised an expedition which sailed at the end of the year. However, by the time its vessel, *Sea Mussel*, had reached the site, the company was deeply embroiled in legal arguments which eventually forced it to withdraw without ever diving on the wreck. Their protagonists were Titanic Ventures, which had been a partner in the successful Franco-American foray in 1987 and laid claim to the *salvor in possession*, a legal term which, if sustained, would mean that they had sole rights to the removal of any artefacts from the wreck. The legal wrangle dragged on until the end of 1993 when Titanic Ventures, now known as R.M.S. Titanic Inc., was finally granted the legal right to work on the wreck and subsequently further dives were arranged in 1993 and 1994 to recover more material.

A small but significant part of the collection gathered over the years featured in a major exhibition at Britain's National Maritime Museum at Greenwich, this display opening on 4 October, 1994 and official guests included a number of survivors of the sinking. When the exhibition finally closed in April 1995, almost three quarters of a million people had been drawn to come and learn the story of the *Titanic* and to view the fascinating collection of pieces drawn up at such great expense from the bottom of the ocean. When it ended, two *Titanic* survivors, Edith Haisman and Eva Hart, joined in a ceremony to dedicate a memorial to the victims of the disaster in the grounds of the museum. Surprisingly, this was the first public memorial to the *Titanic* to be erected in London. In August 1996, RMS Titanic Inc. and the Discovery Channel launched a scientific investigation to try and resolve some remaining mysteries and unsatisfactory explanations. They consulted many prominent experts and, with the aid of a sonar scan, finite element testing analysis and metallurgical testing, they found the hidden gash caused by the iceberg. It was confirmed that the area of damage was just 12.6 sq ft, an area so small, many couldn't believe that it could sink a ship the size of *Titanic*. This finally substantiated the original calculations by Edward Wilding that the damage was no more than 12 sq ft. Most of this damage was found hidden by sediments, the small gashes not being clean and linear but a sporadic type damage. The team also determined that the forces created by flooding and the steel metallurgy had brought about the hull's failure, and that she broke into three pieces during her plunge to the bottom. R.M.S. Titanic Inc. are currently involved in a scheme to mount a permanent *Titanic* display aboard a barge which could then be towed to ports around the world, enabling even more access to one of the world's greatest dramas.

Stuart Williamson ©94

# APPENDICES

## 1 Films

*RIGHT: The busy scenes at Southampton docks as passengers arrive for the voyage of a lifetime..*

*BELOW: Kate Winslet - Rose - on James Cameron's amazingly realistic* Titanic.

The sheer scale of events, the tales of cowardice and courage and the dramatic polarisation between poverty and luxury, have attracted many story tellers to attempt to recount the story of the *Titanic*. However, nothing lends itself so perfectly to this purpose than the medium of film. As early as 1912, the year she went down, a German film entitled *In Nacht und Eis* (by Mime Misu) reconstructed the events of 14 April, 1912.

However, all of the films take second place to James Cameron's remarkable *Titanic*, starring Leonardo DiCaprio and Kate Winslet. Before its release on video, in less than a year, its worldwide receipts approached $2 billion. The stills from the film on the next pages do scant justice to the incredible special effects, which — allied to a punctillious attention to detail, an excellent cast, and a dramatic story — make the film so powerful. To achieve the special effects, Cameron built a massive model — nearly full size — on the coast in Baja California, Mexico. This model sat in a tank of 17 million gallons of seawater.

PREVIOUS PAGE: *Rose De Witt Bukater, played by Kate Winslett, arrives and steps from her carriage to reluctantly join the ship that will carry her to an unwanted marriage.*

ABOVE: *This three quarter size model of the Titanic was actually made of wood and was never in more than three feet of water.*

RIGHT: *Jack Dawson (Leonardo diCaprio) celebrates after winning a ticket to cross the Atlantic on the Titanic.*

Below: *Every effort was made to copy the original ship as closely as possible. Harland & Wolff's plans and drawings, depicted earlier in this book, were followed and the resulting set was minutely detailed.*

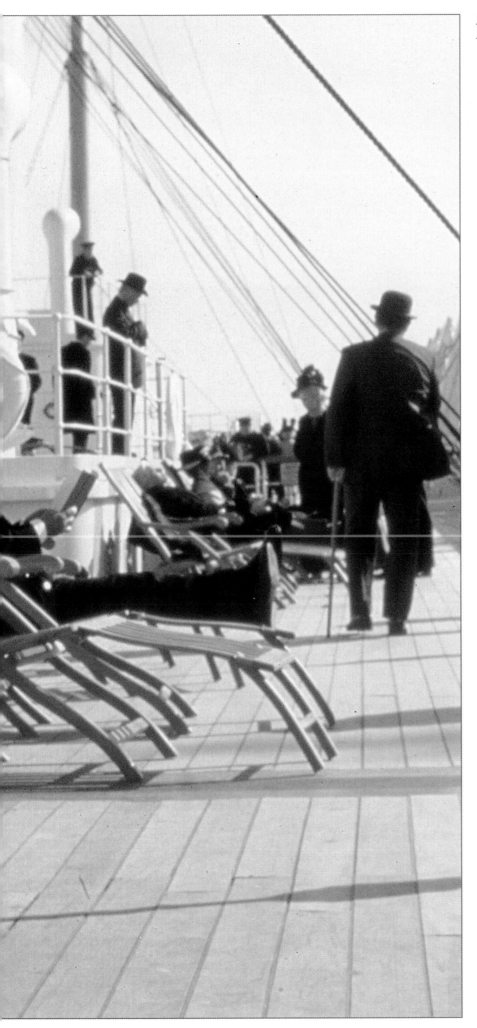

*LEFT: Jack and Rose on the first class Promenade deck.*

ABOVE: A still from the famous scence on the bow.

RIGHT: First class, the 'Unsinkable' Molly Brown played by Kathy Bates. In reality, Molly Brown was a curious character who aspired to the upper classes yet could not bear their snobbery and condescention.

*Above: Cameron's movie critiques the Victorian class system. In this scene Jack is snubbed at the foot of the grand staircase by Rose's mother Ruth De Witt Bukater (Frances Fisher) and her fiancee Cal (Billy Zane). Following the formal dinner Jack takes Rose to a much more liberated party in steerage.*

TOP: *Rose being sketched by Jack while wearing nothing but the 'Heart of the Ocean' as the* Titanic *speeds towards her doom with all lights blazing (*ABOVE*).*

*RIGHT: Jack and Rose battle their way through the freezing water as the Titanic sinks beneath them. The set for the grand staircase was in fact built over a million-gallon tank full of seawater and was lowered into it for this scene to provide a realistic sinking effect.*

*ABOVE: Molly and Ruth panic as the death of the Titanic becomes inevitable. Women from first class represented a relatively high proportion of survivors*

ABOVE: *The set is raised and lowered hydraulically and flooded with tens of thousands of gallons of water to recreate the Titanic's demise. The poop deck set was tilted from almost horizontal to 90 degrees in a matter of seconds. This made dangerous and confusing work for actors, camera crew and stunt people.*

464

*ABOVE: Winslett, diCaprio and Cameron. At the time of going to press, Titanic is the biggest earning movie on record, with takings in excess of $1.8 billion, dwarfing the $200 million that it cost to produce and the £1 million that the original Titanic was insured for.*

It was all a far cry from 1953, when Hollywood made its first all-star cast version of events called *Titanic*. The film was directed by Jean Negulesco, and starred Barbara Stanwyck, Clifton Webb, Brian Aherne and Robert Wagner. The film places the Sturges family at the centre of the drama, and we follow their exploits as Mrs. Sturges, a first class passenger played by Barbara Stanwyck, takes her two children back to America tired of her brutally elitist husband and the endless social whirl of Europe. She longs for her boy to 'walk to school, not picked up each morning by a carriage with two ponies'. Mr. Sturges (Clifton Webb) has other ideas; on finding out that she has fled aboard *Titanic*, he buys a ticket at Cherbourg from a Basque man who is emigrating with his family. The man will follow on the next White Star Liner with the small fortune he has been paid for his steerage ticket.

Sturges quickly moves from steerage to first class, allowing us (briefly) to examine the vast socio-economic divide, in fact Sturges makes a rather interesting quip as he pushes onto the first class Promenade deck; The steward tells him he cannot enter, Sturges mutters, 'Don't worry, I won't embarrass myself, I know how to act'. We then settle into the journey with them, based around the rituals of dining, playing bridge or checkers, or strolling the first class Promenade deck with its many liaisons and flirtations. At the peak of the family drama, the eldest Sturges child, their daughter, makes it perfectly clear that she will return to Europe with her father. The battle then turns to the young boy of ten or eleven. Desperately Mrs. Sturges plays her trump card; the boy is fathered by another man. Sturges rejects the boy saying he wants no further part in his life, adding that he has always thought she was common and now, in addition, rather disgusting. Mrs. Sturges' struggle is mirrored in the subplot of an alcoholic priest who has been fired from the

*BELOW: The launch of* Titanic *depicted in the film* A Night to Remember. *The launch was in reality a lower key affair without the usual champagne bottle-breaking.*

*RIGHT: Captain Smith informs Ismay, the White Star Line's chairman, that the ship is doomed; from the film* A Night to Remember.

*FAR RIGHT: Many women were reluctant to leave their husbands and the safety of the ship. Perhaps the best known example of this is Ida Straus. Survivor Colonel Archibald Gracie recalled that she refused to get into a boat, saying 'No! I will not be separated from my husband. As we have lived, so will we die. Together!' Again, this still is from the film* A Night to Remember.

clergy and is shamefully returning home with the bad news, his life also in tatters. We observe Captain Smith and Lightoller at work (the captain mainly being shown in the context of social engagements). When the ship strikes the berg this has a profound affect upon Sturges who up until this point has been aggressive to all concerned, seeking solace in games of bridge. As *Titanic* starts to go down, he stoically organises his family's evacuation knowing full well he is probably doomed. His display of valour resolves twenty years of acrimony with his wife and they declare their undying love. Sturges then makes himself busy assisting the crew in lowering the other lifeboats and then, suddenly, he remembers the Basque family who are down in steerage — they are confused, crying and refusing to wear lifebelts, Sturges organises their safe evacuation too. Unknown to anybody the Sturges' boy has followed Mr. Sturges example and given his seat to a middle aged woman. They meet on deck, and as the band play and all the passengers sing(!) they huddle together, father reclaiming his son, his son overjoyed to have won back the affections of his father, and proudly they die together like righteous men. Strangely this version makes no mention of Ismay or Andrews whatsoever, electing to lay the blame upon Captain Smith's shoulders, with much being made of Lightoller's attempts to reduce speed and Smith mocking his concerns in front of Colonel Astor. The film feels rather stagy as there are few exterior shots of *Titanic* at sea with the most ridiculous moment being the total lack of pandemonium on deck even

moments before she breaks up. As you would imagine from the time it was made, the iceberg gash runs the length of the ship, and she goes down rather gently in one piece.

A better attempt followed in 1958. In 1955 public attention had been aroused once again by a best selling account of the sinking entitled *A Night to Remember* written by Walter Lord. Lord's treatment of events of that night were written in a dramatic style which captured the public imagination and it was subsequently made into a highly successful film of the same name. *A Night to Remember* directed by Roy Ward Baker, was a British film whose technical adviser was none other than Fourth Officer Boxhall, the longest surviving of the ships officers. The film subtly and most powerfully builds up to its well realised conclusion through a collage of vignettes, rather than placing great emphasis upon a small group of individuals. The film was acutely aware of the class ridden nature of the evacuation, refusing to shy away from the fact that money and status still counted even when facing imminent death. There is one scene where the steerage passengers begin a revolt, frustrated by their hopeless situation as the First Class passengers are politely escorted to their lifeboats. The structure and technique of the film is in more of a documentary style than any other concerning the sinking, and its tension is built with a controlled pace that allows precisely chosen images to speak to the audience concisely: a frantic first class passenger snatches her lucky charm from her suite ignoring her precious jewels, a

*ABOVE: That people were playing cards when the vessel struck the iceberg is evinced by the statement by Alfred Fernand Omont (see page 364). In the subsequent inquiries a number of first class passengers testified to have seen or been involved in a game of bridge before the final plunge into the depths. Nevertheless, this is a ficticious scene from* Atlantic.

sweet trolley rolls down the inclining floor of the deserted first class dining room. Depending on ones viewpoint *A Night to Remember* is probably still the most realistic and engaging account of the disaster to date. In 1964 the passenger Molly Brown was immortalised in her own spin-off story, *The Unsinkable Molly Brown*, and in 1980 followed the disastrous *Raising the Titanic*. Inevitably all other films about liners sinking, or survivors huddled inside a tiny lifeboat, would somehow allude to that night of 14 April, 1912, even if they did so unconsciously, Stanley Kramer's *Ship of Fools* (1965) and Hitchcock's *Lifeboat* (1944) both spring to mind.

The latest cinematic rendition of the event is, of course, James Cameron's 1997 blockbuster, *Titanic*. Cameron was born in Kapuskasing, Ontario, Canada, and grew up in Niagara Falls. In 1971 he moved to California where a decade later he landed a job at Roger Corman's New World Pictures on the strength of his first short film. It was here that he honed many skills — particularly miniature building and art direction. In 1982 Cameron wrote *The Terminator* and after a two year struggle scraped the $6 million production costs together to film it. The rest, as they say is history — critically acclaimed as a landmark science fiction movie and grossing $80 million world wide into the bargain, it lead to directing jobs on *Rambo: First Blood Part 2*, *Aliens*, *The Abyss*, *Terminator 2*, *True Lies* and of course *Titanic*. Cameron has earned a reputation as an accomplished producer/director of action movies and it is easy to see what attracted him to the story of the *Titanic* , a historical event that is loaded with meanings and which offers a huge canvas with the potential for great action. The film was planned and shot as an old fashioned Hollywood epic and reputedly finished as the most expensive film ever made with estimates beginning at $200 million. The scale of the movie was in fact so large that Twentieth Century Fox and Paramount collaborated on the picture, with Paramount stepping in as production costs escalated. The story begins underwater on the wreck of the *Titanic*, with a present day version of *Alvin* and *Jason Junior* attempting the salvage of a safe in a first class cabin which the expedition boss, Brock Lovett (Bill Paxton), is sure contains a priceless diamond known as 'The Heart of the Ocean'. Interestingly, Cameron became obsessed with the wreck — diving on it himself a dozen times, which probably explains why so much screen time is devoted to this part of the story. To Lovett and his team's despair, the safe contains only a sketch of a naked woman wearing the stone around her neck. Enter the story's protagonist, Rose DeWitt Bukater (Gloria Stuart) a 101 year old survivor of the disaster, who sees the picture on television and is subsequently airlifted to the north Atlantic to tell them her story. It is she as a young girl who is wearing the diamond necklace and we begin the sequence of flashbacks describing how she survived the sinking and the mystery of the stone begins to unravel. Cameron has tried to use the distance this device creates to give the film a fairy tale feel, but its most profitable use is when we are given a precise computer generated account of exactly how *Titanic* went down; later, when we watch it happen, we can concentrate more completely on the terror. Southampton 1912; the young Rose played by Kate Winslett arrives and steps from her carriage looking every bit the movie icon, she reluctantly boards the ship that will take her to wed her rich

*BELOW: The women and children rule seemed to be more rigorously enforced on the port side. At least one husband said goodbye to his wife, and then plunged into the icy waters. In the case of Mr Hoyt, who jumped into the water after seeing his wife safely on board and swam in the dark to where he guessed that the boat might be passing, his guess proved correct and he was pulled on board Collapsible D.*

fiancee, Cal (Billy Zane), when they arrive in America. Cal who is as arrogant as he is rich, is the answer to her mothers dreams as her own husband died leaving them nothing but their double barrelled name and huge debts. We cut to a pub on the Southampton quayside where Jack Dawson (Leonardo DiCaprio) is playing poker for a steerage ticket. Jack Dawson is a penniless, free spirited artist, who has been earning a living sketching prostitutes in Paris. He wins the ticket for himself and a companion from two Swedish emigrants and just makes it aboard the departing liner. Later that night Rose tries to throw herself over the stern distraught by the idea of marrying a man who treats her like an expensive possession. Jack manages to talk her out of it and the seeds of romance are sown. His reward for this is dining first class at her table, where Cal and Rose's mother do their utmost to humiliate him, after which Jack takes Rose to a much more liberated party down in steerage. Cal's valet, Lovejoy (David Warner) begins tailing them for his master, and their meetings are forced to become ever more clandestine. Ruth De Witt Bukater (Frances Fisher) starts to apply pressure fearful that this class crossing romance will leave them penniless, and as is typical of many incidents throughout the film, Cameron loads the scene with as much meaning as he can possibly cram in; Rose is having her corset done up. Ruth DeWitt Butaker enters the cabin, she dismisses the maid and takes over the job herself. As she lectures her daughter on the importance of marrying well to save the family from poverty and embarrassment, she pulls harder and harder on the strings of the corset, therefore restricting Rose's body inside it in the same way she seeks to restrict her life in an unwanted marriage. On the bridge, Captain Smith (Bernard Hill) yields to Bruce Ismay's (Jonathan Hyde) demands to make the ship go faster. Rose asks Jack to sketch her nude and she leaves the sketch in Cal's safe. The lovers then flee, pursued by Lovejoy, from first class through steerage, to the crews quarters, the boiler rooms and eventually hide out in the stow. Cameron makes great use of this chase sequence to explore the rest of the ships anatomy having set most of the previous drama in the first class cafe, dining room and promenade decks. Once in the stow the two make love in the back of a luxurious motor car. However, up in the crow's nest the lookouts have spotted ice: Murdoch orders the ship hard a starboard, engines are reversed, she squares up to the iceberg and then slowly comes around but it is too late. *Titanic* glances the berg, sheering off huge chunks on to the deck. Stunned, Smith hurries back up on to the bridge. We return to the drama of the lovers, where Jack is planted with the 'Heart of the Ocean' and arrested as a thief (once again Cameron plays for the visual metaphor; Cal sees Jack as a thief (after all, Rose is his property). With the ship rapidly going down Jack finds himself handcuffed to a pipe in the master at arms office. Thomas Andrews tells Smith that the ship is doomed and also tells Rose, confirming knowingly how right she was when noting that the lifeboats could only provide for half the souls on board. The crew distribute lifebelts, and nonchalance slowly turns to panic. In steerage, panic turns quickly to fury as the third class passengers are locked behind iron gates. Up on deck women and children are being loaded into the boats and it is around this time that Bruce Ismay is seen getting into a boat full of women while watched by a repulsed officer. Below, Rose rescues Jack and they make their escape through flooded steerage passageways and smash down a metal gate. Rose gets into a lifeboat convinced that Jack will follow shortly in the next one. Cal has bribed his way into a boat and is about to board when he sees that Rose has left her boat to rejoin Jack, and then he suddenly remembers that the Heart of the Ocean is in the pocket of his coat that he draped across her shoulders. Furious, yet more twisted by their love he chases the pair down below with a pistol aiming to shoot them both. On deck, Murdoch shoots a crazed

*BELOW: The weather conditions — remarkable flat calm with virtually no swell — and the general size and sturdiness of the vessel, contributed greatly to the ease with which the lifeboats were launched, despite the obvious lack of organisation on the Boat deck. Getting on board the lifeboats was trickier — particularly from the parts of the Promenade deck that had been enclosed. The weather would only start to liven as Carpathia took on the survivors.*

passenger and then takes his own life with a gun shot to the head. His pistol empty Cal turns his attention to self preservation and climbs on board a lifeboat using a child to justify his place. *Titanic* begins to break up and Rose and Jack cling to the stern rail as the most visually stunning shots of the film play out. As the *Titanic* breaks in two, the stern achieves the perpendicular and bodies tumble and fall to their death all around Rose and Jack who then slide under with the sinking ship. After bobbing up from her suction they find some driftwood in the freezing sea of bodies which will only support Rose. Jack slowly freezes to death in the water. Back in the present day the elderly Rose tosses the 'Heart of the Ocean' diamond overboard and dies peacefully in her cabin. Her soul descends to join Jack and the other deceased crew and passengers of the *Titanic*. In making the film, Cameron built a three quarter size set which he then sank section by section on location in Mexico. This enormous floating set was used in conjunction with images shot of various sized models and enhanced by different techniques of computer generated graphics. Back in the studio Cameron built a huge hydraulic stern section that he could manipulate altering angles until finally it would stand vertical. From this vertical hydraulic platform stunt men physically dropped and tumbled over crash mats which were then airbrushed in by computer to look like components of the ship's stern. The meticulously designed interiors recreated the ship in fantastic (and more importantly, accurate) detail. The first class cabins and the atrium domed grand staircase were indeed exceptional. Wherever possible Cameron used the original companies who built furnishings and fittings for the original vessel. It is difficult not to draw parallels with the film and the ship itself, the biggest and most expensive ship of its time — and the biggest and most expensive film of its day. Perhaps we may also draw some parallels from the class system then and the power structure on a big working movie set. News leaked out of friction between the extras (read steerage) and director and producers (first class). Rumours spread that they were working ridiculously long hours in unacceptable conditions, although an independent investigator found nothing to substantiate this. According to the press at the time of production, a disgruntled chef even spiked the director's and producer's food with a mind expanding drug! The two big studios probably felt that with an investment of that size any news was good news and like Bruce Ismay of the White Star Line they were just happy to keep *Titanic* in the headlines.

Cameron adopted the traditional approach of interpreting the sinking as these things: an allegory for capitalism, divine retribution for human presumption and a symbol of the destruction of a privileged way of life as an omen of the changes that World War I was to bring. There are references to the mood of cosmopolitanism prevalent at the time, Rose's interest in the new art scene with her ownership of a Picasso, who Cal sneers 'will never amount to anything'. Her character also foreshadows the rise of feminism which was to have such a profound effect on the rest of the century. The film contains moments of breathtaking if not indulgent cinematography; Leonardo DiCaprio standing at the guard rail on the ship's bow with his arms outstretched, revelling in the air and in the total freedom of the ocean, and then moving along and through the whole length of the ship as we see people walking the decks in scrupulous detail. Some of its most successful scenes are shared with *A Night to Remember* — Thomas Andrews (Victor Garber) wracked with guilt, pondering his shame as he contemplates the picture on the wall in the first class smoking room. The attempts by crowds in the latter stages of the sinking to swamp the final lifeboats also try to achieve the same stark terror. Cameron's version also possibly had its love story roots in the 1955 version's subplot where Miss Sturges is courted by a rather boyish and uncouth tennis player. Of course Cameron takes the idea further as his characters are from the extremes of the class system, whereas in the 1955 version they are only from the extremes within first class.

Possibly to pay homage to the earlier film, Cameron borrows a line of dialogue from the *Titanic* of 1955 when one passenger remarks 'Why do the British find it necessary to announce dinner as if it were a cavalry charge?'

A serious shortcoming is that the script fails to authentically recreate the dialogue and manners of the era, and with Cameron's fastidious approach to recreating everything else of the period, this is obviously something he tried but failed to do. Perhaps we may also question the use of two young fictitious characters as his protagonists when there was a wealth of true stories that could have been dramatised. The films greatest strengths are when it is depicting the demise of the ship. Cameron dares to linger on objects and people throughout (which accounts for the film's great length), but it is when the ship is stricken that its minor and major characters, previously shackled by bad dialogue and positioning, explode into dramatic life. The destruction is awesome and takes on a truly terrifying immediacy, which successfully captures the full visceral terror. In these last moments characters expose themselves more wholly than in the two and three quarter hours that have previously elapsed. Rose punching a steward and Cal grabbing a baby as a passport to his survival are but two examples. The film both triumphs and fails in different ways, but then, how you do show all those fascinating stories of courage or harrowing suffering in just three and a quarter hours and still conform to accepted film storytelling methods? *Titanic* is respectful of its subject matter giving at least some characterisation to Ismay, Andrews and Smith. For the record, Bruce Ismay is painted as a coward who encouraged his Commodore to retire on a high note by sailing the ship faster. Captain Smith himself is portrayed as a man out of his depth rather than a seaman suffering from overconfidence and perishes alone on the Bridge accordingly. The film exceeded all box office expectations and won eleven Oscars, Cameron himself picking up three. maybe it is worth noting that all of them were in a technical category. The big studios had meetings to try and prevent a movie of this scale becoming the blockbuster norm but, as we have seen in history, there is always a human desire to be the very biggest, and the very best. Each time a new feature film, documentary film or book appears on the subject, public interest is rekindled, and as long as those renditions are faithful and engaging they will ensure that the story of what happened on that calm, clear night of 14 April 1912 will live on for generations.

# 2 Chronology

1847

White Star Line is founded.

1868

18 January

White Star Line is bought by Thomas Henry Ismay, father of J. Bruce Ismay. Agreements are reached with Gutsav Schwabe to bankroll White Star, provided that Harland & Wolff is contracted to build all new White Star liners.

1891

J. Bruce Ismay is admitted into the White Star Partnership.

1892

Thomas Ismay retires, leaving Bruce as Chairman

1902

American financier J. Pierpont Morgan's International Mercantile Marine Company (I.M.M.) buys White Star Line for £10 million. J. Bruce Ismay remains Chairman and Managing Director.

1904

J. Bruce Ismay is named President of I.M.M., at age 41.

1907

Summer

J. Bruce Ismay and Lord Pirrie, a partner in Harland & Wolff, meet at a dinner party at Pirrie's residence in London. They begin to formulate plans for two ocean liners that will surpass anything built to date. The names *Olympic* and *Titanic* are chosen. Sometime later, a third ship, at first called *Gigantic*, is added to the plans.

June

J. Bruce Ismay meets the New York Harbour Board to construct a pier long enough to accommodate a ship the proposed size of *Titanic* and *Olympic*. About the same time, Lord Pirrie instructs the Harland & Wolff architects to begin preliminary designs on *Olympic* and *Titanic*. He also begins plans to enlarge the Belfast shipyards to berth ships of such size.

July

Construction begins at Harland & Wolff's yards to combine three slips into two slips with a 220 ft high gantry, the largest ever built. It is supplied by J. Arrol of Liverpool.

1908

29 July

Ismay and Pirrie, among others, meet at Harland & Wolff to view the plans for *Olympic* and *Titanic*.

31 July

White Star Line and Harland & Wolff sign the building contract for *Olympic*, *Titanic*, and *Gigantic* (later renamed *Britannic*).

16 December

The keel plate (number 400) for *Olympic* is laid at Harland & Wolff's Belfast yard.

1909

31 March

The keel plate for *Titanic* (number 401) is laid.

1910

20 October

*Olympic*'s hull is launched and towed to the fitting out basin.

1911

31 May — 12:13 p.m.

*Titanic*'s 26,000 ton hull is launched at Harland & Wolff's shipyard, watched by over 100,000 people. She reaches a speed of 12 knots before six anchor chains and two piles of cable drag chains weighing 80 tons each bring her to a halt. As is White Star's practice, there is no christening.

3:00 p.m.

White Star Line representatives officially take possession of *Olympic*. Bruce Ismay, J. P. Morgan, and many other V.I.P.'s set sail for Liverpool aboard *Olympic*. *Titanic* is towed to the fitting out basin.

11 September

*Olympic* departs Southampton on her fifth voyage, commanded by Captain Edward James Smith, who would later command *Titanic*. While in the Splithead Channel she collides with the British cruiser H.M.S. *Hawke*. Both ships are badly damaged.

## 1912

### 3 February

*Titanic* is dry-docked in the Thompson Graving Dock, where she is fitted with her three massive propellers and the final coat of paint is applied to the hull, the final phase of her fitting out. Finishing touches are begun on the interior and the Marconi Radio is installed, tested and assigned the call letters MGY.

## THE MAIDEN VOYAGE

### Tuesday, 2 April

*Titanic* sets sail from Belfast and begins her sea trials. The most significant of these trials was a full speed turn, which encompassed a circle 3,850 ft in diameter and total forward movement of 2,100 ft. This means that, at 22 knots, it took *Titanic* four-tenths of a mile to turn 90 degrees. Board of Trade surveyor Francis Carruthers approved the tests and White Star took possession of *Titanic*. A small fire started in boiler room 6 that would smoulder for weeks in the coal dust of the starboard bunker.

### Friday, 5 April — 12:15 a.m.

*Titanic* arrives at the Southampton dock dressed in flags and pennants. She is berthed in slip 44.

### Saturday, 6 April

Crew hiring begins at the White Star and the Union halls. Hundreds of people jam the halls hoping for a job after the coal strike, which had ended the same day. Loading of cargo also begins. Crew begins loading the coal needed for the voyage.

### Sunday, 7 April

Crew finishes loading 4,427 tons of coal into *Titanic*'s coal bunkers. Work stops for the day, as it is Easter.

### Monday, 8 April

Fresh food is loaded. 75,000 lb of meat, 11,000 lb of fish, and 1,750 quarts of ice cream are brought into the huge refrigerated storerooms.

*Top and Above: A tasteless contemporary game — From Liverpool to New York without touching the icebergs!*

### Tuesday, 9 April

Board of Trade surveyor Captain Clark completes the final inspection of *Titanic*. Captain E.J. Smith also performs his own inspection with Second Officer Charles Lightoller and builder Thomas Andrews. All officers except Captain Smith slept this night on *Titanic*.

### Wednesday, 10 April — 7:30 a.m.

Captain Smith boards *Titanic* and receives the sailing report from Chief Henry Wilde. Bruce Ismay boards sometime after breakfast and tours the finished ship.

### 9:30 a.m.

The first train with first, second, and third class passengers arrives from Waterloo Station. Captain George Bowyer, *Titanic*'s Pilot, boards and the pilot's flag is run up the flagpole.

11:45 a.m.
*Titanic*'s siren sounds, signalling her departure.

12:05 p.m.
*Titanic*'s mooring ropes are cleared and tug boats begin towing her from the dock. Movement of *Titanic*'s huge mass in the harbour causes all six mooring ropes of the liner *New York* to snap. The *New York* swings towards *Titanic* and the tug *Vulcan* catches her bow, narrowly avoiding a collision. After a delay, *Titanic* is towed from harbour and begins the 24 mile crossing of the English Channel.

5:30 p.m.
*Titanic* arrives at Cherbourg, France, with all lights blazing. Passengers board tenders and are ferried onboard.

8:30 p.m.
*Titanic*'s anchor is raised and she sets sail for Queenstown, Ireland, around the southern coast of England.

Thursday, 11 April — Early morning
Thomas Andrews and the nine-member 'guarantee group' from Harland & Wolff's yards hold a full dress drill of the watertight safety doors.

11:30 a.m.
*Titanic* lowers anchor in Queenstown Harbour, two miles from land. Tenders *America* and *Ireland* deliver more passengers and mail.

1:30 p.m.
*Titanic*'s starboard anchor is raised for the last time, and she sets sail for New York.

2:30 p.m.
The ship's pilot, Captain Bowyer, is dropped off at the Daunt light-ship.

Late afternoon
*Titanic* passes the Old Head of Kinsale and blows her whistles at onlookers. She then heads out to open sea.

Friday, 12 April — Daybreak
*Titanic* is well on her way to the north Atlantic, running at 21 knots. She covers 386 miles on her first day at sea.

Afternoon
*Titanic* receives many wireless messages of congratulations, most including warnings of ice. Some passengers find that the wind is very cold and prefer to stay inside.

Late evening
*Titanic*'s Marconi Wireless Radio fails. Wireless officers Phillips and Bride work through the night to repair it.

Saturday, 13 April — 10:30 a.m.
Captain Smith begins his daily inspection of the ship. During his inspection of the engine room, Chief Engineer Bell reports the fire in boiler room 6 is finally extinguished; however, the bulkhead part of the bunker shows signs of heat damage. Captain Smith orders oil to be rubbed on the damaged one-inch thick steel.

Noon
*Titanic* has covered 519 miles in the last 24 hours.

SINKING

Sunday, 14 April — Early morning
*Titanic* continues on course into the heart of the north Atlantic. She covers another 546 miles on this day.

Mid-morning
*Titanic* receives a warning from *Caronia* of ice ahead. Later, another message from the Dutch liner *Noordam* also warns of 'much ice'.

Early afternoon
The *Baltic* reports 'large quantities of field ice' 250 miles ahead of *Titanic*. Captain Smith would later show this message to Bruce Ismay. One survivor account tells that Smith and Ismay talked at lunch about making New York a day early and grabbing headlines. Another message is received from *Amerika* warning of icebergs, but this message is not forwarded to Captain Smith.

6:00 p.m.
Captain Smith alters course to South 86 West True, heading south-west of original course, but maintains full speed.

7:30 p.m.
The *Californian* sends a third message warning of ice 50 miles ahead of *Titanic*.

9:20 p.m.
After meeting with Second Officer Lightoller and discussing the unusually calm seas and clear air, Captain Smith retires to his room. Officer Lightoller then cautions lookouts to be careful of ice until morning. *Titanic*'s speed at this time is 22 knots.

9:40 p.m.
A heavy ice pack and iceberg warning is received from the *Masaba*. Wireless officers Phillips and Bride ignore the message and proceed with sending personal messages from the passengers.

10:00 p.m.
Second Officer Lightoller is relieved by First Officer Murdock. *Titanic* is running at 22 to 24 knots with 24 of her 29 boilers lit.

10:55 p.m.
*Californian* reports that they have been stopped by ice 10-20 miles north of *Titanic*, reported position 40.2°N 50.7°W. Wireless officer Phillips tells them 'Keep out! Shut up! You're jamming my signal! I'm working Cape Race', and the *Californian* shuts down its set for the night.

11:30 p.m.
Lookouts Fleet and Lee note a slight haze appearing ahead.

11:40 p.m.
Lookout Fleet telephones the bridge yelling 'Iceberg right ahead!' and rings the crow's nest bell three times. Sixth Officer Moody acknowledges and relays the message to Murdock, who orders 'Hard-a-starboard' and telegraphs the engine room 'Full Stop' followed by 'Full Astern'.

11:40:40 p.m.
*Titanic* begins to turn slowly to port but strikes an underwater spar jutting from the iceberg on the starboard side 12 ft back from the bow. The one-inch thick plates of steel are scraped for 300 ft along *Titanic*'s side and 5–20 ft below the waterline, buckling or tearing a hole in compartment 1, two holes in compartment 2, another hole that crosses the bulkhead 3 between compartments 2 and 3,

another across bulkhead 4, and another across bulkhead 5 between boilers 5 and 6 and stoke hold 9. Water pressure from outside is pumping water into the vessel at the rate of 7 tons per minute (almost 2,000 gallons).

11:40:50 p.m.
First Officer Murdock orders 'Full to Port', trying to corner *Titanic* around the remainder of the iceberg. He also throws the electric switch closing the watertight compartment doors. Passengers on the upper decks watch the iceberg as *Titanic* passes by.

11:43 p.m.
Captain Smith arrives on the bridge and orders Thomas Andrews, Chief Wilde, and Officer Boxhall to go below and inspect the damage.

11:55 p.m.
The post office on G deck is flooded, trapping and drowning several workers. Thomas Andrews reports that five compartments are flooded to the waterline and advises Captain Smith that *Titanic* can float with four compartments filled, but not five.

Monday, 15 April — 12:00 a.m.
Officer Boxhall takes *Titanic*'s last position (41.46°N, 50.14°W), which Captain Smith takes to the wireless room and orders the distress call 'C.Q.D'.

12:05 a.m.
The squash court is now flooded. *Titanic*'s bow is only 15 ft above the 28°F water. The engine crew has started shutting down the boilers. Captain Smith orders the lifeboats uncovered and life jackets distributed. 25 minutes after the collision, 140 tons of freezing water now fills the forward compartments and begins to overflow bulkhead 6, which only goes up to E — the Upper deck — and flood the adjoining compartments.

12:07 a.m.
Cunard liner *Carpathia* responds to *Titanic*'s distress calls. She is 58 miles south-east of *Titanic* and will take over four hours to arrive.

12:15 a.m.
Wallace Hartley and his band begins playing ragtime music in the first class lounge on Promenade deck.

12:25 a.m.

Captain Smith orders the lifeboats filled, women and children first. First Officer Lightoller commands the lowering crews, forward boats first and moving aftward.

12:45 a.m.

Lifeboat 7 is launched from the starboard side with 27 people. It can hold 65. Quartermaster George Rowe fires the first distress rocket under direction of Officer Boxhall. The rockets are fired from the bridge railing of the Boat deck, near emergency boat 1. Aboard the *Californian*, Chief Officer Stone reports seeing rockets 10 miles to starboard to Captain Lord, who then orders him to try contacting the ship by Morse lamp, not wireless (this was later disputed by Captain Lord during the official investigations).

12:50 a.m.

Officer Boxhall sights a vessel (possibly the *Californian*) off in the distance, but all attempts to reach her with Morse lamps are futile and she disappears.

12:55 a.m.

Lifeboat 5 is launched from the starboard side with 40 people aboard. Lifeboat 6 is launched from the port side with 25 people.

1:00 a.m.

Lifeboat 3 is launched from the port side with 32 people (including 11 crew members).

1:10 a.m.

Lifeboat 8 is launched from the port side with 27 people aboard. Emergency boat 1 is launched from the starboard side with 12 people. It can hold 40.

1:15 a.m.

Captain Smith tries to recall the half full lifeboats, but none return. *Titanic*'s name, painted on the bow, is now at the waterline and water is beginning to flow over the top of the bulkhead 8 at E deck (Upper deck) level. *Californian* officers Stone and Gibson see several rockets and report them to Captain Lord (who later denied this account) they also try repeatedly to signal they distant ship with Morse lamps.

1:20 a.m.

Lifeboat 10 is launched from the port side with 47 people.

About this time, Thomas Andrews is seen staring at a painting in the first class smoking room. He does not reply when asked to leave.

1:25 a.m.

Panic is setting in as Lifeboat 14 is launched from the starboard side with 54 people, including Officer Lowe, who fires three shots in the air from his pistol to keep passengers on the Lower deck (G) from jumping onto the boat. Lifeboat 16 is launched from the port side with 42 people.

1:30 a.m.

Lifeboat 12 is launched from the port side with 32 people and Lifeboat 9 is launched from the starboard side with 48 people. *Titanic* begins to list to starboard while her decks get continually steeper.

1:35 a.m.

Lifeboat 11 is launched from the starboard side with 56 people. Wireless operator Phillips sends his last message, then abandons the radio room and heads aft.

1:40 a.m.

Lifeboat 13 is launched from the starboard side with 54 people and lifeboat 15 is launched with 57 people. Collapsible boat C is launched from the starboard side with 32 people (including White Star Chairman J. Bruce Ismay). It can hold 49 and is the last boat lowered to the water on this side of the ship.

1:45 a.m.

Emergency boat 2 is launched from the port side with 20 people (it can hold 40).

1:50 a.m.

Lifeboat 4 is launched from the port side with 34 people.

2:00 a.m.

The water has risen to just 10 ft below the Promenade deck and the bow railings are now under water. About this time, Captain Smith is last seen standing on the flooding bridge. Wallace Hartley's band begins their last song, 'Nearer, My God, To Thee'.

2:05 a.m.

Collapsible boat D is lowered from the port side with 44 people. This is the last boat to be lowered from the deck of

*Titanic*. Some survivors reported that an officer (possibly Murdock) shot at rushing passengers, hitting at least one, then turned the gun on himself. There are still over 1,500 people left aboard *Titanic* as water pours over the forward section of A deck. Remaining passengers climb to the aft section, which has now started to rise out of the water.

2:10 a.m.
Collapsible boats A and B are freed from their tie downs but the rising water sweeps them off the deck. Passengers are seen jumping from the aft steerage loading door to the freezing water 100 ft below. *Titanic*'s propellers are now completely out of the water.

2:15 a.m.
Father Thomas Byles gives confession to passengers gathered on the aft end of the Boat deck. Loud crashes are heard as objects in the interior of the ship slide toward the submerged bow.

2:18 a.m.
The lights flicker once, then go out as the electric generators fail. *Titanic*'s hull splits from the deck to the keel between the third and fourth funnels. The stern section falls back to the water, then rises again as the bow breaks off and begins its descent.

2:20 a.m.
The stern section floods and goes down 'like an elevator', 2 hr 30 min after the collision. Over 1,500 remaining passengers plunge into the icy water. Aboard the *Californian*, Officers Stone and Gibson watch as a distant ship apparently travels beyond the horizon.

2:21 a.m.
About 20 people in the water climb into the partially submerged Collapsible A and another 30 climb atop the overturned Collapsible B. Anyone in the 28°F water is now suffering from shock and the onset of hypothermia. The stern section implodes 200 ft down due to external pressure and nowhere for the trapped air to go.

2:25 a.m.
After four minutes in the freezing water, and assuming an average body weight of 140 lb, most people in the water are experiencing numbing of the extremities, shortness of breath, tunnel vision and absolute terror. These assump-

tions are based on medical reports of hypothermia victims.

2:28 a.m.
About this time, the bow crashes to the seabed 12,600 ft below. *Titanic* lands intact and upright, sinking 20-25 ft into the mud. Since it was flooded when it sank, the pressure equalised and it did not suffer the implosion that the stern did. Current position: 41°43'57"N 49°56'49"W (13.5 miles from last reported position).

2:30 a.m.
After ten minutes in the water, the average person is shivering uncontrollably, unable to speak coherently, and unable to process any information. They are running on pure instinct, trying to survive at any cost, and climbing atop one another to get out of the water. Children at this point have lost consciousness.

2:31 a.m.
The stern hits the bottom, 2,000 ft (1/3 mile) away from the bow. Current position: 41°43'35"N 49°56'54"W.

2:35 a.m.
Most adults have stopped trying to swim and are just staying afloat with their lifebelts. The screams have begun to subside as people begin to slip into unconsciousness.

2:50 a.m.
Most people in the water are dead or unconscious by now, having succumbed to hypothermia after 30 minutes in the 28°F water. Survivors in the lifeboats are huddled together, some rowing to keep warm.

3:00 a.m.
Officers and crew members begin to gather the boats together. Some survivors are transferred from lifeboat 14 to the others, then Officer Lowe heads for the people in the water looking for other survivors. Six people are pulled from the water, barely alive. 14 people are pulled from the partially submerged Collapsible A before it is cast adrift with three dead bodies still aboard. Lifeboats 4 and 12 rescue 28 survivors from overturned Collapsible B.

3:30 a.m.
*Carpathia*'s rockets are sighted.

4:10 a.m.
Lifeboat 2 arrives at the *Carpathia*.

4:45 a.m.
Lifeboat 13 arrives at the *Carpathia*.

5:10 a.m.
Lifeboat 5 arrives at the *Carpathia*.

5:30 a.m.
Aboard the *Californian*, Captain Lord arrives on the bridge and asks about the ship from last night. Officer Stewart points out the ship, noting that there are no signals now (what they saw was the *Carpathia*). Captain Lord awakes Wireless Officer Evans and asks him to turn on the wireless. After being advised of *Titanic*'s sinking by the *Frankfort*, *Californian* heads for the site at full steam.

6:00 a.m.
Lifeboats 3 and 6 arrive at the *Carpathia*.

6:30 a.m.
Collapsible C arrives at the *Carpathia* with J. Bruce Ismay aboard.

7:00 a.m.
Collapsible D arrives at the *Carpathia*.

8:00 a.m.
Lifeboat 11 arrives at the *Carpathia*.

8:20 a.m.
*Californian* arrives.

8:30 a.m.
Lifeboat 12 arrives at the *Carpathia*. Officer Lightoller is the last survivor to come aboard.

8:50 a.m.
*Carpathia* leaves for New York with 705 survivors aboard. *Californian* is asked to stay and search for bodies from the water. Both ships are flying their flags at half-mast.

9:00 a.m. approx
J. Bruce Ismay sends to White Star Line's New York office: 'Deeply regret advise you *Titanic* sank this morning after collision with iceberg, resulting in serious loss of life. Full particulars later.' Ismay signed his telegrams using his name in reverse 'YAMSI'. *Titanic* operator Bride offers to help in the sending survivor lists and messages to families.

11:00 a.m.
*Californian* leaves the area bound for Boston.

THE AFTERMATH

18 April — 9:00 p.m.
*Carpathia* arrives in New York with *Titanic*'s 705 survivors. *Californian* arrives the same day in Boston.

19 April
American hearings investigating the disaster begin at the Waldorf Astoria in New York. *Californian* officer Gibson sells his story to the local papers, detailing how officers aboard *Californian* saw the rockets and reported then to Captain Lord, who failed to take prompt action. Although many aspects of his story are denied by other officers, the press blames Captain Lord for the disaster.

22 April
The S.S. *Macay Bennet* is sent from New York to recover the last of the bodies. 328 corpses are recovered by 15 May.

2 May
The British Board of Trade Inquiry begins.

25 May
The U.S. investigation ends, with no clear fault for the disaster found. Captain Lord of the *Californian* is found negligent and blamed for the great loss of life, having not responded to reports of rockets by his officers.

3 July
The British Inquiry ends. Although no clear blame for the disaster is decided, Captain Lord is described as 'negligent' in his handling of the rocket reports from his officers.

April, 1913
As a result of the U.S. and British inquiries, the International Ice Patrol is created to locate and break up large icebergs in the north Atlantic. New regulations are passed for Marconi Wireless Operations, namely that all ship-board radios will be manned 24 hours a day.

26 February, 1914
*Britannic*, the third of White Star's 'Olympic' class, is launched. At 48,158 gross registered tons, she is bigger than her sister ships, *Olympic* and *Titanic*. This increased

size is due to new safety features added to the hull after *Titanic* sank.

13 November, 1915
At the start of W.W.I, *Britannic* is recommissioned as a hospital ship. Her nearly completed interior staterooms are refitted as operating rooms. She is declared fit for war duty on 12 December.

12 December, 1915
*Britannic* arrives in Liverpool under heavy escort. She is outfitted for her duties as a hospital ship with 2,034 berths and 1,035 cots for casualties. A medical staff of 52 officers, 101 nurses, 336 orderlies, and a crew of 675 men and women. The ship is commanded by Charles A. Bartlett.

23 December, 1915
*Britannic* departs Liverpool on her maiden voyage. She is bound for Mudros on the Isle of Lemnos, where she is due to join the *Mauretania*, *Aquitania*, and her sister, *Olympic*, in the Dardanelles (Turkey) Service. Joined later by the *Statendam* the five ships together were capable of carrying 17,000 sick and wounded or 33,000 troops

21 November, 1916
On her sixth voyage, *Britannic* hits a German mine while steaming through the Kea Channel off the coast of Greece and sinks in only 55 minutes. The explosion apparently occurred at the watertight bulkhead between holds 2 and 3. At the same time, boiler rooms 5 and 6 began taking water. This was roughly the same damage as that sustained by her sister the *Titanic*. With 1,100 people on board, only 30 are lost when two lifeboats are launched while the ship is still under way and are sucked into the propellers. On a special note, Violet Jessop was on board assigned as a nurse. She was also on the crew of *Olympic* when it collided with *Hawke*, and she was onboard *Titanic* as a stewardess. She was a survivor, too, of the lifeboat incident.

17 July, 1918
*Carpathia* is struck by two German torpedoes 170 miles from Bishop's rock off of the Isles of Scilly. As the crew man the lifeboats, the ship is struck by a third torpedo. Five crew members are killed instantly. The remainder of the crew and *Carpathia*'s 57 passengers are picked up by the H.M.S. *Snowdrop* and returned to Liverpool. The *Carpathia* sinks at 12:40 a.m. on that morning.

TITANIC TODAY

9 July, 1986
Ballard returns to the wreck aboard *Atlantis II* with the submersible *Alvin* and the remote vehicle *Jason. Junior* The first clear pictures of *Titanic* in 74 years are taken. The R.O.V. *Jason Junior* takes pictures and explores the remains of the grand staircase and ballroom. Ballard says he will not disturb the site in any way and leaves on the forward Promenade deck a bronze plaque honouring the dead.

1987
The U.S. Senate passes a bill stating that 'no *Titanic* artefacts may be imported into the United States', a weak attempt at curbing salvage operations.

22 July, 1987
I.F.R.E.M.E.R.'s mother ship, *Nadir*, successfully launches the deep sea submersible *Nautile* which makes 32 consecutive dives to the wreck site. Using a remote controlled robot similar to *Jason Junior* called *Robin*, *Nautile* records new photos and video.

17 June, 1991
A Canadian-Russian team explores *Titanic* and films with the new IMAX camera.

1993
The R.M.S. Titanic Inc. expedition with submersible *Nautile* spends 15 days at the wreck site and recovers some 800 artefacts.

1994
R.M.S. Titanic Inc. returns with *Nautile* and recovers coal from the debris field.

August 1996
R.M.S. Titanic Inc. returns led by George Tulloch. The expedition tries and fails to retrieve a piece of the hull.

December 1997
Launch of James Cameron's movie *Titanic*.

August 1998
R.M.S. Titanic Inc. Recover the 'Big Piece,' a 23 ft by 14 ft section of the outer hull for exhibition in their public display of *Titanic* artefacts.

# 3 Crew List

OFFICERS

Captain

Smith, Edward John

Chief officer

Wilde, Henry Tingle

First officer

Murdoch, William McMaster

Second officer

*Lightoller, Charles Herbert

Third officer

*Pitman, Herbert John

Fourth officer

*Boxhall, Joseph

Fifth officer

*Lowe, Harold Godfrey

Sixth officer

Moody, James Pell

QUARTERMASTERS

*Bright, Arthur John

*Hitchens, Robert

*Humphreys, James

*Olliver, Alfred

*Perkis, Walter J.

*Rowe, George Thomas

*Wynn, Walter

DECK CREW

A. B. Seamen

*Anderson, J.

*Archer, Ernest

Bradley, F.

*Brice, W.

*Buley, Edward J.

Church, G.

*Clench, Fredrick

Clench, G.

Crouch, F.

Davis, Stephen J.

Evans, Frank O.

*Forward, J.

*French, William

*Hagan, John

Holman, H.

*Hopkins, Robert

*Horswill, Albert

Edward James

*Jones, Thomas

*Lucas, William

Lyons, William H.

Matherson, D.

*McCarthy, W.

*McGough, James (Paddy)

*Moore, George

*Osman, Frank

Parks, Sam

*Pascoe, C. H.

*Peters, W. C.

*Pigott, P.

*Poigndestre, John

*Scarrott, Joseph

Smith, W.

Taylor, C.

Terrell, Bertram

*Weller, William

*White, Ralph

LOOKOUTS

*Evans, Alfred Frank

*Fleet, Frederick

*Hogg, George Alfred

*Jewell, Archie

*Lee, Reginald Robinson

*Symons, George

MISCELLANEOUS

Boatswain Nichols, Alfred

Boatswain's mate

*Haines, Albert

Carpenter Maxwell, John

Joiner Hutchinson, John H.

Lamptrimmer *Hemmings,
  Samuel Ernest

Masters at arms

*Bailey, W.

King, T. W.

Mess-room steward

Mathias, M.

Storekeeper *Foley, Jack

Surgeon

O'Loughlin, William, F. H.

Assistant surgeon

Tamlyn, Fredrick

Window cleaners

*Harder, William

Sawyer, R. J.

Simpson, J. Edward

POSTAL CLERKS

Gwinn, William

March, John Starr

Smith, John Richard Jago

Williamson, James Bertram

Woody, Oscar S.

ENGINEERING CREW

Leading Firemen

*Barrett, Fredrick

Davies, T.

Ford, Thomas

*Hendrickson, Charles

Mason, J.

Mayo, W.

Pugh, P.

Small, William

*Threlfall, Thomas

Ward, J.

Webber, F.

FIREMEN

Abraham, C.

Adams, R.

Allen, H.

Bailey, G. W.

Ball, W.

Barlow, C.

Barnes, Chas

Barnes, J.

Barrett, F. W.

*Beauchamp, George

Bendell, T.

Bennett, G.

Benville, E.

Bessant, W.

Biddlecombe, C.

Biggs, E.

Black, A.

Black, D.

Blackman, H.

Blake, T.

Blancy, J.

Blann, Eustace

Bradley, P.

Brigge, W.

Brown, J.

Brown, J.

Burroughs, A.

Burton, E.

Butt, W.

Camner, J.

Cherrett, W.

Chorley, J.

*Clark, W.

Coffey, John (deserted in
  Queenstown)

*Collins, Samuel

*Coombes, G.

Cooper, H.

Copperthwaite, B.

Corcoran, D.

Cotton, A.

*Crimmins, J.

Cross, W.

Cunningham, B.

Curtis, A.

*Diaper, J.

*Dilley, J.

*Doel, F.

Doyle, F.

*Dymond, Frank

*Flarty, E.

Fraser, J.

Geer, A.

*Godley, G.

Golder, M. W.

*Graham, T.

Graves, S.
Grodidge, E.
*Hagan, J.
Hall, J.
Hallett, G.
Hands, B.
Hannam, G.
Harris, E.
*Harris, F.
Hart, Thomas
Hasgood, R.
Head, A.
Hodges, W.
Hosgood, R.
Hunt, T.
Hurst, C. J.
Instance, T.
Jacobson, John
James, Thos
Jarvis, W.
Joas, N.
*Judd, C.
*Kasper, F.
Kerr, T.
Kinsella, L.
Lahy, T.
Light, C.
Light, W.
*Lindsay, W.
Lloyd, W.
*Major, W.
Marrett, G.
Marsh, F.
*Mason, F.
May, Arthur
*Mayzes, T.
McAndrew, Thos
McAndrews, W.
McCastlen, W.
McGarvey, E.
McGaw, E.
McGregor, J.
McQuillan, William
McRae, William
Milford, George
Mintram, W.
*Moore, J.

Morgan, T.
*Murdoch, W.
Nettleton, G.
Noon, John
Norris, J.
Noss, B.
*Noss, H.
*Nutbean, William
*Oliver, H.
*Othen, C.
Paice, R.
Painter, Charles
Painter, F.
Pand, G.
*Pearce, J.
*Podesta, J.
*Priest, John
*Pusey, Robert
Reeves, F.
*Rice, C.
Richards, H.
Rickman, G.
Roberts, G.
Sangster, C.
Saunders, T.
Saunders, W.
Scott, Archibald
*Self, E.
*Senior, Harry
Shea, Thos
*Shiers, Alfred
Smither, H.
Snellgrove, G.
*Sparkman, H.
Stanbrook, Augustus
*Street, A.
Stubbs, H.
Sullivan, S.
Taylor, J.
*Taylor, James
Taylor, T.
*Taylor, William Henry
Thomas, J.
*Thompson, John
*Thresher, G.
Tizard, A.
Toung, F.

*Triggs, R.
Turley, R.
Vear, H.
Vear, W.
Wardner, F.
Wateridge, E.
Watson, W.
Williams, E.
Witcher, A.
Witt, H.


GREASERS
Baines, Rich
Bannon, John
Beattie, F.
Bott, W.
Castleman, E.
Couch, J.
Eastman, C.
Fay, F.
Gardner, F.
Goree, F.
Gregory, D.
*Hurst, Walter
Jago, J.
Jukes, J.
Kearl, C.
Kelly, J.
Kenchenten, Fredrick
Kirkham, J.
McInerney, T.
Moores, R.
Morris, A.
Olive, C.
Palles, T.
Phillips, G.
Pitfield, W.
*Pregnall, George
*Ranger, Thomas
*Scott, Fred
Self, A.
Stafford, M.
Tozer, J.
Veal, A.
*White, Alfred
Woodford, H.

ELECTRICIANS
Chief electrician
Sloan, P.
Electrician
White, Alfred
Assistant electricans
Ervine, George
Jupe, Herbert
Kelly, William
Middleton, Alfred
Junior Electrician
Alsopp, Alfred S.


ENGINEERS
Chief Engineer Bell, Joseph
Deck engineer Creese, H.
Assistant deck engineer
McReynolds, W.
Senior second engineer
Farquharson, W.
Senior second assistant
    engineer Wilson, Bertie
Second engineer Hesketh,
    James H.
Junior second assistant
    engineers
Shepherd, Jonathan
Harvey, Herbert G.
Senior third engineer
    Hosking. G. F.
Senior third assistant
    engineer Hodge, C.
Junior third engineer
Dodd, E. C.
Junior third assistant
    engineers
Coy, F. E. G.
Fraser, J.
Senior fourth engineer
Hodgkinson, L.
Senior fourth assistant
    engineer Dyer, Henry R.
Junior fourth engineer
    Smith, James M.
Junior fourth assistant
    engineers
Ward, J. M.

Dodd, R.
Junior fifth assistant
    engineer Mackie, W. D.
Extra fifth assistant
    engineer Millar, R.
Senior sixth assistant
    engineer Magee, W.
Junior sixth assistant
    engineer Millar, T.

## MESS STEWARDS
Blake, Seaton
Coleman, J.
*Fitzpatrick, C. W.
Gunnery, G.
*Knowles, T.
May, A. W.

## MISCELLANEOUS
Boilermaker
Chisnall, G.
Junior boilermaker
Fitzpatrick, H.
Writer Duffy, William
Auto Ferrary,
Plumber Rous, A.

## STOREKEEPERS
Foster, A.
Kenzler, A.
Newman, C.
Rudd, Henry

## TRIMMERS
*Allen, E.
*Avery, J.
Bevis, J.
Billows, J.
*Binstead, Walter
*Blake, P.
Brewer, H.
Brooks, J.
Calderwood, H.
Carr, R.
Carter, F.
Casey, T.
Coe, H.

Cooper, J.
Crabb, H.
Dawson, J.
Dickson, W.
*Dillon, Thomas Patrick
*Dore, A.
Eagle, A. J.
Elliott, Everett Edward
Evans, W.
Ford, H.
*Fredricks, W.
*Fryer, A.
Gordon, J.
Gosling, B.
Gosling, S.
Green, G.
Harris, F.
Haslin, J.
*Hebb, A.
Hill, J.
Hinton, W.
*Hunt, Albert
Ingram, C.
Kearl, G.
Lee, H.
Long, F.
Long, W.
Maskell, L.
*McGann, James
*McIntyre, William
Mitchell, B.
Moore, R.
Morgan, A.
Morrell, R.
Morris, W.
*O'Connor, John
*Pelham, G.
*Perry, E.
Perry, H.
Preston, Thomas
Proudfoot, R.
Read, J.
Reed, R.
Saunders, W.
*Sheath, F.
Shilaber, C.
Skeats, W.

Smith, E.
Snooks, W.
*Snow, E.
Steel, R.
Stocker, H.
Webb, S.
White, F.
*White, William George
Wilton, William
Witt, F.
Woods, H.

## VICTUALLING & MISCELLANEOUS CREW
Boots
Bully, H.
*Chapman, J.
Fellows, A.
*Guy, J.
Henry, W.
Jackson, H.
Perrin, W.
Scott
Stebbing, S.

Butchers
Barker, T.
Barrow, H.
Hensford, J.
Maytum, Alfred
*Mills, C.
Roberts, F.
Topp, T.
Wiltshire, W.

Cooks & Chefs
Chief baker
*Joughin, Charles
Assistant bakers
Barker, A.
Barnes, W.
Chitty, G.
*Neale, H.
Smith, J.
Wake, S.
Chief night baker
*Belford, Walter

Second baker Giles, J.
Extra second baker
Davies, J.
Third baker Hines, G.
Extra third baker
*Burgess, Charles
Carver
Scavino, C.
Chefs
Proctor, Chester
Rousseau, P.
Chef's assistant
*Mauge, Paul
Assistant chef
Bochetez, J.
Assistant confectioner
Leader, A.
Cook and mess
Stubbings, H.
Entree cooks
Coutin, A.
*Maynard, John
Assistant entree
Monteverdi, J.
Fish cook Vicat, J.
Assistant fish
Dornier, S.
Grill cooks
Caunt, W.
Lovell, J.
Herb cook Kennell, C.
Larder cooks
Bolhens, H.
Slight, W.
Pastry cook
Jaillet, H.
Assistant pastry
Desvernini, L.
Pass cook Simmons, W.
Roast cooks
Charboison, A.
Jones, H.
Assistant roast
Cornaire, M.
Sauce cooks
Bietrix, G.
*Windebank, J.

Assistant sauce
Jouanmault, G.
Ship's cook Gill, P.
Assistant ship's cook
Johnson, H.
Assistant cooks
Coombs, C.
Gollop, C.
Lock, A.
Thorley, W.
Welch, W. H.
Soup cook Janin, C.
Assistant soup
Vilvarlarge, P.
Vegetable cook
Hutchinson, J.
Assistant vegetable cooks
Ayling, E.
Buckley, H.
*Ellis, J.
Orr, J.

KITCHEN STAFF
Abbott, E.
Akerman, J.
Allen, E.
Aspelagi, G.
*Ball, Percy
Beere, William
Berthold, Florentini
Blumet, J.
Bradshaw, J.
Bull, W.
Bunmell, F.
*Burrage. A.
*Colgan, J.
*Collins, John
Edwards, C.
Fei, Carlo
Hall, F.
*Hardwick, R.
Harris, E.
Hatch, H.
Hiscock, S.
Hogue, E.
Hopkins, F.
Humby, F.

Ings, W.
Jones, A.
Kieran, M.
King, G.
Levett, G.
Light, C.
Marks, J.
Marriott, J. W.
*Martin, A.
Morgan, W.
Pacherat, J.
Parsons, E.
*Pearcey, Albert Victor
Phillips, J.
Platt, W.
*Prentice, Frank M.
Ricks, Cyril S.
Rogers, E. J.
Ross, R.
*Seward, H.
Shaw, H.
*Simmonds, A.
Smith, C.
Thompson, H.
Tietz, C.
Tucker, B.
Walpole, John
Williams, A.
Wrapson, H.
MISCELLANEOUS
Assistant attendants
Back, C.
Barber
*Weikman, August H.
Assistant barber
White, A.
Baggage master
Bessant, E.
Barber Klein, H.
Barman Price, E.
Baths
Hinckley, G.
*Widgery, James
Bell boys
Barrett, A.
Harris, C. H.
Watson, W.

Cashier
Bowker, Miss Little
Second cashier
*Martin, Miss
Clerks
Ashcroft, A.
Campbell, D. S.
Rice, J. R.
Clothes presser
Olive, E. R.
Assistant clothes presser
Halloway, S.
Coffee man Voegelin, H.
Assistant coffee man
Gros, Claude
Controller
Jeffery, W.
Assistant controller
Vine, H.
Glass man
Salussolia, Giovenz
Assistant glass man
Testoni, Ercole
Gymnasium
McCawley, T. W.
Ice man Mattman, A.
Interpeter Muller, L.
Library Kelland, T.
Lift attendants
Allan, F.
Carney, William
King, A.
Pacey, R.
Lounge attendant
Burke, R.
Manager Gatti, L.
First Marconi operator
Phillips, John George
Second Marconi operator
*Bride, Harold
Matron Wallis, Mrs.
Nurse
*Stap, Miss Sarah Agnes
Page boy Turvey, C.
Printer Mishellany, A.
Assistant printer
Corben, E. T.

Pursers
Denison, ?
McElroy, Herbert Walter
Second Purser
Barker, Reginald L.
Pursers' clerk
King, Ernest
Racquet-court attendant
Wright, Fredrick
Reception room attendant
Dolby, J.
Assistant reception room
    attendant Holland, T.
Stenographer
Turner, G. F.
Telephone operator
Perkins, L.
Veranda café
*Stewart, John (Jack)
Assistant veranda café
Broome, Athol
Assistant waiters
Feltham, G.
Fletcher, P. W.
Wine butler Zarracchi, L.
Turkish Bath Attendants
*Caton, Miss
Crosbie, J. B.
Ennis, W.
*Slocombe, Mrs. Maud
Taylor, L.

WAITERS
Allaria, Baptiste
Banfi
Basilico, G.
Baxter, F.
Bazzi, L.
Bernardi, B.
Beux, D.
Bochet, G.
Crovelle, Louis
De Breucq, M.
Dennarsico
Donati, Italio
Gilardino, V.
Gullio, Casali

Monoros, J.

Nannini, F.

Pedrini, Alex

Perotti, Alfonsi

Petrachio, A.

Petrachio, S.

Piatti, L.

Piazza, P.

Poggi, E.

Ratti, E.

Rigozzi, A.

Rotto, Angelo

Sacaggi, G.

Sesea, Gino

Urbini, R.

Valassori, Ettera

Vioni, R.

STEWARDS

Saloon Stewards

Ahier, P.

Allsop, F.

*Baggott, A.

Bagley, E.

Bailey, G.

Barker, E.

Barringer, A.

Barrows, W.

Benhem, T.

Best, E.

Boughton, E.

Boyd, J.

Boyes, H.

Bristowe, H.

*Brown, Edward

Brown, W.

*Burke, William

Burr, E.

Butt, Robert

Butterworth, J.

Cartwright, J.

Casswill, C.

Cave, Herbert

Charman, John

Cheverton, W. F.

Coleman, A.

Conway, P.

Cook, George

*Crafter, F.

Crisp, H.

*Crowe, George F.

Dashwood, W.

Davies, R. J.

Deeble, A.

Derrett, A.

Deslands, P.

Dineage, J.

Doughty, W.

Dyer, W.

Evans, George

Frankin, A.

Fenton, F.

*Fropper, R.

*Gibbons, J. W.

Goshawk, A.

*Hartnell, Frederick

Harris, C. W.

*Harrison, A.

Hawkesworth, John

Helnen, J.

Hendy, E.

Hoare, Leo

House, W.

Howell, A.

Jenner, H.

Jenson, C. V.

*Johnson, James

Jones, A.

Jones, Reginald V.

*Keene, P.

Ketchley, H.

Kingscote, W. F.

Kitching, A.

*Knight, George

Lake, W.

Lane, A. E.

Lawrence, A.

Lefever, G.

*Littlejohn, A.

Lloyd, H.

*Lucas, W.

Lydiatt, C.

*MacKay, Charles D.

McGrady, James

*McMicken, A.

McMullen, J.

Mellor, A.

Middleton, M. V.

Moore, A.

Moss, William

Nicholls, T.

Orpet, W.

Osborne, W.

Parsons, R.

Perriton, H.

*Phillimore, Harold

Pryce, W.

Pusey, J.

Randall, F.

Ranson, Jas

*Ray, Frederick Dent

Revall, W.

Ridout, W.

Robinson, J.

Rogers, M.

Rowe, M.

Rummer, G.

Russell, R.

*Ryerson, W. E.

Samuels, W.

Saunders, D. E.

Scovell, R.

Shea, J.

Simmons, F. G.

Skinner, E.

Smillie, J.

Smith, R. G.

Stagg, J. H.

Stroud, E. A.

Stroud, H.

Strugnell, J

Symonds, J.

Taylor, W.

*Thomas, A. C.

*Thomas, B.

*Toms, F.

Turner, L.

Veal, T.

*Ward, William

Warwick, F.

Weatherstone, T.

*Wheelton, E.

White, L.

*Whitely, Thomas

Whitford, A.

Wormald, T.

*Yearsley, H.

Yoshack, J.

BEDROOM STEWARDS

Allan, R.

Anderson, W.

Barlow, G.

Beedman, G.

Bishop, W.

Bogie, L.

Bond, W.

Boothby, W.

Brewster, G. H.

Byrne, J.

Clark, T.

*Crawford, Alfred

Crumplin, C.

*Cullen, C.

*Cunningham, Andrew

Davies, Gordon

Donoghue, F.

*Etches, Henry Samuel

*Faulkner, William

Ford, F.

Geddes, R.

Gill, S.

Hamblyn, Ernest William

Hayter, A.

Hewett, T.

Hill, J.

Hogg, C.

Janaway, W.

MacKie, G.

McCarty, F.

McMurray, W.

O'Connor, T.

Penrose, J.

Petty, Edwin Henry

Pook, R.

Reed, C.

Roberts, H.

Siebert, Sidney C.

Smith, C.
Stone, E.
Stone, E.
Swan, W.
*Thessinger, A.
Ward, E.
Ward, P.
Wareham, R.
Wittman, H.

STEWARDS
Ashe, H. G. H.
Barton, S.
Baxter, H. R.
*Bennett, Mrs.
*Bliss, Miss
Bristow, Robert C.
Brookman, J.
Cecil, C.
Chitty, G.
Cox, Denton
Crispin, W. G. H.
*Daniels, S.
Edbrooke, F.
Ede, G. B.
Egg, W. H.
Evans, George
Fairall, H. Saloon
Finch, H.
*Foley, W. C.
Ford, E.
Fox, W. T.
*Gold, Mrs Kate
*Gregson, Miss
*Halford, R.
Hill, H.
*Hylands, Leo J.
Ide, H.
Ingrouville, H.
*Jessop, Miss Violet
Knight, L.
*Lavington, Miss
Leonard, M.
*Lewis, Arthur
*Leather, Mrs Elizabeth
Mabey, J.
Mantle, R.

*Marsden, Miss
*Martin, Mrs.
*McLaren, Mrs.
Mullen, T.
Nichols, A.
Pearce, A.
*Port, F.
Prideaux, J. A.
*Prior, H. J.
*Pritchard, Mrs.
*Pugh, Alfred
Rice, P.
*Roberts, Mrs.
*Robinson, Mrs. Annie
Ryan, T.
*Savage, C. J.
Sedunary, Sidney
Sevier, W.
Slight, H. J.
*Sloan, Miss Mary
*Smith, Miss
Snape, Mrs.
Talbot, George
Fredrick Charles
Taylor, C.
Walsh, Miss
Thayler, M.
White, J. G. H.
Willis, W.
*Wright, W. G. H.

ASSISTANT STEWARDS
Wood, J. T.
*Williams, W.
*Wheat, Joseph Thomas
*Terrell, F.
Robertson, G.
Penny, W.
*Nichols, W. K.
Owens, L.
Lacey, Bert W.
Kerley, W. T.
Humphreys, H.
Gunn, J.
Dean, G.
Christmas, H.
*Andrews, Charles E.

BATH STEWARDS
Broom, H.
Major, E.
*Morris, F.
*Rule, Samuel J.
Pennell, F.

MISCELLANEOUS
Chief steward
Latimer, Andrew J.
Chief second steward
Dodd, George
Assistant second steward
Hughes, H.
Chief second class steward
*Hardy, John
Chief third class steward
Kiernan, James W.
Third class steward
*Hart, John Edward
Assistant bedroom stewards
Harding, A.
Longmiur, J.
Captain's steward
Paintin, J. Arthur
Deck steward Edge, F.
Deck steward, Ismay's
    Secretary Freeman,
    Ernest E. S.
Assistant deck stewards
Boston, W.
Hawksworth, W.
Hospital steward
Dunford, W.
Smoke-room steward
Webb, Brooke
Second class smoke-room
    steward *Witter, James
Assistant S. R. steward
Hamilton, E.

BAND
(All employed by
Messrs C. W. and F. N.
Black of Liverpool)
Bandmaster
Hartley, Wallace Henry

Cellists
Bricoux, Roger
Taylor, Percy, C.
Woodward, J. W.
Pianist Brailey, Theodore
First violinist
Hume, John (Jock) Law
Violist Krins, George
Bass violist Clarke, J. Fred C.

OTHER CREW
The following, who had
'signed on,' did not go on
the voyage:
Haveling, A.; Sims, W.;
Penny, V.; Blake, C.; Slade,
A.; Slade, Thos.; Salde, D.;
Burrows, W.; Shaw, J.;
Holden, F.; Brewer, B.; di
Napoli, E.; Fish, B.;
Kilford, P.; Dawes, W.W.;
Ettlinger, P.; Fisher, R.;
Manley, A.; Mewe, W.J.;
Dawkins, P.; Bowman,
F.T.; Coffey, J.

The following were taken
on as substitutes:
Dodds, Renny; Kinsella,
L.; Geer, A.; Hosgood, E.;
Lloyd, W.; Witt, H.; Black,
D.; Windebank, A.; Locke,
A.; Brown, J.; O'Connor,
F.; Dickson, W.; Gordon, T.

*ABOVE: The officers of the* Titanic.
*Standing, from left to right: Herbert McElroy, Chief Purser; Charles Lightoller, Second Officer; Herbert Pitman, Third Officer; Joseph Boxhall, Fourth Officer; Harold Lowe, Fifth Officer (all survived). Seated, from left to right: James Moody, Sixth Officer; Henry Wilde, Chief Officer; Captain Smith; William Murdoch, First Officer (all drowned).*

*RIGHT: First Officer William Murdoch.*

## Chief Officer Henry Tingle Wilde

Described by none other than Charles Lightoller — one of the officers 'demoted' to accommodate Wilde — as 'one of the bravest men who ever stepped on deck,' Wilde was 38, very experienced and well respected.

However, his sudden appointment has always remained a mystery. Wilde was actually Chief Officer of the *Olympic*, the *Titanic*'s sister ship, but for some reason Captain Smith decided he was the man to be at his right hand during the *Titanic*'s maiden voyage. The transfer took place at short notice and he did not join the *Titanic* until the day before her scheduled sailing. It caused a re-shuffle amongst the other senior officers and, even if there was no resentment in evidence, it meant that the senior staff had not had time to 'gel' into a team.

Certainly he was a man of courage, steeped in the tra-ditions of the sea and the eitquette of his time. He gave the order to issue small arms to the officers as the evacuation of women and children began. And, although the White Star Line's owner Bruce Ismay was condemned for escap-

ing on a lifeboat, witnesses testified that it was Chief Officer Wilde who man-handled Ismay into a boat when no further women came forward. He remained at his post and went down with the ship.

## First Officer William McMaster Murdoch

The *Titanic's* first officer became one of the central characters as the tragic drama unfolded. A 39-year-old Scot, from Dalbeattie in Galloway, he came from a long line of mariners. His father Samuel Murdoch had been a master mariner and by 1912 William himself had already served on six White Star Line vessels. His reputation was as a canny and dependable man.

In 1903 as second officer on the RMS *Arabic* his cool head and quick thinking had averted a disaster when a ship was spotted bearing down on the *Arabic* out of the darkness. He ignored a command to steer hard-a-port and the two ships passed within inches of one another. Any alteration in course would have actually caused a collision.

His promotion had been steady and he rose to the position of Chief Officer within the Line. However, for the maiden voyage of *Titanic*, he had been forced to step down to first officer to make way for Captain Smith's own choice as chief officer, Henry Wilde.

Murdoch was on watch when the iceberg was spotted. He instantly gave orders to alter course, but the warning had come at least 30 seconds too late. When the evacuation got under way, Murdoch took charge of lifeboats on the starboard side. He remained cool as the crush to escape became ever more chaotic, shouting 'Stand back, stand back . . . it's women first' as his purser and sixth officer fired their sidearms into the air to prevent a stampede of anxious men. The epic film by James Cameron portrays Murdoch as a man who panicked, shot a passenger and then put the gun to his own head. But those who were there say he was a five-star hero who gave his lifebelt and gun to another passenger to help them before being swallowed by the dark, icy waters.

## Second Officer Charles Herbert Lightoller

A young man who loved adventure, the lure of the sea had gripped him at an early age and he set out on a life of travel which seemed permanently intermixed with trouble.

At sea he had survived knife fights and four previous shipwrecks. Several times he had almost drowned and he spent some time as a castaway on a desert island. His nose for adventure led him into the gold-fever country of the Yukon where he had prospected, obviously quite unsuccessfully, and he enjoyed a brief period as a cowboy on the Canadian prairies.

Lightoller had been born into a well-off family in Lancashire, England, but the family fortune made in the cotton industry had been all but lost when Lightoller left school. His mother died and his father left for a new life in New Zealand, so Lightoller went to sea. He joined the White Star Line in 1900, holding a Master's certificate, and his skills were soon recognised by the company which prided itself on recruiting the cream of the crop.

He also played a leading role in events on that tragic night. He steadfastly helped passengers into lifeboats and with great courage stayed on to the end. Incredibly, a succession of flukes — the type of luck which had been the hallmark of his previous adventures — meant that he survived to be rescued by the Carpathia. He went on to command a destroyer during the First World War, sinking a U-boat, and in 1940 he rescued stranded Allied soldiers from the beaches of Dunkirk in his own cabin-cruiser, the *Sundowner*.

## Wallace Hartley

There were none more implaccable as events unfolded than band leader Wallace Hartley. A consumate professional, he gathered his men around him and played as the great liner slowly sank. There is no doubt that their calming influence helped to prevent a greater panic.

Wallace was born in Dewsbury, Yorkshire, an English county noted for its no-nonsense approach. And Wallace was certainly not one to make a drama out of a crisis. He was well-known and popular with music lovers in many parts of the country and had conducted orchestras in Harrogate, Bridlington and Leeds. He chose to entertain at sea to broaden his horizons and had joined the *Titanic* as musical director from the Mauretania.

He had made his home in Colne, Lancashire, and was engaged to be married to a lady from Boston Spa, near Wetherby, the great Yorkshire horse-training town. There has been much speculation about which tune the band were playing when they, too, finally succumbed to the waves. Some say it was the hymn 'Nearer My God to

Thee,' others say it was the popular waltz 'Autumn.'

In the confusion, it could have been either. Or one followed by the other. But in a strange quirk, Wallace had told a fellow musician aboard the *Mauretania* that he felt he would meet his end at sea one day. And that as the last moments approached, he would instruct his orchestra to play 'Nearer My God To Thee.'

## Marconi Operator Harold Bride

Young Harold Bride was number two to Marconi operator Jack Phillips. He was a keen and willing assistant to the older man and had learned his trade as a wireless operator back home in Bromley, Kent. Just 23 he was driven by the excitement of being in the forefront of communications technology and swelled by the adrenalin of adventure which came with a position on board the *Titanic* rather than some routine job in a small town Post Office.

Bride and his mentor Phillips were not employed by the White Star Line, but by the Marconi International Marine Communication Co. The pair would make sure the wireless was manned continuously while at sea, working shifts of six hours on and six hours off duty. Bride was an assuming chap. He had to be to work for Marconi. The company philosophy was that any man who showed signs of suffering from 'a swelled head' was no longer of any use.

Quiet then, but most certainly dedicated, Bride stayed at his post, together with Phillips throughout the night despatching urgent communiques about *Titanic*'s distress. As Phillips worked tirelessly at the Marconi, Bride fastened a lifebelt around him, as Phillips himself was too deep in concentration to notice.

He was only slightly built, but when another seaman, in despair, tried to steal his boss's lifebelt, young Bride attacked him and knocked him cold. When the Captain relieved the two men of their duties, Phillips continued to send the distress signal. Bride took his chances in the water along with the others and was fortunate enought to be saved.

## Stewardess Violet Jessop

First Class stewardess Violet Jessop was a bright, vivacious and very attractive 24-year-old when she signed on for the *Titanic*'s maiden voyage. She had joined the White Star Line a year earlier and had gained a considerable amount of experience in looking after the whims and fancies of well-heeled ladies.

A hard worker from an ordinary Suffolk family, Violet was wide-eyed and awestruck at the sheer majesty of the ship's opulent surroundings. Everyone on board was bound by the strict social conventions of the time. None more so than young Violet. When disaster struck, she recalled later, she dithered about which dress to put on — rejecting one with frills as being too fussy for the occasion.

Along with other women, she was fortunate to be put aboard lifeboat number 16 as the ship neared its end. But, it says much for her spirit that the incredible tragedy did not prevent Violet from returning to sea. Indeed, she was back on the water a fortnight after the 1912 inquiry into the disaster. During the First World War she served as a nurse aboard the hospital ship *Britannic* which hit a mine and sank in the Aegean Sea. Again, she survived.

Violet lived to the age of 83, a kind-hearted woman alone with her memories. She never married, although she did turn down a proposal from a wealthy New Yorker. Her one and only love had been a ship's engineer called Ned, who she met on her first sea voyage. Alas, life on the oceans kept them apart.

Colonel John Jacob Astor

The sheer opulence of *Titanic* was ideal for celebrated patrons like Colonel John Jacob Astor, one of the richest men in America. At 47, the heir to the fabulous Astor empire of property and manufacturing he had been described as 'the world's greatest monument to unearned increment.'

A familiar figure in the world's financial circles in his bowler hat and overcoat he was also an adventurer and inventor. During the Spanish-American War he financed and fought with his own units, equipping them with the latest weaponry and recording much success. Though he lived in the family mansion on Fifth Avenue, New York, he was happy to 'rough it' with his own troops and certainly earned their unending respect.

He was also the talk of polite society. In 1909 it was revealed that his wife had divorced him in secret and two years later he began a romance with 18-year-old New Yorker Madeleine Force. The couple married, amid much controversy so, as much to escape the Press as anything else, he took his new bride for an exotic honeymoon in Egypt. He was returning after spending the winter there when he boarded the *Titanic* for home. He did ask if he could join his wife in the liefboat because she was 'in a delicate condition' but accepted the refusal with calm dignity. His last act was to place a baby in the last lifeboat, raising his hand in salute, and joining other doomed men on the bridge.

Fourth Officer Joseph Boxhall

Boxhall had just arrived on the bridge for his watch when the collision occurred. He was a middle-ranker of not inconsiderable experience. But in the minutes after the *Titanic* struck the iceberg, his actions caused controversey for decades afterwards.

Boxhall, from Hull, England, was ordered to establish the ship's position. Under pressure he used his skills of dead reckoning and the ship's known speed and course to deliver his verdict. Sadly he was incorrect by a few vital miles. And although his error is unlikely to have cost lives, it created a misunderstanding which has been debated almost ever since.

That aside, Boxhall was considered hard working and reliable. He was put in charge of lifeboat No 2 and had the presence of mind to load it with signal rockets. Subsequently his was the first liefboat to be picked up.

Benjamin Guggenheim

'The second wealthiest man aboard' is how Benjamin Guggenheim was described by those chronicling the maiden voyage of the *Titanic*. He was the son of an immigrant who started life in America in 1847 selling shoelaces in Philadelphia. In a short space of time the Guggenheim's had amassed a vast fortune estimated at around $100 million, based on interests in mining, smelting and banking.

Certainly Benjamin Guggenheim felt totally at home amongst the clutch of super-rich industrialists promenading on the first class deck. He was noted as something of a playboy, however, and was said to be travelling with his Pairsian mistress.

The unfolding tragedy was noted for much chivalry and heroism and, in some cases, arrogance and cowardice. The story of Bejamin Guggenheim is a first class example of the former.

He and his secretary both changed into evening dress

so that they were 'prepared to go down like gentlemen.' As people scrambled for places aboard the departing lifeboats, Guggeheim told a steward: 'Tell my wife I played the game out straight and to the end. No woman shall be left aboard this ship because Ben Guggenheim is a coward.'

## Countess of Rothes

The countess enjoyed a lifetime of privilege which only members of the British aristocracy could comprehend. Her father, Mr Thomas Dwyer Edwardes, was the owner of Prinknash Park in Gloucestershire. It was a country seat of distinction, dating from 1530. In 1900 the pretty young Miss Edwardes married the Earl of Rothes, a Scottish peer of the realm, and enjoyed the extra privileges of title as well as wealth.

As many others found out that night, however, wealth counts for nothing when cruel fate takes such a devastating turn. A mother of two boys, the robust Lady Rothes was more than equal to the challenge thrust upon her. Put into a lifeboat without sufficient crew she showed remarkable strength of character by immediately taking to the oars. Lady Rothes, who was on her way to meet her husband the Earl in America, rowed all night and became known by all as 'the plucky little Countess.'

After they were rescued by the Carpathia she showed tremendous compassion by caring for the unfortunate women and children from steerage who had managed to survive.

## Ted and Ethel Beane

Newlyweds, they were amongst the many loving couples separated with the words: 'Sorry, sir. It's women and children only.' The couple from Norwich, Norfolk, were making their way to the United States to start a new life together. Ted was a 32-year-old bricklayer who had for

some time been sharing his time between Norfolk and America.

He had met Ethel, an attractive 19-year-old barmaid at the Lord Nelson pub in Norwich where she worked, and eagerly proposed marriage. The wedding took place a few days before the couple were due to embark on the adventure of a lifetime aboard the great new steamship *Titanic*. Ted had previously travelled third class as he crossed the Atlantic, but had saved especially hard to provide second class berths for himself and his new wife. They embarked with all their worldy possessions safely stowed aboard.

However, they were luckier than many. When Ted was turned back from lifeboat 13 with his wife, he decided to dive into the water and swim for one of the lifeboats which had been despatched only half full. He reached one, and was pulled from the water to discover he had swum out, amidst the chaos, to the one carrying his wife.

*BELOW: Mrs. Dean carrying Millvina, with her brother Bertram.*

## Bertram Dean

He was a publican in the East End of London. Life was hard pulling pints for ungrateful drinkers in the mean, grimey streets of a poor working class district and he dreamed of providing a better existence for his wife and family. So it was that in 1912 this determined man sold his pub and bought third class tickets to America for himself, his wife Georgetta, and children Bertram Jr, and baby Millvina, who was but three weeks old when she lost her father in the tragedy.

A cousin, Alfred Norbury, had moved to Kansas in 1871 and Bertram's plan was to join him there and start a small business as a tobacconist. His dream died that fateful night. His wife and two children were saved and his daughter went on to become one of the last survivors of the tragedy.

Millvina later recalled: 'My father had no choice but to stay on board. It was women and children first, then First Class passengers. My father told my mother that he hoped to see her later, but that was the last time she ever saw him. It was awfully sad for her.'

## Henry Morley

Shop owner Henry Morley was a pillar of respectability. Handsome and well mannered he and his young wife kept pretty much to themselves as the excited passengers in second class began the process of introductions and chatting amiably at mealtimes. Everyone assumed that they were naturally reserved. It was a reserve borne out of a guilty secret, however, because 37-year-old Morley's young companion was not his wife, but a 19-year-old shopgirl with whom he was eloping.

News of their situation would have scandalised shipboard society, just as it had scandalised the community in Worcester from where the couple had vanished. Morley had fallen in love with the young girl Kate Phillips who worked in one of his four shops. He sold two of his shops to elope with her on the *Titanic*, leaving the other two to support his wife and 12-year-old daughter. The pair intended to make a new life in San Francisco.

When disaster struck, Morley accepted his fate stoically, like many other men on board, while Kate was helped into one of the lifeboats. Later, as she recovered with a kind family in New York, Kate discovered she was carrying Morley's child which had been conceived on board ship. Their daughter Ellen was born almost nine months after the *Titanic* sank.

*ABOVE: Photograph of Boat 1's occupants, taken aboard* Carpathia. *Back row, left to right — Saloman, Stengel; Middle row: Hendrickson, Lady Duff-Gordon, Francatelli, Sir Duff-Gordon, Taylor; Seated: Symons, Horsewell, Collins, Pusey.*

## Sir Cosmo and Lady Lucile Duff-Gordon

Lady Lucile became one of the prominent players after describing to the *Titanic* inquiry how she saw an officer shoot a male passenger who was trying to force his way onto one of the lifeboats. Certainly she and her husband Sir Cosmo Duff-Gordon would have been in a position to see — they were amongst the first to escape the sinking ship in No 1 Lifeboat, along with Lady Duff-Gordon's secretary, seven crewmen and two male passengers.

The Duff-Gordons were out of the 'top drawer' of British society and the type, no doubt, who would have felt it was their right and privilege to have safe passage in a lifeboat containing only 12 people. Lady Duff-Gordon was a noted fashion expert and was called on a a costumier to the British Royal Court. Sir Cosmo was a typical self-posessed Society man with all the best connections.

The inquiry was anxious to learn why Sir Cosmo gave the lifeboat crew members £5 each. Some said it was a bribe to prevent them rowing back to pick up more survivors and risk being dragged down with the *Titanic's* vortex. However, Sir Cosmo said he merely wished to help the men replace their kit which had gone down with the ship.

## Mr and Mrs Isidor Straus

In all of the dramatic personal stories none were more romantic than that of Mr and Mrs Isidor Straus. Mr Straus was a very wealthy man, but one of strong principle. He was a Bavarian Jew and had built his fortune through shrewd commerce and banking and his partnership in the world-famous Macy's department store. Unlike some, his wealth had not made him pompous or selfish. He was a noted philanthropist, campaigner for social reforms and a great friend of the late US President Cleveland.

Straus was returning from a winter holiday with his wife at Cap Martin on the French Riviera. They were a devoted couple and friends described them as a real-life Darby and Joan. When the time came to embark in the lifeboats Mrs Straus refused to leave her husband's side. She told friends: 'I've always stayed with my husband, so why should I leave him now?' Mr Straus was told that no-one would object if an old man took a place in the lifeboat, too, but with immense courage he replied: 'I will not go before other men.' The pair went to their deaths arm in arm.

494

towards the surface like a missile. He bobbed out into the waves and made his way towards a liferaft, swimming from one piece of floating wreckage to another. Eventually he reached the others and later recalled: 'Men who seemed long ago to have forgotten how to address their creator recalled the prayers of their childhood and muttered them over and over through the night.'

Major Archibald Willingham Butt

US President Taft paid tribute to his own personal aide de camp, Major Archibald Butt, who proved himself to be a genuine hero as the ship went down. Major Butt had served with distinction in the army and had been personally selected by President Taft to join his staff. The major was a colourful figure amongst the mainly formally-attired men in First Class, wearing his impressive dress uniform complete with medals and ribbons. Impervious to the rising state of panic, Butt organised a foursome at cards in the first class saloon awhere he played until 2am.

Survivors recalled him taking charge of a section of the ship, issuing orders and pacifying those who panicked with his own stoical calm. He was an impressive presence and President Taft said: 'I never really had any hope of seeing him again. Archie was a soldier and he was always where he was wanted. I knew Archie would be amongst those lost. He would be on deck doing his duty to the end.'

Colonel Archibald Gracie

The last man to be saved was United States Army Colonel Archibald Gracie. He was a handsome man, in his late 30s, with a well-groomed moustache of which he was inordinately proud. Although he was also rightly proud to be serving his country, he came from a gentrified family in Arkansas where he owned a large cotton plantation in Jefferson County.

As news of the impending disaster spread he calmly cancelled his booking for a private squash lesson with the well-known professional Frederick Wright. A true officer, he took his chances and went down with the ship only to be saved by a dramatic turn of events. As he was being dragged down, an underwater explosion propelled him

John Sage and family

Amongst the masses travelling in steerage was a family of 11 from Peterborough, England. John Sage, his wife and their nine children aged from five to 25, were heading for Florida to start a new life. Sage had been a shopkeeper and had run the village inn at Gaywood near King's Lynn, Norfolk, before moving to Peterborough.

Mr Sage, 50, had spent some time farming in Saskatchewan with his eldest son, George, before returning to England to take all his family to the United States. He had bought a fruit farm at jacksonville, Florida, and the family left Britain filled with hope and expectation.

William Thomas Stead

Described as 'the greatest journalist of his age', the writer William Thomas Stead was one of the more flamboyant personalities on board. He numbered Queen Alexandra amongst his admirers and was an idealistic man who was full of life and energy.

Stead had previously shown the courage of his convic-

tions when he was jailed after falling foul of the law over some vitriolic journalistic revelation. Though an intellectual, Stead also had the rare gift of making people laugh and his company was much sought after on board *Titanic*. He was last seen helping ladies into the waiting boats, offering reassurance that everything would turn out.

His integrity was never questioned although he did harbour spritualist beliefs which some of his contemporaries did not understand. After his death a medium claimed to have been in contact with Stead who had said he had asked the band to play 'Nearer My God To Thee' as the ship sank.

Jacques Futrelle

French novellist Jacques Futrelle was parted from his wife as the lieboats departed but he was determined to 'play by the rules' and not secure an escape for himself. He died in the way a hero in one of his novels might have done. His wife did not want to leave but he told her: 'For God's sake go. It's your last chance.'

Futrelle was over 6ft tall but described by everyone as a gentle giant. He began his career writing for newspapers but then started writing novels. He invented a detective in the Sherlock Holmes mode who became known as The Professor. His book, The Thinking Machine, was one of the most successful books of its time in America.

# 4 Passenger List

Compiled by the White Star Line on May 9, 1912 Survivors are marked *

FIRST CLASS, *Allen, Miss Elizabeth Walton
Allison, Mr. H. J.
Allison, Mrs. H. J. and *Maid
Allison, Miss L
*Allison, Master T. and *Nurse
*Anderson, Mr. Harry
*Andrews, Miss Cornelia I.
Andrews, Mr. Thomas
*Appleton, Mrs. E. D.
Artagaveytia, Mr. Ramon
Astor, Colonel J. J. and Manservant
*Astor, Mrs. J. J and *Maid
*Aubert, Mrs. N. and *Maid
*Barkworth, Mr. A. H.
Baumann, Mr. J.
*Baxter, Mrs. James
Baxter, Mr. Quigg
Beattie, Mr. T.
*Beckwith, Mr. R. L.
*Beckwith, Mrs. R. L.
*Behr, Mr. K. H.
*Bishop, Mr. D. H.
*Bishop, Mrs. D. H.
Bjornstrom, Mr. H.
Blackwell, Mr. Stephen W.
*Blank, Mr. Henry
*Bonnell, Miss Caroline
*Bonnell, Miss Lily
Borebank, Mr. J. J.
*Bowen, Miss
*Bowerman, Miss Elsie
Brady, Mr. John B.
Brandeis, Mr. E.
*Brayton, Mr. George
Brewe, Dr Arthur Jackson
*Brown, Mrs. J. J.

*Brown, Mrs. J. M.
*Bucknell, Mrs. W. and *Maid
Butt, Major Archibald W.
*Calderhead, Mr. E. P.
*Candee, Mrs. Churchill
*Cardoza, Mrs. J. W. M. and Maid
*Cardoza, Mr. T. D. M and manservant
Carlson, Mr. Frank
Carran, Mr. F. M.
Carran, Mr. J. P.
*Carter, Mr. William E.
*Carter, Mrs. William E. and Maid
*Carter, Miss Lucile
*Carter, Master William T. and Manservant
Case, Mr. Howard B.
*Cassebeer, Mrs. H. A.
Cavendish, Mr. T.W.
*Cavendish, Mrs. T. W. and *Maid
Chaffee, Mr. Herbert F.
*Chaffee, Mrs. Herbert F.
*Chambers, Mr. N. C.
*Chambers, Mrs. N. C.
*Cherry, Miss Gladys
*Chevre, Mr. Paul
*Chibnafl, Mrs. E. M. Bowerman
Chisholm, Mr. Robert,
Clark, Mr. Walter M.
*Clark, Mrs. Walter M.
Clifford, Mr. George Q.
Colley, Mr. E. P.
*Compton, Mrs. A. T.
*Compton, Miss S. P.
Compton, Mr. A. T., Jr.
*Cornell, Mrs. R. G.
Crafton, Mr. John B.
Crosby, Mr. Edward G.
*Crosby, Mrs. Edward G.

*Crosby, Miss Harriet
Cummings, Mr. John Bradley
*Cummings, Mrs. John Bradley
*Daly, Mr. P. D.
*Daniel, Mr. Robert W.
Davidson, Mr. Thornton
*Davidson, Mrs. Thornton
*de Villiers, Mrs. B.
*Dick, Mr. A. A.
*Dick, Mrs. A. A.
*Dodge, Dr. Washington
*Dodge, Mrs. Washington
*Dodge, Master Washington
*Douglas, Mrs. F. C.
Douglas, Mr. W. D.
*Douglas, Mrs. W. D. and Maid
Dulles, Mr. William C.
*Earnshew, Mrs. Boulton
*Endres, Miss Caroline
*Eustis, Miss E. M.
Evans, Miss E.
*Flegenheim, Mrs. A.
*Flynn, Mr. J. I.
Foreman, Mr. B. L.
Fortune, Mr. Mark
Fortune, Mrs. Mark
*Fortune, Miss Ethel
*Fortune, Miss Alice
*Fortune, Miss Mabel
Fortune, Mr. Charles
Franklin, Mr. T. P.
*Frauenthal Mr. T. G.
*Frauenthal, Dr. Henry W.
*Frauenthal, Mrs. Henry W.
*Frolicher, Miss Marguerite
Futrelle, Mr. J.
*Futrelle, Mrs. J.
Gee, Mr. Arthur
*Gibson, Mrs. L.-

*Gibson, Miss D.
Giglio, Mr. Victor
*Goldenberg, Mr. S. L.
*Goldenberg, Mrs. S. L
Goldschmidt, Mrs. George B.
*Gordon, Sir Cosmo Duff
*Gordon, Lady Duff and *Maid
*Gracie, Colonel Archibald
Graham, Mr.
*Graham, Mrs William G
*Graha, Miss Margaret
*Greenfield, Mrs. L. D.
*Greenfield, Mrs. W. B.
Guggenheim, Mr Benjamin
*Harder, Mr. George A.
*Harder, Mrs. George A.
*Harper, Mr. Henry Sleeper and *Manservant
*Harper, Mrs. Henry Sleeper
Harris, Mr. Henry B.
*Harris, Mrs. Henry B.
Harrison, Mr. W. H.
*Haven, Mr. H.
*Hawksford, Mr. W. J.
Hays, Mr. Charles M.
*Hays, Mrs. Charles M. and maid
*Hays, Miss Margaret
Head, Mr. Christopher
Hilliard, Mr. Herbert Henry
Hipkins, Mr. W. E.
*Hippach, Mrs. Ida S.
*Hippach, Miss Jean
*Hogeboom, Mrs. John C.
Holverson, Mr. A. O.
*Holverson, Mrs. A. O.
*Hoyt, Mr. Frederick M.
*Hoyt, Mrs. Frederick M.
Holt, Mr. W. F.
Isham, Mrs. A. E.

*Ismay, Mr. J. Bruce and Manservant
Jakob, Mr. Birnbaum
Jones, Mr. C. C, Julian, Mr. H. F.
Kent, Mr. Edward A.
Kenyon, Mr. F. R.
*Kenyon, Mrs. F. R.
*Kimball, Mr. E. N.
*Kimball, Mrs. E. N.
Klaber, Mr. Herman
Lambert-Williams, Mr. Fletcher Fellows
*Leader, Mrs. F. A.
Lewy, Mr. E. G.
*Lindstroem, Mrs. J.
*Lines, Mrs. Ernest H.
*Lines, Miss Mary C.
Lingrey Mr Edward
Long, Mr. Milton C.
*Langley, Miss Gretchen F.
Loring, Mr. J. H.
*Madill, Miss Georgette Alexandra
Maguire, Mr. J. E.
*Marechal, Mr. Pierre
Marvin, Mr. D. W.
*Marvin, Mrs. D. W.
McCaffry. Mr. T.
McCarthy, Mr. Timothy J.
*McGough, Mr. J. R.
Meyer, Mr. Edgar J.
*Meyer, Mrs. Edgar J.
Millet, Mr. Frank D.
Missahan, Dr. W. E.
*Missahan, Mrs. W. B.
*Missahan, Miss Daisy
*Moch, Mr. Pkdtp E.
Moch, Mr. Phillip E.
Molson, Mr. H. Markland
Moore, Mr. Clarence and Manservant
Natsch, Mr. Charles
Newell, Mr. A. W.
*Newell, Miss Alice
*Newell, Miss Madeline
*Newsom, Miss Helen

Nicholson, Mr. A. S.
*Omont, Mr. F.
Ostby, Mr. E. C.
*Ostby, Miss Helen R.
Ovies, Mr. S.
Parr, Mr. M. H. W.
Partner, Mr. Austin
Payne, Mr. V.
Pears, Mr. Thomas
*Pears, Mrs. Thomas
Penasco, Mr. Victor
*Penasco, Mrs. Victor and Maid
*Peuchen, Major Arthur
Porter, Mr. Walter Chamberlain
*Potter, Mrs. Thomas, Jr.
Reuchlin, Mr. Jonkheer, J. G.
*Rheims, Mr. George
*Robert, Mrs. Edward S. and *Maid
Roebling, Mr. Washington A., 2nd
*Rolmane, Mr. C.
Rood, Mr. Hugh R.
*Rosenbaum, Miss
Ross, Mr. J. Hugo
*Rothes, the Countess of and *Maid
Rothschild, Mr. M.
*Rothschild, Mrs. M.
Rowe, Mr. Alfred
Ryerson, Mr. Arthur
*Ryerson, Mrs. Arthur and *Maid
*Ryerson, Miss Emily
*Ryerson, Miss Susan
*Ryerson, Master Jack
*Saalfeld, Mr. Adolphe
*Schabert, Mrs. Paul
*Seward, Mr. Frederick K.
*Shutes, Miss E. W.
*Silverthorne, Mr. S. V.
Silvey, Mr. William B.
*Silvey, Mrs. William B.
*Simonius, Mr. Oberst Altons

*Sloper, Mr. William T.
Smart, Mr. John M.
Smith, Mr. J. Clinch
Smith, Mr. R. W.
Smith, Mr. L P.
*Smith, Mrs. L P.
*Snyder, Mr. John
*Snyder, Mrs. John
*Soloman, Mr. A. L.
*Spedden, Mr. Frederick O.
*Spedden, Mrs. Frederick O. and *Maid
*Spedden, Master R. Douglas and *Nurse
Spencer, Mr. W. A.
*Spencer, Mrs. W. A. and Maid
*Stahelin, Dr. Max
Stead, Mr. W. T.
*Steffanson, B. B.
*Steffanon, H. B.
*Stehli, Mr. Max Frolicher
*Stehli, Mrs. Max Frolicher
*Stengel, Mr. C. E. H.
*Stengel, Mrs. C. E. H.
Stewart, Mr. A. A.
*Stone, Mrs. George M. and *Maid
Straus, Mr. Isidor and Manservant
Straus, Mrs. Isidor and *Maid
Sutton, Mr. Frederick
*Swift, Mrs. Frederick Joel
Taussig, Mr. Emil
*Taussig, Mrs. Emil
*Taussig, Miss Ruth
*Taylor, Mr. E. Z
*Taylor, Mrs. E. Z.
Thayer, Mr. J. B.
*Thayer, Mrs. J. B. and *Maid
*Thayer, Mr. J. B., Jr.
Thorne, Mr. G.
*Thorne, Mrs. G.
*Tucker, Mr. G. M., Jr.

Uruchurtu, Mr. M. R.
Van der Hoef, Mr. Wyckoff
Walker, Mr. W. Anderson
Warren, Mr. F. M.
*Warren, Mrs. F. M.
*Weir, Mr. J.
White, Mr. Percival W.
White, Mr. Richard F.
*White, Mrs. J. Stuart and *Maid and Manservant
Wick, Mr. George D.
*Wick, Mrs. George D.
*Wick, Miss Mary
Widener, Mr. George D. and Manservant
*Widener, Mrs. George D. and *Maid
Widener, Mr.. Harry
*Willard, Miss Constance
Williams, Mr. Duane
*Williams, Mr. R. N., Jr.
*Woolner, Mr. Hugh
Wright, Mr. George
*Young, Miss Marie

SECOND CLASS PASSENGERS

Abelson, Mr. Samson
*Abelson, Mrs. Hanna
Aldworth, Mr. C.
Andrew, Mr. Edgar
Andrew, Mr. Frank
Angle, Mr. William
*Angle, Mrs.
Ashby, Mr. John
Baily, Mr. Percy
Baimbridge, Mr. Chas. R.
*Balls, Mrs. Ada E.
Banfield, Mr. Frederick J.
Bateman, Mr. Robert J.
*Beane, Mr. Edward
*Beane, Mrs. Ethel
Beauchamp, Mr. H. J.
*Becker, Mrs. A. O. and *three children
*Beesley, Mr. Lawrence

*Bentham, Miss Lilian W.
Berriman, Mr. William
Botsford, Mr. W. Hull
Bowenur, Mr. Solomon
Bracken, Mr. Jas. H.
Brito, Mr. Jose de
*Brown, Miss Mildred
Brown, Mr. S.
Brown, Mrs.
*Brown, Miss E.
Bryhl, Mr. Curt
*Bryhl, Miss Dagma
*Buss, Miss Kate
Butler, Mr. Reginald
Byles, Rev.nomas R. D.
*Bystrom, Miss Karolina
*Caldwell, Mr. Albert F.
*Caldwell, Mrs. Sylvia
*Caldwell, Master Alden G.
*Cameron, Miss Clear
Carbines, Mr. William
Carter, Rev. Ernest C.
Carter, Mrs. Lillian
Chapman, Mr. John H.
Chapman, Mrs. Elizabeth
Chapman, Mr. Charles
*Christy, Mrs. Alice
*Christy, Miss Juli
Clarke, Mr. Charles V.
*Clarke, Mrs. Ada Maria
Coleridge, Mr. R. C.
Collander, Mr. Erik
*Collett, Mr. Stuart
Collyer, Mr. Harvey
*Collyer, Mrs. Charlotte
*Collyer, Miss Marjorie
Corbett, Mrs. Irene
Corey, Mrs. C. P.
Cotterill, Mr. Harry
Davies, Mr. Charles
*Davis, Mrs. Agnes
*Davis, Master John M.
*Davis, Miss Mary
Deacon, Mr. Percy
del Carlo, Mr. Sebastian
del Carlo, Mrs.
Denbou, Mr. Herbert

Dibden, Mr. William
*Doling, Mrs. Ada
*Doling, Miss Elsie
Downton, Mr. William J.
*Drachstedt, Baron von
Drew, Mr. James V.
*Drew, Mrs. Lulu
*Drew, Master Marshall
*Duran, Miss Florentina
*Duran, Miss Asimcion
Eitemiller, Mr. G. F.
Enander, Mr. Ingvar
Fahlstrom Mr. Arne J.
Faunthorpe, Mr. Harry
*Faunthorpe, Mrs. Lizzie
Fillbrook, Mr. Charles
Fox, Mr. Stanley H.
Funk, Miss Annie
Fynney, Mr. Jos.
Gale, Mr. Harry
Gale, Mr. Shadrach
*Garside, Miss Ethel
Gaskell, Mr. Alfred
Gavey, Mr. Lawrence
Gilbert, Mr. William
Giles, Mr. Edgar
Giles, Mr. Fred
Giles, Mr. Ralph
Gill, Mr. John
Gillespie, Mr. William
Givard, Mr. Hans K.
Greenberg, Mr. Samuel
Hale, Mr. Reginald
*Hamalainer, Mrs. Anna
    and *Infant
Harbeck, Mr. Wm. H.
Harper, Mr. John
*Harper, Miss Nina
*Harris, Mr. George
Harris, Mr. Walter
Hart, Mr. Benjamin
*Hart, Mrs. Esther
*Hart, Miss Eva
*Herman, Miss Alice
*Herman, Mrs. Jane
*Herman, Miss Kate
Herman, Mr. Samuel

*Hewlett, Mrs. Mary D.
Hickman, Mr. Leonard
Hickman, Mr. Lewis
Hickman, Mr. Stanley
Hiltunen, Miss Martha
Hocking, Mr. George
*Hocking, Mrs. Elizabeth
*Hocking, Miss Nellie
Hocking, Mr. Samuel J.
Hodges, Mr. Henry P.
Hoffman, Mr. and *two
    children (Loto and Louis)
*Hold, Mrs. Annie
Hold, Mr. Stephen
Hood, Mr. Ambrose
*Hosono, Mr. Masabumi
Howard, Mr. Benjamin
Howard, Mrs. Ellen T.
Hunt, Mr. George
*Ilett, Miss Bertha
*Jacobsohn, Mrs. Amy P.
Jacobsohn Mr. Sidney S.,
Jarvis, Mr. John D.
Jefferys, Mr. Clifford
Jefferys, Mr. Ernest
Jenkin, Mr. Stephen
*Jervan, Mrs. A. T.
*Kantor, Mrs. Miriam
Kantor, Mr. Sehua
Karnes, Mrs. J. F.
Keane, Mr. Daniel
*Keane, Miss Nora A.
*Kelly, Mrs. F.
Kirkland, Rev. Charles L
Kvillner, Mr. John Henrik
*Lahtinen, Mrs. Anna
Lahtinen, Mr. William
Lamb, Mr. J. J.
*Lamore, Mrs. Ameliar
Laroche, Mr. Joseph
*Laroche, Mrs. Juliet
*Laroche, Miss Louise
*Laroche, Miss Simonne
*Lehman, Miss Bertha
*Leitch, Miss Jessie
Levy, Mr. R. J.
Leyson, Mr. Robert W. N.

Lingan, Mr. John
Louch, Mr. Charles
*Louch, Mrs. Alice Adela
Mack, Mrs. Mary
Malachard, Mr. Noel
Mallet, Mr. A.
*Mallet, Mrs.
*Mallet, Master A.
Mangiavacchi, Mr. Emilio
Mantvila, Mr. Joseph
Marshall, Mr.
*Marshall, Mrs. Kate
Matthews, Mr. W. J.
Maybery, Mr. Frank H.
McCrae, Mr. Arthur G.
McCrie, Mr. James
McKane, Mr. Peter D.
*Mellers, Mr. William
*Mellinger, Mrs. Elizabeth
    and *Child
Meyer, Mr. August
Milling, Mr. Jacob C.
Mitchell, Mr. Henry
Morawick, Dr. Ernest
Mudd, Mr. Thomas C.
Myles, Mr. Thomas F.
Nasser, Mr. Nicolas
*Nasser, Mrs.
Nesson, Mr. Israel
Nicholls, Mr. Joseph C.
Norman, Mr. Robert D.
*Nye, Mrs. Elizabeth
Otter, Mr. Richard
*Oxenham, Mr. P. Thomas
*Padro, Mr. Julian
Pain, Dr. Alfred
*Pallas, Mr. Emilio
Parker, Mr. Clifford R.
*Parrish, Mrs. L Davis
Pengelly, Mr. Frederick
Pernot, Mr. Rene
Peruschitz, Rev. Jos. M.
Phillips, Mr. Robert
*Phillips, Miss Alice
*Pinsky, Miss Rosa
Ponesell, Mr. Martin
*Portaluppi, Mr. Emilio

Pulbaun, Mr. Frank

*Quick, Mrs. Jane

*Quick, Miss Vera W.

*Quick, Miss Phyllis

Reeves, Mr. David

Renouf, Mr. Peter H.

*Renouf, Miss Lillie

*Reynolds, Miss E.

Richard, Mr. Emile

*Richards, Mrs. Emily

*Richards, Master William

*Richards, Master George

*Ridsdale, Miss Lucy

Rogers, Mr. Harry

*Rogers, Miss Selina

*Rugg, Miss Emily

Sedgwick, Mr. C. F. W.

Sharp, Mr. Percival

*Shelley, Mrs. Imanita

*Silven, Miss Lyyli

*Sincook, Miss Maude

*Sinkkenen, Miss Anna

Sjostedt, Mr. Ernest A.

*Slayter, Miss H. M.

Slemen, Mr. Richard J.

Smith, Mr. Augustus

*Smith, Miss Marion

Sobey, Mr. Hayden

Stanton, Mr. S. Ward

Stokes, Mr. Phillip J.

Swane, Mr. George

Sweet, Mr. George

*Toomey, Miss Ellen

*Trant, Miss Jessie

Tronpiansky, Mr. Moses A.

*Troutt, Miss E. Celia

Tupin, M. Dorothy

Turpin, Mr. William J.

Veale, Mr. James

*Walcroft, Miss Nellie

*Ware, Mrs. Florence L

Ware, Mr. John James

Ware, Mr. William J.

*Watt, Miss Bertha

*Watt, Mrs. Bessie

*Webber, Miss Susie

Weisz, Mr. Leopold

*Weisz, Mrs. Matilda

*Wells, Mrs. Addie

*Wells, Miss J.

*Wells, Master Ralph

West, Mr. E. Arthur

*West, Mrs. Ada

*West, Miss Barbara

*West, Miss Constance

Wheadon, Mr. Edward

Wheeler, Mr. Edwin


THIRD CLASS, BRITISH
SUBJECTS EMBARKED
AT SOUTHAMPTON

Abbott, Eugene

*Abbott, Rosa

Abbott, Rossmore

Abbing, Anthony

Adams. J.

*Aks, Filly

*Aks, Leah

Alexander, William

Allen, William

Allum, Owen G.

*Badman, Emily

Barton David

Beavan, W. T.

Billiard, A. van

Billiard, James (child)

Billiard, Walter (child)

*Bing, Lee

Bowen, David

Braund, Lewis

Braund, Owen

Brocklebank, William

Cann, Erenst

Carver, A.

Celotti, Francesco

*Chip, Chang

Christmann, Emil

*Cohen, Gurshon

Cook, Jacob

Corn, Harry

*Coutts, Winnie

*Coutts, William (child)

*Coutts, Leslie (child)

Coxon, Daniel

Crease, Ernest James

Cribb, John Hatfield

*Cribb, Alice

*Dahl, Charles

Davies, Evan

Davies, Alfred

Davies, John

Davies, Joseph

Davison, Thomas H.

*Davison, Mary

Dean, Mr. Bertram F.

*Dean, Mrs. Hetty, *Dean,
  Bertran (child), *Dean,
  Vera (infant)

Dennis, Samuel

Dennis, William

*Derkings, Edward

*Dowdell, Elizabeth

*Drapkin, Jenie

*Dugemin, Joseph

Elsbury, James

*Emanuel, Ethet (child)

Everett, Thomas J.

*Foo, Choong

Ford, Arthur

Ford, Margaret

Ford, Mrs. D. M.

Ford, Mr. E. W.

Ford, M. W. T. N.

Ford, Maggie (child)

Franklin, Charles

Garthfirth, John

Gilinski, Leslie

*Godwin, Frederick

Goldsmith, Frank J.

*Goldsmith, Emily A.

*Goldsmith, Frank J. W.

Goodwin, Augusta

Goodwin, Lillian A.

Goodwin, Charles E.

Goodwin, William F.
  (child)

Goodwin, Jessie (child)

Goodwin, Harold (child)

Goodwin, Sidney (child)

Green, George

Guest, Robert

Harknett, Alice

Harmer, Abraham

*Hee, Ling

*Howard, May

*Hyman, Abraham

Johnston, A. G.

Johnston, Mrs.

Johnston, William (child)

Johnston, Mrs. C. H. (child)

Johnson, Mr. A.

Johnson, Mr. W.

Keefe, Arthur

Kelly, James

*Lam, Ali

Lam, Len

*Lang, Fang

Leonard, Mr. L

Lester, J.

Ling, Lee

Lithman, Simon

Lobb, Cordelia

Lobb, William A.

Lockyer, Edward

Lovell, John

MacKay, George W.

Maisner, Simon

McNamee, Eileen

McNamee, Neal

Meanwell, Marian O.

Meek, Annie L.

Meo, Alfonso

Miles, Frank

*Moor, Beile

*Moor, Meier

Moore, Leonard C.

Morley, William

Moutal, Rahamin

Murdlin, Joseph

Nancarrow, W. H.

Niklasen, Sander

Nosworthy, Richard C.

Peacock, Alfred

Peacodc., Treasteall

Peacock, Treasteall (child)

Pearce, Ernest

Peduzzi, Joseph

Perkin, John Henry

Peterson, Marius
Potchett, George
*Rath, Sarah
Reed, James George
Reynolds, Harold
Risien, Emma
Risien, Samuel
Robins, Alexander
Robins, Charity
Rogers, William John
Rouse, Richard H.
Rush, Alfred George J.
Sadowitz, Harry
Sage, John
Sage, Annie
Sage, Stella
Sage, George
Sage, Douglas
Sage, Frederick
Sage, Dorothy
Sage, William (child)
Sage, Ada (child)
Sage, Constance (child)
Sage, Thomas (child)
Sather, Sinon
Saundercock, W. H.
Sawyer, Frederick
Scrota, Maurice
Shellard, Frederick
Shorney, Charles
Simmons, John
Slocovski, Selman
Somerton, Francis W.
Spector, Woolf
Spinner, Henry
*Stanley, Amy
Stanley, E. R. Mr.
Storey, T. Mr.
*Sunderland, Victor
Sutehall, Henry
Theobald, Thomas
Thomas, Alex
*Thorneycrolt, Florence
Thorneycroft, Percival
Tomlin, Ernest P.
Torber, Ernest
*Trembisky, Berk

*Tunquist, W.
Ware, Frederick
Warren, Charles W.
Webber, James
*Wilkes, Ellen
Willey, Edward
Williams, Harry
Williams, Leslie
Windelov, Einar
Wiseman, Philip

NON-BRITISH
EMBARKED AT
SOUTHAMPTON
*Abelseth, Karen
*Abelseth, Olaus
*Abramson, August
Adahl, Mauritz
*Adolf, Humblin
Ahlin, Johanna
Ahmed, Ali
Alhomaki, Ilmari
Ali, William
Anderson, Alfreda
*Anderson, Erna
Anderson, Albert
Anderson, Anders
Anderson, Samuel
Anderson, Sigrid (child)
Anderson, Thor
*Anderson, Carla
Anderson, Ingeborg (child)
Anderson, Ebba (child)
Anderson, Sigvard (child)
Anderson, Ellis
Anderson, Ida Augusta
Anderson, Paul Edvin
Angheloff, Minko
Asplund, Carl (child)
Asplund, Charles
*Aspland, Felix (child)
Asplund, Gustaf (child)
*Asplund, Johan
*Asplund, Lillian (child)
Asplund, Oscar (child)
*Asplund, Selma
Arnold, Joseph

Arnold, Josephine
Aronsson, Ernest Axel A.
Asim, Adola
Assam, Ali
Augustsan, Albert
Backstrom, Karl
*Backstrom, Marie
Balkic, Cerin
Benson, John Viktor
Berglund. Ivar
Berkeland, Hans
Bjorklund, Ernst
Bostandyeff, Guentcho
Braf, Elin Ester
Brobek, Carl R.
Cacic, Grego
Cacic, Luka
Cacic, Maria
Cacic, Manda
Calie, Peter
Carlson, Carl R.
Carlsson, Julius
Carlsson, August Sigfrid
Coelho, Domingos
   Fernardeo
Coleff, Fotio
Coleff, Peyo
Cor, Bartol
Cor, Ivan
Cor, Ludovik
*Dahl, Mauritz
Dahlberg, Gerda
Dakic, Branko
Danbom, Ernest
Danbom, Gillber (infant)
Danoff, Sigrid
Danoff, Yoto
Dantchoff, Khristo
Delalic, Regyo
Denkoff, Mito
Dimic, Jovan
Dintcheff, Valtcho
Dyker, Adoff
*Dyker, Elizabeth
Ecimovic, Joso
Edwardsson, Gustaf
Eklunz, Hans

Ekstrom, Johan
*Finote, Luigi
Fischer, Eberhard
Goldsmith, Nathan
Goncalves, Manoel E.
Gronnestad, Daniel D.
Gustafson, Alfred
Gustafson, Anders
Gustafson, Johan
Gustafsson, Gideon
Haas, Aloisia
*Hadman, Oscar
Hagland, Ingvald O.
Hagland, Konrad R.
Hakkurainen, Pekko
*Hakkurainen, Elin
Hampe, Leon
*Hankonen, Eluna
Hansen, Claus
*Hansen, Janny
Hansen, Henry Damgavd
Heininen, Wendla
Hendekevoic, Ignaz
Henriksson, Jenny
*Hervonen, Helga
*Hervonen, Hildwe (child)
*Hickkinen, Laina
*Hillstrom, Hilda
Holm, John F. A.
Holten, Johan
Humblin, Adolf
Ilieff, Ylio
Ilmakangas, Ida
Ilmakangas, Pista
Ivanoff, Konio
*Jansen, Carl
Jardin, Jose Netto
*Jensen, Carl
Jensen, Hans Peter
Jensen, Svenst L.
Jensen, Nilho R.
*Johannessen, Bernt
*Johannessen, Elias
Johansen, Nils
*Johanson, Oscar
*Johanson, Oscal L.
Johansson, Erik

Johansson, Gustaf

Johnson, Jakob A.

*Johnson, Alice

*Johnson, Harold

*Johnson, Eleanora (infant)

Johnsson, Carl

Johnsson, Malkolm

Jonkoff, Lazor

Jonsson, Nielo H.

Jusila, Katrina

Jusila, Mari

*Jusila, Erik

Jutel, Henrik Hansen

Kallio, Nikolai

Kalvig Johannes H.

Karajic, Milan

*Karlson, Einar

Karlson, Nils August

Kekic, Tido

*Kink, Anton

*Kink, Louise

*Kink, Louise (child)

Kink, Maria

Kink, Vincenz

Klasen, Klas A.Mona,
    Mae A.

Klasen, Hilda

Klasen, Gertrud (child)

Laitinen, Sofia

Laleff, Kristo

*Landegren, Aurora

Larson, Viktor

Larsson, Bengt Edvin

Larsson, Edvard

Lefebre, Frances

Lefebre, Henry (child)

Lefebre, Ida (child)

Lefebre, Ida (child)

Lefebre,Mathilde (child)

Leinonen, Antti

Lindablom, August

Lindell, Edvard B.

Lindell, Elin

Lindahl, Agda

*Lindqvist, Einar

*Lulic, Nicola

Lundahl, John

*Lundin, Olga

*Lundstripm, Jan

*Madsen, Fridjof

Maenpaa, Matti

Makinen, Kalle

*Mampe, Leon

Marinko, Dmitri

Markoff, Marin

Melkebuk, Philemon

*Messemacker, Guillaume

*Messemacker, Emma

*Midtsjo, Carl

*Mikanen, John

Misseff, Ivan

Minkoff, Lazar

Mirko, Dika

Mitkoff, Mito

Moen, Sigurd H.

*Moss, Albert

*Mulder, Theo

Myhrman, Oliver

Naidenoff, Penko

Nankoff, Minko

Nedeco, Petroff

Nenkoff, Christo

Nieminen, Manta

Nilsson, August F.

*Nilson, Berta

*Nilson, Helmina

Nirva, Isak

*Nyoven, Johan

*Nyston, Anna

*Odahl, Martin

*Orman, Velin

*Olsen, Arthur

Olsen, Carl

Olsen, Henry

Olsen, Ole M.

Olson, Elon

Olsson, John

Olsson, Elida

Oreskovic, Luka

Oreskovic, Maria

Oreskovic, Jeko

*Osman, Mara

Pacruic, Mate

Pacruic, Tome

Panula, Eino

Panula, Ernesti

Panula, Juho

Panula, Maria

Panula, Sanni

Panula, Urhu (child)

Panula, William (infant)

Pasic, Jakob

Pentcho, Petroff

Paulsson, Alma C

Paulsson, Gosta (child)

Paulsson, Paul (child)

Paulsson, Stina(child)

Paulsson, Torborg (child)

Pavlovic, Stefo

*Pekonemi, E.

Pelsmaker, Alfons de

Peltomaki, Nikolai

*Persson, Ernst U.

Peterson, Johan

Peterson, Ellen

Petranec, Matilda

Petterson, Olaf

Plotcharsky, Vasil

Radeff, Alexander

Rintamaki, Matti

Rosblom, Helene

Rosblom, Salfi (child)

Rosblom, Viktor

Rummstvedt, Kristian

Salander, Carl

*Salkjellsvik, Anna cor-
    rected

Salonen, Werner

*Sandman, Johan

*Sandstrom, Agnes

*Sandstrom, Beatrice
    (child)

*Sandstrom, Margretha
    (child)

Sdycoff, Todor

*Sheerlinck, Jean

Sihvola, Antti

Sivic, Husen

*Sjoblom, Anna

Skoog, Anna

Skoog, Carl (child)

Skoog, Harald (child)

Skoog, Mabel (child)

Skoog, Margret (child)

Skoog, William

Slabenoff, Petco

Smiljanic, Mile

Sohole, Peter

Solvang, Lena Jacobsen

*Sop, Jules

Staneff, Ivan

Stoytcho, Mihoff

Stoyehoff, Ilia

Strandberg, Ida

*Stranden, Jules

Strilic, Ivan

Strom, Selma (child)

Svensen, Olaf

Svensson, Johan

*Svensson, Coverin

Syntakoff, Stanko

Tikkanen, Juho

Todoroff, Lalio

*Tonglin, Gunner

Turcin, Stefan

*Turja, Anna verified by her
    grandson, not "Turgo"

*Twekula, Hedwig

Uzelas, Jovo

Waelens, Achille

Van Impe, Catharine (child)

Van Impe, Jacob

Van Impe, Rosalie

Van der Planke, Augusta
    Vander

Van der Planke, Emilie
    Vander

Van der Planke, Jules
    Vander

Van der Planke, Leon
    Vander

Van der Steen, Leo

Van de Velde, Joseph

Van de Walle, Nestor

Vereruysse, Victor

Vook, Janko

Wende, Olof Edvin

*Wennerstrom, August

Wenzel, Zinhart
Vestrom, Huld A. A.
Widegrin, Charles
Wiklund, Karl F.
Wiklund, Jacob A.
Wirz, Albert
Wittenrongel, Camille
Zievens, Renee
Zimmermann, Leo

EMBARKED AT
CHERBOURG
*Assaf, Marian
Attala, Malake
*Baclini, Latila
*Baclini, Maria
*Baclini, Eugene

*Baclini, Helene
Badt, Mohamed
*Banoura, Ayout
Barbara, Catherine
Barbara, Saude
Betros, Tannous
Boulos, Hanna
Boulos, Sultani
*Boulos, Nourelain
Boulos, Akar (child)
Banous, Elias
Caram, Joseph
Caram, Maria
Shabini, Georges
Chehab, Emir Farres
Chronopoulos, Apostolos
Chronopoulos, Demetrios

Dibo, Elias
Drazenovie, Josip
Elias, Joseph
*Elias, Joseph
*Fabini, Leeni
*Fat-ma, Mustmani
Gerios, Assaf
Gerios, Youssef
Gerios, Youssef
Gheorgheff, Stanio
Hanna, Mansour
Jean Nassr, Saade

Johann, Markim
*Joseph, Mary
*Karun, Franz
*Karun, Anna (child)
Kassan, M. Housseing
Kassem, Fared
*Kassein, Hassef
Kalil, Betros
*Khalil, Zahie
Kraeff, Thodor
Lemberopoulos, Peter
Malinoff, Nicola

*Bruce Ismay escapes in one of the last lifeboats in* A Night to Remember. *He received a very bad press for surviving the tragedy, rather than go down with his captain and his ill-fated ship. However, the inquiries found him not to have acted improperly, and found that White Star had been within the BoT guidelines.*

*Meme, Hanna
Monbarek, Hanna
*Moncarek, Omine
*Moncarek, Gonios (child)
*Moncarek, Halim (child)
Moussa, Mantoura
*Naked, Said
*Naked, Waika
*Naked, Maria
Nasr, Mustafa
*Nichan, Krikorian
*Nicola, Jamila
*Nicola, Elias (child)
*Novel, Mansouer
Orsen, Sirayanian
Ortin, Zakarian
*Peter, Catherine Joseph
Peter, Mike
Peter, Anna
Rafoul, Baccos
Raibid, Razi
Saad, Amin
*Saad, Khalil
Samaan, Hanna
Samaan, Elias
Samaan, Youssef
Sarkis, Mardirosian
Sarkis, Lahowd
Seman Betros (child)
Shedid, Daher
Sleiman, Attalla
Stankovic, Jovan
Tannous, Thomas
Tannous, Daler
Thomas, CharlesP
*Thomas, Tamin
*Thomas, Assad (infant)
Thomas, John
Tonfik, Nahli
Torfa, Assad
Useher,Baulner
*Vagil, Adele Jane
*Vartunian, David
Vassilios, Catavelas
Wazli, Yousif
Weller, Abi
*Yalsevae, Ivan

Yazbeck, Antoni
*Yazbeck, Salini
*Youssef, Brahim
Youssef, Hanne
*Youssef, Maria (child)
Youssef Georges (child)
Zabour. Tamini
Zabour, Hileni
Zakarian, Maprieder

EMBARKED AT
QUEENSTOWN

Barry, Julia
Bourke, Catherine
Bourke, John
*Bradley, Bridget
*Buckley, Daniel
Buckley, Katherine
Burke, Jeremiak
Burke, Mary
Burns, Mary
Canavan, Mary
Carr, Ellen
Car, Jeannie
Chartens, David
Cannavan, Pat
Colbert, Patrick
Conlin, Thos. H.
Connaghton, Michel
Connors, Pat
*Conolly, Kate
Conolly, Kate
*Daly, Marcella
*Daly, Eugene
*Devaney, Margaret
Dewan, Frank
Dooley, Patrick
Doyle, Elin
*Driscoll, Bridget
Emmeth, Thomas
Farrell, James
Foley, Joseph
Foley, William
Flynn, James
Flynn, John
Fox, Patrick
Gallagher, Martin

*Gilnegh, Katie
*Glynn, Mary
Hagardon, Kate
Hagarty, Nora
Hart, Henry
*Healy, Nora
Horgan, John
Hemming, Norah
Henery, Delia
*Jenymin, Annie
Kelly, James
*Kelly, Annie K.
*Kelly, Mary
Kerane, Andy
*Kennedy, John
Kilgannon, Thomas
Kiernan, John
Kiernan, Phillip
Lane, Patrick
Lemom, Denis
Lemon, Mary
Linehan, Michel
*Madigan, Maggie
Mahon, Delia
*Mannion, Margareth
Mangan, Mary
*McCarthy, Katie
*McCoy, Agnes
*McCoy, Alice
*McCoy, Bernard
*McCormack, Thomas
*McDermott, Delia
McElroy, Michel
*McGovern, Mary
McGowan, Katherine
*McGowan, Annie
McMahon, Martin
Mechan, John
*Meeklave, Ellie
Moran, James
*Moran, Bertha
Morgan, Daniel J.
Morrow, Thomas
*Mullens, Katie
*Mulvihill, Bertha
*Murphy, Norah
*Murphy, Mary

*Murphy, Kate
Naughton, Hannah
Nemagh, Robert
O'Brien, Denis
O'Brien, Thomas
*O'Brien, Hannah
O'Connell, Pat D.
O'Connor, Maurice
O'Connor, Pat
O'Donaghue, Bert
*O'Dwyer, Nellie
*O'Keefe, Pat
*OLeary, Norah
O'Neill, Bridget
O'Sullivan, Bridget
Peters, Katie
Rice, Margaret
Rice, Albert (child)
Rice, George (child)
Rice, Eric (child)
Rice, Arthur (child)
Rice, Eugene (child)
*Riordan, Hannah
Ryan, Patrick
*Ryan, Edw.
Sadlier, Matt
Scanlan, James
Shaughnesay, Pat
*Shine, Ellen
*Smyth, Julian
Tobin, Roger

# 5 Cargo Manifest

Acker, Merrall & Condit
75 cs anchovies, 225 cs
mussels, 1 cs liquor, 50 cs
wine
Adams Express Co.
4 rolls linoleum, 3 bales
leather, 1 cs hats, 6 cs
confectionery, 5 cs books, 1
cs tin tubes, 2 cs soap, 2 cs
boots
Adams Express, Limited
35 cs books
Aero Club of America
1 cs machinery, 1 cs
printed matter
Altman, B. & Co.
1 cs cotton
American Express Co.
a quantIty of oak beams,
9 cs books, 3 cs cameras &
stands, 1 cs canvas, 1 cs
cheese, 30 bundles cheese,
2 cs cognac, 1 barrel earth,
1 cs Edison gramaphones,
1 package effects, 1 cs
elastics, 6 cs film, 2 barrels
glassware, 4 cs hosiery,
43 cs merchandise,
2 parcels merchandise,
2 barrels mercury, 1 cs
packed packages, 8 cs
paste, 1 cs plants, 3 cs
printed matter, 3 cs prints,
1 cs rubber goods, 2 cs
samples, 1 cs sero fittings,
1 cs speedometers, 1 cs
straw braids, 3 cs straw
hats, 3 cs tissues, 1 cs tweed
American Motor Co.
1 package candles
American Shipping Co.
5 cs books
Anderson Refridg, Mach. Co.
11 cs refridgeration appratus

Arnold & Zeiss
134 cs rubber
Arnold, F.R. & Co.
6 cs soap
Austin, Nichols
25 cs olive oil, 14 cs mushrooms
Bardwill Bros.
8 cs laces
Baring Bros. & Co.
63 cs rubber, 100 bgd gutta
Baumert, F.X. & Co.
50 bundles cheese
Baumgarten, W. & Co
3 cs furniture
Bernard, Judas & Co.
70 bundles cheese
Blechoff, H. & Co.
35 bags rough wood
Blum, J.A.
3 cs silk goods
Brasch & Rothenstein
2 cs lace collars, 2 cs books
Broadway Trust Co.
3 cs coney skins (rabbit)
Brown Bros & Co.
76 cs dragon's blood,
15 cs rabbit hair, 3 cs gum,
100 cs shelled walnuts,
100 bales shelled walnuts
Budd, S.
1 parcel merchandise
Calhoun, Robbins &, Co.
1 cs cotton laces, 1/2 cs
brushware
Carbon Machinery
Equipment Co.
1 cs clothing
Carter, W.E.
1 cs auto (i.e. 1 car)
Cauvigny Brush Co.
1 cs brushware
Claflin, H.B. & Co.
12 cs cotton lace

Cobb, G.H.
1 cs lace tissue
Cohen, M. Bros.
5 pkg skins
Corbett, M.J. & Co.
2 cs hat leather
Costa, F.
1 cs silk goods
Crown Perfume Co.
3 cs soap perfume
Downing, R.F. & Co.
1 cs felt, 1 cs metal, 2 cs
tennis balls, 1 cs engine
packing, 1 cs iron jacks,
1 cs bulbs, 1 cs hosiery
Du Bois, Geo. C.
16 hogshead wine
Dubois, Geo. F.
6 cs vermouth, 4 cs wine
Dublin, Morris &
Kornbluth
2 pkg skins
Dujardin & Ladnick
10 bx melons
Engs. P.W. & Sons
190 cs liquor, 25 cs syrups
Flietman & Co.
1 cs silk goods
First National Bank of
Chicago
300 cs shelled walnuts
Fouger, E.
41 cs filter paper
Fuchs & Lang
Manufacturing
4 cs printers blank
Gallia Textile Co.
1 cs lace goods
Gillman, J.
4 bales skins
Goldster, Morris
11 cs feathers
Gross, Engle Co.
61 cs tulle

Haupt & Burgi
50 bundles cheese
Heidelbach, Ickelheimer
& Co.
11 cs shelled walnuts
Hempstead & Sons
30 cs plants
Heyliger, A.V.
1 cs velvet
Hollander, H.
185 cs wine, 110 cs brandy
International News Co.
10 package periodicals
International Trading Co.
1 cs surgical instruments,
1 cs ironware
Isler & Guve
4 bales straw,
53 pkg straw
Johnson, J.G. Co.
2 cs ribbons
Judkins & McCormick
2 cs flowers
Knauth, Nachod &, Kuhne
107 cs mushrooms,
1 cs pamphlets
Kronfeld, Saunders & Co.
5 cs shells
Kuyper, P.C. & Co.
1 cs elastic cords,
1 cs leather
Lasker & Bernstein
117 cs sponges
Lazard Freses
1 bale skins, 25 cs
sardines, 3 cs preserves
Leeming, T. & Co.
7 cs biscuits
Lemke & Buechner
1 parcel merchandise
Lippincott, J.B. & Co.
10 cs books
Lustig Bros.
4 cs straw hats

Mallouk, H.

1 cs laces

Maltus & Ware

19 cs orchids, 15 cs alarm apparatus

Manhattan Shirt Co.

3 cs tissues

Marshall Field & Company

1 cs gloves

Mathews, G.T. & Co.

2 cs books and lace

Meadows, T. & Co.

5 cs books, 3 bx samples, 1 cs parchment

Meadows, Thomas & Co.

3 cs hosiery

Metzger, A.S.

2 cs tulle

Milbank, Leaman & Co.

2 cs woollens

Mills & Gibb

20 cs cottons

Moquin Wine Co.

1 cs liquor, 38 cs oil

Munro, J. & Co.

22 cs mushrooms, 15 cs peas, 3 cs beans, 10 cs mixed vegetables, 10 cs peas, 25 cs olives, 12 bundles capers, 10 bundles fish, 20 bundles merchandise

Muser Bros.

3 cs tissues

Naday & Fleisher

1 cs laces

National City Bank of New York

11 bales rubber

NY & Cuba SS Co.

12 cs butter, 18 cs oil, 2 hogsheads vinegar, 19 cs vinegar, 6 cs preserves, 8 cs dried fruit, 2 cs wine

New York Motion Picture Co.

1 cs film

Nicholas, G.S. & Co.

1 cs merchandise

Nottingham Lace Works

2 cs cotton

Oelrichs & Co.

2 cs pictures

Pape, Chas. & Co.

1,196 bags potatoes

Park & Tilford

1 cs toothpaste, 5 cs drug sundries, 1 cs brushware

Peabody, H.W. & Co.

13 bales straw goods,

Percival, C.

50 bundles cheese

Petry, P.H. & Co.

1 cs tulleetry, 10 bundles cheese

Phoenix Cheese Co.

30 bundles cheese

Pitt & Scott

4 cs printed matter, 1 cs machinery, 1 cs pictures, 1 cs books, 1 cs merchandise, 1 cs notions, 1 cs photos

Prost. G.

1 cs auto parts

Rathenberger & Co.

190 bundles cheese

Rawstick Trading Co.

28 bags sticks

Reynolds & Dronig

15 bundles cheese

Richard, C.B.

1 cs films

Rosenthal, Leo J. &, Co.

4 cs cotton

Rusch & Co.

1 cs velvets

Rush & Co.

1 cs hair nets

Rydeman & Lassner

1 cs tulle

Sanger, R. & Co.

3 cs hair nets

Sauer, J.P. & Co.

318 bags potatoes

Schall & Co.

25 cs preserves

Sheldon & Co.

40 bundles cheese

Sheldon, G.W. & Co.

1 cs machinery, 1 cs elastics, 2 cs books, 1 bx golf balls, 5 cs instruments

Sherman Sons & Co.

7 cs cotton

Shieffelin & Co.

17 pkg wool fat

Simon, A.I. & Co.

1 cs raw feathers

Snow's Express Co.

3 cs books

Spaulding & Bros.

34 cs athletic goods

Spencerian Pen Co.

4 cs pens

Spielman Co.

3 cs silk crepe, 1 cs gloves

Stechert, G.E. & Co.

12 pkg periodicals

Stern, S.

60 cs salt powders

Sterns, R.H. & Co.

1 cs cretonne

Stone, C.D. & Co.

50 bundles cheese

Strohmeyer & Arpe

75 bales fish

Suter, Alfred

18 cs machinery

Thomas & Pierson

2 cs hardware, 2 cs books, 2 cs furniture

Thorburn, J.M. & Co.

3 cs bulbs

Thorer & Praetorius

1 bl skins

Tice & Lynch

5 cs books, 1 bag frames,

1 cs cotton, 2 cs stationery

Tiedeman, T. & Sons

2 cs silk goods

Tiffany & Company

1 cask china

Tolson, A.M. & Co.

1 cs gloves

Uchs & Hegnoer

3 cs silk goods

US Export Co.

1 cs scientific instruments, 1 cs sundries, 3 cs test cords, 1 cs briar pipes, 1 cs sundries, 2 cs printed matter

Van Engen E.H. & Co.

1 cs woolens, 1 parcel

Van Renssaller, C.A.

10 hogshead wine, 15 cs cognac

Vandegrift, F.B. & Co.

63 cs champagne

Vandegrift, F.B. (personal)

1 cs merchandise

Victor & Achiles

1 cs brushware

Wakem & McLaughlin

25 cs biscuits, 6 bales cork, 43 cs wines

Wells Fargo Co.

3 cs books, 2 cs furniture, 1 cs pamphlets, 1 cs plants, 1 cs eggs, 1 cs whiskey

Wilson, P.K. & Sons

2 cs linens

Wimpfheimer, A. & Co.

3 cs leather

Witcombe, McGrachlin, & Co.

856 rolls linoleum

Wright & Grahm Co.

437 casks tea

Young Bros.

1 cs feathers

# 6 Bibliography

Ballard, Robert D & Archbold, Rick; *The Discovery of the Titanic*; Orion, 1995.

Beasley, Lawrence; *The Loss of the S.S. Titanic: its Story and its Lessons*; 7C's Press, 1973.

Beasley, Lawrence; *The Story of the Titanic as Told by its Survivors*;Dover Publications, 1960.

Behe, George; *Titanic, Psychic Forewarnings of a Tragedy*; Stephens, 1988.

Biel, Steven; *Down With the Old Canoe; A Cultural History of the Titanic Disaster*; W.W. Norton, 1996.

Boyd-Smith, Peter; *Titanic from Rare Historical Reports*; Brooks Books, 1992.

Browne, Father Frank; *Father Browne's Titanic Album: A Passenger's Photographs and Personal Memories*; Wolfhound, 1997.

Bullock, Shan F; *Thomas Andrews, Shipbuilder*; 7C's Press, 1973.

Cahill, Richard A.; *Disasters at Sea: Titanic to Exxon Valdez*; Century, 1990.

Davie, Michael; *The Titanic: Full Story of a Tragedy*; Bodley Head, 1986.

Denny, Ronald C; *Shadow of the Titanic, A Survivor's Story*; Greenwich University Press, 1994.

Deakin, Nicholas; *The Enterprise Culture and the Inner City*; Routledge, 1993.

Eaton, John P. & Haas, Charles A.; *Titanic: Destination Disaster: The Legends and the Reality*; Stephens, 1987.

Gardiner, Robin & Van der Vat, Dan; *The Riddle of the Titanic*; Weidenfield & Nicolson, 1995.

Garrett, Richard; *Atlantic Disaster: The Titanic and Other Victims of the North Atlantic*; Buchan & Enright, 1986.

Gibbs, Philip; *The Deathless Story of The Titanic*; Peter Way Ltd, 1972.

Hilton, George Woodman; *Legacy of the Titanic*; Stanford University Press, 1995.

Hoffman, William & Grimm, Jack; *Beyond Reach: the Search for the Titanic*; Paul Harris, 1984.

Hutchinson, Gillian; *The Wreck of the Titanic*; Adax, 1994.

Jessop, Violet; *Titanic Survivor: The Memoirs of Violet Jessop, Stewardess*; Sutton, 1998.

Lynch, Don; *Titanic: An Illustrated History*; Hodder and Stoughton, 1992.

Marriott, Leo; *Titanic*; P.R.C. Publishing, 1997.

Marsh, Ed W.; *James Cameron's Titanic*, Boxtree, 1998.

Martin, Simon; *The Other Titanic*, David & Charles, 1980.

Padfield, Peter; *The Titanic and the Californian*, Hodder and Stoughton, 1965

Pellegrino, Charles R.; *Her Name Titanic: The Untold Story of the Sinking & Finding of the Unsinkable*, Robert Hale, 1990.

Read, Leslie; *The Ship that Stood Still, The Californian and her Mysterious Role in the Titanic Disaster*; P Stephens, 1993.

*The Titanic's bows and spare anchor are revealed in the blackness of the depths.*

510

*The Hollywood version of Phillips operating the Marconi wireless to send out the distress signal which was picked up by the* Carpathia.

Roston, Sir Arthur; *The Loss of the Titanic*; Titanic Signals Archive, 1991.

Thresh, Peter; *Titanic*; Parkgate, 1992.

Tibballs, Geoff; *The Titanic, The Extraordinary Story of the Unsinkable Ship*; Carlton, 1997.

Ticehurst, Brian; *Titanic's Memorials Worldwide: Where are They Located? A Listing*; B&J Printers, 1996.

Wade, Wyn Craig; *The Titanic: End of a Dream*; Weidenfield & Nicolson, 1980.


Official Documents

Great Britain, Parliament, Shipping Casualties; *Loss of the Steamship Titanic: Report of the Formal Enquiry*;H.M.S.O. 1912.

Great Britain, Marine Accident Investigation Branch; *R.M.S. Titanic; Reappraisal of Evidence Relating to the S.S. Californian*; H.M.S.O. 1992.

Great Britain, Wreck Commissioner's Office; *Formal Investigation into the Loss of the S.S. Titanic*, 10 volumes; H.M.S.O. 1912.

Mercantile Marine Service Association; *A Petition on Behalf of the Late Captain Stanley Lord, ex S.S. Californian*; The Association, 1968.

United States, Congress, Senate, Committee on Commerce; *Titanic Disaster: Report of the Committee on Commerce*; Government Print 1912.

# INDEX

# Acknowledgments

For kindly supplying the reproductions in this book, we gratefully acknowledge the assistance of the following:

Beken of Cowes: 205, 234 *top*, 235-237, 246, 421 *bottom*

Bison Picture Library: 8-9, 30, 48, 52, 53, 54, 55, 56, 58, 78, 80, 82, 209-224, 488 *top*, 489, 490 *top*, 491 *bottom*, 492 *top*, 493, 494, 495 *top and bottom right*

The British Titanic Society: 19, 77 *top*, 260, 307 *bottom*, 309, 492 *bottom*

Carlton International Media Limited: 448-449, 450-469, 471, 499, 501, 510

Simon Clay: 209, 210, 211, 212, 213, 216, 217, 218, 219, 224

These photographs taken by Simon Clay with kind permission of the White Swan Hotel in Alnwick: 214-215, 220, 221, 222-223

Corbis:

    Ralph White, 433, 434 *bottom and top*, 436-437, 438-439, 441, 442, 443, 446-447

    Todd Gipstein; RMS Titanic, Inc., 435, 440

FM Browne SJ Collection/Irish Picture Library: 156 *top and bottom*, 157 *top*, 163 *middle and bottom left*, 185 *top*, 196-197 *top and bottom*, 207, 242-243, 248-251, 253, 258, 259, 261-301, 303-306, 307 *top*, 310, 318, 319, 337, 339, 346 *top*, 351, 357, 373, 376-377, 383, 490 *bottom*, 495 *bottom right*

Harland & Wolff: 14-15, 17, 20-22, 24-25, 26-27, 57, 86-111, 113, 116-125, 127-154, 157 *bottom*, 158-162, 163 *top and bottom*, 164-184, 185 *bottom*, 186-191, 198-204, 206, 208, 240-241, 247, 384-417

The Hulton Getty Picture Collection: 76, 77 *bottom*, 83, 112, 114, 115, 126, 192-193, 195 *top and bottom*, 196 *top*, 238, 239, 313, 315, 316-317, 321, 335, 343, 345, 347, 348, 349, 354-355, 356, 362, 448 *bottom*, 491 *top*

IMAX Corp: 18

Imperial War Musuem: 225 *top*, 228-233, 234 *bottom*, 422, 423, 424, 425, 426, 427, 430, 431, 225 *bottom*, 226-227

Low Films International, Inc.: 508-509

Mary Evans Picture Library: 85

National Maritime Museum, Greenwich, London: 50-51, 59-74, 197 *bottom*, 357, 376-377, 418-419, 420 *bottom*, 420-421

Images reproduced by courtesy of the Public Record Office: 252, 254-257, 320, 322, 323, 325-329, 324, 330-333, 340, 341, 346 *middle and bottom*, 358, 360-361, 364, 367, 381, 382, 475

Stuart Williamson: 6-7, 10-11, 12-13, 16, 445

Titanic Heritage: 245 *top*

University of Liverpool: 244-245